La Florida

Catholics, Conquistadores, and Other American Origin Stories

Kevin Kokomoor

Thanks so much

La Florida Forever!

KDK

Palm Beach, Florida

Pineapple Press
An imprint of Globe Pequot, the trade division of
The Rowman & Littlefield Publishing Group, Inc.
4501 Forbes Blvd., Ste. 200
Lanham, MD 20706
www.rowman.com

Distributed by NATIONAL BOOK NETWORK

British Library Cataloguing-in-Publication Information available

Library of Congress Cataloging-in-Publication Data

Names: Kokomoor, Kevin, author.
Title: La Florida : Catholics, conquistadores, and other American origin stories / Kevin Kokomoor.
Description: Palm Beach, Florida : Pineapple Press, [2023] | Includes bibliographical references and index. | Summary: "La Florida explores a Spanish thread to early American history that is unfamiliar or even unknown to most Americans. As La Florida uncovers, it was Spanish influence, not English, which drove America's early history. By focusing on America's Spanish heritage, the book's collection of stories complicates and sometimes challenges how Americans view their past, which author Kevin Kokomoor refers to as 'the country's founding mythology.'"—Provided by publisher.
Identifiers: LCCN 2023003543 (print) | LCCN 2023003544 (ebook) | ISBN 9781683343523 (hardback ; alk. paper) | ISBN 9781683343530 (epub)
Subjects: LCSH: Catholic Church—United States—Influence. | Florida—History—Spanish colony, 1565–1763. | Spain—Colonies—America—History. | United States—Civilization—Spanish influences. | Southern States—History—Colonial period, ca. 1600–1775.
Classification: LCC F311 .K65 2023 (print) | LCC F311 (ebook) | DDC 975.9/01—dc23/eng/20230216
LC record available at https://lccn.loc.gov/2023003543
LC ebook record available at https://lccn.loc.gov/2023003544

™ The paper used in this publication meets the minimum requirements of American National Standard for Information Sciences—Permanence of Paper for Printed Library Materials, ANSI/NISO Z39.48-1992.

To Warren

Acknowledgments

If *La Florida* seems like a strange book, the past few years have been strange times. Although COVID-19 was a terrible epidemic with horrific consequences, for me I guess in the end its isolation also ultimately proved productive. I taught classes online at a time when we weren't supposed to come on campus at the university where we worked, for almost any reason whatsoever. To pass the time, I wandered with my dog around the golf course I lived on every day for months. I played golf. I re-learned how to fly fish. To make extra money, I worked for a food delivery service, shopping and delivering food across the Myrtle Beach area. I fixed up an old Bronco, which I now drive everywhere. I had a roommate, Bob, who put up with all of this. I also continued to reconnect with my ex-wife, who soon moved down to live with me, and who gave birth to our first son, Warren, late in 2021.

I also obviously wrote. *La Florida* is, in other words, the quasi-academic quarantine side-project of an international epidemic. Strange times indeed. Yet, while most of the writing was done alone, in my room, there are still plenty of thanks to be given now that I see it all in print. I would like to thank Coastal Carolina University for doing everything it could to keep vulnerable faculty like me employed and productive. I give tremendous thanks in particular to the librarians and professionals at Coastal Carolina University's Kimbel Library. Michelle Lewis, Bill Carter, Joseph Taylor, and the rest of the incredible Access Services staff at the Kimbel Library, worked through countless book requests over semesters of work. *La Florida* absolutely would not have been possible without their assistance.

I also continue to thank the same familiar faces—the several historians, colleagues, mentors, and friends, who have shaped my career, and whose guidance I will always seek. John Belohlavek and Andrew Frank continue to encourage and critique my work, and I will always value their insight. To them I would like to add Robbie Ethridge. Robbie has had a hand, in one way or another, in almost everything I have produced academically. Even though I never formally studied under her, as I did with John and Andrew, I consider her no less a mentor. As has always been the case, I am thankful for the careful read and thoughtful consideration Robbie always gives anything I send her.

I would also like to thank Sian Hunter, whose encouragement helped me overcome some early setbacks. It is only because of our encouraging conversations and her professional recommendations that *La Florida* ever got to print. Timothy Fritz, a colleague and friend, looked over the manuscript and helped me continue to polish it, for which I am indebted. Thanks also to Chris Gunn, Aneilya Barnes, and the rest of the history department at Coastal Carolina University, for their continued support and friendship. Thanks to Giles Anderson, who saw as much potential in the project as I did, and who took a chance on me in pitching it. I look forward to working with him in the future.

Finally, a huge thanks my family, who continually support me no matter what. To my parents, to my brother and sister, to my grandparents, to Jenny, and now to Warren, I love you all!

Contents

Introduction: The Thanksgiving Day . . . Massacre? . . . . **ix**

I. Connections **1**

1 The La Florida Letdown **3**

Caribbean Connections 7

Central American Dreams 15

2 The Treacherous Gulf **29**

The Treacherous Gulf 33

Las Flotas 49

II. Origins **65**

3 Catholic Origins **67**

Spiritual Conquest in a New World 71

"Possessing" La Florida 81

La Matanza 93

4 Enslaved Origins **103**

Caribbean Slavery, La Florida Slavery 107

Slaves, Slavers, and Conquistadores 121

III. Transformations **135**

5 The Mississippian Encounter **137**

The Word *Pestilence* 141

The Everyday Theft 147

Caciques and Conquistadores 161

Two Towns Destroyed 171

6 Spanish-American Places **183**
From Martyrs to Models 187
Spanish-American Places. 201
Creole-American Places 217
7 Native Lasts, Native Firsts **231**
Smallpox and Slave Raids 235
A Southeastern Coalescence 249
Los Cimarrones. 257

IV. Legacies **273**
8 American Saints, American Legends **275**
American Saints 279
American Legends 291
9 An Anglo-American Counterpoint **301**
The Lost Pirate Colony of Roanoke 307
America's First Underground Railroad 319
Deerskin Diplomacy 335
10 La Florida Foodways **349**
BBQ, La Florida Style 353
The Cowboys of the Big Sink. 361
Citrus aurantium, La Florida's Fruit 371

Conclusion: "20. and Odd Negroes" **385**

Bibliography **393**

Index **411**

Introduction

The Thanksgiving Day . . . Massacre?

Consider one of America's foundational stories, the story of the First Thanksgiving. As the story goes, the first Thanksgiving was celebrated in the fall of 1621 after a very tough first year in Plymouth Plantation. According to Pilgrim Edward Winslow it was a harvest celebration that came after the townspeople processed all their crops and some men went out hunting. Not only did the men return with plenty for everyone to eat but also with groups of local Wampanoag Natives led by a chieftain, Massasoit. Not only would Massasoit and his people prove immensely influential in the colony's early survival, but the headman would also continue to play a role in the colony's development for the rest of his life. For now, his hunters added to the Pilgrim feast by bringing provisions of their own, including a few deer. According to Winslow, this was how the First Thanksgiving came to be.

With Winslow was Governor William Bradford, who penned his remembrance of the same fall harvest sometime later. Like Winslow, Bradford described things taking shape after the men and women gathered up their "small harvest" and were "well recovered in health and strength and had all things in good plenty." The residents went about winterizing Plymouth and otherwise preparing for the upcoming cold season by stockpiling food. All that summer "there was no want," and as autumn came, Plymouth enjoyed more abundance. Fish were everywhere, as were migratory fowl. Then there were deer, corn, and of course turkey, "of which they took many." This was the setting for Bradford's celebration.[1]

These two descriptions are actually the only two that speak in any detail of America's "First Thanksgiving." The two sources are not conflicting, yet they also do not exactly say a lot. Only one mention in Bradford's account, made in passing, lays the foundation for the ubiquitous turkey dinner most Americans today consider central to Thanksgiving Day. For hundreds of years since, historians have done wonders to fill in the celebration's likely particulars. Groups of colonists and Natives enjoyed a multi-day, coming-and-going affair of eating, drinking, shooting, and of course giving thanks. Even though no one referred to any of this as a "Thanksgiving" festival, there was plenty of thanks to be given. There were thanks to be given for the abundance of food that the Pilgrims and their Native guests enjoyed, which both sources related. The summer had gone so well, Bradford explained, and the bounty was so excellent that settlers got in the habit of writing "so large of their plenty here to their friends in England" that the picture they painted was simply not true. Nevertheless, the 1621 Plymouth feast was probably one to behold. Pilgrim-Native relations would not remain that pleasant forever.

But what if none of this was, in fact, the "First Thanksgiving"? It most certainly was New England's first harvest festival, and it might have even been the first communal celebration of thanks made in all of the English New World. But ask a historian of Spanish colonial history about America's First Thanksgiving, and the date would probably be some time in the late summer or early fall of 1565, more than a half-century before Plymouth Plantation was even a thought. Over the course of September 1565, Pedro Menéndez de Avilés established four separate "feast days of commemoration" after his successful landing at the future site of the town of St. Augustine. Any one of these, you could say, could be the First Thanksgiving.

The first of Menéndez's feast days was St. Augustine's Day, which he named after the day he first sited land. The first continuously occupied settlement in what is now the continental United States still bears that name. The second was Our Lady's Day, the day Menéndez landed at the site of that town, and where he held the first Mass. That, very well, might be the date of the First Thanksgiving. Today a church originally founded by these first Spaniards, Nombre de Dios, still stands in that spot. Third and fourth were St. Matthew's Day and All Saints' Day, two celebrations with much darker legacies based on what transpired in the following days and weeks. Could one of them be the First Thanksgiving?[2]

If calling a feast one of "commemoration" sounds awfully close to one of "Thanksgiving," it is because they were. Every one of these feasts certainly were just as much about giving thanks as the Pilgrim feast beheld by Winslow or Bradford. Each of Menéndez's four feast days was very much an act of public religious thanksgiving, but if we need to whittle it down to one feast exactly, it was at one of the first two, celebrated on September 8, when a chronicler described how Menéndez "had the Indians fed and dined himself." According to noted Florida historian Michael Gannon, aside from being the date of the establishment of America's first church, this feast "was the first community act of religion and

Thanksgiving in the first permanent settlement in the land."[3] If the celebration was a giving of thanks that included both Europeans and Natives, then Gannon was right. This was, as a matter of objective historical fact, America's First Thanksgiving.

If historians have taken liberties with Winslow's and Edwards's short explanations to describe the extent and importance of the Pilgrims' harvest celebration, then so, too, have historians like Gannon taken liberties with Menéndez's feast days. The phrase "had the Indians fed and dined himself" is literally all that is mentioned of Menéndez's festival. Not even a complete sentence! Which Natives partook of this celebration? Probably local Timucuans, but how many is uncertain. How exactly were the thanks given? Probably in a long and elaborate Mass, accompanied with lots of iconographic Catholic materials and loads of Latin. It would have been a solemn event that Natives would have found thoroughly confusing and probably pretty boring. What was served at this giving of thanks? Maybe the First Thanksgiving turkey if the Timucuans brought some, but probably fish and venison instead. Spaniards would have produced a classic Iberian soup made from salted pork or some other heavily cured ham and dried garbanzo beans and would have accompanied it with a strong Spanish wine. Perhaps some flour biscuits and honey were passed around for dessert. This Spanish feast would have been a far cry from turkey and pumpkin pie indeed.

Thanksgiving fare aside, far better understood and far more questionable were the events for which Menéndez was giving thanks. America's first governor was giving thanks for the recent successes that made the colony possible. The first two, St. Augustine's Day and Our Lady's Day, seem innocent enough. They marked a safe Atlantic crossing and the expedition's successful way up through the treacherous Caribbean Sea and the Gulf of Mexico passages. Considering how many sailors either died or simply disappeared along that journey each year, those were no small feats, and thanks were due. Those events, however, were not where his thanks ended. Almost every one of the Spanish men and women in St. Augustine were also thankful for Menéndez's recent military victories over the French, the victories that solidified St. Augustine's place as a first in North American history. His trip across the Atlantic was not done merely for the sake of European "discovery," after all; Menéndez founded St. Augustine to keep Spain's European competition from settling it first, and in that undertaking he had succeeded in remarkably bloody fashion. St. Augustine's first days, to be certain, were nothing to be proud of by modern sensibilities. To Menéndez, however, as well as to the hundreds of friars, soldiers, and settlers that accompanied him to St.

Augustine, these victories were nothing less than miraculous. Might these be the thanks given at the First Thanksgiving?

Menéndez's third feast day, St. Matthew's Day, was dedicated to the spectacular massacre he had just performed near the present-day city of Jacksonville. As soon as he and his men landed at St. Augustine, Menéndez set his eyes upon a group of French Huguenot Protestants and their fortified settlement, Fort Caroline, which lay just to the north. Menéndez wasted little time, marching his soldiers for days through swamps and driving rain, to surprise that den of pirates and heretics. When he did, he proceeded to slaughter all but a handful of women and children, and quickly shipped those horrified survivors away, not because he feared his men might take advantage of the women, but because he could not stand the presence of Protestants among him. This was the occasion of a marvelous Spanish feast, the St. Matthew's Day feast. Perhaps this was the setting of the First Thanksgiving.

Or perhaps it was the fourth feast, the All Saints' Day feast, which commemorated how Menéndez's men proceeded to hunt the battered French survivors of his first attack up and down the beach like animals. Of course, you could say the French were far from innocent in this affair. In fact, if the shoe were on the other foot, you could argue they would have done the exact same thing. Under their leader, Admiral Jean Ribault, they had taken ships down the coast to attack St. Augustine at the very same time Menéndez was marching his men north to attack him. Instead of a surprise attack by sea, Ribault's ships got caught in the very same storm that drenched the Spaniards, and the French ended up marooned on the beach. When Menéndez found the Frenchmen, they were dying of starvation, dying of thirst, dying of being stuck on a beach in the middle of nowhere. Despite their origination intent, the hapless French were now no longer a threat to anyone, yet that was exactly where Menéndez's troops set about systematically and pitilessly executing almost every single one of them, including Admiral Ribault. After accepting their surrender, Menéndez's men bound the castaway French soldiers and led them over the dunes in small groups so they could not hear each other scream. The executioners did not even bother to waste ammunition on their heretical French Protestant foes, who were now entirely at their mercy. No, they did their work slowly and methodically with lances and clubs, killing scores of unarmed prisoners and leaving their bodies to rot right there on the beach. For this great victory Menéndez proclaimed an All Saints' Day feast.

Some Thanksgiving this was! Comparatively speaking, it was not as though Edward Winslow, William Bradford, or anyone else was on hand to give thanks in November of 1621 at Plymouth Plantation had not seen their share of death. More than two thirds of the women on the Mayflower were dead by that First Thanksgiving, part of an overall majority of the entire colony that did not survive its first year. For all the different things to give thanks for in 1621, most Englishmen and -women probably gave thanks simply for being alive. Yet even that loss of life could never compare with the first few months of St. Augustine's existence. La Florida was a colony founded in wild bloodshed, and Menéndez gave thanks for every drop of blood spilled. Perhaps this is the reason why Americans gloss over Spanish La Florida so easily when recounting their country's earliest traditions. Who could blame them? Menéndez's Thanksgiving celebrations were a boring Mass at best, and the celebration of a cold-blooded killing spree at worst. Who would possibly want to make those qualities the foundation of the most American of traditions?

On the other hand, little more than a decade after the Pilgrim feast, Native relations had soured so badly that war was increasingly inevitable. First would be the Pequot War, followed by the much larger and more destructive King Philip's War, which saw Puritans effectively ethnically cleanse Southern New England of its Native population. In that light, perhaps La Florida's neglect is not all about the violence of St. Augustine's founding. Pilgrims certainly could get violent, too, as the horrific 1636 Mystic Massacre aptly demonstrates. Maybe La Florida's neglect reflects more fundamental assumptions about America's social, cultural, and religious roots. Perhaps the reason for the historical triumph of the Protestant harvest festival as "First Thanksgiving" is that, still to this day, Americans consider their country not only a Protestant nation but a nation founded by Protestants. In that light, Menéndez's feast celebrations become even more horrifying yet. Not only was he a Catholic, but at least two out of the four of his feast days were dedicated to the massacre of Protestants! French Huguenots studied many of the same Reformation texts as did their English Puritan relatives. They were the same kinds of heretical separatists that landed at Plymouth. Had Menéndez encountered any Pilgrims on the beach in La Florida, he almost certainly would have killed them too. How could a Protestant nation have such a violent anti-Protestant origin story? Imagine teaching that story to a middle school social studies class.

At first, the recounting of these first La Florida moments reads like an entertaining but otherwise academically useless exercise in historical counternarrative. Yet as the year 2021 fades into the past, Americans will have sat down to commemorate the four hundredth anniversary of the First Thanksgiving, even though as a matter of simple historical fact, it will not have been the four hundredth anniversary of the First Thanksgiving. Such an anniversary only makes sense if Americans completely ignore the European settlement that was already long in existence in North America by the time Pilgrims landed at Plymouth. Is the state in which that Spanish presence originated—Florida—no less a part of the United States of America than Massachusetts? Not at all. Nevertheless, such has been the case as long as the Thanksgiving Day holiday has existed in America, so perhaps no attempt at historical revisionism will ever replace Massachusetts with Florida, Plymouth with St. Augustine, Protestants with Catholics, or buckle hat–wearing Pilgrims with murderous Spaniards, as the foundation for America's favorite meal. Several of the profession's most prominent historians certainly have tried. Yet, oddly enough, this book is an attempt to do just that. Just as La Florida represented America's first European colony, so too does Spanish colonial history represent America's first Euro-American history.

If, at its heart, *La Florida* seeks to challenge English firsts with Spanish firsts, then why open with Plymouth and America's First Thanksgiving? After all, wasn't British America already in existence by that point, farther south, in Virginia? Why not begin with Jamestown? Because *La Florida* claims to rediscover and recenter the Spanish in America's founding stories, and perhaps there is no more powerful founding story than that of the First Thanksgiving. What *La Florida* does not claim to do is provide a complete revisionist history of the early Southeast, or even a chronological history of colonial Florida. It is not primarily a Native American history of early America, or a history of slavery there. It is not designed to be academically comprehensive in any way. Its narrative is not built upon the discovery or usage of new sources. Neither does it frame older sources in novel ways. While it certainly is still academic in nature, its narrative is approachably written and synthetic in design. It relies far heavier on secondary historical and anthropological work than the primary record, which is tapped only to give life to particular historical actors or bring unique historical moments to life.

There is plenty that *La Florida* does not claim to do. What it does claim to do, on the other hand, is get its readers questioning America's founding mythology. Highlighting America's Spanish connections and Spanish firsts puts non-English and non-Protestant voices center stage in the epic saga of America's earliest years. When the religious forces of push and pull enticed the first Europeans to America's shores, they were Catholic, not Protestant, forces. The first settlers to establish themselves in America permanently were not religious Anglican outcasts or ambitious London merchants. They were Spaniards, looking to La Florida at first to replicate their successful conquests elsewhere in the Spanish empire, then second to secure the riches of those conquests by claiming La Florida's Gulf and Atlantic coastlines.

To do those things, *La Florida* blends popular stories of Native empires, food traditions, and shipwrecked castaways with academically honest discussions of race, violence, and colonialism. In the process of their attempts at American colonization, Spaniards were the first to introduce slavery into North America and build their societies around concepts of race. The first ships that would connect Africa to North America in the Atlantic slave trade originated in Spanish and Portuguese outposts on the West coast of Africa and terminated in St. Augustine. Spanish settlements during this period also set into motion the first ecological changes that would sweep across the continent. Spanish colonizers brought the first plants, animals, and diseases to American shores, the latter of which would lead to the dislocation and even destruction of entire Native polities. That chaos also, however, led to the creation of new Native identities, like Seminoles, a Native identity now practically synonymous with Floridian identity. Spanish colonization was devastating, but it also produced some of America's most iconic regional foodways, like Florida citrus or Southern barbecue. The legacies of the very first years of Spanish colonization in North America, which began early in the sixteenth century, reverberate both in Florida and in the larger Southeast today.

La Florida's stories represent nontraditional narratives that should have Americans questioning their country's founding mythology. Although this book is not overly argumentative in that respect, there is an important question worth considering when reading it: these stories are lively, relatable, relevant, and entertaining. They are the kinds of stories people love to read. Why, then, are they so often undervalued, or discounted altogether? Probably because they consider American founders that spoke Spanish, not English. That were Catholic, not Protestant. That were in Florida, not Massachusetts or Virginia. They are stories inconsistent, in other words, with the commonly understood and universally accepted narrative of America's beginnings—a mythology that many Americans accept as objective historical fact. Most Americans believe that their country's religious traditions started with Pilgrims in Massachusetts, or that its ugly history with racial slavery began with tobacco in Virginia. Yet, revealing the role non-English others played in America's earliest moments creates a more complex, complete, and interesting history of important American legacies. Spanish actions had tremendous consequences in the transformation of North America.

A few last points of clarification are necessary—a few more things *La Florida* will claim to do or not do. First, it will always attempt to portray the experiences of all actors in the *La Florida* story. While it is a history of Florida and the Southeast, and not specifically a Native history of Florida and the Native Southeast, nevertheless *La Florida* does attempt to recover a Native voice. This, any historian will tell you, can be tricky. Native voices in such early and far-flung places are difficult to uncover. Just as rare are the voices of America's first African and Creole peoples, which *La Florida* also attempts to uncover. Then, on the other hand, there are the Spanish voices. Spaniards, like other European colonizing powers of the time, were notorious bureaucrats, even when stationed in backwater outposts like St. Augustine or Pensacola. While the records they produced are not so rare, very seldom did those Spaniards pontificate on the lives of the enslaved, the missionized, or otherwise colonized. When they did, very seldom were their words particularly insightful. Church documents venerated friars' Catholic values and disparaged Native cultural, social, and faith traditions. Political and economic documents referenced slavery casually, and in passing, and when they did, their words oozed with racial and cultural prejudices. Just as bad are the writings of eyewitnesses like enthusiastic de Soto chroniclers, like Gracilaso de la Vega. Reading their narratives, as one author put it, is like reading "a lot of highly creative interpretations of historical events," and that's putting it generously.[4] In short, the lives of Native, African, and Creole groups are no easier constructed in La Florida than they are anywhere else in early America. Their lives and their stories are explored in every chapter, at every turn, to every extent. While these moments will never prove satisfying, they are all the sources will allow.

Lastly, and perhaps most importantly, although *La Florida* presents a Spanish-centered look at Southeastern America, it is no way supposed to narrate a Eurocentric story of colonial triumphalism. It is heavy in both irony and sarcasm; do not mistake any of that for genuine veneration of the Spanish, or legitimization of either Spanish actions or the ideologies that drove them. Nowhere, in fact, should the Spanish be perceived as the heroes of its stories. The Native peoples of La Florida were not somehow its invaders. They were the defenders of their homes and their ways of life. And Spaniards were not righteous Christian warriors or the religious saviors of ignorant Native peoples. They were not a culturally or even a technologically superior people. What they were was a devastating colonizing power that entirely changed the trajectory of the American Southeast. No more, no less.

The religious, ethnic, and racial bigotry exhibited by Spanish colonizers went to depths unfathomable by modern sensibilities, and the world those colonizers sought to build in La Florida was one of unparalleled intolerance and exploitation. The violence wrought by the Spanish upon the Native Southeast, for instance, could be described at times as almost apocalyptic. Many Native peoples survived this period of calamity, as generations of Native scholars have argued. As *La Florida* will suggest, however, many did not. Likewise, to suggest that the American slave trade really began as the La Florida slave trade is to acknowledge an even longer and uglier history of racial oppression in what would become the United States of America than is already admitted. The Spanish, in short, while central to *La Florida*, are nothing to be celebrated. Indeed, while they are almost always the primary actors in the stories that follow, they also almost always play the villains.

Structurally and narratively speaking, *La Florida* charts a somewhat unorthodox and potentially confusing course. Like a journey through "The Treacherous Gulf" (the title and subject of an early chapter), it will take skill to navigate. The book comprises four separate parts: "Connections," "Origins," "Transformations," and "Legacies." Each part moves thematically more than it does chronologically, meaning the same time period can be covered more than once. "Connections," for instance, begins at contact and moves through a century of Spanish expansion, only to have "Origins" loop around and begin basically at the same place again. So on with "Transformations," and "Legacies." Because the chapters in each part hinge on interpretive themes, there can be significant chronological overlap between and among them, and they can jump back and forth a bit. Things may even seem redundant at first, yet each chapter in each part serves its own purpose.

Within the four parts are ten separate chapters in total, each of which speaks to the Spanish La Florida that began in 1513 and ended with the evacuation of the colony in 1763. Scholars refer to this tidy two-and-a-half-century stretch as the "first" Spanish period. Although this might seem like an obscure and insignificant stretch of time, the government of the United States of America will have to control Florida for more than another generation before it can claim an ownership longer than the period under consideration here—Spain's *first* of *two* claims to ownership.

In "Connections," the first two chapters open the book by discussing contact, and they do that by tying Florida's discovery and ultimate settlement to Spanish happenings elsewhere. The first begins with Caribbean-based conquistadores hopping from island to island searching for the next conquest. The second charts the importance of La Florida to Spanish authorities who sought to protect the treasure routes that they used to transport the plundered riches of the New World back to Spain. As the opening chapters demonstrate, the continent's history of colonization was really first a Caribbean, South American, and maritime history. It is Spanish colonial history.

Next, in "Origins," chapters 3 and 4 describe important American beginnings with more particular thematic connections between La Florida and Spanish colonization elsewhere in the New World. Chapter 3 focuses on the influence of the unrelenting, unyielding, and surprisingly violent Catholic Church. Church officials played central roles in the conquest of the New World, which they hoped to extend to La Florida. Chapter 4 discusses the role of captivity and enslavement in the discovery and settlement of La Florida. North America, this chapter suggests, was discovered not in the search of a fountain of youth, but in the search for slaves, placing slavery and captivity at the heart of American history from its earliest days. Both chapters explore America's first years of European discovery, exploration, and colonization, by describing just how typically and violently Spanish it all was.

Chapter 5 begins an important new thread that considers the consequences of this contact. This begins "Transformations," which charts the interactions between Spanish conquistadores and Mississippian Chiefdoms, the two worlds that often collided together during the earliest moments of contact and colonization. In the short term these interactions were tense and disruptive at best. At worst, they frequently led to incredible violence. In the long term, they were nothing short of transformative, setting into motion the collapse of Southeastern America's Native world. Chapter 6 follows those moments of contact by following the slow colonization of Spanish La Florida. While in no way comparable in size to larger colonies like New Spain, La Florida was still a Spanish colony. It featured all the familiar trappings of a Spanish colonial society, from its churches to its orderly roads to its highly structured and extremely oppressive racial caste system.

Chapter 7 returns to Native America and takes a sobering look at the legacies of Spanish colonialism. Across the turn of the eighteenth century, Southeastern America's Native polities withered away under a constant barrage of epidemic disease, only to be assaulted by a slave trade that originated with Spain's American soon-to-be archrival—English Carolina. The final destruction of the Mississippian World was not the end of America's Native presence, however, but the beginning of a process of coalescence that brought the remnants of broken and scattered communities together into new peoples with names Americans still recognize, like Cherokees and Choctaws. In the modern-day state of Florida, this process continued with the creation of Seminoles, a group now seemingly synonymous with Florida's modern identity. Seminoles represent the powerful, modern legacy of Spanish La Florida. This chapter is one of the few that carries the La Florida story out of the first Spanish period, but it does so by reminding readers of the La Florida origins of the Seminole people.

Chapter 8 begins the last section, "Legacies," by looking at the history behind some Florida place names, as well as some of its most important legends, including the infamous "Fountain of Youth." Chapter 9 is a more sobering look at the larger theme of Anglo-Hispanic rivalry, begun earlier, by discussing Florida's impact on English settlement in North America. Roanoke, it suggests, was founded by British privateers interested in raiding Spanish shipping off the coast of La Florida. Disrupting Spanish shipping just off of La Florida, in other words, gave birth of the idea of Virginia. In future generations it was the Carolinas that defined the Anglo-Spanish rivalry. Considering slavery, for instance, while Spanish La Florida was the first enslaved place in North America, it was also the location of the first free African American community, a community that was purpose-built to undermine slavery in the expanding British Lowcountry. Spanish offers of freedom to British slaves created America's first traditions of slave resistance, including the first "Underground Railroad," which ran south to St. Augustine. The possibility of finding freedom there was also at least partially responsible for precipitating the Stono Rebellion, the British South's first major slave insurrection. Lastly, the Spanish presence in St. Augustine and Pensacola also allowed regional Natives, like Creeks, to negotiate with British traders in South Carolina and Georgia for higher trade prices and more advantageous trade relationships. This competition generated a Native policy referred to as "play-off diplomacy," and a period understood as the high-water mark in terms of Native power and sovereignty in the Colonial Southeast.

The last chapter ends with a somewhat lighter take on America's hidden Spanish heritage: it looks at a few of the foods in Florida and the larger Southeast that people regularly enjoy, but do not necessarily recognize as having distinctly Spanish roots in this period. Swine herding, free-range cattle ranching, and citrus farming were all Spanish traditions that are now recognizable American traditions. Most Floridians might have tasted a good smoked fish dip in their lifetimes, but few will have recognized that smoked fish, a process mastered by La Florida's Native peoples, can lay claim to America's first barbecue tradition. It certainly inspired Euro-Americans, beginning with the Spanish, to apply the technique to more familiar fare, like hogs. The rest, it almost goes without saying, is culinary history.

Some chapters are more whimsical in nature and construction, and others more academically rigorous. They all, however, when taken together support the common theme that many of America's firsts were not necessarily English firsts, Protestant firsts, Massachusetts or Virginia firsts. America's Euro-American story was first set into motion by Spaniards, years that included moments and processes of incredible historical weight. Many of the modern-day legacies of those shaping forces may have faded away, but not all have, and one does not have to take a stroll through St. Augustine to evoke them. A good pulled pork sandwich or even a glass of orange juice will do.

Notes

1. These two sources for the first Thanksgiving come from Bradford, *Bradford's History*, 127-128; and Dexter, *Mourt's Relation*, 132-135.
2. Bushnell, *Situado and Sabana*, 37.
3. Gannon, *The Cross in the Sand*, 26-27.
4. Cofer, "A Brief Account of the Adventures of My Appropriated Kinsman," 655.

I. CONNECTIONS

1 The La Florida Letdown

In 1540 Hernando de Soto's men excitedly arrived in Cofitachequi, a Mississippian chiefdom located near modern-day Camden, South Carolina. For de Soto and his hundreds of men, the journey to Cofitachequi had not been an easy one. They had fought their way out of peninsular Florida under a hail of arrows only to teeter on the edge of starvation as they passed through a stretch of the Savannah River basin. It was a place, as even local chieftains admitted, barren of either food or people for de Soto to steal it from. Despite those warnings, de Soto and his men pressed on. That made the misery of the stretch—the Georgia Stretch—one entirely of the Spaniards' own making. They had practically run from peninsular Florida to the Carolina Piedmont. Even odder, no one was chasing them. Rather, it was gold de Soto's men were chasing. These Spaniards were chasing rumors of La Florida's endless mineral riches, and Cofitachequi was apparently where they would find it.

Earlier, Native captives in the chiefdom of Apalachee, near present-day Tallahassee, had assured the Spaniards that fabulous amounts of gold and silver awaited them at Cofitachequi, accounts which de Soto clearly found convincing. There "they thought to load themselves down with rich treasure and return to Spain," according to one of de Soto's chroniclers. Such claims were no doubt calculated by the Apalachee to get the unwanted Spanish as far away from them as possible. The last winter had been a devastating one for the Apalachee, with de Soto's men running through the chiefdom's corn stores, affronting and even kidnapping its leadership, and perpetrating all manner of horrors on its men and women. Thankfully, if the rumor of Cofitachequi was indeed a plan to rid Apalachee of this Spanish scourge, then at least it worked. Hernando de Soto and his men marched so quickly through Georgia that the months spent there were the most peaceful of any on his entire entrada. Very seldom in the sixteenth-century Southeast did things go as smoothly as they did along the Georgia Stretch.

Then there was Cofitachequi, a sizeable Mississippian community nestled on the banks of the Wateree River. Once there, fed and rested, de Soto's men wasted little time pressing their hosts about the riches of which they had been promised. They pointed to their jewelry when trying to communicate with the Natives, showing them whatever gold, silver, or precious stones they had on them. Obliging her guests, the Chieftainess of Cofitachequi summoned men to bring out what she was sure they were asking for, the metals "that were in her country of the colors that the Spaniards wanted, which were yellow and white, because they showed her gold rings and pieces of silver," as well as pearls and any other precious stones she thought they might value. Soon enough Natives appeared with beautiful sheets of hammered copper "of a very resplendent golden color"—the supposed gold. And for silver the Natives produced slabs of mica, which at first sight "were white and shone like silver" but were light as a feather. After holding, they crumbled in the Spaniards' hands.[1]

One can almost see the look on de Soto's face, or feel the pit in his stomach, when his guests presented him with the supposed riches of Cofitachequi. This stuff was worthless. At least there were pearls, and plenty of them, as could plainly be seen by de Soto and his men. They covered the bodies of their Native hosts and even filled burial pits. Pearls however assuaged de Soto little in that moment of almost unimaginable disappointment. He, who had already experienced the glory of conquest in Peru and the wealth of its corresponding riches, had not risked his reputation, his finances, and his life to sail to La Florida for strings of burnt freshwater pearls. Neither had his men fought their way out of basically the entire modern state of Florida, and then crawled through much of the modern state of Georgia, for sheets of copper. They had all done these things on the guarantee of gold and silver that their previous exploits had convinced them were in La Florida. After several months looking, however, and having moved through several large chiefdoms and coming up empty, de Soto and his men were slowly coming to realize that their confidence was misplaced. La Florida, for this newest wave of Spanish attempted conquest, was a letdown.

De Soto's epic moment of letdown in modern-day South Carolina is one important chapter in the European origin story of America that begins in 1492 and has a decidedly Spanish Caribbean and Latin American feel to it. Before there was anything else of European or African origin in what would become the United

States of America, there was La Florida. And long, long before that became the American South, it constituted the unknown northern edges of the Caribbean and then modern-day Mexico. Here, the discovery of La Florida and the first attempts to settle it are seen from that perspective. They were first the culmination of waves of Spanish expansion into the Caribbean, beginning with Columbus's original voyages of discovery. Only modest successes there by the most stubborn, violent, enterprising conquistadores, however, led to expansion and exploration elsewhere. Those desires ultimately generated the first waves of interest in La Florida, which was at that time considered another island of possible potential. Consequently, the attempts were led by already wealthy, seasoned, and disappointed Caribbean explorers, one among them being Juan Ponce de León. When those initial attempts to extend the Caribbean did not bring the easy returns to which Spaniards were accustomed, a La Florida still largely unknown in size and scope to Europeans was written off as just another island of underwhelming potential, and conquistadores looked elsewhere.

That continued until the Spanish conquest of the Aztec and Incan empires in Central Mexico and Peru, respectively, each of which like a shot of adrenaline instantly revived interest in La Florida and fueled new waves of Spanish exploration. These waves brought more violent and more haunting characters to the shores of the North American continent—Pánfilo de Narváez and Hernando de Soto, to be specific—but figures no more successful in their goals of realizing fabulous wealth. Thus, La Florida's origin story is one of connections, not only to the Caribbean, but to Central and South America as well.

The first, Narváez, had been humiliated in his own attempt to conquer the Aztec Empire. The second, Hernando de Soto, had played a significant but still subordinate role in the conquest of the Incas. Both men expected that their leadership roles in the successful exploration, conquest, and settlement of La Florida would mend their reputations and catapult them into the pantheon of Spanish warrior-legends. Each of these men tempted La Florida because they already had histories in the New World, histories which explain their determination to explore and attempt to conquer a recently discovered and unknown territory at great risk. Spanish successes elsewhere in Central and South America, in short, provided the motivation for conquistadores of a second rate to try their luck in La Florida. By the end of these settlement attempts at midcentury, the limits of La Florida as they had been charted and explored were tremendous, extending a claimed Spanish Caribbean empire all the way to the Appalachian Mountains.

Note

1. Clayton, Knight, and Moore, eds., *The De Soto Chronicles*, 231, 279-280; Clayton, Knight, and Moore, eds., *The De Soto Chronicles*, 2: 262, 294-295; Hudson, *Knights of Spain*, 176-179.

Caribbean Connections

Over the course of several voyages, beginning of course in 1492 and stretching into the sixteenth century, Christopher Columbus became the first European to lay eyes on the modern-day Bahamas and Hispaniola—the latter of which is now home to the Dominican Republic and Haiti. Next for Columbus to behold was Puerto Rico, Jamaica, Cuba, various other smaller surrounding Caribbean islands, and eventually the Caribbean coast of Central America. La Florida's story might have begun on one of his first two voyages, in say 1492 or 1494, when Columbus was the closest he would ever be to either the East Coast of peninsular Florida or the Gulf of Mexico. Had he continued northwest through the Bahamas on his first sail, rather than turning south to Cuba, he most likely would have gotten his ships caught in the Gulf Stream, as Juan Ponce de León would do two decades later. Or had he continued west along the southern coast of Cuba in 1494, the Yucatan Current would have sucked his ships into the Gulf of Mexico. Either would have led him, in all likelihood, to the coast of La Florida. Instead, in both instances he went elsewhere, turning back in 1494 to the more familiar islands of his previous adventures, leaving both the Gulf of Mexico and La Florida to the exploits of later Spaniards.[1]

Those original discoveries were ultimately the product of Spanish and Portuguese desires to directly contact markets in Asia and India, markets that were being accessed at the time through a system of overland trade routes now known collectively as the Silk Road. Portuguese explorers took a more traditional tack to get around that road, working down the west coast of Africa, across the Cape of Good Hope, and then up the East Coast of Africa to India. When they eventually did so, it ushered in a multi-century era of Portuguese imperialism.[2] Columbus, of course, charted a far more radical course, but with the same goal in mind—finding his way to the Pacific. That goal kept him and the waves of Spanish explorers that followed him occupied during what seemed to be a constant stream of Caribbean discovery. For years Spaniards kept discovering the southern edges of the New World because they kept trying to get around it.[3]

Economics, however, can only partly explain the waves of Spanish conquistadores that flooded into the Caribbean in Columbus's wake. Columbus's 1493 return, it turns out, coincided almost perfectly with the closing of a defining chapter in Hispanic history, which left thousands of potential conquistadores rudderless and adrift in their homeland. The year 1492 not only marked Columbus's arrival of the "New World," but the final victory achieved by Spaniards in a centuries-long struggle to reclaim their corner of the "Old World." In 1492 the combined forces of King Ferdinand of Aragon and Queen Isabella of Castile completed the Spanish *Reconquista* after capturing the last Islamic outpost at Granada, a campaign that also gave rise to the Catholic Spanish monarchy. In the wake of that glorious victory, however, legions of men who had known nothing but faith and conquest were left idle. These men were "never so happy" as when they were at war, according to one historian, gaining land and title by taking it from their enemies.

They were a class of men, in sum, who had been defined by war, but now there was no more war. These hidalgos faced an existential crisis—without such a struggle to define them, what would they do? Thus, the New World was destined to suffer as perhaps the world's first immigrant safety valve, and for men who embodied the most extreme qualities of toxic masculinity perhaps in all of world history, no less. The *Reconquista* would continue into the New World, beginning with Columbus. Theirs was a mission, as contemporary Bernal Díaz del Castillo explained, "to serve God and His Majesty; to bring light to those that dwell in darkness, and to get rich, as all men desire." In other words, they would conquer unknown lands and subjugate unknown people, and they would do so to glorify the Spanish Crown, to glorify the Catholic Church, and of course to glorify themselves. These were the men, unfortunately, which Columbus's European discoveries unleashed upon the Caribbean, and who would make it from there to La Florida.[4]

Explorers but also conquerors, these men poured into the New World with a relentless drive for conquest and wealth, moving from Caribbean Island to island, then to the Isthmus of Panama, then down the Atlantic Coast of South America.[5] Still others began to double back, hoping to make their names and their fortunes subduing the Native populations of the Caribbean islands and exploiting them to generate wealth. These waves of discovery and destruction, however, turned out to be the New World's first bubble. Although there was some mineral wealth to be had in these initial years of brutal conquest, beginning on Hispaniola, there was not as much as was anticipated. Caribbean "placer" successes became moderate and then even disappointing, based on initial accounts of riverine gold that were soon exhausted. Hopes of easy mineral wealth turned to establishing *encomiendas* in order to exploit Native labor on sugar or tobacco plantations. Eventually, however, the luster of the New World began to fade. Instead, as one historian described, "America remained a half-forgotten reality that disappointed the pioneers, because it failed to produce either immediate wealth or a route to the Spice Islands."[6]

Nevertheless, successive expeditions slowly branched out into the Caribbean basin, moving from Hispaniola to Puerto Rico in 1508 and Jamaica a year later, bringing Spaniards ever nearer to the Gulf of Mexico and peninsular Florida. With the invasion of Cuba by Diego Velázquez de Cuéllar in 1511, the discovery of La Florida just to the north became inevitable.[7] La Florida was destined to be next, a place discovered and exploited by those Caribbean conquistadores who had already settled elsewhere, who were disappointed by what they found, and who sought more.

It was only a few years later, in fact, in 1513, when a frustrated group of these Cuban- and Puerto Rican–based Spaniards led the expedition that named mainland North America. Juan Ponce de León organized the exploration, continuing another Spanish Caribbean trend into North America: those who went to La Florida were usually not beginners. As for de León, he certainly was no stranger to the Caribbean, having sailed with Columbus on his second voyage in 1493. As a mariner and a soldier, one of the New World's original gold placers, a rancher, and then a plantation owner, de León had through brutal exploitation of Natives amassed a small Caribbean fortune. Yet, in true hidalgo fashion, he quickly resettled from Hispaniola to Puerto Rico after word spread of gold there, extending his holdings onto multiple islands. He even briefly governed Puerto Rico before being ousted in a legal struggle spearheaded by the competing Columbus family, who claimed control of everything Christopher Columbus originally discovered. Forced from his governorship, the Spanish King consoled de León by authorizing him to explore the northern edges of the Caribbean, already reported to contain a new island named "Bimini," which had been visited briefly by a wayward Spanish mariner or two only a few years previous. Rich but out of his position of power and yearning for more, Juan Ponce de León looked to Bimini. What he found was La Florida.[8]

As de León's decision to wager it all on La Florida foretold, this new unknown was a place to test Caribbean Spaniards unhappy with their current position, and who usually sailed from Caribbean ports. As it turned out, almost all of the Spaniards to test their luck there lost everything there, including their life, another trend de León would pioneer.[9]

While reconnoitering the Gulf Coast, de León and his men received small quantities of a low-grade gold from the nearby Calusa Indians and were invited to stay for more, which they obviously did. Instead, they were buffeted by wave after wave of canoe-based assault in what seemed to be a well-coordinated ambush. De León left without giving much of a fight but soon retained a governorship, or *adelantado* title, to La Florida and the elusive "Bimini," even though he chose not to pursue it. Instead, he returned to Puerto Rico to firm up Spanish control there—at least the violent subjugation of Puerto Rico had produced moderate wealth for him already.[10]

For the moment, de León chose the very un-hidalgo-like path of easiest return. As a consequence, La Florida, its identity tied inexorably to that of the larger Caribbean, was written off as another underwhelming island in what had become, by the second decade of the sixteenth century, somewhat of an underwhelming New World. That was the case for almost another half-decade. Only with the discovery and conquest of the present-day country of Mexico did La Florida's prospects brighten. Mariners Francisco Hernández de Córdoba and Juan de Grijalva took note of the populated Gulf Coasts of the Yucatan and Central Mexico when they cruised up and down it in 1517–1518.[11] One year later, Hernán Cortés landed on the Gulf Coast of present-day Mexico, founded Vera Cruz, and marched inland to Tenochtitlan and began the destruction of the Aztec Empire. Cortés's consequent establishing of Mexico City and New Spain generated a gold boom that had, by the 1520s, made a handful of conquistadores almost unimaginably rich, and transformed the Spanish government of Charles V into a European superpower almost overnight.[12]

In Mexico City, Cortés served as *adelantado*. His title was a type of governorship issued by the Spanish King, and one that usually came with incredible perks. It granted for the successful conqueror some combination of a share of whatever riches were gained, the right to lands or slaves, or some sort of title of nobility. This was clarified in Cortés's *capitulación*, a contract for conquest, and in Cortés's case, it had made him a very rich and very powerful man. For enterprising hidalgos there was no greater honor than attaining such power and prestige. Juan Ponce de León received a *capitulación* in 1513 that granted him the *adelantado* title and secured for him, among other provisions, "the gold and other metals and profitable things" he might find in La Florida, tax free for the first year. Taxes on gold would increase over time, but de León was also guaranteed a tenth of any other revenue the entire region would produce. While de León was disappointed in his first time to capitalize on such a deal, Hernán Cortés certainly was not, and he died having amassed tremendous wealth, political power, and a "marques" title. Waves of hopeful hidalgos yearned for a similar opportunity, intoxicated by the possibility of triumphant combat and similar fame and untold fortune. Some looked to the south, into Mayan and Incan territory, and some looked to the north, returning a Spanish gaze onto La Florida, forever connecting the possibilities of that place with the successes in Central Mexico.[13]

By the time would-be *adelantados* like Juan Ponce de León returned their gaze to La Florida, its sprawling contours were also coming into clearer view. While its interior had gone unchallenged, the waters off of La Florida were teeming with merchant activity. Antón de Alaminos, a member of Columbus's final voyage to the Caribbean and a member of de León's voyage in 1513, emerged as a workhorse of a mariner and one of the pioneers of La Florida exploration, charting much of the Gulf Coast by 1519. Alonso Álvarez de Pineda came next, reaching the Gulf Coast of peninsular Florida near present-day St. Marks, charting most of the eastern Gulf Coast down to modern-day Naples, then doubling back all the way to the Mississippi River. Together these charts revealed the rough limits of peninsular Florida, generating for the Spanish government the first comprehensive chart of a La Florida that spanned from the Texas Gulf Coast to the Atlantic Ocean.[14] Perhaps new ideas of La Florida's expansiveness were what spurred Juan Ponce de León onto his second La Florida attempt. Again it was Caribbean- and Gulf-based exploration that would fuel La Florida expansion, and again this attempt at expansion would end in failure.

A permanent settlement in La Florida would surely lay the foundation for a sprawling empire comparable to New Spain, de León certainly gambled, and he planned his newest conquest accordingly. Several ships, 250 horses and all other manner of livestock, and around 200 men would make this journey.[15] Again de León chose the southwest coast of peninsular Florida, perhaps because he was already familiar with the environment but also certainly because the region had produced for him at least some gold already. This time, de León was certainly confident; if the Calusa were intent on resisting, he would be prepared.

The irony in this approach was twofold. First, there was no gold to be had in southwest peninsular Florida. Whatever gold the Calusa gave de León in 1513 was gold they most likely had received in trade from Taino or Arawak Natives, visiting from elsewhere in the Caribbean. Second and far worse for de León, by 1521 waves of Spanish violence and enslavement had already devastated much of the northern Caribbean. Whoever had not been enslaved from islands like the Bahamas was fleeing to places like southern peninsular Florida, forgotten and relatively unaffected by Spanish conquest. Any news being brought by Taino or Arawak refugees to Calusa territory was not going to reflect well on a man like Juan Ponce de León, in short, who has been described in recent scholarship as "red-haired, robust, and full of vinegar," and as a "robust redhead who loved bullying Indians."[16] De León was a particularly ambitious Spanish hidalgo with a long and multi-island record of violence, intimidation, and Native exploitation. It was almost certainly the clear lack of compassion for Natives, and not his red hair, that sealed Juan Ponce de León's fate on the Florida coast.

Although de León came to La Florida to stay in 1521, he spent so little time physically on the beach that scholars aren't clear as to whether his settlement ever actually existed. The expedition was overwhelmed and repulsed by a force of Calusa warriors almost immediately upon landing. According to one Spanish chronicler, the Calusa broke up the effort immediately "and killed part of the Christians, and more than twice as many of the Indians died." Eventually, however, they forced de León to beat a hasty retreat. De Leon himself "badly wounded" by an arrow had agreed to retreat to Cuba "to be cured, if he could," and then "with more people and strength to return to this conquest." Instead, he died, along with others that were wounded or sick, bringing the first attempt by Spaniards to colonize La Florida to an unceremonious end.[17]

Although 1521 would mark the end of the first attempt to settle La Florida and indeed the end of de León himself, Spanish interest in La Florida was only on the rise. That very same year a lesser-known settlement in a different part of the Spanish territory was beginning to take shape, drawing into focus the enormous extent of this unexplored land. That was the year an entirely different set of Spaniards, led by Francisco Gordillo and Pedro de Quejo, arrived on the coast of modern-day South Carolina. Fittingly, they were slave raiders, working together and sailing on reports of the previous exploits of another slave raider by the name of Francisco de Salazar. Doing so, the two made landfall near the Santee River. Soon they made their way north along the coast and into Winyah Bay, near modern-day Georgetown.[18] Their expeditions were quick, but the reports they brought back with them set into motion larger designs for the region known as "Chicora."

News spread quickly. By 1523 Lucas Vázquez de Ayllón, then a judge in Hispaniola who had funded Francisco de Salazar's original voyage, gained royal authorization to settle the region. Two years later Ayllón dispatched Quejo on a reconnoitering sail and Quejo gave him more than he bargained; on his cruise he mapped the Atlantic Coast from Cumberland Island, Georgia, all the way north to the Delaware Bay. Quejo also snatched up Natives from four separate language groups along the coast, hinting at what the Spanish had in store for the Native population of South Carolina. For Ayllón, more sources of local intelligence, possible future interpreters, and certainly potential laborers. For groups like the Waccamaw or Pee Dee, new sources of disease and destruction. Certainly, Ayllón's developments boded far better for the ends of Spanish explorers who were really just Caribbean plantation owners and slave raiders than for the Southeast's Native peoples.[19]

For the second time, an unknown La Florida was being probed by a Caribbean Spaniard seeking to improve his lot through discovery and hopefully conquest. Ayllón finally attempted such a settlement in 1526, and at over 600 people his expedition was sizeable. According to one contemporary, the Spanish hidalgo spirit was nowhere lacking in enterprise, "for the entire Spanish nation is in fact so keen about novelties that people go eagerly anywhere they are called by a nod or a whistle, in the hope of bettering their condition, and are ready to sacrifice what they have for what they hope."[20] Although by that point he was little more than a Dominican bureaucrat, Ayllón was no stranger to Caribbean conquest. As a member of Pánfilo de Narváez's disastrous expedition in 1520 to oust Hernán Cortés from New Spain, however, Ayllón had tasted only failure.[21] It was through his settlement of La Florida that Ayllón hoped to advance from his modest success as a colonial lawyer to the glory of an *adelantado*.

Upon landing at Winyah Bay, however, Ayllón was disappointed by what he found. These swamps were unsuitable for settlement in just about every possible way, prompting Ayllón to split his expedition up and move south. Despite the maze of islands, bays, and meandering rivers, the land and sea party had no trouble reconnecting along the Georgia coast near Sapelo Sound, where Ayllón founded San Miguel de Gualdape.[22] A brief settlement resulted, but riches were not what Lucas Vázquez de Ayllón found in Guadalpe. There in September, it was gone by October. By that time disease had claimed Ayllón and countless others, and the remainder were mutinying. By the time the survivors abandoned Guadalpe and retreated to the expedition's port of origin, Santo Domingo, only a quarter of the original expedition remained. While this settlement could claim to be the earliest settlement attempt in what would become a British North American, as historian Paul Hoffman reminds us, for the Spanish it was yet another La Florida letdown.[23]

Notes

1. Kamen, *Empire*, 41-43; Sledge, *The Gulf of Mexico*, 43-44.

2. Hart, *Comparing Empires*, 14-18; Spate, *Spanish Lake*, 1-15; Hazlewood, *The Queen's Slave Trader*, 28-30; Sugden, *Sir Francis Drake*, 12; Schwaller, *The History of the Catholic Church*, 33-36; Knight and Hurley, eds., *An Account*, xxxiv.

3. Kamen, *Empire*, 41-43; Schwaller, *The History of the Catholic Church*, 36; Weber, *The Spanish Frontier*, 31; Sugden, *Sir Francis Drake*, 12; Hoffman, *Florida's Frontiers*, 20-21.

4. Kamen, *Empire*, 5-6, 14-19, 57; Schwaller, *The History of the Catholic Church*, 13-18, 37; Lynch, *New Worlds*, 6; Knight and Hurley, eds., *An Account*, xxxix; Hudson, *Knights of Spain*, 3-11; Weber, *Spanish Frontier*, 19-20; Jennings, *New Worlds of Violence*, 30-31.

5. Kamen, *Empire*, 85-86.

6. Kamen, *Empire*, 82; Elliott, *Empires*, 105.

7. Kamen, *Empire*, 44, 82-84, 98; Hoffman, *Florida's Frontiers*, 21-22; Sledge, *The Gulf of Mexico*, 44.

8. Turner, "Juan Ponce de León," 2-5, 11, 17-18, 20-27; Kamen, *Empire*, 85; Weddle, *Spanish Sea*, 39-47; Weber, *The Spanish Frontier*, 31-33; Milanich, *Laboring in the Fields of the Lord*, 57-59; Jennings, *New Worlds of Violence*, 37-38; Davis, "Ponce de León's First Voyage," 8-14, 16; Arana, "The Exploration of Florida," 1-2.

9. Turner, "Juan Ponce de León, 2-5, 11, 17-18, 20-27; Weddle, *Spanish Sea*, 39-47; Weber, *The Spanish Frontier*, 31-33; Milanich, *Laboring in the Fields of the Lord*, 57-59.

10. Turner, "Juan Ponce de León," 24-27; Weber, *The Spanish Frontier*, 33-34; Weddle, *Spanish Sea*, 47, 56-57; Davis, "Ponce de León's First Voyage," 20.

11. Hoffman, *Florida's Frontiers*, 22.

12. Kamen, *Empire*, 44, 82-85, 88, 98-105.

13. Hudson, *Knights of Spain*, 6, 8, 31-32; Restall, *Seven Myths*, 27-43, 65-66; Schwaller, *The History of the Catholic Church*, 38-39; Hudson, *Juan Pardo*, 5; Weber, *The Spanish Frontier*, 23; Kamen, *Empire*, 95-96; Jennings, *New Worlds of Violence*, 36, 38. For de León's *capitulación*: Davis, "Ponce de León's First Voyage," 9-14; Davis, "Ponce de León's Second Voyage," 53-56.

14. Weber, *The Spanish Frontier*, 34; Hoffman, *Florida's Frontiers*, 22-24; Weddle, *The Spanish Sea*, 41, 61-62, 99-100; Hudson, *Juan Pardo*, 5-6; Arana, "The Exploration of Florida," 5.

15. Turner, "Juan Ponce de León," 27-28; Hoffman, *Florida's Frontiers*, 23-24.

16. Weddle, *Spanish Sea*, 39; Sledge, *The Gulf of Mexico*, 44.

17. Turner, "Juan Ponce de León," 29; Weber, *The Spanish Frontier*, 34; Kamen, *Empire*, 244; Weddle, *Spanish Sea*, 39, 47-48; Sledge, *The Gulf of Mexico*, 44. For contemporary accounts of the voyage and direct quotes: Oviedo, *Historia*, 3: 622-623; Worth, *Discovering Florida*, 63; Davis, "Ponce de León's Second Voyage," 59-62.

18. Hoffman, *Florida's Frontiers*, 24.

19. Hoffman, *Florida's Frontiers*, 26-29; Jennings, *New Worlds of Violence*, 37-38.

20. Martyr, 2: 269-270.

21. Weddle, *Spanish Sea*, 116-118; Jennings, *New Worlds of Violence*, 37-39.

22. Hoffman, *Florida's Frontiers*, 26-28.

23. Hoffman, *Florida's Frontiers*, 26-29; Hoffman, "Lucas Vazquez," 36-49; Weber, *The Spanish Frontier*, 35-37; Milanich, *Laboring in the Fields of the Lord*, 59-63. Hoffman describes Guadalpe in the most detail in *A New Andalucia*, pt. 1, particularly pp. 66-80.

Central American Dreams

In theory, Spain claimed all of North America by its right of discovery, all the way from the Gulf Coast of New Spain, around the peninsula of Florida, and northward all the way to New England. While those extreme claims were no more than claims, both de León and Ayllón had tested them, attempting settlements on both the Gulf and Atlantic coasts.[1] Both had been failures, yet La Florida's popularity seemed only to grow with its size. As was the case with its original Caribbean connection, conquests made by Spaniards elsewhere in the New World were more than enough to influence the minds of prospective Spanish conquistadores. This time, the connections were to Central and South America—to New Spain and Peru.

Only one year after Ayllón's failure at San Miguel de Guadalpe, for instance, Panfilo de Narvaez arrived on the Gulf Coast of Peninsular Florida, not far from where de León made his La Florida attempts. Narváez, "aggressive and brutal, as well as impulsive and stupid," in the words of one historian, was the embodiment of Spanish hidalgo culture, and the embodiment of the connection between La Florida and Spanish conquest elsewhere. Narváez was a seasoned veteran of Spanish conquest with a brutal and aggressive repute, having participated in the destruction of Native chiefdoms on Hispaniola and Cuba, and having gained land on the latter island in reward for his successes.[2] Those early achievements, however, were eclipsed only a few years after by his failures in New Spain, setting the scene for his arrival in La Florida.

After the Córdoba and Grijalva expeditions confirmed the existence of large Native societies along the coast of modern-day Mexico, further Spanish exploration came quickly. In 1520 Narváez legally assumed command of such an effort when Cuba's governor, Diego Velázquez de Cuéllar, reversed his support of his original choice, Hernán Cortés. When Cortés defied the governor in 1519 and sailed for the Mexican coast anyway, Cuéllar ordered Narváez to catch up with the renegade and deal with him. To ensure success, the governor supplied Narváez with an impressive fleet and over a thousand well-supplied men, far more than Cortés commanded. By the time Narváez arrived on the coast, Cortés had already left to march inland, toward Tenochtitlan, leaving only a contingent of men at Vera Cruz. Not only did Narváez fail to recruit that army, but when Cortés did return to confront his challenger, the two squared off violently and Cortés, as unmatched as he was, prevailed. Outmaneuvered and humiliated by Cortés's smaller force and crippled by the loss of an eye in the process, Narváez was then forced to watch his competitor's stunning successes in Tenochtitlan from a prison cell in Vera Cruz. For a man who was already rumored to be as cocky as he was ruthless, what Narváez suffered at the hands of Cortés on the coast of Mexico was a degree of disgrace far worse than death. He would be driven almost to insanity in the next few years searching for an opportunity to regain his honor and, hopefully, amass a similar fortune. La Florida provided him the chance.[3]

Spanish colonialism shifted from the Caribbean to the mainland of New Spain and its surroundings almost immediately after Cortés's destruction of Tenochtitlan and establishment of Mexico City. This was Narváez's moment. Charles V obliged, awarding Narváez the title *adelantado* of La Florida and authorized him to complete the conquest of New Spain's unknown northern edges. His was one of two expeditions that fitted out almost simultaneously, and for largely the same purpose: to extend Cortés's victories and secure the perimeters of the Gulf Coast. Narváez would go to La Florida, and Francisco de Montejo to the Yucatan.[4] The riches found in Central Mexico, the bruised egos of failed conquistadores, and a royal need to better understand the Gulf Coast all combined to produce a second wave of expeditions much more consequential than the first Caribbean ones.

While both the Narváez and Montejo expeditions failed to find treasure or secure any of the Gulf of Mexico, Narváez's failures far surpassed Montejo's. What unfolded in La Florida truly was a nightmarish fiasco with an almost movie-like drama to it.[5] Perhaps memories of defeat and ignominy in New Spain were what pressed Narváez onward even after friends counseled him otherwise.[6] The warnings certainly proved prophetic. After stopping in Santo Domingo and Cuba, dealing with a hurricane, and building up his supplies and provisions, Narváez finally arrived in La Florida in 1527. He landed an impressive expedition consisting of near six hundred Spaniards and dozens of horses on the Gulf Coast of peninsular Florida, somewhere in the vicinity of Tampa Bay. Things at first certainly looked bright. In one of the abandoned houses they encountered on this first day, "we found a rattle of gold there among the nets."[7] Perhaps this place would turn out to be Narváez's Vera Cruz after all.

The men of the land expedition soon found more evidence of gold in this place that otherwise held absolutely no lure for a Spaniard—a sandy, unimpressive pine barren where there wasn't even corn for the horses. Local Natives were quick to describe the paramount chiefdom Apalachee, to the north near present-day Tallahassee, as the place to find what the Spanish were looking for—a place "in which there was much gold, and they made signs to indicate that there were very great quantities of everything we held in esteem." Almost certainly a ploy to get their uninvited guests to leave, the enticement worked. Off to Apalachee Narváez and the expedition went, where the men were sure "there was great bounty." In a fateful move that was contested strenuously by many of his men, Narváez split the expedition into two separate groups, dispatching his supply ships ahead to scout a particular bay, probably Tampa Bay, which was reported to be a promising location for settlement. The land expedition would link back up with the ships there. That of course never happened. The ships never remade contact with Narváez and the three hundred men with him, even after scouring the west coast of peninsular Florida for a year searching.[8] The loss of the ships and the provisions on them made the immediate success of Narváez's entrada critical. Either they would succeed in La Florida, or they would all probably die.

The Narváez entrada slowly moved north from the beach and toward Apalachee. Their route had them crossing the Withlacoochee and Suwannee Rivers, passing through vast swamps that made it clear this would be no easy journey. By the time it reached the outskirts of the main towns, the expedition was already in trouble. The men rejoiced and Narváez confidently expected his first taste of mineral wealth. It was there "where we desired to be, and where they told us there were so many foodstuffs and so much gold," wrote Treasurer Álvar Núñez Cabeza de Vaca, and so "it seemed to us that a great portion of our hardship and weariness had been lifted from us." Oh, but how wrong he was. Although the Florida panhandle was filled with impressive stands of pine and oak, teemed with wildlife, and supported complex hierarchical corn-based societies, there was not even a hint of gold. Narváez had been deceived, and now his men were in real trouble.[9]

After almost a month at Apalachee and having clearly outstayed their welcome by that point, the men pushed onward to another town, Aute, under basically a hail of arrows. Rather than fight the approaching Spaniards, most nearby Natives simply disappeared, leaving the hundreds in Narváez's army to wander blindly, withering away slowly from starvation, exposure, and disease. Aute, abandoned and half-burned, provided the men with much needed food stores, but no good news.[10] Apalachee and Aute, La Florida's first major towns to be subjected to Spanish occupation, were both busts. While de León never lived to realize La Florida had no gold, Narváez unfortunately did.

From this already disappointing start, the expedition quickly descended into utter chaos. Just south of Tallahassee the healthy, limping along on jaded horses and burdened by carrying the masses of sick and dying, reached their breaking point. Their departure from Aute marked the end of one phase of the Narváez entrada—by the time the men reached the coast near present-day St. Marks, they were done with La Florida. "Having arrived and seen the little prospect there was for going forward," there was only one solution: they had to get out, and fast. One cannot mistake the clear disappointment in de Vaca's writings, after only a few months in La Florida, as the men departed the burned-out Aute and made for the coast. "I refrain here from telling this at great length," de Vaca would later write of that particular leg of the hike, "because each one can imagine for himself what could happen in a land so strange and so poor and so lacking in every single thing that it seemed impossible either to be in it or to escape from it."[11]

After consulting with each other, the men resorted to building rudimentary ships, a herculean task considering they had neither shipbuilding tools nor anyone who knew how to build a ship. There was only one carpenter in the expedition. One man said he could make a rudimentary forge using hollow pieces of wood and deerskin as a bellows. While that probably seemed crazy, "since we were in such straits that anything that had some semblance of a solution seemed to us a good thing, we said that he should set to the task." Soon men were at work making nails and working tools from their stirrups, crossbows, "and other iron objects we had," transforming their camp into a makeshift shipyard. After weeks of work, they managed to fashion several rafts from pine, sealing them with palmetto fiber and pine pitch, rigging them with sails made from their clothing and with ropes made from the tails and manes of their horses, and manning them with cypress oars. What a site this shipyard would have been to behold. In the meantime, men raided Aute for corn, "and every third day a horse would be killed and distributed among those who were working on building the ships and those who were sick." The hide from the horses' legs was even stripped, cured, sewn up, and filled with water.[12]

When the five rafts were complete almost two months had passed. Another forty men were dead, and every horse had been eaten. It was on these rafts, each holding near fifty men, that the naked and starving survivors pushed off on the next leg of the expedition. The rafts, no larger than thirty feet long, were packed with men so tightly they could barely move, and they sat so low in the water that only inches of the keels showed. "And so great can necessity prevail that it made us risk going in this manner and placing ourselves in a sea so treacherous," de Vaca explained, without even a single navigator.[13]

On this second leg of the journey, much longer and far more treacherous than the first, the expedition's ever-dwindling number of men tested the Gulf of Mexico. They made their way through the swamps down to the coast and pushed out into the open water, determined to sail the length of La Florida's coastline all the way to New Spain. With only handfuls of raw corn to eat and constantly hovering on the brink of death by thirst, the men slugged on at the mercy of the winds and waves, creeping west just off the Gulf Coast. In his long string of failures, it was during this leg of the expedition where Narváez would suffer the ultimate one. After over a month on the water, the rafts were struck by the currents of the Mississippi River, whisking them apart from each other and out to sea. The healthier men on Narváez's raft, able to row faster back to land, began pulling away from the other two rafts, one of which was commanded by de Vaca. At shouting distance de Vaca asked what he and his men should do, "since I saw the small possibility, we had to follow him." Narváez answered that "it was no longer time for one man to rule another, that each one should do whatever seemed best to him in order to save his own life," which, consequently, was exactly what he intended to do. The expedition now in shambles, it was officially every man for himself. With that adieu, somewhere west of the Mississippi River, de Vaca lost sight of Narváez, never to lay eyes on him again.[14]

According to conflicting reports, Narváez was either swept out to sea at the mouth of the Mississippi, or he was pulled out to sea by the tides from Matagorda Bay, Texas, in the middle of the night. Either way, his dreams of wealth and power came to an unceremonious end as he drifted hopelessly into the oblivion of the Gulf of Mexico. The coast would claim La Florida's second *adelantado*, as it would in time claim almost every one of his men. Led now by de Vaca, the survivors slowly trekked for years along the beaches and barrier islands of Texas and Mexico, destitute, half naked. For half a decade they suffered various degrees of captivity and abuse at the hands of multiple Native groups. They ran across the remains of their lost shipmates, ate cactuses to survive, and slowly perished from starvation, exposure, and violence. When a group of Spanish slave raiders ran across the survivors in Sonoran Mexico, only four of the original army remained, and they were so tattered and tanned that they dumbfounded their rescuers.[15]

The "epitome of all colonial disasters" in the words of one historian, this entrada was by far the worst disaster of a Spanish expedition anywhere in the New World.[16] Most of the protracted story of the Narváez expedition, in fact, is actually really just the Álvar Núñez Cabeza de Vaca story, for after the parting of Narváez's raft at the Mississippi, relatively early in the ordeal, his thread of the story ends. Cabeza de Vaca, on the other hand, survived every one of the expedition's seven more years of torment. After relating his tales in Mexico City personally to both Cortés and the new viceroy, de Vaca finally set sail for Europe, arriving in Lisbon a full decade after setting sail with Narváez from the Spanish coast just to the south. Importantly, however, once home he would publish his narrative of the journey, *La Relacion*, much of which he evidently wrote down. Evidently *La Relacion* began when de Vaca first tried to explain a storm that destroyed a few of his ships before the expedition even got to the Florida coast. A Spanish authority responded to the report by suggesting de Vaca continue the habit of writing such happenings down. He clearly did, and as one historian put it, "the Crown official could hardly have expected an account such as Cabeza later produced."[17]

One would suppose that such an epic and well-documented failure would have dashed the ambitions of anyone thinking of trying their luck on La Florida any time soon. Surprisingly, however, Cabeza de Vaca's accounts of the sprawling and densely populated kingdoms that stretched along the Gulf Coast seemed to intrigue more than they dissuaded. De Vaca would not speak publicly about anything other than a hostile and utterly worthless land that produced only privation and death. That, however, was not what people seemed to hear. His tales made it to the Spanish Court and eventually to the ears of Hernando de Soto even before they were published publicly. According to one contemporary de Soto chronicler, in private de Vaca supposedly told de Soto that it was "the richest land in the world."[18] A fortuitous talk indeed—only a few years later the newest La Florida's *adelantado* landed, to repeat on an even a larger scale the failures of his predecessors.

De Soto's expedition was the largest, the longest, the most sweeping, and the most destructive entrada in an era of destructive entradas. Historians certainly consider it the most consequential as well.[19] And much more so than the rest, de Soto was the living connection between La Florida and Spanish colonialism elsewhere in the Americas. He was the embodiment of an aggressive and violent hidalgo, a man who would use La Florida to ascend to the highest levels of wealth and esteem. He had already tasted such success in the New World, arriving there in the earliest and most violent days of modern-day Panama as a young man, "with nothing else his own except his sword and shield." Obviously, he rose quickly through the ranks. He had served in Nicaragua and later was a captain in the Pizarro brothers' subjugation of the Incan empire, a defining moment in the Spanish conquest of the New World more transformative than even Cortés's conquest of New Spain.[20]

Almost from the moment Pizarro arrived back in Spain, laden with the mineral wealth of the Incan Empire, accounts spread to the eager ears of more would-be conquerors, no more so than de Soto. Although by the early 1530s his role in the Incan conquest had already made him a very wealthy man, even that sort of wealth could not quench the desire for Cortés- or Pizarro-like fame and fortune, which led de Soto to petition King Charles V for a larger expedition very quickly after returning to Spain himself. If he had stayed in Peru "he would forever be a subordinate," wrote historian Charles Hudson, which was no sort of ambition. No, he would be an equal to Pizarro, or he would die trying. Eager for success in La Florida, Charles V turned to de Soto, naming him Governor of Cuba as well as *adelantado* of Florida, "with the title of marquis to a certain part of the lands he might conquer," according to one contemporary, "thirty leagues in length and fifteen in breadth," according to another, "in whatever place he might choose from that which he could conquer at his own expense." Such a *capitulación*, published in Spain, was everything for which de Soto could have hoped. Gripped by reports of the Narváez expedition and not at all discouraged by them, de Soto resolved to wager not only his wealth but his reputation on what had eluded several prospective conquistadores already—the conquest and colonization of La Florida.[21]

In 1539 his expedition, consisting of over six hundred men, landed in familiar territory in the vicinity of Tampa Bay, very near where Narváez had come ashore. Although his choice of beachhead was similar, unlike the several failures that preceded him, de Soto had no plans to hug the coast. He specifically sought out the mound building, hierarchical, corn-based chiefdoms that were mentioned by Ayllón and witnessed to some extent by Narváez and Cabeza de Vaca. Such hierarchies and physical structures had been the key so far to incredible riches, both in Central Mexico and now in South America, and there was no reason for de Soto to believe the Mississippian chiefdoms of La Florida would not control similar sources of mineral wealth. The key to the attempted colonization of La

Florida continued to be its connection to Caribbean, and now to South American, precedents. De Soto, a seasoned veteran of Spanish conquest and by far the most successful one to make his way through La Florida, was only doing so in the hopes of recreating wealth he had tasted elsewhere.[22]

Like those that came before him, de Soto and his men quickly found encouraging reports of gold that exceeded even those of Narváez's or de León's early days. When he inquired about mineral wealth around Tampa Bay, he like Narváez was pointed inland. "That land had gold in abundance and when those people came to make war . . . they wore hats of gold resembling helmets." Like Narváez, de Soto quickly made his way to Apalachee, and like Narváez he was disappointed with what he found. There were no gold-helmeted warriors there. After an entire winter of bloody occupation, de Soto and his men finally departed for present-day South Carolina, Cofitachequi, where the "chieftainess," a woman, collected tribute, and "gold in abundance." According to one account, they learned from a Native that not only was there gold, but that it was "taken from the mines, melted, and refined," just like in Central and South America, which their Native guest described in such detail that it stunned his Spanish interrogators. It was "just as if he had seen it done, or else the devil taught him." According to another, the men actually showed off their own jewelry, "gold jewelry and pieces of silver and fine stones set in rights that were found among some of the captains and principal soldiers," so that they made sure the Natives knew what they were talking about. At Cofitachequi "there was a great deal of metal like the yellow and the white," and also pearls, so much that merchants actually trafficked them. "Our Spaniards were very pleased and rejoiced at this news, desiring to see themselves at once in Cofitachequi in order to be masters of so much gold and silver and so many precious pearls." Smitten by such accounts, the expedition was soon on its way.[23]

From Apalachee de Soto and his men passed through Altamaha and Ocute settlements, Mississippian chiefdoms with the kind of social hierarchies he would have hoped to find. Quick to move on, however, to its final destination, the expedition endured a difficult trek across a barren Savannah River basin—the modern-day Georgia-South Carolina border—and then through central South Carolina. By the time the men arrived across the Wateree River from Cofitachequi, the expedition was in dire straits, finding "only hunger and more hunger."[24] And again, although what the men found there was certainly not nothing, it was still tremendously disappointing. The pearls shown de Soto and his men were valuable, of course, and Cofitachequi seemed to be made out of them. Natives wore them on necklaces, fashioned them into figurines, and even buried them in their graves. Hundreds of pounds were right there for the taking, while one chronicler described de Soto grabbing specimens by "double handfuls" that were "the size of large chick-peas."[25] Perhaps, his men dared to think, if de Soto altered his expectations a bit, they alone might make the region worthwhile. But pearls were not gold and pearls were not silver, and de Soto, seeking another treasure like "the lord of Peru," had "no wish to content himself with good land or with pearls." With that, the expedition pushed on.[26]

So, although he had already succeeded more than Narváez, Ayllón, or de León had before him, a desire for riches in pearls was not what Hernándo de Soto brought with him from his time in Peru. Everything about the Mississippian Southeast was as it should be—the hierarchies, the mound structures, and the prestige of its chieftains. Everything told of familiar wealth. The only problem was that there wasn't any.

Not finding what he needed in Cofitachequi, de Soto stayed only days, moving northwest to Chiaha and Chisca into the Tennessee River Valley. He did so upon rumors of copper and possibly some gold, the hopes of which reveal how far de Soto's expectations were slipping; copper with perhaps a bit of gold was a far cry from the vast stores of gold he was sure would be in his possession by that time.[27] Deluded by dreams of Peru, de Soto was doomed. At Chiaha the men heard accounts of "mines of the yellow metal" that they sought, but upon the return of a scout, found that mines were of brass. "Having received an account of the gold mines that they went to discover," along they went to the southwest, back into Georgia and toward Alabama, this time to Coosa.[28]

Beginning his trek on the southwest coast of Florida, de Soto searched for his Peruvian wealth on an epic quest that led him across the Southeast, passing initially through the Flint, Oconee, Ocmulgee, Savannah, Wateree, and Catawba river basins, near the foothills of the Appalachian Mountains, all before crossing over into the Tennessee River watershed, then moving southwest into the Alabama, Tombigbee, and Mississippi river valleys. In doing so, he passed through several of the Southeast's largest Mississippian chiefdoms, including Apalachee, Ocute, Cofitachequi, Coosa, and Chicaza.[29] At times he moved quickly through a region when headmen gave him what he wanted, or at least pointed convincingly enough to the richer areas farther up the road. That was at least the case early in the expedition, when all were confident that gold or other sources of mineral wealth were right around the next corner. As de Soto slowly came to realize otherwise, however, his entrada grew more violent as he grew more desperate.

The various chiefdoms that he encountered all had plenty of corn, but no gold or silver, leaving a frustrated de Soto to lash out quicker at each proceeding village. Despite his brutal tactics or perhaps because of them, resistance only intensified, and neighboring Natives retaliated with equal ferocity. After sustaining only minor losses in his travels from the coast of La Florida up through Apalachee, to Cofitachequi, then back southwest to Coosa, the situation slowly deteriorated. His over-aggressive actions in Mavila, in present-day Alabama, triggered a daylong uprising that changed the face of the entire expedition. The battle cost de Soto more than a dozen lives and a considerable amount of the expedition's resources. The Native death toll was somewhere in the thousands.[30]

Ironically, a swift retreat was possible after Mavila, one that de Soto obviously chose not to take. One of his captains just happened to be awaiting the expedition right down the coast, not too far from Mavila, and with him was a ship destined for Havana. De Soto, however, deliberately withheld this potentially conquest-ending information from his men. The pearls that were to be sent to Cuba by that ship had just been destroyed, and the men, although victorious at Mavila, were thoroughly demoralized. Already nearing mutiny, if they caught wind of such a possible avenue of escape most would surely take it, leaving de Soto's expedition in shambles. After hearing wind of desertion, he resorted to shaming his men. If it did not produce gold or silver, and if its survivors were left again only to recount its horrors, de Soto feared La Florida would "acquire such a reputation that no man would desire to go thither when people might be needed." The "excessive hardships" the men "had endured hitherto in the discovery of that country would be lost." He certainly also feared for himself, should he depart empty handed. He would be "stripped of his grandeur, authority, and reputation," and his money "spent in vain." Consequently, wrote another of his chroniclers, "he determined not to give news of himself so long as he did not find a rich land." Instead of giving up on La Florida, de Soto pressed on.[31]

Although determined to press on, it was clear even to de Soto's most ardent chroniclers that he was not the same man, wandering through La Florida "from one place to another without order or purpose, like a man tied to life and desirous of ending it, until he died," which would happen eventually. In the meantime, however, the violence of the entrada intensified.[32] Chicaza communities assaulted the party along the border of Tennessee and Mississippi. The men suffered Mavila-like casualties and, worse yet, the expedition was devastated logistically by the loss of horses and supplies. "If, perchance, any one still had had any clothing left from the fire at Mavilla, it was now all burned up in that place."

Caught off guard by the night raid, many of the men left were basically naked, and now it was freezing. "The whole night was passed turning from one side to the other" next to fires "without sleeping, for if they were warmed on one side they froze on the other." For an army already demoralized, this was certainly a new low.[33] Indeed, by the time the men departed Chicaza, crossed the Mississippi River, and moved into present-day Arkansas and east Texas, it was clear to all that La Florida was more than just a letdown—it was a failure. Then the really bad news. Scouts returned having found no signs of corn, no trails, no people, no nothing. Most of the soldiers were probably aware of the fate of the Narváez survivors if they had not read Álvar Núñez Cabeza de Vaca's account directly. No one was interested in writing volume two. It was after hearing these reports that de Soto's spirit finally seemed to break. He soon fell ill and died. His followers sank him into the Mississippi River, and his bones are still probably somewhere in its muck.[34]

With the expedition's leader dead and the prospect of riches long gone, the surviving half of the de Soto entrada, now led by Luis de Moscoso Álvarado, quickly abandoned the cause. Starving soldier–built ships floated down the Mississippi, and like the Narváez survivors years previous, escaped to Mexico City.[35] Ultimately, without finding any mineral wealth and without securing any part of La Florida, de Soto's entrada achieved nothing more than any of his predecessors. La Florida was now more legend than letdown.

Notes

1. Weber, *The Spanish Frontier*, 37-38, 50.

2. Weddle, *Spanish Sea*, 116-119, 163-164; Hoffman, "Narvaez and Cabeza de Vaca in Florida," 50-51.

3. Weddle, *Spanish Sea*, 116-119, 164; Kamen, *Empire*, 102; Elliot, *Empires*, 4-5; Hoffman, "Narvaez and Cabeza de Vaca in Florida," 51.

4. Kamen, *Empire*, 88, 98; Weddle, *Spanish Sea*, 163-164; Hoffman, "Narvaez and Cabeza de Vaca in Florida," 51-52.

5. The Narváez expedition is covered in: Milanich, *Laboring in the Fields of the Lord*, 62-68; Kamen, *Empire*, 244-245; Hoffman, "Narvaez and Cabeza de Vaca in Florida"; Weddle, *Spanish Sea*, 185-207; Hoffman, *Florida's Frontiers*, 29-31; Weber, *The Spanish Frontier*, 42-45. For Francisco de Montejo's attempts, see: Weddle, *Spanish Sea*, 163-182.

6. Weddle, *Spanish Sea*, 185; Hoffman, "Narvaez and Cabeza de Vaca in Florida," 52-53.

7. Adorno and Pautz, eds., *The Narrative of Cabeza de Vaca*, 54; Hoffman, "Narvaez and Cabeza de Vaca in Florida," 52-53; Weddle, *Spanish Sea*, 185-191; Hoffman, *Florida's Frontiers*, 29-31.

8. Adorno and Pautz, eds., *The Narrative of Cabeza de Vaca*, 56-60; Weddle, *Spanish Sea*, 185-191; Hoffman, "Narvaez and Cabeza de Vaca in Florida," 54-58; Hoffman, *Florida's Frontiers*, 29-31; Weber, *The Spanish Frontier*, 42-43.

9. Adorno and Pautz, eds., *The Narrative of Cabeza de Vaca*, 64, 67; Hoffman, "Narvaez and Cabeza de Vaca in Florida," 58-61; Weddle, *Spanish Sea*, 185-191; Hoffman, *Florida's Frontiers*, 29-31; Weber, *The Spanish Frontier*, 43.

10. Adorno and Pautz, eds., *The Narrative of Cabeza de Vaca*, 69.

11. Adorno and Pautz, eds., *The Narrative of Cabeza de Vaca*, 70-71.

12. Adorno and Pautz, eds., *The Narrative of Cabeza de Vaca*, 71-73.

13. Adorno and Pautz, eds., *The Narrative of Cabeza de Vaca*, 74; Weddle, *Spanish Sea*, 191-193; Weber, *The Spanish Frontier*, 42.

14. For this stretch of the journey, see: Adorno and Pautz, eds., *The Narrative of Cabeza de Vaca*, 74-82; Hoffman, "Narvaez and Cabeza de Vaca in Florida," 63-64; Weddle, *Spanish Sea*, 185-207; Hoffman, *Florida's Frontiers*, 29-31.

15. Weddle, *Spanish Sea*, 194-207; Hoffman, *Florida's Frontiers*, 29-31.

16. Weddle, *Spanish Sea*, 164.

17. Weddle, *Spanish Sea*, 187.

18. Clayton, Knight, and Moore, eds., *The De Soto Chronicles*, 48; Hudson, *Knights of Spain*, 45-46; Hoffman, "Narvaez and Cabeza de Vaca in Florida," 64-65; Weddle, *Spanish Sea*, 164; Hudson, "The Hernando de Soto Expedition, 1539-1542," 74-75.

19. The definitive work on the de Soto expedition remains Hudson, *Knights of Spain*, and also the older: Duncan, *Hernando de Soto*. Shorter, briefer studies of his entrada that are relied on here are: Hoffman, *Florida's Frontiers*, 31-38; Hudson, Smith, DePratter, "The Hernando de Soto Expedition," 74-103; Weddle, *Spanish Sea*, 208-233; Weber, *Spanish Frontier*, 49-55; Milanich, *Laboring in the Fields of the Lord*, 68-76.

20. Kamen, *Empire*, 105-111; Hudson, *Knights of Spain*, 40-45, 47; Clayton, Knight, and Moore, eds., *The De Soto Chronicles*, 47.

21. Hudson, *Knights of Spain*, 39-47; Hudson, Smith, and DePratter, "The Hernando de Soto Expedition," 74; Hudson, *Juan Pardo*, 8; Kamen, *Empire*, 76, 88, 120; Weddle, *Spanish Sea*, 209-211; Clayton, Knight, and Moore, eds., *The De Soto Chronicles*, 47; Clayton, Knight, and Moore, eds., *The De Soto Chronicles*, 2: 71.

22. Weber, *The Spanish Frontier*, 40.

23. Clayton, Knight, and Moore, eds., *The De Soto Chronicles*, 64, 74; Clayton, Knight, and Moore, eds., *The De Soto Chronicles*, 2: 249; Hudson, Smith, and DePratter, "The Hernando de Soto Expedition," 81.

24. Hudson, Smith, and DePratter, "The Hernando de Soto Expedition," 82-83; Clayton, Knight, and Moore, eds., *The De Soto Chronicles*, 2: 272-281.

25. Clayton, Knight, and Moore, eds., *The De Soto Chronicles*, 231, 279-280; Clayton, Knight, and Moore, eds., *The De Soto Chronicles*, 2: 262, 295-297.

26. Clayton, Knight, and Moore, eds., *The De Soto Chronicles*, 83-84.

27. Hudson, Smith, and DePratter, "The Hernando de Soto Expedition," 83-87.

28. Clayton, Knight, and Moore, eds., *The De Soto Chronicles*, 2: 317, 320.

29. Hoffman, *Florida's Frontiers*, 32-33.

30. Ethridge, *From Chicaza to Chickasaw*, 26-29, and for the battle of Mavila in particular, 42-59; Hudson, *Knights of Spain*, 237-249; Hudson, Smith, and DePratter, "The Hernando de Soto Expedition," 87; Weber, *The Spanish Frontier*, 52-53.

31. Clayton, Knight, and Moore, eds., *The De Soto Chronicles*, 104; Clayton, Knight, and Moore, eds., *The De Soto Chronicles*, 2: 356-357.

32. Clayton, Knight, and Moore, eds., *The De Soto Chronicles*, 2: 357-358.

33. Clayton, Knight, and Moore, eds., *The De Soto Chronicles*, 108; Hudson, *Knights of Spain*, 265-270; Hudson, Smith, and DePratter, "The Hernando de Soto Expedition," 90.

34. Hudson, *Knights of Spain*, 349-352; Hudson, Smith, and DePratter, "The Hernando de Soto Expedition," 90-94; Clayton, Knight, and Moore, eds., *The De Soto Chronicles*, 243.

35. Weber, *The Spanish Frontier*, 53-55; Milanich, *Laboring in the Fields of the Lord*, 75-76.

2 The Treacherous Gulf

In the fall of 1527 Álvar Núñez Cabeza de Vaca got caught up in a Caribbean storm that struck while he was preparing for Pánfilo de Narváez's La Florida expedition. He was not in La Florida yet, but at a port on the south of Cuba named Villa de la Satisfima Trinidad, or Trinidad for short. He was there with two ships trying to add to the expedition's stores while the rest of the men waited nearby in Santiago de Cuba. But all of this, as they say, was about to change.

De Vaca's ships were moored offshore, with all his men on them, when very quickly one morning "the weather showed signs of becoming ominous, and it began to rain and the sea became so turbulent" that although de Vaca gave the men permission to ride things out onshore, they were all already too scared to leave the ships. The shoreline was over three miles away and the conditions were deteriorating so quickly that they decided to hunker down aboard "in order to avoid the wet and cold." At first de Vaca did the same, declining residents' invitations go to ashore, "saying that I could not leave the ships." Finally, upon the pleading of both the townspeople and his own men, who "strongly urged me to go so that haste be made and the provisions be brought as quickly as possible," he relented. De Vaca braved the winds and the waves and made it ashore to Trinidad.

What a fateful decision he made. Not long after his departure the winds grew so strong that no one else could leave the ships even if they wanted to. They were so strong indeed that the crews were not even able to run the ships aground in shallow water, a known seafaring tactic of last resort that would have at least saved the ships. Instead, the men would have to ride the storm out at their moorings for at least one whole day. Meanwhile there was de Vaca, in town, "and at this time the sea and the storm began to swell so much that there was no less tempest in the town than at the sea, because all the houses and churches blew down." Apparently, this was quite a storm. The wind and the rain left the townspeople huddling together in small groups under whatever cover they could find, "our arms locked with one another, in order to save ourselves from being carried away by the wind." They dared not leave, "since the storm was so great that even the trees, like the houses, fell." So it went all night. There was no refuge to be had, de Vaca wrote, where anyone could feel safe "for even half an hour." In that town "such a fearful thing had never been seen."

De Vaca made it through the night, surviving what could have been any one of the several varieties of Caribbean storms that wracked places like Trinidad with regularity. Judging from that report it was probably a hurricane or at least a tropical storm, even though it was late in the season. It also could have been an unusually strong northern front, the kind that regularly swept south from the Gulf from fall to spring. Whatever it was, from the severity of de Vaca's descriptions, it was clearly a good one. The town's provisions were lost, much of the livestock was dead or scattered, and the town itself lay in ruins. "The land was left in such a state that it was a great pity to see it: the trees fallen, the woods destroyed, all stripped of leaves and grass."

The sites de Vaca witnessed on shore, however, paled in comparison with what confronted him when he returned to the waterfront to check on his men. He found nothing. When he saw mooring buoys but no ships, the storm's true devastation came into focus. While he survived, evidently the rest of his men did not. He and the townspeople with him "knew they had been lost," and reluctantly began a search for the wreckage. He was puzzled by not finding much until he came upon a rowboat stuck in the trees miles inland from the coast. Farther down the beach two of his men were found in a pile of beach wreckage, "and the bodies were so disfigured from the blows of the rocks that they could not be recognized."

Other than that grisly sight and a few shredded articles of clothing, the rest of the men and the ships they were holed up in had vanished from the face of the earth. In one day a Caribbean storm had made two entire ships disappear, taking their crews and the expedition's supplies with them to the bottom of the Caribbean Sea. Sixty men and twenty horses were lost, de Vaca recounted. Those that had gone ashore with him, "probably about thirty persons, were all that remained of the ones there had been on both ships." Soon to arrive was Narváez, who had also weathered the storm down the coast but had fared much better. While the remainder of the ships and supplies were intact, the men were so terrified by what they had just witnessed "that they greatly feared embarking again," and they begged Narváez to let them wait out the rest of the storm season on the island, which he did. They would not embark again until February. De Vaca and his men had gotten a taste of the treacherous Gulf.[1]

By the time news of de Soto's failure made its way back to Spain, several waves of conquistadores had died trying to get rich off of La Florida. Not only had they all failed, but the survivors of each of their expeditions all returned with the same disappointing intelligence—La Florida was a total bust. It was a "graveyard of hopes," in the words of one prominent Florida historian.[2] Still, Spain sent wave after wave of potential colonizers, and eventually in 1565 one of them succeeded in creating something of permanence—St. Augustine. But why? The answer lies with trouble in the Gulf, including storms like the one Cabeza de Vaca and Narváez survived off the coast of Cuba. While La Florida was proven to be no place of outrageous riches, it still had clear strategic value to the Spanish Crown because of the Gulf of Mexico's treachery. Accordingly, the Treacherous Gulf is not exactly a chapter about La Florida, but a chapter about the water off of La Florida, the dangers it held and the important role it played in the continued reasons Spaniards were determined to create a permanent European presence along its coastline.

The Gulf of Mexico was a part of the route mariners took through the Caribbean basin for centuries. By the middle of the sixteenth century, it was the highway of the Spanish New World, and as Cabeza de Vaca and Narváez had come to witness with their own eyes, things there did not always go as planned. As more Spaniards plundered the New World, as more ships carried trade goods to Spanish colonial settlements along the Caribbean rim and carried gold and silver back to Spain, bad things happened with more frequency. More ships went down in storms on bad weather days, and more pirates began harassing them on the good weather days. In order to save the lives of shipwrecked mariners, recover lost treasure, and deter piracy, Spanish colonial officials renewed their commitment to settling La Florida.

While previous attempts by conquistadores to conquer La Florida focused on their personal desires for wealth and power, these new attempts were for reasons of colonial interests elsewhere. Finally, with the establishment of St. Augustine, one such attempt succeeded. As salvage expert and naval historian Robert Marx suggested, without the discovery and exploitation of mineral wealth by Spaniards in Central and South America the treasure fleets never would have existed, and without the treasure fleets "the whole course of American history would have taken a different turn."[3] In other words, St. Augustine and Spanish La Florida never would have existed. Thus, a maxim of Florida real estate, understood well by modern tourists and residents alike, was created: the value of waterfront property. As it turns out, beachfront real estate was just as important to the Spanish government in the sixteenth as it is now in the twenty-first century state of Florida.

Notes

1. Adorno and Pautz, eds., *The Narrative of Cabeza de Vaca*, 49–52.
2. Lyon, *The Enterprise of Florida*, 44.
3. Marx, *Shipwrecks in the Americas*, 22.

The Treacherous Gulf

SPAIN'S NEW WORLD COMMERCE WAS REFERRED TO OFFICIALLY AS THE *CARrera de Indias*, or the Indies trade, and it was big business by the middle of the sixteenth century. Spanish cargo ships arrived in the Caribbean loaded with trade goods meant for colonists, and returned to Spain with valuables of all sorts, plundered from plantations, ranches, and mines across the Caribbean and Central America. In order to control all aspects of that developing trade, Isabella and Ferdinand established the *Casa de Contratacion*, the House of Trade, in Seville in 1503. Ships arriving from the New World could be better monitored and protected by being forced to operate through a central system, either by using Seville's port Sanlúcar de Barrameda on the Guadalquivir River, or the city's larger port directly on the Atlantic at Cádiz. From there colonial officials could keep a watchful eye on what came and went from the New World. Departing ships would need to gain documentation there, smuggling could be kept to a minimum, and taxes could be calculated accurately. Gold and silver shipments could also be offloaded safely and accounted for properly. Even the secrets of Spanish travel and trade could be protected by controlling access to the New World in such a way. Seville's importance as Spain's logistical hub would grow as a result of the House of Trade, which operated for more than two centuries.[1]

Outbound ships usually stopped for provisioning at Atlantic islands like the Canaries after leaving port in Spain. From there, utilizing both Atlantic trade winds and current systems they would make the Atlantic crossing, arriving at the southern Caribbean islands two to three months later. By the first few decades of discovery the trip was a regular one and not the most dangerous, relative at least to say the journey from the Philippines to Acapulco, which was much longer and more unpredictable. Still, it could be a possibly months' long journey that depended on ocean and atmospheric conditions that were entirely out of the mariners' control. Once sighting land in the lower Caribbean, the ships would then utilize trade winds and the Caribbean current system to take them where they needed to go.[2]

The Caribbean current system contains several smaller component currents. It begins with Atlantic water flowing west into the Caribbean basin, between the islands of Puerto Rico and Hispaniola to the north and the coast of South America to the south. Continuing west, the current is eventually forced by the contours of the basin to curl north, moving through the Yucatan channel, between the western end of Cuba and the eastern edge of the Yucatan Peninsula. At this point it is briefly known as the Yucatan current. Columbus was close to discovering the channel in 1494 and might actually have experienced the current. Convinced that Cuba was not an island, however, and part of a more foreboding landmass, he returned east to Jamaica rather than flow with it into the Gulf of Mexico.[3]

Once passing through the Yucatan channel and into the Gulf of Mexico, the current changes names again. Part of it moves sharply to the west to the east coasts of Mexico and Texas, while another portion of it continues north for a bit longer into the center of the Gulf. The former waters become the Mexican current, while the latter become the Loop current. The Mexican current flows clockwise, paralleling the Gulf Coasts of Mexico, Texas, and Louisiana. At some point along this circuit the Mexican current reconnects with the larger Loop current, which circles in a quick clockwise fashion in the center of the Gulf of Mexico basin. The currents combine and curl south, paralleling the west coast of peninsular Florida. Once past the Florida Keys the current makes an abrupt turn east, becoming the Florida current as it pours through a narrow path between the Keys and Cuba. This is the beginning of the Florida Straits. The current moves swiftly east through this channel before again swiftly changing course, this time turning north, between the east coast of Peninsular Florida and the Bahamas. While still being known as the Florida current, and moving through the Florida Straits, at this point it could also be called the Bahamian current, moving through the Bahamian channel. It is also known by this point simply as the Gulf Stream. The Gulf Stream continues north along the east coasts of Peninsular Florida, Georgia, and the Carolinas, until moving into the Atlantic around North Carolina's Outer Banks.[4]

Any ship in the centuries-long era of sail that entered the Caribbean basin had to deal with several sections of this current system in order to return home. Once pushing off from the Canaries, for instance, a typical journey to Vera Cruz took a Spanish ship to the southern Caribbean around Dominica. From there it would take the Caribbean to the Yucatan to the Mexican current in order to make port on the east coast of Mexico, most likely at San Juan de Ulúa, the major fortification in the harbor at Vera Cruz. On its return to Europe it would have to catch the Mexican current again, hugging the coasts of Mexico and Texas to the northeast almost all the way to the coast of Florida near present-day Pensacola in order to avoid unfavorable winds, and from there connect to the Loop current. By doing so it would cruise down almost the entire length of the west coast of peninsular Florida, and all the way around the Keys and into the Florida Straits, finally making port in Havana.[5] Regardless of where a ship made port, however, from Santo Domingo to Portobelo, it would have to deal with at least the final portion of the system—the Florida Straits and the Gulf Stream—in order to reenter the Atlantic Ocean.

Around midcentury an English expedition under John Hawkins passed into the Gulf and recorded his journey. At first Hawkins dismissed the current as he passed between the Keys and Cuba. It was not as strong as he had expected. As soon as his ships began the transition into the Bahamian channel, however, his men "felt such a current, that bearing all sailes against the same, yet were driven backe againe a great pace," and Hawkins temporarily lost sight of his ships.[6] Although he was probably the first Englishman to write about it, successive expeditions along the same stretch began as early as 1513, when Antón de Alaminos first recorded the Gulf Stream and the Florida Straits when sailing with de León. The current was so strong one of the ships was separated and drifted out of sight, as would happen to Hawkins years later. Alaminos charted a current "so strong that it drove them back, though they had a favorable wind." Despite the seeming danger, Alaminos used the current to his advantage on the expedition's return trip to the Bahamas.[7]

Alaminos and others, as they probed Cuba and the Yucatan, finally gained all of the puzzle pieces when they passed through the Yucatan channel, realizing the potential of a regional system that could be used to their advantage. Once Spanish explorers discovered and charted the system, they uncovered the sixteenth-century equivalent of Interstate 95—a sea lane running Spanish shipping out of the Caribbean, up the east coast of Florida to the Carolinas, and then into the Atlantic and back toward Spain. For that reason, the La Florida discovered and explored in the sixteenth century retained its importance to Spain even when its financial prospects were revealed as worthless. Because its coastline stretched through critical portions of a burgeoning transatlantic trade system, so, too, would it remain critical to the Spanish government.

The more Spanish sailors charted them, the more regular and predictable the currents became. They were also incredibly powerful. That made them surprisingly deadly even when sailors knew what to expect, taking the lives of countless mariners seemingly each year of the Indies trade and making the return trip to Spain the deadliest portion of the entire circuit. The length of time it took ships to navigate the Caribbean basin was an important contributing factor. Pushing off from Portobelo in the southern Caribbean, for instance, a Spanish vessel could not expect to make port again in Spain for upward of five months. In general, it could take almost twice as long to complete the homebound as the outbound leg. Burdened by a smaller crew, heavier ships, and wear and tear issues like the growth of barnacles or marine worms, the ships moved even slower. The stretch from Vera Cruz to Havana, slowly skirting almost the entire rim of the Gulf of Mexico, took almost a month alone.[8]

The sheer time involved in the journey amplified the danger that faced any mariner in the Gulf—the warm waters themselves and the unpredictable storms that strengthened over them almost instantaneously. Over the several month exodus from the Caribbean, ships would be at the mercy of several tricky current systems, often fighting contradictory winds, and all the while at the mercy of Caribbean storms. Both the Gulf of Mexico and the larger Caribbean were, and still are, notorious for storms. Consider the catastrophe that struck in 1554. Four Spanish ships left Vera Cruz and were immediately caught in a strong storm just off the coast of modern-day Galveston, Texas. Of the *San Andres*, the *Santa María de Ycair*, the *San Esteban*, and the *Espiritu Santo*, only the *San Andres* sailed away. The wrecks of the other three were in shallow water right off the coast, so shallow in fact that the masts of one could be seen from shore. Because the ships wrecked so close to the beach a good amount of the four hundred passengers survived, comprising a mix of soldiers, church laypeople, and civilians, including women and children. A detachment of them took a small boat back down to Vera Cruz. The vast majority, over 250 in total, attempted to walk along the beach to the next nearest Spanish outpost, not knowing that the closest one, Tampico, was hundreds of miles away. Even under the best of circumstances most of them probably would have died of exposure before making it. The journey was not made under the best of conditions, however, and most of the survivors did not have time to die of exposure. Almost every one of them was killed by coastal Natives, a death toll equivalent to those men of the Narváez expedition.[9]

The 1554 catastrophe took place on a particularly treacherous stretch of coastline, and death at the hands of Natives was simply its punctuation point. Although it had relatively stable currents the western Gulf was otherwise open water, vulnerable to both tropical cyclones that built over the Caribbean and "northerner" winter fronts that swept south from mainland North America.

There was little notice when a storm was approaching, and few areas of refuge. As Hawkins described while in port at Vera Cruz, "there is not in all this coast another place for shippes to arrive in safety, because the North winde hathe there such violence." Unless ships were in the harbor, fastened safely by mooring cables, anchors, and shorelines, "there is no remedie for these North windes but death." Then there was hurricane season, which stretched from late summer into the fall months. "It is necessary to go to the West Indies by way of the Cape Verde Islands before September owing to storms and heavy seas," went one set of contemporary sailing directions. "It is necessary also to pass the Gulf of Florida at the very latest in July, as the hurricanes are heavy there in August." The founder of St. Augustine, Pedro Menéndez de Avilés, said almost the exact same thing, warning his own son not to mess with the month of August.[10] These overlapping seasons meant there was almost no safe time to actually be in the Gulf if you were going to be in it for months at a time, and the 1554 wreck was a testament to the danger of a quickly approaching storm, for which there was almost no warning and little chance of surviving.

Things only got worse from there. With particularly strong currents pouring through a tight geological funnel, and with few safe harbors past Havana, the Florida Straits and the Gulf Stream were by far the most feared stretches of the Caribbean system. First were the straits. Almost all of the water that flowed from the Atlantic Ocean into the Caribbean basin reentered the Atlantic by passing through this remarkable stretch of water, less than one hundred miles wide from Key West to the coast of Cuba. It was a notoriously hazardous stretch, predictable under most circumstances because of its current but also extremely unforgiving. All of that water had, over millions of years, cut a tight and well-defined trench in the sea floor. Depths along the edges of the straits rose from the unchartable to single digits within hundreds of yards and were lined with coral reefs and shoals. While beautiful by twentieth-century diving and fishing standards the Florida Straits were, to sixteenth-century mariners, a death trap.

The currents swept close to the coast, giving navigators little option but to follow the coastline of keys that could, with any one wrong move, destroy them. Spanish mariners also valued sighting known objects for navigational accuracy, which provided a predictable cruise but also had ships hugging within eyeshot of shoals and reefs, dramatically increasing the danger posed by contradictory winds of any sort.[11] Even with a favorable wind, the currents were too strong for captains to reverse course or run too hard against them, and adjustments had to be made quickly to avoid at best grounding, which on a reef meant having the hull of their ship ripped apart from underneath them. The stretch of the modern-day Florida Keys was so notorious that the first Spaniards to lay eyes on them did not hesitate to name them the Martyrs, "for the reason that many men have suffered on them," as one castaway would later write, and that the rocky outcroppings, perhaps coral, "at a distance, look like men in distress." Many a shipwrecked Spaniard "was to suffer and die there in years to come," went another.[12] That was the case, according to Robert Marx, in 1521 with the wreck of the *San Anton* and in 1550 with the *Visitacion*, both going down along this notorious stretch of La Florida.[13]

The turn to the north and the resulting cruise up the southeast coast of peninsular Florida offered little respite. The reefs that are known today for their beauty lay just to the east of the northernmost Keys, including Islamorada, Key Largo, and Key Biscayne, just off present-day Miami and right at the critical turn north into the Gulf Stream. No more than sixty miles to the east of the present-day city of Miami lays Bimini, and just to the southeast, the imposing edge of the Grand Bahamian Bank. This stretch is also where the Antilles current, flowing west along the northern coast of Hispaniola and Cuba and below the Bahamas, enters the Gulf Stream. With the addition of that water, the Gulf Stream current from modern-day Miami to Cape Canaveral is perhaps the strongest anywhere along the entire circuit. According to an account from de León's 1513 cruise, the men originally tried to sail against the current in this vicinity and were immediately unsuccessful. The men attempted heading south along the southeast coast of peninsular Florida near present-day Palm Beach, where they "doubled the cape of La Florida, which they named Cabo de Corrientes [Cape of Currents], because the water ran so swift there that it had more force than the wind, and would not allow the ships to go forward, although they put out all sails."[14] Not only were the currents particularly strong there; that was right where coral reefs were the most treacherous to the west, and the Bahamian bank closest to the east. The "Cape of Currents" was a fitting name indeed for such an unforgiving stretch of water.

That was the stretch in which ships were temporarily lost in both de León's and Hawkins's cruises—a testament to the current's strength—and the stretch that personally scared the latter mariners to death. Desperate to bring on fresh water as they transitioned from the Gulf into the Florida Straits, Hawkins hoped to find Havana but overshot it, leaving his ships to try the Keys. He hoped to do so early, before the turn to the north, "for, to go further to the Eastward, we could not for the shoals, which are very dangerous; and because the current shooteth to the Northeast" and so the expedition "durst not approach them." Several ships went down along the Bahamian bank before the mid-sixteenth century, providing ample evidence of the turn's risky nature.[15]

Not even after making the turn to the north were ships safe. The coast of eastern peninsular Florida, exposed to the raw power of the southern Atlantic, was just as prone to bad weather as any other section of the coastline. The open Atlantic brought shipping into sustained threat of the worst of those storms, the kind a Frenchman on the coast of La Florida described as "a species of whirlwinds or typhoons, which sailors call 'houragans,'" which from time to time came on "suddenly and inflict terrible damage on the coast." Hawkins called them "Furicanos" while Menéndez recalled explaining to his own son "that in the whole month of July he could come out of the Bahamian Channel, because in the beginning of August, some years, they often have very great hurricanes."[16] Getting hit by even a small Atlantic hurricane coming in from the Atlantic was almost invariably a death sentence. Shoals and even patches of reef continue to line the east coast of peninsular Florida all the way up to present-day Stuart. This section claimed the *San Nicholas* in 1551 when it went down off modern-day Fort Pierce. Three years later two ships wrecked near the same place on two separate occasions, while in 1556 another ship was suspected to have gone down near Cape Canaveral. Not until they pushed out into open waters off the coast of northern peninsular Florida or Georgia were mariners finally clear of the dangers of La Florida's coastline. By that time, they had been negotiating the Caribbean current system possibly for months.[17]

As was the case in 1554, ships went down on reefs and shoals so close to shore that survivors were not uncommon. Cast away on remote and hostile coastlines, however, simply not drowning did not mean a survivor was really meant to survive a shipwreck. Of course, death by exposure on the beach was a possibility, but according to many reports most survivors of shipwrecks did not have enough time to die of thirst. As waves of failed conquistadores had already discovered, the shores of La Florida were not at all an uninhabited wasteland; coastal Native peoples like the Tocobaga or Calusa on Florida's southwest coast, or the Ais on the southeast, had violent reputations that bordered on the legendary. The harsh treatment Spaniards endured at the hands of Natives, of course, paled in comparison with the carnage wrought on Caribbean Natives by Spaniards, and by the late sixteenth century coastal Natives were probably thoroughly and rightfully sick of seeing Spaniards creeping along the coastline, no matter their condition. Their penchant for finishing off the exhausted and starving foreigners they found littering their shores was certainly rightly earned. Remarking at midcentury was Hawkins, who explained that the Natives of the southern Peninsula, probably Calusa or perhaps Tequesta, were notoriously violent—"of more savage and fierce nature, and more valiant then any of the rest," and had killed scores of Spaniards already. If he was indeed referring to the Calusa, then he was only one of the many who took note of the tribe for their notorious ill-treatment of shipwrecked survivors.[18]

Also produced along this same coast of peninsular Florida were long-enslaved captives who did manage to survive, producing in the process some of the region's first and most detailed ethnological accounts. Juan Ortiz, whom de Soto encountered in the first days of his entrada, was a captured and enslaved member of Narváez's expedition who endured a decade of servitude in the area around Tampa Bay. Ironically, Juan Muñoz was captured from de Soto's expedition right around the same time Ortiz was found. Muñoz was in turn enslaved, only to be found by Spanish missionaries a decade later, in 1549. Even more ironic, that same year Hernándo d'Escalante Fontaneda was shipwrecked on the Keys. He would survive almost two decades of captivity among the Calusa to be rescued by Menéndez hundreds of miles from St. Augustine. Fontaneda would also produce a memoir, making the most of his years of torment. Forty more survivors of his wreck, however, were not so lucky. One of them was his brother. Even then, decades later, he continued to press for the further protection of the trade routes, all the way around the peninsula of Florida, where the royal armadas "that go to Peru, New Spain, and other parts of the Indies, which pass, of necessity, along that shore and channel of the Bahama, where many vessels are wrecked, and many persons die."[19] Fontaneda, unfortunately, was speaking from personal experience.

Such horror stories were in no way confined to southwest peninsular Florida. Unnamed wrecks in 1525 and 1545 along other stretches of modern-day Florida ended in the massacre of hundreds of sailors.[20] A few years after Fontaneda's wreck, in 1551, the *San Juan* went down at an unnamed location off the coast of peninsular Florida, leaving over twenty castaways presumably to die there at the hands of Natives.[21] Then came the disastrous 1554 wreck, which ended in the slaughter of hundreds of survivors, including priests, women, and children. As late as 1564 two more Spanish Fontaneda characters had been found—spared castaways who were found enslaved but alive, living among Natives for well over a decade.[22] From these alarming accounts it is clear why the settling of the La Florida coastline, even if it did not produce riches, emerged as a major humanitarian necessity that grew out of sustained travel through the Gulf of Mexico. Mariners went down along the coastline of La Florida so frequently that rescuing them, as well as preventing Natives from massacring them, was reason enough to establish a physical presence along the heavily used trade routes. Possibly thousands of lives could be saved.[23]

Another obvious factor of the 1554 wreck was the combined cargo in the holds of the three ships that went down. The usage of large and deep galleons to transport goods left thousands of pounds of valuables of all sorts underwater in instances of wrecks. They included barrels of valuable cochineal dyes, animal hides, and above all else, well over one million pesos worth of gold and silver. The loss of such riches was catastrophic; they threatened to financially devastate the Crown and private merchants alike, both of whom used the ships to transport valuables to and from the colonies. Laden as they were with riches of all types, the ships were part of the larger mixed merchant and military flotillas that had been shuttling the wealth of the Caribbean and of New Spain back to the mother country for decades. Much of the gold and silver was destined for the Spanish Crown, which would use it to pay back loans, finance its wars, and purchase power on foreign markets. Most of the other goods, like tobacco products, sugar, pearls, hides, etc., had been produced in the New World by slave labor and shipped to Spain to be taxed and then sold all over the world.[24] When a ship went down, the work of enslaved Natives and Africans went with it, and the lost wealth represented basically the whole reason for the Spanish to be in the New World in the first place.

This mixed merchant convoy system was known as the *Flota de Indies*, the Indies Flotilla, or colloquially simply the "Treasure Fleets." The *Flota*'s precursors could be seen as early as 1519, when Cortés himself first used the Gulf Stream to transport Aztec gold back to the Spanish Court, doing so practically as soon as Antón de Alaminos first charted it. As Spaniards expanded their colonial presence in the New World they established plantations, mines, and even royal mints, and shipments moving both ways increased. Ships brought trade goods to the colonies, emptied their hulls, and transported the products of enslaved or coerced Native workers back to Spain. These ships faced all sorts of obstacles, both natural and man-made, and once the flow of them became steady, it generated the need for a unified, protected system of transportation. The result was the *Flota* system, which hit its peak at the turn of the seventeenth century. It is difficult to measure just how much wealth in gold and silver alone made the journey. Widespread smuggling means the true numbers could be much higher. According to one 1626 account, however, in the roughly one century period from 1519 to 1617, it "amounted to 1536 millions."[25]

The epic, world history–altering transfer of that wealth followed, charted by a familiar course. At least once a year for decades, a convoy of Spanish merchant ships and massive armed galleons would depart Spain and arrive in the Caribbean, first probably an outlying Caribbean Island like Dominica, Hispaniola, or later, Puerto Rico. Loaded with merchant orders meant for colonial markets, the ships would split off onto two main routes. One route, known as the *Tierra Firma Flota*, hopscotched across ports in the lower Caribbean, like Cartagena, Nombre de Dios, and Portobelo. There merchants would offload the goods bound for them and would then transfer onboard the products of local *haciendas* and ranches in order to get them to market in Seville. Sailors would also trade with the Manila Galleons, an entirely separate caravan of ships that arrived regularly on the Pacific Coast of modern Panama from the Philippines. From that trade, the same ships would trade currency and other goods for the spices, silks, etc., of Spain's Asian markets. Most important, perhaps, while at these ports the ships would take on tons of officially minted silver from the mines of Peru.[26] Shoving off again they would catch the Yucatan current and then a portion of the Loop current, sweeping around the Gulf of Mexico to arrive at Havana.

A separate route was taken by the *Nueva España*, or the New Spain Flota. Ships along that route would pick up trade goods like tobacco, sugar, and rum from island ports like San Juan, Santo Domingo, or Santiago de Cuba on their way through the northern Caribbean basin. Once clearing the western end of Cuba these ships would take the Yucatan current north to the Mexican current, turn a sharp west, and make port on the Gulf Coast of Mexico, usually at Vera Cruz. There they would offload trade goods meant for Mexico City and take on the loot of New Spain's gold and silver mines. According to Hawkins, when he visited Vera Cruz in 1567, he saw a dozen ships in the harbor, "which had in them by the report two hundred thousand pound in gold and silver." What he witnessed was the New Spain Flota. Shoving off, the fleet would take the Loop current in a sweeping circuit, hugging the Gulf Coast shores of modern-day Texas, Louisiana, Alabama, and Florida before turning south and traveling down the west coast of peninsular Florida. The two fleets would regroup in Havana harbor and prepare for the return voyage to Spain. There the merchant ships would regroup with a security escort of heavily armed naval galleons, some of which might even include hundreds of marines. Pushing out of the harbor they would catch the current heading east, beginning their journey through the Florida Straits, north up the Gulf Stream, and out into the Atlantic.[27]

The 1554 wrecks, scattered along the Texas shore, were a part of the New Spain Flota. They were caught in what was most likely a hurricane soon after embarking from Vera Cruz. In that respect the three ships were not simply one of the many that went down at some point along a treacherous, monthslong trek across the Caribbean. They also proved that unexpected patches of rough weather not only wrecked ships and stranded survivors; they produced financial nightmares that crippled both private and royal interests. And the 1554 losses, although they were particularly costly, were not isolated incidents. At least some ships of the New Spain Flota were lost near Vera Cruz to storms in 1545, 1553, 1555, and 1558, proving how treacherous the open waters of the Gulf truly were. The 1555 loss was doubly tragic, for onboard the *Santa María la Blanca* was near a million pesos in gold and silver that had just been salvaged from the 1554 wreck along the Texas coast.[28]

Several costly wrecks went down in the Florida Straits. In 1544 the *Santa María de la Isla* went down off Havana after making port in Nombre de Dios. Another in 1555, laden with goods from Panama, most likely Nombre de Dios, was lost off Matanzas. Both presumably sailed with the Tierra Firma Flota, and both presumably went down with hulls full of silver. Just to the north, the 1550 *Visitacion* wreck in the Keys was part of the New Spain Flota. The years 1556 and 1563 were particularly bad for the Tierra Firma and New Spain Flotas, respectively. In 1556 four ships went down off the coast of Havana, while in 1563 six ships went down off the southern coast of the island.[29]

Yet more treasure went down along the edges of the Bahaman Channel. In both 1554 and 1555 ships of the Tierra Firma Flota got separated in the channel and were never seen again. Those wrecks, in addition to the 1554 catastrophe in Texas, marked a dark year indeed. On the Florida side of the channel, an unnamed 1556 wreck off Cape Canaveral was associated with the New Spain Flota, while the 1551 *San Nicholas* went down at Fort Pierce after stopping at both Cartagena and Nombre Dios. It presumably sailed with the Tierra Firma Flota and was almost certainly burdened with valuable cargo. Perhaps that was the wreck Fontaneda would later write about himself, noting how the Ais and Jeaga Natives of east peninsular Florida got rich "only by the sea, from the many vessels that have been lost well laden with these metals," one of which was "in the year '51." The unnamed Cape Canaveral ship was said to have gone down with over a million pesos in the form of gold and silver bars. When Hawkins visited the French in peninsular Florida shortly before the Spanish destroyed it, he found the Frenchmen walking around with gold and silver that clearly came from such wrecks. He described how the men made their way down the southwest, presumably near Calusa territory, "having found the same dangerous, by means of sundry banks, as we also have found the same: and there finding masts which were wracks of Spaniards coming from Mexico, judged that they had gotten treasure by them." Not even after clearing the Bahamas were the fleets safe. Ships from the New Spain Flota wrecked on the reefs of Bermuda in 1550 and 1563, and ships traveling with the Tierra Firma Flota did so in 1551 and 1560.[30]

Every one of these ships went down not only at the cost of lives but carrying something of extreme value to both Spanish merchants and the Crown. Much of that cargo was certainly ruined, like the dyes, hides, and logwood that went down with the three 1554 wrecks off Galveston. The gold and silver, however, were not so perishable, and they needed to be recovered. As soon as he heard word of the wreck, Viceroy Diego de Velasco immediately dispatched an expedition from New Spain to salvage what it could. By the time the wreckers arrived, salvaging operations dispatched by other more local authorities had already begun. They continued for months; still, because of shifting sands and the deteriorating condition of the ships, workers recovered less than half the gold and silver listed on the manifests.[31]

In the case of the 1554 wrecks, the remains were so close to settled areas of the coast—at most only a few days' sail from Vera Cruz—that Spanish salvagers could get to them almost immediately. Wrecks elsewhere along the coast of La Florida were much more difficult to reach, and that was if Spaniards ever learned where they went down at all. A wreck of a Tierra Firma galleon having gone down somewhere along peninsular Florida in 1551, for instance, was recorded as being salvaged almost completely by Spanish authorities shortly after its loss, even though this would appear to be the same wreck looted by coastal Natives. The 1554 Fort Pierce wreck, on the other hand, was discovered and looted at least partially by local Ais Natives. Others simply disappeared.[32]

Results were mixed at best because there was no reliable settlement past the coast of Mexico from which authorities could either hear of a wreck or dispatch salvage crews to recover what was lost. Only years later would Spaniards ever learn of the location of a wreck in the mid-sixteenth century, for example, when Fontaneda described it in his memoir. He recounted a Calusa headman traveling across the peninsula to loot an unnamed wreck on the east coast, which Fontaneda described as including "as much as a million dollars, or over, in bars of silver, in gold, and in articles of jewelry made by the hands of Mexican Indians."[33]

The riches, divvied up among Native headmen, would never find their way back to Seville. While establishing an outpost along such a critical stretch of water was certainly important for rescuing shipwrecked mariners, Spanish authorities also recognized that there was a tremendous amount of money at stake as well.

Making matters worse, the increase in trade ships plying the waters of the Caribbean basin naturally brought an increase in piracy. Current American popular culture, obsessed as it is with pirates, opens almost every pirate legend or curse with some sort of "buried treasure," and there is, of course, a clear historical foundation to such fantasy: this period of the Spanish Flotas, when ships plied crystal-clear and coral-lined waters, packed down with gold and silver. It was the Spanish *Carrera de Indias*, in short, that generated the first waves of piracy in the New World. Only two years after the first Spanish galleon shipped Aztec gold back to the Spanish Crown, in fact, French corsairs picked one off in the Gulf of Mexico in 1521. French Pirate Jean Fleury took another two ships off the coast of Portugal a year later. Other historians place the first recorded act of piracy against Spanish shipping as taking place off Panama in 1536.[34] Regardless, with the large-scale establishment of gold and silver mines in Central Mexico and South America, piracy got very popular, and very quickly.

The thought of plundering the Spanish Caribbean caught the eye of the French in particular, whose attacks hit a frenzy by the mid-sixteenth century. Not only did they single out straggling ships, but they also targeted entire ports. Pirates, including Jean-François Roberval and François le Clerc, sacked various Caribbean ports, including San German, Puerto Rico, and Santiago de Cuba, before turning to Santa Marta and Cartagena in 1543 and 1544. Meanwhile, Jacques Sores seized Havana after attacking various other Spanish outposts across the Caribbean basin. Le Clerc and Sores both used their attacks to ransom their way to riches, and Le Clerc so thoroughly devastated Santiago de Cuba that it never fully recovered. Worse yet was the loss of Havana, Spain's logistical Caribbean hub and the rendezvous point for the treasure fleets. That was a particularly humiliating ransom for colonial authorities to pay. French privateers also sacked a coastal town in Honduras in 1558 and then Campeche in 1561.[35] Attacking the "Spanish Main," a term used to describe the coastline of the Spanish New World, turned out to be a lucrative business indeed.

Although slow to act, Spanish authorities responded in several ways. They commissioned an official escort fleet to guard the home stretch of the fleets' return voyage, protecting ships as they moved from the Canaries and Azores to port in Spain.[36] They also invested in many of their New Spain and Tierra Firma ports, building fortifications that still overlook the entrances to sizeable harbors on the Caribbean coastline, like Nombre de Dios, Portobelo, and Trujillo. One can visit the imposing fortifications at Cartagena and Vera Cruz in particular to witness the severity of the piracy threat to the colonial outposts that served essentially as Spain's New World bank vaults. The works are impressive. Several overlapping fortifications also protected the harbors of San Juan, Puerto Rico, and Havana, Cuba, two of the Flotas' largest ports of rendezvous. Outposts on the La Florida coastline, Spanish authorities hoped, would soon add to the list of those fortifications.

The piracy threat was also one of the primary reasons the Crown adopted the Flota system. Ships loaded with gold and silver required protection, which was far too costly to provide to each and every ship that might set sail from the New World individually. Instead, authorities grouped them together and provided them with armed escorts. There was, in the view of the *Casa de Contratacion*, safety in numbers, and so the Spanish government sent scores of ships, at least once a year, along the coast of La Florida on their way back to Seville.[37] That created a desire to develop coastal communities not unfamiliar to modern Floridians: coastal communities near the modern cities of Pensacola, Tampa, Naples, Miami, and St. Augustine are some of the most popular in twentieth-century North America because of the aesthetic beauty of their coastlines. As it turns out, La Florida's waterfront real estate in the sixteenth century was no less coveted. It was some of the most important real estate in the New World because it was the key to the transportation of New Spain's imperial wealth.

Notes

1. Elliot, *Empires*, 108-110; Lyon, *The Enterprise of Florida*, 8-9; Lowery, *The Spanish Settlements*, 4-5; Marx, *Shipwrecks*, 4-6; Walton, *The Spanish Treasure Fleets*, 30-35.
2. Elliot, *Empires*, 108-110; Marx, *Shipwrecks in the Americas*, 17.
3. Sledge, *The Gulf of Mexico*, 43-44. For the Caribbean current: https://oceancurrents.rsmas.miami.edu/caribbean/caribbean.html. For the Yucatan channel: https://oceancurrents.rsmas.miami.edu/caribbean/yucatan.html.
4. For the Mexican current: https://oceancurrents.rsmas.miami.edu/caribbean/mexican.html. For the Loop current: https://oceanservice.noaa.gov/facts/loopcurrent.html and https://oceancurrents.rsmas.miami.edu/atlantic/loop-current.html. For the Florida Strait and the Gulf Stream: https://oceanservice.noaa.gov/facts/gulfstreamspeed.html and https://oceancurrents.rsmas.miami.edu/atlantic/gulf-stream.html. For secondary historical sources: Weddle, *Spanish Sea*, 42.
5. Marx, *Shipwrecks in the Americas*, 18-19.
6. Burrage, ed., *Early English and French Voyages*, 117-118.
7. Weddle, *Spanish Sea*, 42, 46; Davis, "Ponce de León's First Voyage," 18.

8. Elliot, *Empires*, 108-109; Marx, *Shipwrecks in the Americas*, 17-19.

9. Weddle, *Spanish Sea*, 246-248; Weber, *Spanish Frontier*, 65-67.

10. Marx, *Shipwrecks in the Americas*, 22; Burrage, ed., *Early English and French Voyages*, 141-142; Notation 2 in Gabriel de Luxan to Philip II, n. 140, in Quinn, ed., *The Roanoke Voyages*, 2: 767; Lyon, *The Enterprise of Florida*, 28.

11. Marx, *Shipwrecks in the Americas*, 19-20.

12. Davis, "Ponce de León's First Voyage," 18-19; Worth, *Discovering Florida*, 199; Weddle, *Spanish Sea*, 42.

13. Marx, *Shipwrecks in the Americas*, 195.

14. Davis, "Ponce de León's First Voyage," 18-19; Davis, "Ponce de León's Second Voyage," 65.

15. Burrage, ed., *Early English and French Voyages*, 117; Marx, *Shipwrecks in the Americas*, 314.

16. Bennett, ed., *Settlement of Florida*, 113; Burrage, ed., *Early English and French Voyages*, 140; Lyon, *The Enterprise of Florida*, 29. For a detailed account of the role hurricanes played in the early Atlantic world, see: Schwartz, *Sea of Storms*, particularly ch. 2.

17. Marx, *Shipwrecks in the Americas*, 195-196; Lyon, *The Enterprise of Florida*, 14-15.

18. Burrage, ed., *Early English and French Voyages*, 119.

19. Weddle, *Spanish Sea*, 39, 189, 220, 242-243, 251; Ferdinando, "A Translation History of Fontaneda," 213-214.

20. Marx, *Shipwrecks in the Americas*, 195.

21. Weddle, *Spanish Sea*, 317.

22. Weddle, *Spanish Sea*, 293.

23. Weddle, *Spanish Sea*, 254-256.

24. Weddle, *Spanish Sea*, 246.

25. Turner, "Juan Ponce de León," 21, 26; Lowery, *The Spanish Settlements*, 5-6.

26. Lowery, *The Spanish Settlements*, 11.

27. Marx, *Shipwrecks in the Americas*, 10-12; Lowery, *The Spanish Settlements*, 11; Walton, *The Spanish Treasure Fleets*, 44-61; Burrage, ed., *Early English and French Voyages*, 141.

28. Marx, *Shipwrecks in the Americas*, 239-241.

29. Marx, *Shipwrecks in the Americas*, 239-241.

30. Marx, *Shipwrecks in the Americas*, 195-196, 300, 314.

31. Marx, *Shipwrecks in the Americas*, 300.

32. Marx, *Shipwrecks in the Americas*, 195-196.

33. Worth, *Discovering Florida*, 206-207.

34. Weddle, *Spanish Sea*, 287; Kamen, *Empire*, 258; Lane, *Pillaging the Empire*, 17; Lowery, *The Spanish Settlements*, 9.

35. Kamen, *Empire*, 258-259; Lane, *Pillaging the Empire*, 17-28; Marley, *Wars of the Americas*, 52-58; Hoffman, *A New Andalucia*, 128-130, 132-136, 140-143, 216, 225; Weber, *The Spanish Frontier*, 65; Weddle, *Spanish Sea*, 287-289; Lowery, *The Spanish Settlements*, 22; Jennings, *New Worlds of Violence*, 62-63; Hudson, *Juan Pardo*, 12.

36. Lowery, *The Spanish Settlements*, 12.

37. Marx, *Shipwrecks*, 9-10; Lowery, *The Spanish Settlements*, 10-11.

Las Flotas

Spanish colonialism fed piracy in the sixteenth century, and by midcentury, piracy was booming. The frequency with which French and British "corsairs" harassed Spanish treasure ships was beginning to transition from menace to disaster, and some of the worst news was coming from far-flung La Florida. For Spanish authorities, an absolute worst-case pirate scenario involved a competing European power actually establishing its own outpost along the La Florida coastline. The long-term consequences would be devastating: a competing foreign base anywhere along La Florida's Gulf or Atlantic coasts would not only place the treasure fleets in routine danger of harassment, but would threaten Spanish imperial interests everywhere from the tobacco, sugar, and pearl regions of the Caribbean all the way up to the cod fisheries of Newfoundland.[1]

That threat was manifested around midcentury when Spanish authorities discovered published French accounts that claimed portions of La Florida based on Giovanni de Verrazano's voyages dating back as early as 1524, which would have placed French-backed explorers along the Atlantic Coast of La Florida two years earlier than Ayllón's failed Guadalpe attempt. While this was worrisome enough, it was also clear the French had no intention of halting their activities, and right on the very stretches of La Florida coastline that the Spanish considered so critical to their own security, no less.[2] Out of sheer necessity, then, Spaniards had to get there first. It was a combination of economic and military exigencies, all based on La Florida's location along the Gulf currents, which drove renewed interest in settling the region.

A threatened French settling of Santa Elena, for instance, was one of the primary reasons King Philip II authorized the Tristán de Luna y Arellano expedition in the 1550s, more than a decade after de Soto's failure in 1542.[3] In 1557 Philip II officially sanctioned the establishment of two separate fortified settlements along the treasure route: one along the south Atlantic at Santa Elena, in modern-day Port Royal, South Carolina, and the other somewhere along the Gulf Coast. When Spanish officials broached the idea, the Viceroy of New

Spain, Diego de Velasco, was quick to agree. These were the plans that laid the foundation of the Spanish attempt to settle Florida's Gulf Coast at the present-day site of Pensacola.[4]

Viceroy de Velasco quickly fit out a preliminary scouting expedition under the command of Guido de Lazavares, who took three ships along the Gulf Coast, feeling out possible settlement locations. De Lazavares only made it to Mobile Bay and slightly farther before returning to Vera Cruz, yet his cruise achieved Don Luis de Velasco's ostensive objective—charting the suitability of several bays on the Gulf Coast. De Velasco moved quickly, green lighting a full-scale attempt to settle one of those bays. Don Tristán de Luna y Arellano was tapped to lead the expedition. By royal order he would establish a presidio—a fortified town—at a site of his choosing on the Gulf, then dispatch a second detachment to march overland to establish Santa Elena. From there a road might be established between the two and towns, connecting the coasts of La Florida and, eventually, continuing west into the northern edges of New Spain.[5]

Tristán de Luna would be the first of several Spaniards to attempt settling Santa Elena and establishing it as the terminus of such a Camino Real, or royal road. While many Spaniards certainly still hoped to colonize the Southeast to their economic advantage, Santa Elena brought the strategic, and not monetary, value of La Florida into clearer focus. First, a position like Santa Elena would provide Spaniards a second port of protection against shipwrecks and piracy as ships exited the Bahamian channel and entered the southern Atlantic. Although South Carolina seems a bit out of the way, the Gulf Stream current continues north from the southern tip of peninsular Florida north along the Atlantic Coast all the way north to the Outer Banks. While many ships pushed out into the open ocean before they reached the coast of modern-day South Carolina, it certainly was possible for them to wait, and if Spaniards had Santa Elena to provide them protection, they probably would. In fact, even the men of de Soto's expedition noticed the location's value as they stood in Cofitachequi, hundreds of miles inland. When pitching the idea of staying there to de Soto, the men argued that "if it were settled, all the ships from New Spain, and those from Peru, Santa Marta, and Tierra Firma, on their way to Spain, would come to take advantage of the stop there, for their route passes by there." Santa Elena, if properly fortified, could mark for Spaniards the conclusion of the treacherous Florida current system.[6]

More intriguing, perhaps, connecting the Gulf and Atlantic coasts of La Florida overland promised Spanish authorities the ability to circumvent the Gulf of Mexico and its currents completely, something that might save untold lives. By the mid-sixteenth century, the idea of an interconnected New Spain and La Florida was not altogether foreign to Spanish explorers. It stretched back at least to Alonso Álvarez de Pineda's 1519 expedition to chart the Gulf of Mexico. On his way into the Gulf, he mapped the east coast of modern-day Mexico and then Texas, and what he saw evidently impressed him. Pineda requested royal authorization to colonize the region north of New Spain, which he referred to as "Amichel," and which, he argued, had plenty of strategic value as well as potential wealth. A few years later, as Pánfilo de Narváez's expedition began to fall apart, both he and Cabeza de Vaca chose to head west, hoping perhaps to find rescue by accessing this region, "the back door into Mexico."[7]

This reasoning made the de Luna expedition a clear departure from previous entradas. Predecessors, including de León, Ayllón, Narváez, and de Soto, were all motivated entirely by personal financial gain. They were all authorized by but not financially supported by the Crown. De Velasco, on the other hand, as the Viceroy of New Spain was officially backing and outfitting the de Luna expedition at royal expense and ordering it to be undertaken for the strategic benefit of New Spain and the Spanish Crown. Although there might be an *adelantado* title in it for the successful settler, in other words, that was not the original motivating factor. The treasure fleets were. De Luna's attempt at Pensacola and Santa Elena marked a new era in the trajectory of La Florida and American history.

As a consequence, the de Luna expedition was perhaps the most sizeable, and by far the most professional, of all the Spanish attempts to colonize La Florida. At the time of its sailing, de Luna's fleet comprised eleven ships, carrying over fifteen hundred people and over two hundred horses. Even more impressive than the expedition's size, however, was the composition of the men. Never before had the would-be colonizers been so experienced, wrote one historian. That began of course with de Luna, a veteran of Spanish conquest in New Spain who had also accompanied Francisco Vasquez de Coronado into the American Southwest. Over five hundred of the expedition's men were trained soldiers, many of whom were veterans of previous conquests, including in Mexico and Peru. Some had even already been in La Florida, and some of the officers had participated in the de Soto entrada. The pilots leading the way were the finest and most experienced in the region, and based on their knowledge and previous experiences, special sailing craft were designed and purpose-built to operate in the shallow waters of the Gulf Coast.[8]

De Luna's colonizing effort was massive, professional, and well supplied, all of which would seem to have guaranteed at least some success. His opening moves, although not without adversity, also went smoothly. While the initial sail from Vera Cruz to Pensacola harbor—what the Spanish referred to as Ochuse—went predictably, the ships then overshot their destination, landing instead near modern-day Apalachicola. After backtracking too far to Mobile Bay, de Luna dispatched cavalry to travel overland to Pensacola Bay and, by late August, had sailed the eleven ships into the bay to meet them. After choosing the site of a fort on a bluff he sent word of the expedition's initial successes to Viceroy de Velasco and began preparations to dispatch the Santa Elena expedition. Perhaps the only thing that could have doomed de Luna at this critical juncture is precisely what arrived less than a month after the establishment of Santa María de Ochuse. A massive storm—almost certainly either a tropical storm or a hurricane—promptly arrived, wrecking seven of de Luna's ships in the harbor, killing scores of settlers, and ruining most of the expedition's supplies. Almost in an instant, with so much destroyed so quickly, Ochuse was "rendered untenable at a stroke."[9]

De Luna salvaged what he could, sending the only remaining seaworthy ships back to Vera Cruz to deliver the bad news directly to de Velasco, and hopefully secure aid. Over the next year, despite multiple attempted resupply efforts, everything slowly fell apart. In an effort to get supplies to Ochuse overland from Mexico, Viceroy Diego de Velasco ended up proving the ridiculousness of a royal road connecting New Spain to La Florida. The cattle he sent got nowhere near Pensacola. Meanwhile, various dispatches of soldiers sent by de Luna moved inland from the coast to Native American settlements in modern-day Alabama, hoping to take advantage of the legendary corn civilizations mentioned in previous entradas. Although scouts made it all the way to towns in the Coosa province of northern Alabama and lived there in relative health, Ochuse would not find its salvation in Mississippian corn. Then, a reprovisioning mission to Cuba, which carried with it de Luna's first attempt to establish Santa Elena by sea, hit what was very likely a second hurricane. All the while, Santa María de Ochuse slowly collapsed. De Luna struggled to keep his settlement from starving, struggled with de Velasco, struggled increasingly with his subordinates, and struggled with his own health. Diego de Velasco eventually ordered him relieved of duty.[10]

In an effort to save the mission, de Velasco appointed Ángel de Villafañe, himself a New Spain veteran and the garrison commander at Vera Cruz, to replace de Luna. That switch took place in March of 1561 after almost a year and a half of hardship and privation. Rather than spend any more time propping up a failing Ochuse, however, Villafañe immediately set off for Santa Elena by way of Havana, trying to fulfill at least that portion of the King's original order. He handpicked his expedition, leaving the remainder of the men to abandon Ochuse behind him. He actually made it to Santa Elena but was immediately disappointed by what he saw. Nothing about Port Royal Sound, which he described as too shallow and too barren, looked promising. Sailing north he passed the Cape Fear River and eventually made it to Hatteras before his ships were wrecked by, incredibly enough, the third hurricane to strike the de Luna expedition in as many years. If ever there was an expedition willed by nature to fail, this one was it. Villafañe returned to Havana and gave up all hope of La Florida, bringing to an ignominious end the most well-planned settlement attempt perhaps in all of New Spain, and one of the first to be bankrolled directly by the Spanish government.[11]

As one historian suggested, this was the La Florida entrada that, had it been successful, had the most potential to change the trajectory of North American history. Had either de Luna or Villafañe succeeded in establishing Ochuse and Santa Elena, and from there established an overland route between the two, Spanish La Florida certainly would have experienced an immediate wave of settlement. The same could be said about the road connecting Zacatecas and Ochuse, which de Velasco attempted to forge in his effort to relieve Ochuse. Had they succeeded, the Gulf Coast would look entirely different.[12] Instead, again La Florida had disappointed. The failure to establish at least Santa Elena, more particularly, signified La Florida's latest, most expensive, and most embarrassing failure yet.[13]

In the immediate aftermath of the de Luna debacle, New Spain officials recalculated La Florida's worth, found it lacking, and abandoned all further efforts at colonization. That did not last long. With imperial competition between Spain and France escalating, the Spanish Crown begrudgingly accepted that it simply could not afford to ignore La Florida, regardless of the hardships it had already caused. In particular it was the Santa Elena dream that continued to keep the hope of La Florida alive. Three more attempts on the Atlantic Coast, in fact, took place in as many years. Two attempts were made at Santa Elena, and a third was made by Lucas Vasquez de Ayllón's own son, Vasquez de Ayllón the Younger, to settle the Bahia Santa María, which the British would later refer to as the Chesapeake Bay. Each of the three, however, failed at various stages that all fell short of actually touching land.[14]

Ultimately, it was the French that forced King Philip's hand. Almost immediately after these last Spanish expeditions had failed, in the early 1560s, Jean Ribault and René Goulaine de Laudonnière arrived near the future location of

St. Augustine. They moved north, establishing Charlesfort at Port Royal before returning to France. It would be ironic that Frenchmen were able to secure the location of Santa Elena in just one attempt, when Spaniards had failed now close to a half-dozen times. But Charlesfort did not last long for the French either. Ribault left men but very little by way of supply, leading to a quick abandonment of Charlesfort. So quick, in fact, that the small Spanish detachment sent from Cuba to destroy it arrived too late. Unfortunately for the Spanish, however, the French proved no less determined than they when it came to the Atlantic Coast. Soon they were back, this time on the St. Johns River, where they established Fort Caroline near modern-day Jacksonville. Worse yet, they "found a nook whence to plunder as many ships as should come from Terra Firma, whether from Mexico, or Peru, or from other parts," according to Fontaneda, whose warnings were no exaggeration. Within a year, in fact, French deserters were caught actually raiding Caribbean shipping off Hispaniola and Cuba, bringing the reality of the French threat home to the Spanish. Although the French mutineers took few prizes and did little damage to the larger Spanish trade, the importance—and continued irony—of their capture cannot be denied. To King Philip II, this was a disaster in the making. These French trespassers and pirates would be dealt with accordingly.[15]

Forced into immediate action, King Philip II dispatched Pedro Menéndez de Avilés with orders to destroy the French settlement and replace it with a permanent Spanish one. Menéndez had risen from within the ranks of the Spanish navy, having fought French privateers through the Indies and slowly earning the esteem of Charles V and then his son, Philip II. As captain-general of the Indies fleet he navigated the treacherous Gulf back to Spain on four separate occasions, making him an uncontested authority about La Florida's currents. Perhaps no one was as much an authority—in 1563 he lost his only son Juan to a suspected hurricane along the coast of peninsular Florida.[16]

In keeping with the times, Philip II granted Menéndez a *capitulación* (also referred to by that point as an *asiento*) that provided La Florida's newest prospective *adelantado* plenty of financial and political incentives for his sacrifice. Menéndez requested guarantees on classic sources of wealth, like mining, sugarcane, or cattle ranching. He considered his position on the Gulf Stream as possibly increasing his trade prospects through Indies trade, and so he requested concessions there, as well. His contract left the door open for *encomienda* and *repartimiento* grants, something Philip had been clearer about banning in the recent past. He even lobbied for the title of marquis, a clear nod to the times and successes of Cortés. Yet while Philip allowed most of this, continuing the tradition of private conquest, Menéndez's mission was not at all simply one of power and prestige. Also in Menéndez's instructions were clear strategic goals. He was required to settle La Florida heavily and with an eye for long-term settlement. He was to fortify the coast, begin the religious conversion of the local Natives, and even import enslaved African laborers to physically build the colony. It was a sprawling and ambitious contract inked between Menéndez and Philip II. Nevertheless, within months it was all in motion. Menéndez established St. Augustine, destroyed the French garrison at Fort Caroline with what you might call in modern military parlance *extreme* prejudice, then traveled north and finally established Santa Elena, something that had eluded Spaniards for decades.[17] By 1565 La Florida, stretching from South Carolina to northern Florida, had a permanent European presence, and it was Spanish.

For a brief time at least, Philip II could claim even more. Menéndez envisioned major Spanish garrisons funded at royal expense at St. Augustine and somewhere north, possibly on the Chesapeake, in order to secure the treasure fleets, shore up claims to La Florida, and protect the flanks of New Spain. Other towns, on the southwest coast of peninsular Florida and at Santa Elena, would be manned more at private expense and in hopes of financial gain.[18] Although not to the letter, Menéndez set out doing much of that within months of landing. He was frequently hopscotching between Havana and both coasts of peninsular Florida, rounding up men and supplies and dropping them off at the resettled Santa Elena, then at smaller garrisons near the modern-day Florida cities of Miami, Fort Myers, and Tampa.[19]

Menéndez paid special attention to the southwest coast of peninsular Florida near present-day Charlotte Harbor. The region had already produced shipwrecked gold and the Calusa were notorious for the way they treated castaways. These represented the two clear strategic reasons for a Spanish presence along the La Florida coast, but Menéndez moved to explore farther. One of the region's rivers, he hoped, might hold the key to a trans-Florida waterway that could do at least some of what the Camino Real promised. By cutting out at least the Florida Straits and the Gulf Stream, such an inland route could save the lives of countless mariners and thousands of pounds of gold and silver. As it turns out, the infamous cross-Florida barge canal, a politically complicated and multi-presidential attempt to cut a waterway through the Florida peninsula in the nineteenth and twentieth centuries, actually had its genesis hundreds of years previous.[20]

Southwest Florida was a fortuitous choice for Menéndez; it was there, around modern-day Fort Myers, where his men ran across the long-castaway Hernándo d'Escalante Fontaneda. Since being shipwrecked in 1549 he had been serving as a quasi-enslaved Calusa interpreter, but quickly returned to the Spanish fold. Unfortunately for Menéndez, the first intelligence Fontaneda provided was to alert a grieving father that there was little hope of finding his son, Juan, alive. Nevertheless, with Fontaneda's help Menéndez was soon able to ransom almost a dozen castaways from Calusa captivity. Scores of bones along one stretch of beach alone alluded to the many more Spanish victims of shipwrecks that had not been so lucky.[21] Although settling La Florida for the sake of shipwreck survivors might have been an objective of secondary importance, it certainly had paid off for Fontaneda and many others.

After recruiting Fontaneda, befriending Calusa headman Carlos, receiving reinforcements from Spain, and establishing a fort in southwest peninsular Florida, Menéndez went about pursuing the ultimate Camino Real objective: an overland connection across peninsular Florida. If Menéndez was able to find an inland waterway cutting through peninsular Florida that connected the Gulf with the Atlantic, La Florida's Spanish potential would be boundless. He did not get far, of course; while it is theoretically possible to traverse the Florida peninsula, from the St. Johns River to Charlotte Harbor through the peninsula's winding rivers and across Lake Okeechobee, in no way was it a trek a Spaniard could have hoped to make in the sixteenth century.[22]

Even farther to the northeast, Menéndez commissioned a small enterprise to the Bahia de Santa María, hoping perhaps it might hold the key to another even more stupendous passage: the fabled Northwest Passage. Spaniards had been in the region and had actually passed by Roanoke Island already, where the British would attempt their colonization a generation later. In 1570 an expedition from Santa Elena entered the James River and stopped around modern-day Newport News. The men landed within miles of the future site of Jamestown before crossing by land from the James to the York River. Eventually they established Ajacán, a small and short-lived Jesuit mission in the shadow of the Powhatan chiefdom John Smith would encounter almost a half-century later.[23]

From Santa Elena, Menéndez also commissioned the Juan Pardo expedition in 1566, which represented the culmination of the grandest strategic plans for La Florida. Juan Pardo was a captain under Menéndez's command and helped establish Santa Elena. This was the man Menéndez chose to open the overland route to northern Mexico and, in particular, the silver mines at Zacatecas. It was more or less the same task delegated to de Luna, demonstrating the importance Spanish officials placed in the Camino Real.[24] If Pardo succeeded, Santa Elena would be the terminus of a sprawling continental road, a gateway along which tons of gold and silver would make their way back to Spain. Hopes for La Florida were high indeed in 1566.

Every one of these missions, of course, failed, and with varying degrees of mortality. The thought of walking from the modern-day state of South Carolina entirely through modern-day Texas sounds laughably absurd. Juan Pardo's expedition was a fraction of the size of either Narváez's or de Soto's attempts, and not nearly as provisioned. His men would have died of exposure before they got within a thousand miles of another Spaniard on the northern edges of New Spain. Who would cook up such a foolish plan? Apparently at the time, colonial authorities considered the task rather straightforward.

Despite Narváez's survivors having trekked through Texas and northern Mexico, and despite de Soto's men having moved through much of the remaining south, geographic knowledge of La Florida's interior was still very much limited when Menéndez landed at Santa Elena. While narratives of the travels existed, few if any maps did. Neither of the entradas were cartographic expeditions, after all. And even if such maps did exist, neither Pardo nor Menéndez would have gotten the opportunity to see them. Authorities in Spain and New Spain withheld whatever information they did have about either the sea lanes around or the interior of La Florida in fear of its falling into the hands of their colonial rivalries. And apparently, they were quite good at keeping secrets—so good, in fact, that even their own explorers had no idea what was there.[25] For that reason, the common perception was that the distance between Zacatecas and Santa Elena was considerably less than one thousand miles. In reality, and by even the most favorable routes, it was more than double that. Spaniards even believed that among the Appalachians of the Atlantic Coast they would find the mountain range that would lead them to Zacatecas. The Sierra Madre Occidental Range, wherein one would find Zacatecas, is a southern subsection of the American Rockies, not the Appalachians.[26] With no maps and limited knowledge of the interior, Menéndez was ordering Juan Pardo on a suicide mission.

Such a fascination with a La Florida Camino Real reveals the true treachery of the Gulf and the discontent there was among Spanish authorities with the Flota system, not more than a few decades in operation. Colonial authorities already depended upon overland routes to connect the silver mines in Zacatecas to New Spain and had relied on roads and enslaved Natives to transport gold and silver from mines in New Spain and Peru to regional ports. There was no reason La Florida could not be folded into such a system, which might later produce attractive regions for further immigration and settlement.[27] Meanwhile, in the short term, countless ships had already gone down in the Gulf or in the Florida Straits, at the loss of countless lives and untold riches. Pirates now lurked about. Any option seemed worth exploring. Even if such an overland road took months to travel, there was no way it could be any more miserable or more dangerous than the epic, nightmarish journey the sailors on the Flotas faced every time they set sail from Vera Cruz.

Juan Pardo's expeditions never amounted to much. They are most notable perhaps because Pardo actually survived them. There were two separate attempts, the first from December 1566 to March 1567, and the second from September 1567 to March 1568. Each included over one hundred soldiers, and each made it well into the interior of South and North Carolina and even into extreme east Tennessee. Neither expedition got anywhere close to the silver mines of Zacatecas. Although Pardo established five separate outposts in the interior of the Carolinas along his route, including small garrisons of soldiers housed in rudimentary forts, they were all gone within months.[28] Small parties of Spaniards made several further attempts into the interior of Georgia and the Carolinas, investigating rumors of inland peoples.[29]

Just as short lived were Menéndez's grand plans for the settlement of La Florida's coastline. Most of his original garrisons began mutinying within months of their postings. Malnutrition, isolation, and poor relations with surrounding Natives all contributed to their demise. San Antonio, the Calusa fortification near present-day Fort Myers, was destroyed after rounds of Spanish punitive execution, the first of which ended the life of the wily Chief Carlos. To the north, the Tocobaga fort was sacked with the loss of the entire Spanish garrison. Forts among the Tequesta and Ais similarly fell along the east coast of peninsular Florida, and Ajacán was destroyed by Chesapeake Natives shortly after its establishment. Whatever grand designs Menéndez held for the region, either strategically or financially, were gone. Spaniards maintained a presence at Santa Elena and St. Augustine, but for the time being, that was all that was left of the European presence in La Florida.[30]

Notes

1. Kamen, *Empire*, 250, 258-259; Hoffman, *A New Andalucia*, 128-130, 132-136, 140-143, 216, 225; Weber, *The Spanish Frontier*, 64-67; Milanich, *Laboring in the Fields of the Lord*, 86.

2. Hoffman, *Florida's Frontiers*, 39; Hudson, *Juan Pardo*, 11-12, 14; Hoffman, "The Chicora Legend," 427-430.

3. Weddle, *Spanish Sea*, 280; Lowery, *The Spanish Settlements*, 13.
4. Weddle, *Spanish Sea*, 255-257.
5. Weddle, *Spanish Sea*, 257-261.
6. Hoffman, *Florida's Frontiers*, 39; "The Account by a Gentleman from Elvas," in Clayton, Knight, and Moore, eds., *The De Soto Chronicles*, 84.
7. Hoffman, *Florida's Frontiers*, 23, 29, 39.
8. Weddle, *Spanish Sea*, 260-261, 265-266.
9. Weddle, *Spanish Sea*, 267-268.
10. Weddle, *Spanish Sea*, 269-276; Hoffman, *Florida's Frontiers*, 39-41; Weber, *The Spanish Frontier*, 67-68; Hoffman, *A New Andalucia*, 147-153, 158-159, 169-171; Milanich, *Laboring in the Fields of the Lord*, 76-78.
11. Weddle, *Spanish Sea*, 276-278; Hoffman, *Florida's Frontiers*, 41-42.
12. Weddle, *Spanish Sea*, 280.
13. Weddle, *Spanish Sea*, 280-281.
14. Hoffman, *A New Andalucia*, 169-202; Hoffman, *Florida's Frontiers*, 42-44; Lyon, *The Enterprise of Florida*, 24-26.
15. Hoffman, *Florida's Frontiers*, 45-46, 48-51; Hoffman, *A New Andalucia*, 205-211, 213-215, 218-219; Milanich, *Laboring in the Fields of the Lord*, 76-78; Weddle, *The Spanish Sea*, 289; Hudson, *Juan Pardo*, 14-15; Lyon, *The Enterprise of Florida*, 33-34, 38-41.
16. Weddle, *The Spanish Sea*, 314-315; Hoffman, *Florida's Frontiers*, 46; Hudson, *Juan Pardo*, 15-16; Lowery, *The Spanish Settlements*, 13; Merás, *Pedro Menéndez de Avilés*, 26-27; Lyon, *The Enterprise of Florida*, 29-32.
17. Hoffman, *Florida's Frontiers*, 46; Lyon, *The Enterprise of Florida*, 43-56; Merás, *Pedro Menéndez de Avilés*, 27; Hudson, *Juan Pardo*, 14-18; Milanich, *Laboring in the Fields of the Lord*, 82-86; Kamen, *Empire*, 248-250.
18. Hoffman, *Florida's Frontiers*, 46; Merás, *Pedro Menéndez de Avilés*, 27; Hudson, *Juan Pardo*, 14-18; Milanich, *Laboring in the Fields of the Lord*, 82-86; Kamen, *Empire*, 248-250.
19. Weber, *The Spanish Frontier*, 70; Hoffman, *Florida's Frontiers*, 51-53; Hoffman, *A New Andalucia*, 241, 248-249, 255-256; Lyon, *The Enterprise of Florida*, 150-157; Milanich, *Laboring in the Fields of the Lord*, 90-92.
20. For later attempts at the "cross Florida barge canal," see Noll and Tegeder, *Ditch of Dreams*.
21. Hoffman, *Florida's Frontiers*, 51-52; Lyon, *The Enterprise of Florida*, 147-150; Weddle, *The Spanish Sea*, 316-317.
22. Weddle, *The Spanish Sea*, 319; Hoffman, *Florida's Frontiers*, 51-53; Hudson, *Juan Pardo*, 18, 125; Lyon, *The Enterprise of Florida*, 168-169, 172-173, 176; Dobyns, *Their Number Become Thinned*, 128.
23. Hoffman, *A New Andalucia*, 233-234, Weber, *The Spanish Frontier*, 69-72; Milanich, *Laboring in the Fields of the Lord*, 92; Hudson, *Juan Pardo*, 16; Williamson, *Powhatan Lords*, 18.
24. Pardo's journeys are covered extensively in Hudson, *Juan Pardo*; also in Hoffman, *Florida's Frontiers*, 52-53; Hoffman, *A New Andalucia*, 239-241, 244, 249; Hoffman, "Narvaez and Cabeza de Vaca in Florida," 65; DePratter, "The Chiefdom of Cofitachequi," 201-203; Weber, *The Spanish Frontier*, 70-71; Milanich, *Laboring in the Fields of the Lord*, 89, 93.
25. Weber, *The Spanish Frontier*, 55-57; Lowery, *The Spanish Settlements*, 6-7.
26. Weber, *The Spanish Frontier*, 70.

27. Hudson, *Juan Pardo*, 128-130.

28. Hudson, *Juan Pardo*, 23-46, 146-152.

29. Worth, "Late Spanish Military Expeditions," 104-122; DePratter, "The Chiefdom of Cofitachequi," 203-204.

30. Weddle, *The Spanish Sea*, 320-321; Lyon, *The Enterprise of Florida*, 150-153, 165-167, 173-177.

MAP 1.1. La Florida and the Caribbean

This map of the Caribbean, made at the dawn of the seventeenth century, describes territory ostensibly governed by the Audiencia of Hispaniola. La Florida, at the top left, demonstrates the region's earliest connections to Spanish colonialism.

"DESCRIPCION DEL DESTRICTO DEL AUDIENCIA DE LA ESPAÑOLA." MADRID, 1601. ACCESSION NUMBER 01808-008. JOHN CARTER BROWN LIBRARY—BROWN UNIVERSITY.

PHOTO 1.1. De Soto in Peru
Hernando de Soto on horseback, confronting Atahualpa as a member of Francisco Pizarro's entrada.

"FERDINANDUS DE SOTO HAUPTMANN..." *[AMERICA. PT. 6. GERMAN] DAS SECHSTE THEIL DER NEUWEN WELT. ODER DER HISTORIEN ... DAS DRITTE BUCH...* RECORD NUMBER 35379-6. JOHN CARTER BROWN LIBRARY—BROWN UNIVERSITY.

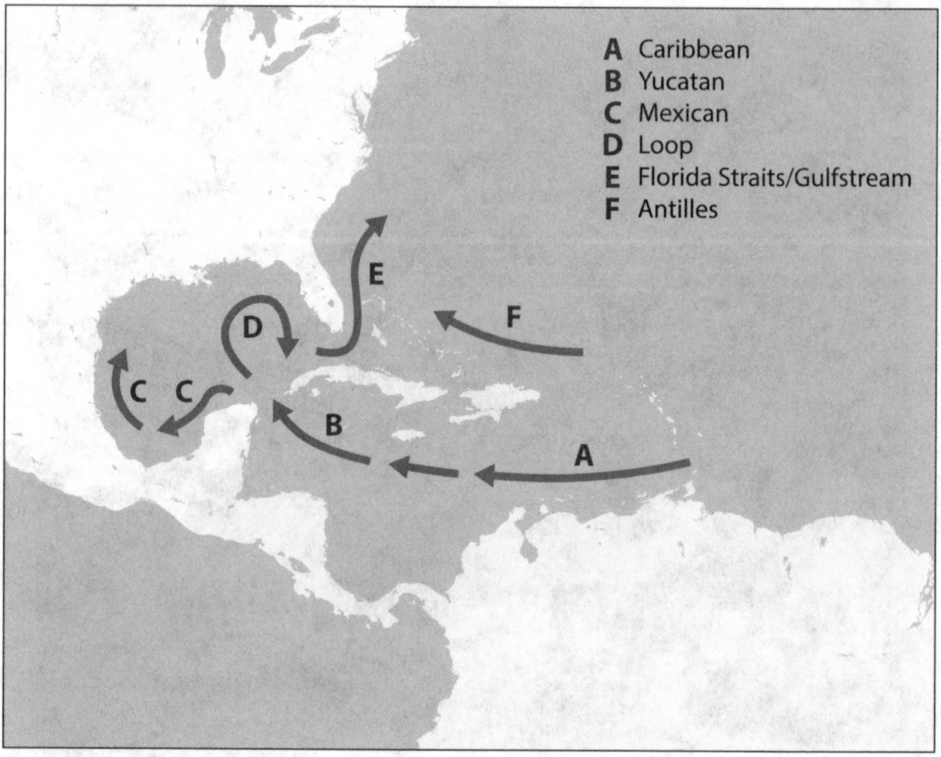

Map 1.2. The Caribbean System

PHOTO 1.2. Early Spanish Shipping
This depiction of an early Spanish sailing vessel also features a potential storm brewing on the horizon.
"PISCES IN MARI ALATI." *[AMERICA. PT 4. LATIN] AMERICAE PARS QUARTA. SIVE, INSIGNIS & ADMIRANDA HISTORIA DE REPERTA PRIMUM OCCIDENTALI INDIA À CHRISTOPHORO COLUMBO ANNO M. CCCXCII* ... RECORD NUMBER 09887-4. JOHN CARTER BROWN LIBRARY—BROWN UNIVERSITY.

PHOTO 1.3. A Hurricane on Hispaniola

A hurricane striking Hispaniola, sending Spaniards fleeing.

"HORRENDA & INAUDITA TEMPESTAS." *[AMERICA. PT 4. LATIN] AMERICAE PARS QUARTA. SIVE, INSIGNIS & ADMIRANDA HISTORIA DE REPERTA PRIMUM OCCIDENTALI INDIA À CHRISTOPHORO COLUMBO ANNO M. CCCXCII* ... RECORD NUMBER 09887-10. JOHN CARTER BROWN LIBRARY—BROWN UNIVERSITY.

II. ORIGINS

3 Catholic Origins

When Pedro Menéndez de Avilés's 1565 armada set sail from Cádiz, Spain's major port on the southern Atlantic Coast, it was reportedly enormous. Rumors of the expedition's purpose, the "destruction of the heretics who had settled in the lands of the King," otherwise known as French Protestant Huguenots, provided no shortage of volunteers. However many actually boarded is unknown; if one account is to be believed, it could have been upward of two thousand. Rough seas scattered the flotilla while crossing the Atlantic, and Menéndez, hoping to catch the French off guard, did not wait for them to regroup once he arrived in the Caribbean. By the time he moved on from Puerto Rico, his army was one third the size it was when it left the Canaries. Nevertheless, it was still sizeable, and the men on board "were persons of much reliance and bravery," even though they were untrained and "raw recruits for the most part."

To season this ragtag army, Menéndez issued the men their harquebuses on the ship. He had them implement a cleaning regiment so they would feel comfortable holding the firearms in their hands and had them shoot "three rounds every day until they reached Florida" so that they would not only get used to shooting, but get good at it. The men built makeshift ranges on the ships and made a competition out of target practice, with "prizes being awarded to the soldiers in the companies who shot best, and to their captains so that they should take great care to make them skillful." All the while the men daily repeated the "Christian doctrine and the litanies," praying and "beseeching Him to grant them victory in everything." This is how Menéndez trained his army of Catholic warriors on their approach to La Florida.

Having safely arrived on the Atlantic Coast of modern-day Florida, the expedition soon landed a handful of men and, after a few tense exchanges with nearby Timucua Natives, learned of the Frenchmen's whereabouts. They were miles to the north, so Menéndez immediately moved the ships that way, stopping at the first good harbor he encountered "with a good beach, to which he gave the name St. Augustine." The men caught sight of the French ships not long after, farther yet to the north, near present-day Jacksonville. To Menéndez's dismay they were the supply ships he had hoped to beat to La Florida. He had failed to do that, and now he had lost the element of surprise, giving Menéndez little hope that the French fort could be taken, "nor their armed harbor." That disturbing turn of events required a war council, Menéndez held on his ship soon after.

While his captains advised returning to Hispaniola for reinforcements, Menéndez was determined not to lose any more of the mission's initiative, particularly in the face of as dangerous an enemy as he considered his Lutheran foe. La Florida had, up to that point, been the scene of repeated and unqualified failure. This expedition absolutely could not fail. Instead, Menéndez decided to confront the French ships immediately, while they were at anchor just offshore and while their crews were busy unloading them. The French lobbed cannon shot through Menéndez's masts and rigging as he sailed up next to them in the night. He positioned his flagship next to the French Admiral Jean Ribault's own ship in preparation for a boarding raid early the next morning. Despite his intentions and in the darkness of the night, Menéndez was first to make contact, with "the trumpets hailing the enemy, and they answered him, hailing him with theirs."

Menéndez enquired officially, "with much courtesy," about the men and their intentions. "We are bringing infantry, artillery and supplies for a fort which the King of France has in this country," one French sailor responded, "and for others which he is to build." Menéndez then asked, were the travelers Catholics or Lutherans and who led them? "They answered that they were all Lutherans of the new religion," and Jean Ribault was their general. The French, then, in turn inquired about Menéndez. The armada he controlled "belongs to the King of Spain and I am the General thereof," Menéndez answered assertively, "and I come to hang and behead all the Lutherans I may find on this sea and in this land; and thus do I bring instructions from my King, which I shall fulfill at dawn when I shall board your ships; and if I should find any Catholic, I will give him good treatment."[1] And with that, you could say, the pleasantries were at an end. Although Menéndez did not achieve his bloody objective that morning, he would not long after.

This section, "Origins," is more thematic than chronological, and charts two important ideas that lay at the heart of La Florida's earliest history: religion and slavery. It opened with an exchange between two religious groups, both of which Americans in the twenty-first century might refer to simply as Christians. In fact, while there certainly are spiritual and liturgical differences between the modern-day Catholic and Protestant churches, the term "heretic" is not usually thrown around by one when describing the other. Yet those were exactly the kind of words that were thrown around off the coast of La Florida in 1565. As the confrontation between Ribault and Menéndez off the coast of modern-day Jacksonville reveals, tolerance across the spectrum of western religious ideology has not always been the case. It also suggests that while economic access to foreign markets, the hidalgo spirit, and the naked desire for wealth and power were all important components to Spanish expansion into the Caribbean and the Americas, they certainly were not the only ones. Another was the Catholic faith.

The fall of the Islamic stronghold of Granada in 1492 did not only signify the final reconquest of Iberia and the emancipation of Spaniards from the rule of religious outsiders. It also represented the triumph of the Catholic faith over infidels—Muslim Moors in the case of the *Reconquista*. By that time Isabella and Ferdinand had already instituted the Spanish inquisition, which they used to convert or banish anyone not of the Catholic faith from what was quickly forming into a Catholic country. Muslims, Jews, Protestants, and any other non-Catholics had to become Catholics, or they had to go. Spain emerged from the *Reconquista* more than just a warrior nation—it was a Catholic warrior nation. Thus, to all of the negative personality traits associated with the hidalgos that would spread across the New World must be added some of western civilization's most extreme traditions of religious intolerance. The faith of men like Menéndez had been forged in bitter struggle with outsiders for centuries, then with Protestant rebels within the faith for decades. Both had crafted men like him into religious conquerors who would see either the submission of both nonbelieving "barbarians" and non-Catholic "infidels" to Catholicism, or their destruction.

The early La Florida expeditions of de León, Ayllón, Narváez, and de Soto were all at least partially motivated by these religious forces. As the Spanish planned it, spiritually ignorant Natives would be given an opportunity to embrace the Pope and the King of Spain as their sovereigns and their masters. If they would not, then they would be forced to embrace them. Backed not only by the Crown but by Catholic doctrines that had "donated" most of the entire non-Christian New World to Spain, and aided by their patron saint, Santiago Matamoros, Spanish warriors and attendant priests sought subjugation to both the Crown and the Church simultaneously.[2] For Spaniards, these political and religious gains were one and the same.

While the early attempts to force Natives into submission were failures, Menéndez, in his vanquishing of the Protestant heretics on La Florida's Atlantic coastline, marked the Catholic Church's first victory in the spiritual conquest on this new religious battlefield. The threat of piracy posed by the French was real, but the threat of the establishment of non-Catholics also forced King Philip's hand, leading him to dispatch Menéndez. La Florida's first *adelantado* was there to wipe the Huguenots out, and wipe them out he did, establishing North America's first European colony dedicated specifically for religious purposes. It was most certainly a Catholic one.

Notes

1. Merás, *Pedro Menéndez de Avilés*, 77-78, 80, 84-87.
2. Lowery, *The Spanish Settlements*, 4.

Spiritual Conquest in a New World

In one of the most familiar paintings of one of the most influential conquistadores to make his mark on the New World, Francisco Pizarro's portrait illustrates the intertwined political and religious ambitions of the Christian warriors that followed Columbus into the Caribbean. In it, Pizarro stands at a table, his left hand on his sword and his right hand on a map. On his chest, prominently displayed, is the unmistakable red cross of St. James. It is one of several paintings of Pizarro that feature the same cross. They represented his membership in the Order of Santiago, one of Spain's oldest and most venerated military fraternities, and one which still exists in the present. Along with the Orders of Calatrava, Alcantara, and Montesa, the Order of Santiago was a knighthood created in the military violence of the twelfth century. It was, in other words, a product of the *Reconquista*. Of the four, however, only the Order of Santiago would gain new meaning in the violent conquest of the New World.

The order was named Santiago after St. James the Great and also after James the Apostle, one of Jesus's original twelve disciples. After Jesus's death James would evangelize Iberia before returning to and being martyred in the Holy Land. St. James, or Santiago, is the patron saint of Spain, and his remains are interred in Santiago de Compostela, in Galicia, Spain. Only many years later, however, did Santiago's likeness undergo a powerful and profoundly militant transformation. That was said to have happened when a mounted Santiago himself appeared before Christian warriors at several critical battles of the *Reconquista*, leading them on to victory over incredible odds. Over time his likeness became a symbol of struggle and perseverance against non-Christian enemies. His standard in the form of the red cross was carried before Spanish soldiers into countless battles, and his name was shouted as a rallying cry. Through those battlefield experiences, Spaniards reshaped St. James the Great into Santiago Matamoros, or St. James the Moor Slayer. Spain's patron saint was not only a symbol of hope but also a warrior figure.[1]

Even when the prestige of the other orders began to ebb after the end of the struggle for which they were created, devotion toward Santiago Matamoros continued to grow. Isabella and Ferdinand and then Charles turned to Santiago Matamoros to rally an increasingly unified country. While his foundation lay in the middle ages and the *Reconquista*, with the support of the sixteenth-century Crown, the Order of Santiago was soon the most prestigious and important knighthood in all of Spain.[2]

Suited to doing battle with nonbelievers, Knights of the Order of Santiago were well positioned to transition from the *Reconquista* to the religious conquest of the New World. Santiago's standard would be worn by the warriors of that conquest, like Pizarro, just as it had been carried before Catholic armies during the *Reconquista*. Pizarro shouted "Santiago!" in Cajamarca as he first reached to seize Atahualpa. Iterations of his name are still visible across the Caribbean and Central and South America—many of the first settlements made by Spanish Christians in the New World were named "Santiago" or "Matamoros," a fitting reminder that if Spaniards did so inspirationally, then they were laying the foundation of brutal conquest, not peaceful colonial coexistence.[3]

On the edges of what was La Florida, Matamoros lays directly across the border from Brownsville, Texas, yet Knights of the Order of Santiago traveled to the New World long before the founding of that border town. According to one account, after Lucas Vázquez de Ayllón applied to the Crown to conquer La Florida and settle San Miguel de Guadalpe in the 1520s, Charles "granted it, honoring him with the habit of the Order of Santiago."[4] While Francisco Pizarro proudly wore the Cross of Santiago into Peru, so would one of his captains, de Soto, wear it into La Florida. In 1538 he applied to join the order "and to live in observance and under the rule and discipline of it, out of devotion that he has for the daring apostle Santiago." To be knighted was no small feat, and so Spanish authorities ordered an inquiry into de Soto's lineage. It would need to be affirmed without a shadow of a doubt that he and his entire family line, as far as could be researched, "have been and are currently and generally reputed to be a people of nobility," according to "traditional Spanish law and custom," and that such lineage had not been corrupted by "the race of Jews, converts, Moors, or peasants." This was actually done, and by the time de Soto marched through La Florida, he carried the Cross of Santiago before him.[5] Pedro Menéndez de Avilés, the founder of St. Augustine, was also a member. In fact, as was the case with Pizarro, the most commonly used portrait of Menéndez features him donning the cross proudly.[6] Just as it was across the New World, many of the would-be conquerors of La Florida were Knights of the Order of Santiago.

The imagery of St. James represented the desire among the Spanish not simply to exploit Native people's land or labor for political or financial gain, but to submit unbelievers to the authority of the Catholic faith. For Spaniards, the religious and political subjugation of the New World was a very much intertwined undertaking, just as the *Reconquista* had been. That began with the Catholic Church, whose authorities played perhaps an even more important role in the official sanctioning of such adventures than the Spanish Crown. Expanding the Catholic faith, they declared, was a mandatory component of any new discovery.

Lands unclaimed by Christians, *terra nullius*, were taken possession of through royal and religious ceremonies of ownership. Church authorities, beginning with the pope, were issuing such directives well before the New World was even discovered, demonstrating a long and intertwined history of exploration and religious conquest. Among them was *Romanus pontifex*, issued by Pope Nicholas V in 1454. It was a response by the Church to the result of Portuguese exploration along the northwest coast of Africa. Portuguese mariners, attempting to find the Spice Islands, were coming up with new, non-Christian peoples, and Church guidance was necessary to determine how they would be dealt with. *Romanus pontifex* upheld the Portuguese ownership of these territories politically but also did far more, authorizing the forcible colonization and possible enslavement of the non-Christians that were being found there. The bull praised "Catholic kings and princes," Pope Nicholas V wrote, who like "athletes and intrepid champions of the Christian faith," would only restrain "infidels, enemies of the Christian name, but also for the defense and increase of the faith vanquish them and their kingdoms and habitations, though situated in the remotest parts unknown to us."[7]

At the heart of such an aggressive declaration was the "positive violence" aspect of the Catholic faith that had developed naturally from the religious wars of the period, of which the *Reconquista* was a part. Catholic clerics were at the same time defensive and also profoundly offensive when it came to religious competition. Any unbeliever—or, worse yet, the believer of a different faith—constituted an existential threat to the Catholic Church and must be dealt with. It was not enough for a Christian warrior to simply defend his faith. As *Romanus pontifex* laid out clearly, such a threat had to be neutralized, no matter where it was. Non-Christians had to be converted, or they had to be destroyed.

The pope issued several bulls related to conquest and colonization in the years between *Romanus pontifex* and 1492, and then issued several more after

Columbus's return. These included two separate *Inter caetera* bulls, *Eximiae devotionis* bull, and *Dudum siquidem* bull, all issued in 1493, which together are known as the "Bulls of Donation." They answered whatever questions the Spanish Crown might still have about how to approach the New World, and the answer was simple—it would go to Isabella and Ferdinand. It was also in *Inter caetera*, published in May of 1493, when Pope Alexander VI also laid out the terms for the forced conversion of Native peoples. The Catholic faith was to be "exalted and be everywhere increased and spread, that the health of souls be cared for and that barbarous nations be overthrown and brought to the faith itself." Previous struggles, he suggested, had laid the foundation for such an undertaking, and future explorers, including Columbus, of course, would "bring under your sway the said mainlands and islands with their residents and inhabitants and to bring them to the Catholic faith."

Finally, in order to do all that, the pope "by the authority of Almighty God" issued the donation for which all these bulls would be known: to "give, grant, and assign to you and your heirs and successors, kings of Castile and León, forever, together with all their dominions, cities, camps, places, and villages, and all rights, jurisdictions, and appurtenances, all islands and mainlands found and to be found, discovered and to be discovered towards the west and south," according to a line drawn down the earth that would be confirmed later in the Treaty of Tordesillas, partitioning up the Spanish and Portuguese worlds. Under the sanction of the Catholic Church, the New World was now Spanish property that could be divided up and distributed as the Crown wished, and a place filled with non-Christians that would be, either by choice or by force, subjected to Christianity.[8]

Ferdinand and Isabella, and then Charles V, wasted little time fulfilling the wishes of the Catholic Church. They chopped this New World up and issued calls for its conquest. Quick to answer were men of hidalgo spirit, but also Catholic warriors convinced at least ostensibly of the danger posed by these "barbarians," and the righteousness of the newly expanded, and now truly global, religious struggle in which they were now a part. The bulls not only gave them legal authority to forcefully enter into an entirely foreign place on the other side of the world, make its wealth theirs, and subject its people to Spanish political culture and the Catholic faith—it ensured that they could do all of those things with the clearest of consciences. Violence could be used, property could be taken, and people could be enslaved, and there would be plenty of all of that.

Even though conquest and colonization was built upon a foundation of violence and exploitation, there were still rules. A *capitulación* had been written up by the proper authorities that officially sanctioned basically whatever needed to be done. Even afterward, a certain decorum had to be followed to make sure that Spanish soldiers proceeded with such violent acts justifiably. Conquest by means of a "just war" began with a legitimate reason to go to war in the first place, *jus ad bellum*. From that moment certain rules had to be followed that concerned how the war was fought, *jus in bello*.[9]

These guidelines, established long before even the *Reconquista*, were remarkably easy for the Spanish to adapt and then perfect. Doing battle against Muslim "infidel" who understood and rejected Christianity, for example, was theoretically straightforward. Spanish warriors could not only do battle with Muslims in southern Spain with clear consciences but use their victories to legally acquire wealth and prestige for themselves and their families as the earned spoils of their righteous struggle. The land, property, and wealth assumed by Catholic warriors during the *Reconquista* had therefore all been taken not just gloriously, but legally. In the Americas, however, Natives had never heard of the Catholic faith. They therefore had no chance to understand it and either accept or reject its truths. An infidel and a barbarian, it turns out, were two separate things entirely, an unfortunate discrepancy Spanish Catholics had to negotiate in the Caribbean. The Natives there also happened to be literally on the other side of the world, and it was hard to justify the danger they posed either to Spain or to Rome in even the most abstract way.[10] An argument for physical conquest and the seizure of land and wealth based on positive violence did not quite fit in the New World, at least not at first.

Church scholars did not take long to solve their moral and religious conundrum. According to the brightest Church scholars, Natives were not intellectually sophisticated enough to properly grasp the Gospel or to properly control land. They did not understand correct notions of land ownership and had failed to utilize their territory correctly. By their "barbaric" and even cannibalistic ways they lived in perpetual sin, necessitating Christian redemption. Perhaps, if the leaders of these Natives acted too brutally against their own people they deserved being overthrown. That made conquistadores not really conquistadores at all, really. There were, in short, only too many rationalizations that legitimized making war on the ignorant and uncivilized. Each one is almost more incomprehensible than the last, but all were totally acceptable to the Catholic Church at the time, and in the end, they were enough.[11]

In a remarkable act of synthesis, blending papal bulls with just war philosophies and even a touch of Aristotle, Spanish authorities developed a uniquely

Spanish legal instrument that paved the way for an immediate and practically guilt-free just war. This was the *requerimiento*, or the requirement. One of the most well-known versions comes from Juan López de Palacios Rubios, dated 1513.[12] Ideally, as soon as a prospective conquistador had just stepped foot into a new territory, he would either read the document, or have a priest or other duly appointed representative read it. He would also have some sort of official on hand to certify that it had, in fact, been read. The reader would begin by declaring that he and his compatriots were acting on behalf of the King and Queen of Castile and León, "subduers of the barbarous nations." After a very cursory lesson on Christianity, the document moved on to the Pope and explained the whole "Bulls of Donation" idea. Therefore their "Highnesses are kings and lords of these islands and land of Tierra-firme by virtue of this donation," the Spaniard would declare. In other words, all these lands and everyone in them, now belonged to Spain and the Catholic Church, just as the Pope had intended. Then the men would move on to the important part: the actual requirement.

> *Wherefore, as best we can, we ask and require you that you consider what we have said to you, and that you take the time that shall be necessary to understand and deliberate upon it, and that you acknowledge the Church as the Ruler and Superior of the whole world, and the high priest called Pope, and in his name the King and Queen Doña Juana our lords, in his place, as superiors and lords and kings of these islands and this Tierra-firme by virtue of the said donation, and that you consent and give place that these religious fathers should declare and preach to you the aforesaid.*

The orator ensured his audience that, if they took the King and Queen as their masters, and accepted the Church as their faith, submitting themselves politically as well as religiously, everything would be just fine. "The men shall leave you, your wives, and your children, and your lands, free without servitude, that you may do with them and with yourselves freely that which you like and think best." On the other hand, however, if their guests rejected the "requisition," the penalties were as severe as they got. With the Christian warriors before them and "with the help of God, we shall powerfully enter into your country," the orator would declare, "and shall make war against you in all ways and manners that we can," including robbing them of their property, enslaving them, and otherwise doing "all the mischief and damage that we can, as to vassals who do not obey, and refuse to receive their lord, and resist and contradict him."

Perhaps the most astounding portion of the whole written document and spoken performance was how it concluded. The "deaths and losses which shall accrue from this are your fault, and not that of their Highnesses, or ours, nor of these cavaliers who come with us." Just one of the many aspects of the *requerimiento* that would have made its reading almost humorous to behold, as historians have since commented, had it not in so many cases immediately preceded such extreme violence. It is important to reiterate, in fact, that the requirement was a real thing. Its reading did actually happen and doing so meant quite a lot to Spaniards. The choices were simple: submission or destruction.[13]

The requirement represented a blending of religious and legal authorities in Spanish culture that was, in turn, the product of the blending of Islamic and Catholic religious and legal cultures that had evolved over the hundreds of years of the *Reconquista*.[14] It also reflected how Catholics had cleverly and rather ironically adopted an instrument of their own conquest and molded it to the exigencies of the conquest they now wished to perform, now that the shoe was on the other foot. For example, the requirement did theoretically create a path to peaceful coexistence, albeit one based on complete submission of one party to the other. If Natives simply accepted the conquistadores' invitation to both embrace the Catholic faith and become vassals of the Spanish Crown, theoretically, they were to be treated peacefully. But really, how likely was that? Consider first the context of its reading, regardless of whatever form the requirement took. Whether it was performed in Latin or Spanish the *requerimiento* was shouted by armed, angry men in a language never heard by the Native population. Incan onlookers watching Pizarro and his men perform the requirement in front of Atahualpa would have been no more confused or dumbfounded by what they were seeing had Martians just landed in a spaceship to begin performing it in Martian.

One such version of the requirement was in fact read to Atahualpa by a friar while Pizarro looked on, and with cavalry lurking in the shadows. After listening patiently, the Incan half-god, half-man potentate of the most complex society in the New World took the bible that the friar had held and referenced, inspected it, and then angrily tossed it aside. The enraged friar turned immediately to Pizarro shouting "Come out! Come out, Christians! Come at these enemy dogs who reject the things of God. That tyrant has thrown my book of holy law to the ground!" March out against him, the friar shouted, "for I absolve you!" The hidden horsemen dashed out and the legendary capture of Atahualpa was on. In that instance the requirement worked, it seemed, just as it was designed. The men with Pizarro had hidden themselves in preparation of a surprise attack, and such an insulting rejection of the requirement—not to mention the desecration of the friar's bible—was everything for which they could have hoped.[15]

The requirement, as the Incan experience would suggest, was a warfare-legitimizing procedure that was based on setting forth standards of understanding, acknowledgment, and acceptance that were impossible for any Native to fulfill. If after receiving their crash course in Christianity and the demand of immediate submission that followed the Natives rejected it, or simply scratched their heads in confusion for too long, then the path was legally clear for the Spanish to conquer a people who had now officially transitioned in title from the barbaric to infidel, a transition that both enabled and demanded violent action. That was how Pizarro later clarified his actions to Atahualpa himself. Pizarro and his men had come "to conquer this land" by command of their king, "that all may come to a knowledge of God and of His Holy Catholic Faith," and for those glorious reasons, God "permits this," referring presumably to the extreme violence that had just devastated Cajamarca, "in order that you may know Him and come out from the bestial and diabolical life that you lead." That was the reason, Pizarro explained to Atahualpa, that his capture had gone so smoothly. "Our Lord permitted that your pride should be brought low and that no Indian should be able to offend a Christian."[16]

The immediacy and severity of such violence differentiated the requirement from even its Muslim predecessor. Where Muslim traditions of jihad demanded religious recognition and obedience and called for armed conflict should the demand be rejected, they did not necessitate immediate conversion, or even sincere belief in the Muslim faith. Muslim clerics did not even recognize a profession of faith made under clear coercion to be a legitimate profession of faith. All of that stands in stark comparison to the Spanish requirement.[17]

Onlookers and academics alike, from the contemporary to today, view the reading of the requirement as an almost joke-like procedural absurdity, which was more about the protocol for invasion than it was an honest attempt to convert Native peoples. By the mid-sixteenth century Spanish theologians would begin raising all sorts of questions relative to the requirement. They challenged not just the legality of the document but many of the assumptions about Native humanity that supported the document. They questioned the applicability of the just war philosophy, and even the pope's Bulls of Donation. If a "just war" was prohibited from causing more damage than it was supposed to prevent, for example, then how on earth could the conquest of the Caribbean, which resulted in the death and enslavement of almost 100 percent of its Native population, have possibly been considered "just"? Religious scholars and philosophers across Europe, including in Spain, would grow bolder in their criticism of both the Catholic Church and Spain's mechanisms of conquest. Those waves of revisionism would come far too late, however, for the Native peoples of the New World, including La Florida.

Notes

1. Rowe, *Saint and Nation*, 20-31; Jennings, *New Worlds of Violence*, 32; Schwaller, *The History of the Catholic Church*, 13, 16-17.
2. Rowe, *Saint and Nation*, 33; Hudson, *Knights of Spain*, 5-6; Schwaller, *The History of the Catholic Church*, 16.
3. Rowe, *Saint and Nation*, 32-34; Diamond, *Guns, Germs, and Steel*, 72.
4. "La Florida," in Clayton, Knight, and Moore, eds., *The De Soto Chronicles*, 2: 65.
5. "Interrogation," in *De Soto Chronicles*, 470-484; "Account of the Northern Conquest," in Clayton, Knight, and Moore, eds., *The De Soto Chronicles*, 251.
6. Jennings, *New Worlds of Violence*, 32.
7. Schwaller, *The History of the Catholic Church*, 35; Bushnell, *Situado and Sabana*, 34.
8. Schwaller, *The History of the Catholic Church*, 39-41; Elliott, *Empires*, 68; Adorno, "The Polemics of Possession," 21-22; Pagden, "The Struggle for Legitimacy," 39; Pagden, "Conquest and the Just War," 50-52; Hart, *Comparing Empires*, 15-16; Spate, *Spanish Lake*, 27-29. Copies of the bulls can be located in Davenport, *European Treaties*, 9-83.
9. Pagden, "Conquest and the Just War," 32, 36; Seed, *Ceremonies of Possession*, 70; Jennings, *New Worlds of Violence*, 59-60.
10. Pagden, "Conquest and the Just War," 36.
11. Pagden, "Conquest and the Just War," 36-45; Elliott, *Empires*, 66-67.
12. Schwaller, *The History of the Catholic Church*, 42.
13. Seed, *Ceremonies of Possession*, 70-71; Jennings, *New Worlds of Violence*, 33.
14. Seed, *Ceremonies of Possession*, 74-79; Jennings, *New Worlds of Violence*, 43-44.
15. Diamond, *Guns, Germs, and Steel*, 71-72; Schwaller, *The History of the Catholic Church*, 56-57.
16. Diamond, *Guns, Germs, and Steel*, 73-74.
17. Seed, *Ceremonies of Possession*, 74-79; Jennings, *New Worlds of Violence*, 43-44.

"Possessing" La Florida

THE READING OF A REFINED *REQUERIMIENTO* WAS SUPPOSEDLY MANDATED BY King Charles V, making the 1513 version available before much of South or Central America had been entered into forcefully by conquistadores, or even encountered by Spanish explorers.[1] Presumably, it was designed precisely for those kinds of occasions. Still, it is unclear the extent to which conquistadores read all of it, waited for an answer, or even cared about it at all, considering what it was designed to accomplish. They were also far away from any colonial authority in any position to direct their actions should Natives actually agree to such terms. Perhaps these reasons help explain why there is not much of a record of the requirement being read in La Florida. At least to some degree, however, it did happen. And had anything gone right for de León, Narváez, or de Soto, his men would have done more than read it; had all of these conquistadores not failed so miserably in La Florida, a moment of confrontation and conflict like that of Cajamarca almost certainly would have transpired somewhere within the present limits of the Southeastern United States.

Immediately upon naming La Florida in 1513, for example, de León landed to claim ownership of the territory, although not much was said about the act and it is unclear whether he had any clergy with him to convey religious possession as well. That seemed to be clarified in his 1514 *capitulación*, where much more detailed instructions were provided. As soon as de León disembarked at the location chosen for his settlement, he was directed to assemble "the chiefs and Indians thereof, by the best device or devices there can be given them" so that he could read and they could bear witness to the several documents that royal and ecclesiastical officials had written up specifically for him—in other words, an official copy of the *requerimiento*. It would advise them, for instance, "that they should come into the knowledge of Our Catholic Faith and should they obey and serve as they are bound to do." De León was to have several notaries and witnesses with him to certify that the document was indeed read, "and the summons must be made once, twice, thrice." If the Natives assented they were to be treated well, and de León was directed "by all the means at your disposal, to convert them to Our Holy Catholic Faith." If they rejected the summons, however, de León was authorized to "make war and seize them and carry them away for slaves." This was absolutely the requirement, directed to be read by the highest church officials, and by Charles V himself. Acknowledging the intertwined religious and political ends to his undertaking, de León would announce for the King just before setting off in 1521 that he was returning to La Florida "if it please God's will, to settle it, being enabled to carry a number of people with which I shall be able to do so, that the name of Christ may be praised there, and Your Majesty served with the fruit that land produces."[2]

As one preeminent scholar of La Florida's early religious history once suggested, this first attempt to establish a church around the present-day location of Charlotte Harbor in southwest Florida was "noble in conception," despite failing immediately. Considering Juan Ponce de León's instructions were to enslave or destroy whoever refused the requirement he was supposed to read as soon as he had the opportunity, "noble" might not be the best way to describe the first attempt by Catholics to plant the gospel in La Florida. Nevertheless, de León would not be the last to try to do so. Lucas Vázquez de Ayllón arrived in present-day South Carolina and Georgia five years later with two priests and another layperson of the Dominican order, and together they constructed the first church in what would become the United States of America, St. Michael, although it would not last long.[3] Pánfilo de Narváez, upon landing in La Florida, supposedly made a formal possession. According to de Vaca, who as a royal official would have been present and would have borne witness, related that Narváez "raised the standard on Your Majesty's behalf and took possession of the land in your royal name and presented his orders and was obeyed as governor just as Your Majesty commanded." According to one historian's unconfirmed account he went much further, reading at least some portion of the requirement. After giving a cursory bible lesson beginning with Adam and Eve, he made his demand. "I entreat and require you to understand this well which I have told you, taking the time for it that is just you should, to comprehend and reflect, and that you recognize the Church as Mistress and Superior of the Universe," and that they consent to have the priests with him "preach these things to you." With Narváez and de Vaca were several Franciscans and an unknown number of unaffiliated Catholic clergy who would have been present for the demand. In the best traditions of the requirement, however, it appeared that if the account was accurate, the demand was read to an abandoned village, its people having fled in the night in their canoes.[4] While ridiculous, such an approach makes sense.

The Narváez expedition soon devolved into a long and ultimately unsuccessful struggle of survival, which spared neither cleric nor royal official. Neither Pánfilo de Narváez nor de Vaca had much of a chance to exert the will of the Spanish Crown, in other words, over anyone in La Florida. Neither could the many Franciscans that came along with them exert the will of the Catholic Church. Although they surely prayed for their own survival and for the deliverance of the expedition, they probably spent little time proselytizing. And while there was evidence of friars making it deep into La Florida on the expedition's retreat, none of them made it to Mexico City. Nevertheless, several years later, after his epic journey brought de Vaca back to Spain, he still wrote to the court that he hoped his narrative might assist others "who in your name might go to conquer those lands" and at the same time bring the region's Natives, whom he previously referred to as "barbarous peoples," to "knowledge of the true faith and the true lord and service to Your Majesty."[5]

De Soto, on the other hand, did have the ability to project Spanish colonialism in the Southeast, which he did for years and with terrific consequences for untold thousands of Natives. Aside from being a Knight in the Order of Santiago, his expedition was also well staffed with the religious representatives necessary for an undertaking that would have made Santiago himself proud. There "went with the fleet twelve priests, eight clerics and four friars," and "all were most exemplary and learned men," went one account. These were no ordinary clerics, either, but those well versed in conversion through force. Soon after landing, de Soto sent a captain and foot soldiers to harass a group of Natives meeting on a nearby island. The officer apparently also "had a fray with them." The whole party, including the clergyman, assaulted the Natives and killed several of them in a pitched fight that wounded many of the Spaniards. Not only were these clergy "learned men," clearly, in the best traditions of Spanish Catholicism, they were fighting men as well.[6]

Hidden among the several accounts of his entrada are only a few clear attempts made by de Soto to subject Native peoples to Christianity, according to either the letter or the intent of the *requerimiento*. One of his first acts of possession, however, provides hints that de Soto was prepared to do so had the opportunity presented itself. After landing horses and equipment and having scouted the surroundings of Tampa Bay, for example, de Soto "took possession of the land in the name of Their Majesties with all the formalities that are required," claiming the land politically but not making any particular mention of any religious prerogative. Interestingly, though, according to several accounts, he also sent one of the Indians he had captured and kept as a guide "to persuade and invite in peace" neighboring headmen. As another chronicler elaborated, de Soto sent messengers to the headman "saying that he begged him to come out peaceably and to consent to have Spaniards for friends and brothers." While the Spaniards "did not have any intention of injuring anyone," the chronicler continued, they were "a warlike people and brave, who, if their friendship was not accepted," they "could do much harm" to the headman and his people. De Soto's intention, described by chronicler Gracilaso de la Vega, "was to reduce through peace and friendship all the provinces and nations of that great kingdom to the obedience and service of the most powerful emperor and king of Castilla, their lord," and he desired to see the headman personally, "to tell him these things more fully."

The use of words like "persuade," "consent," and "reduce" paint a troubling picture indeed for the meeting de Soto had in store for his Native guests. It is of course impossible to determine if what he was preparing was any more aggressive than what he had already said publicly, but at such a time of contact more of the requirement's formalities might certainly have been observed. Ultimately, we will never know; the Native headmen did not appear, and that moment of contact and possible conquest never developed. According to one account the messengers never delivered the invitation. According to another they did, and the response was a flat rejection of de Soto's overtures and everything they entailed. One chieftain "by no means desired friendship or peace with such people, but rather mortal and perpetual warfare," and as far as what de Soto's men had said "about giving obedience to the king of Spain," among other choice words he replied, "that he himself was king in his own country and there was no necessity for becoming the vassal of another who has as many as he."[7]

These first exchanges, made within months of de Soto's landing, brought the reality of the political and religious conquest of La Florida home to its would-be conquerors. Such a straightforward rejection of de Soto's terms, had it actually happened that way, certainly cleared the way legally for any violence his men would partake in that instance. De Soto's men certainly would partake in plenty of violence in peninsular Florida, but not necessarily there, in that place. Why? Perhaps having just landed in a sprawling place, with few Native allies of his own and with no outward sign of extreme wealth to be gained by it, de Soto was simply not in any position to wage a conquest of destruction in that moment. Perhaps he had other things on his mind. Herein lies the complexity of such a potentially important moment of contact and exchange in early America.

Gracilaso de la Vega actually spent quite some time pondering this inconsistency. Despite being directed to do so by the Catholic Church and even by the Pope directly, and wearing the Cross of Santiago on his chest, de Soto's unwillingness to immediately engage in religious conquest raises important questions about the true place of Catholic conversion in the process of colonization. While the requirement was supposed to be central to any conquest, it clearly took a back seat for men like de Soto to the search for gold and silver. An excellent example of this prioritization came months later, while de Soto's men were slugging it out in Apalachee. He dispatched thirty horsemen back to their beachhead on the coast to bring up more supplies. When the horsemen arrived, they were again met by a gracious and extremely helpful Mocoso, a Tocobaga headman, leaving de la Vega to regret how "it was a great pity" that the men did not attempt to evangelize him, "for in view of his good judgment few persuasions would have been needed to take him out of his heathenism and convert him to our Catholic faith." That, in turn, they anticipated "would have been an auspicious beginning for hoping that such seed would produce much grain and a bountiful harvest."

As de la Vega explained, however, it had already been decided among the leadership that doing so was not in the original plan. Although he did not elaborate more fully on how such a decision was made, considering there were several clergymen with the expedition who probably would have dissented, de la Vega explained that de Soto had determined that the spiritual conquest of La Florida would take a back seat to its physical conquest, temporarily at least. De Soto's right to conquer La Florida also came with the option of exploring it without settling it. Legally, de Soto apparently had the right to wander as long as he wanted, and to overlook in the moment the gross religious affronts his men witnessed. Only after "having conquered and made an establishment in the land" would the priests sweep in and begin their work, making it understandable why the clergy did not immediately preach or otherwise administer religious sacraments when it appears they should have.[8]

Such an admission by de la Vega would have angered clerics back in Spain, but it does seem obvious enough given de Soto's ambitions. While spiritual conquest was central to the Spanish Catholic identity, and even though he personally wore the Cross of Santiago, de Soto had not wagered his fame and fortune on a religious pilgrimage. From other sources, however, it is clear it still did happen.

Somewhat conflicting accounts, for instance, describe de Soto's attempt to do so near Ochese, in modern-day Georgia.

Well on their way to Cofitachequi and moving fast, de Soto still "left a wooden cross raised very high in the middle of the public place." According to another account it was placed atop a ceremonial mound. In a Mississippian community like Ochese, that mound would have been in the center of the entire community and would have been visible by everyone. In a more detailed recollection, Gracilaso de la Vega described something much more similar to the actual requirement. Messengers met de Soto's men at the outskirts of town, bringing gifts and inquiring into de Soto's intentions. His response was that he was a "Captain of the great King of Spain," and "that in his name he came to give them to understand the sacred faith of Christ, and that they would know him and be saved, and give obedience to the apostolic church of Rome and to the Supreme Pontiff and Vicar of God who resides there, and that in the temporal world they should recognize as king and lord the Emperor, king of Castile, our Lord, as his vassals, and that they would treat them all well, and with peace and justice, like his other Christian vassals." The raising of a wooden cross was one thing. If Gracilaso de la Vega is to be believed, then what de Soto did outside of Ochese was to attempt to read the requirement.

Rodrigo Rangel's shorter chronicle did not detail such a moment, bringing its veracity into question. Instead, "as time did not allow more," de Soto, through an interpreter, only apparently gave the most cursory religious lesson on the cross's significance. It was "a memorial" to the crucifixion of Christ, "who was God and man and created the heavens and the earth and suffered to save us, and therefore," he declared, the Natives "should reverence it." They signified they would, and so he left. This was repeated upon arriving at the next major chiefdom, Ocute. There "a cross was placed," and the residents "appeared to receive it with much devotion and adored it on their knees, as they saw the Christians do."[9]

If what Rodrigo Rangel meant by "as time did not allow more," was that de Soto and his men were marching as fast through the region as they could without their horses dropping dead underneath them, then perhaps what happened at Ochese was not as tense as it sounded. The Spaniards were on their way to the supposed gold and silver fields of Cofitachequi, making their interactions in Ochese and Ocute understandably brief. Stopping only to eat and sleep, there was little motivation even among the clerics in the expedition to halt their march in order to instruct the Natives on Christianity. Evangelizing the Natives was important, but it was not that important, a reminder that once on the ground in

La Florida, what primarily motivated de Soto was material wealth, not Christian souls.

Then there was the battle of Mavila, one of the bloodiest single days in American history, and a pivotal moment in de Soto's entrada. In it is a very different record of religious interaction. De Soto's men were ambushed at the fortified town of Mavila, in the chiefdom of Tascalusa, in modern-day Alabama, leading to a fight that arguably resulted in the utter destruction by de Soto of an entire Mississippian chiefdom. After the first attack by Tascalusa, Mavila quickly descended into chaos, with Spanish and Natives "savagely killing and wounding each other" in a battle that raged for the entire day.[10] The Spanish, in the panic that ensued after Tascalusa's surprise, were forced to retreat from the palisade. They soon regrouped and de Soto organized them into fighting companies in preparation for a full assault on the densely populated, heavily fortified town. After reentering the palisade, the battle was fierce and consisted of close-quarter, house-to-house, and many times hand-to-hand combat. While the Spaniards had several clear advantages in horses, armor, and metal weaponry, they were also heavily outnumbered by Native warriors, both inside and outside of the town, who were extremely skilled with their own weapons and who fought with a ferocity that terrified de Soto's men. In no way was it certain to the Spaniards that they would prevail.

It was at this point, after four hours of fierce and bloody combat, that de Soto instantly connected the past of Spain's religious struggle to the battle before him in La Florida. No doubt wearing the Cross of St. James on his chest he summoned none other than Santiago Matamoros himself. "So as to increase the fears of the enemy and the spirit and courage of his men," he mounted a horse and, with another man, went about "calling the names of Our Lady and St. James the Apostle and shouting loudly to their men to make way." Doing so the two riders led a mounted charge, lances in hand, that "broke through the enemy squadron from one side to another as it was fighting in the principal street and in the plaza," spearing Native warriors all along the way, "like the brave and skillful soldiers that they were." The two riders, de Soto and Nuño Tovar, "although they fought all day," charged Native warriors several times, "and were present at the most dangerous crises of this battle," received only a few wounds, "which was no small, good fortune."[11]

This account of the summoning of Santiago de Matamoros evoked in an instant the continued religious foundations of conquest that, it seemed, had been relegated by a desire for political conquest and material wealth. Just as they had done in the most pitched battles of the *Reconquista*, Spain's Christian warriors had summoned their patron saint, and with his aid they once again proved victorious.[12] And there was no doubt, "few or no battles between Spaniards and Indians have taken place in the New World that would equal this one," Gracilaso de la Vega would later write. It was a terrifying moment of colonializing violence which, for the Spaniards, was nothing less than a miracle. There were signs all around them, de la Vega would recall. During one of de Soto's and Tovar's mounted charges an arrow pierced Tovar's lance in a way that made the whole thing resemble a cross, a miraculous omen at a pivotal moment during a victorious battle.

At the end of the day scores of de Soto's men had been killed and well over one hundred badly wounded. Accounts of the wounds alone were staggering, which each of the chroniclers made a point to recall. One placed the number at "seven hundred arrow wounds," while another counted almost two thousand separate wounds. "There was an almost countless number of such wounds, for there was scarcely a man who was not wounded, and most of them had five or six wounds, and many ten or twelve." The point? For each of the chroniclers, there was no doubt this was a miraculous religious victory. Exhausted, terribly wounded, and without medical supplies or even food, the survivors were in dire straits, and they continued to seek assistance in their faith. In their hearts and aloud, de la Vega described, "they called on God to protect and succor them in that affliction, and our Lord as a merciful Father aided them, by giving them an invincible spirit in that hardship, which the Spanish nation always had above all the nations of the earth to support" in its most trying times. And ultimately it "was God's will that they were healed shortly of very dangerous wounds," another concluded.[13] The battle of Mavila, an atrocity orders of magnitude greater than the Battle of Horseshoe Bend, the Sand Creek Massacre, or Wounded Knee, was not that at all to de Soto and his men. It had proven to the Spaniards that their cause was indeed righteous, and that Santiago de Matamoros continued to fight for them.

Far less evidence of any sort of religious proselytization exists after Mavila. Perhaps the only example came well after the men had moved west across the Mississippi River. There the expedition approached Casquin, where the headman, suffering a drought, asked for religious favor. De Soto readily assented, and in the presence of the headman had a carpenter fashion a cross "from the tallest and thickest pine tree that could be found in the vicinity." The cross, which "came out most handsomely because it was so tall," couldn't be lifted by one hundred men, de la Vega described, and the chieftain "should believe that he would lack nothing if he had true faith in it." When the time came to position their cross the men of the expedition formed a processional with the "priests, clerics, and friars" at the front, "chanting the litanies and chorus" with the soldiers following behind them responding. They drove the enormous cross into the center of the community's largest ceremonial mound, "and we all went with much devotion, kneeling to kiss the foot of the cross," in front of thousands of Casquin onlookers. The celebration took four hours.[14] The planting of that cross, in their moment of trial, probably meant more to the Spaniards than to the people of Casquin.

De Soto's actions at Casquin were the exception when it came to religious evangelism in the last years of the expedition. For that, there are two equally obvious explanations. First, while the battle of Mavila cost dozens of Spanish lives, a great deal of the expedition's animals, equipment, and foodstuffs were also seized by the Natives or destroyed. Included in those supplies were the bags of wheat flower and the jugs of wine the men carried "very carefully and reverently for celebrating mass," as well as "the chalices, altars, and ornaments they were carrying for divine worship." This loss immediately confronted the men with fundamental "questions in theology," as de la Vega put it. How could they celebrate such a basic Catholic tradition as communion if they had none of its required components? And according to their own admission, they had absolutely none of them. They considered consecrating "bread made of maize," but in the end they balked at the idea, citing "sacred canons" that made it clear that "the bread shall be of wheat and the wine from grapes." In fear of adopting some compromise that might prove more insulting to the Church than simply forgoing Mass, and without any of the other physical requirements, like "chalices and altars for celebrating it," the men reluctantly chose the latter. They would have Mass, without really having Mass.

Priests improvised the best they could. They set up makeshift altars for Sunday and feast day venerations. They draped themselves in buckskin ornaments, read all the required sacred texts and gave their "discourse or sermon," and in doing so partook in what the men came to call a "dry mass." It was clear, though, that the men recognized what was lost. With "this sort of ceremony they conducted in the place of Mass they consoled themselves in the affliction they felt at being unable to adore Jesus Christ our Lord and Redeemer in the sacramental elements." This was how the Catholic Church would endure among de Soto and his men for the remainder of the entrada. "This lasted for three years, until they left La Florida for Christian lands."[15] While they did their best, in short, it was clear to the men that their best was nowhere near good enough, and for the rest of their days they suffered existentially for it. How could even the most fervent evangelists among de Soto's men expect to instruct Natives on Christianity and administer to them its necessary sacraments if they were forced to do such a poor job of practicing it themselves?

As equally clear, after Mavila followed another attack at Chicaza, which destroyed whatever military advantage the Spanish still maintained. At that point, de Soto and his men were simply no longer in any position to impose their will on Native communities. Most of the horses were gone, removing the men's largest tactical edge. Their numbers were dwindling, and almost everyone by that point was seriously wounded. De Soto's army was, by the time it approached the Mississippi, a shadow of what it had been when it arrived in La Florida. For Gracilaso de la Vega, this was basically the end of the de Soto expedition, even though its men would trudge on for another few years. Not only had de Soto been broken, but the twin mandates from which he derived his authority were clearly going to go unfulfilled. He failed "to lay the foundations for a most glorious and beautiful kingdom for the Crown of Spain, and for the increase of the holy Catholic faith, which is what is to be most regretted."[16]

In other words, according to Gracilaso de la Vega religious motivations were just as important as the search for political power or economic advancement. These were the influences that drove Spaniards to La Florida and motivated them to exert tremendous violence on the Native populations there—violence that we will approach in future chapters. Thankfully for the Native populations of La Florida that survived these entradas, none of it stuck.

Notes

1. Jennings, *New Worlds of Violence*, 43-44.
2. Davis, "Ponce de León's First Voyage," 36-37; Davis, "Ponce de León's Second Voyage," 57.
3. Gannon, "Altar and Hearth," 20-21.
4. Adorno and Pautz, eds., *The Narrative of Cabeza de Vaca*, 48, 54; Oviedo, *Historia*, 3: 615; Gannon, "Altar and Hearth," 21-22.
5. Adorno and Pautz, eds., *The Narrative of Cabeza de Vaca*, 46-47.
6. "La Florida," in Clayton, Knight, and Moore, eds., *The De Soto Chronicles*, 2: 74; Gannon, "Altar and Hearth," 23; "Account of the Northern Conquest," in Clayton, Knight, and Moore, eds., *The De Soto Chronicles*, 257; Robertson, "Preface," in Clayton, Knight, and Moore, eds., *The De Soto Chronicles*, 27-28.
7. "Account of the Northern Conquest," in Clayton, Knight, and Moore, eds., *The De Soto Chronicles*, 255; "La Florida," in Clayton, Knight, and Moore, eds., *The De Soto Chronicles*, 2: 143-144.

8. "La Florida," in Clayton, Knight, and Moore, eds., *The De Soto Chronicles*, 2: 229, 355. Rodrigo Rangel's account gives a slightly different response: "Account of the Northern Conquest," in Clayton, Knight, and Moore, eds., *The De Soto Chronicles*, 289; Hoffman, "The Chicora Legend," 425.

9. "The Account by a Gentleman from Elvas," in Clayton, Knight, and Moore, eds., *The De Soto Chronicles*, 77; "Account of the Northern Conquest," in Clayton, Knight, and Moore, eds., *The De Soto Chronicles*, 270-273; Robertson, "Preface," in Clayton, Knight, and Moore, eds., *The De Soto Chronicles*, 27; Hudson, *Knights of Spain*, 159.

10. "La Florida," in Clayton, Knight, and Moore, eds., *The De Soto Chronicles*, 2: 338.

11. "La Florida," in Clayton, Knight, and Moore, eds., *The De Soto Chronicles*, 2: 341-342.

12. According to Rangel's account Luis de Moscoso rallied men during the Napetuca massacre. "Come on, men, Santiago, Santiago, and at them." See "Account of the Northern Conquest," in Clayton, Knight, and Moore, eds., *The De Soto Chronicles*, 265.

13. "La Florida," in Clayton, Knight, and Moore, eds., *The De Soto Chronicles*, 2: 343, 346, 348, 351; "The Account by a Gentleman from Elvas," in Clayton, Knight, and Moore, eds., *The De Soto Chronicles*, 104.

14. "Relation of the Island of Florida," in Clayton, Knight, and Moore, eds., *The De Soto Chronicles*, 239-240; "Account of the Northern Conquest," in Clayton, Knight, and Moore, eds., *The De Soto Chronicles*, 300-301; "La Florida," in Clayton, Knight, and Moore, eds., *The De Soto Chronicles*, 2: 391-393.

15. "La Florida," in Clayton, Knight, and Moore, eds., *The De Soto Chronicles*, 2: 353-354; Robertson, "Preface," in Clayton, Knight, and Moore, eds., *The De Soto Chronicles*, 28; Gannon, "Altar and Hearth," 25.

16. "La Florida," in Clayton, Knight, and Moore, eds., *The De Soto Chronicles*, 2: 358.

La Matanza

If the Catholic Church failed to establish a La Florida beachhead in the earliest decades of contact and colonization, Christian warriors did eventually find their first success with the establishment of St. Augustine. That victory would not come directly at the expense of Natives, however, but of competing European Christians. When Pedro Menéndez de Avilés founded St. Augustine in 1565 it was in direct response not only to the presence of French pirates but also French Protestants; the faith of the French squatters that appeared in La Florida in the years before St. Augustine represented a threat that was just as dangerous as the damage they sought to do to Caribbean shipping. While the Protestant faith would come to dominate the British colonies in the eighteenth and nineteenth centuries, it was a Protestant-Catholic struggle that defined contact in the two centuries previous. That divide was no trifling difference at the time of La Florida's founding—not only were its founders Catholic, but St. Augustine was founded in bloody struggle with Protestants, the first of whom Menéndez butchered in La Florida like animals. Once again, the European settling of La Florida was steeped in Catholic ambition.

For Spaniards, a distrust of non-Catholics had been building for hundreds of years and was central to the very identity of a man like Menéndez. For the origins of that distrust, we return to the *Reconquista*, a violent process of political, cultural, and religious coalescence in the Iberian world. It was one in which the multiethnic residents of a once-complicated political and religious region were united under the combined kingdoms of Portugal, Castile, and Aragon, but also under the authority of the Catholic Church. That was the process Ferdinand and Isabella completed with the conquest of Grenada in 1492, galvanizing a cohesive Spanish identity that was deeply intertwined with the Catholic faith and a fear of non-Catholics. The *Reconquista* had proved the superiority of the Catholic Church, which in turn had Spain's political and religious rulers casting a doubtful eye on the region's other popular faiths, namely, Islam and Judaism. While both of those faiths had been a part of

Iberian society for generations, they now constituted threats to the newly unified Catholic monarchs.

What had been a complicated and relatively tolerant region faded away in the later years of the *Reconquista* as Christian armies regained corners of the Iberian Peninsula, leaving Spaniards with a "One Faith, One Law, One King" philosophy that had terrible consequences for all non-Catholics. Jews and Muslims both suffered under the Spanish Holy Office of the Inquisition, which Ferdinand and Isabella first established with the assistance of the Pope in 1478. Religious outsiders were forced to either convert or leave, demands that increasingly took place under the threat of torture or death. Thousands chose the former, yet that only created the troubling and possibly subversive threat of hidden non-Catholics in Spanish society. Converts were often accused of only doing so half-heartedly, producing a sort of second-class citizenship in Spain that paved the way for blood purity requirements that defined social and political advancement.

The *Limpieza de Sangre*, which translates literally to cleanliness of blood, created procedures for proving the heritage of those with political aspirations. In order to rise through the ranks of Spanish society, a hopeful would have to prove that their Catholic blood had not been tainted by Islamic, Jewish, or otherwise heretical influence for four generations. A foreboding development for the future of the Americans indeed—the *Limpieza de Sangre* requirements created a Spanish caste system that would quickly make its way with conquistadores into the New World. The Catholic monarchs were followed up by Charles V, who not only embraced the Catholic Church but was pronounced the Holy Roman Emperor, its head of state. From him the charge was passed on to his son, Philip II, no less a defender of the Catholic orthodoxy than was his father.[1] Spain by this point was not only the primary exemplar of Catholicism in the world but was dedicated to extending church influence throughout the world.

Although Philip II had charged Menéndez with settling St. Augustine as a bulwark against regional piracy, it was not to be overlooked that the particular group of pirates he was to chase out were not Catholics. They were members of a French Protestant denomination known as Huguenots. For Philip and Menéndez both, the French squatters in La Florida were among the worst subsets of religious dissidents—the followers of notorious apostates Martin Luther and John Calvin. Although Lutherans and Calvinists grew into separate branches of the Reformed Christian faith, both were highly critical of the orthodoxy of the Catholic Church, and both influenced the growth of French Huguenots.

Consider Luther, whose criticism of Church orthodoxy is seen as one of the kicking-off points of the entire Reformation. Ramping up his writings in the early sixteenth century, Luther's attacks on the dogma and corruption of the Catholic Church, including the Pope, also constituted an attack on the Spanish Crown. Atop the Catholic Church sat not only Pope Leo X but Charles V of Spain, who as both King and Holy Roman Emperor would also have something to say about Luther's criticism of his power. Both he and the Pope demanded Luther retract his charges. When Luther did not, the Pope excommunicated him while Charles V oversaw the issuing of the 1521 Edict of Worms, declaring Luther an outlaw and an enemy of the Church, and called for his capture and presumable execution "as a notorious heretic." The centrality of Charles V not only in the Church but in what became the Counter-Reformation—Spain's response to radical Reformed ideology—helps explains why his son, Philip II, pursued the French heretics so violently into La Florida during his own reign.[2]

By the time Philip II took power the Reformation was only speeding up, generating a European "flood tide of heresy" for the new king, in the words of one historian. That was particularly the case in a politically disheveled France, where Crown weaknesses could not keep such radical teachings from spreading. Lutheran thought, although condemned by French Catholics and increasingly by the French Crown, spread like wildfire, gaining theological footholds in universities, and making its way in literature through the countryside. When French theologian John Calvin entered the scene in the 1540s, adding his voluminous criticisms to the emerging canon, it seemed clear that Reformed ideology was in France to stay, even in the face of more violent repression on behalf of an increasingly threatened King Francis I. In spite of that violence and after Francis's death, Reformed churches flourished from the mid-sixteenth century to 1562, the year French Huguenot colonizers stretched out into the Atlantic.[3]

Admiral Gaspard de Coligny represented both of those developments. An influential Huguenot, Grand Admiral of France, and a personal friend to King Charles IX, Coligny helped organize the country's failed attempt to build a Protestant colony in Portuguese Brazil in the 1550s, near present-day Rio de Janeiro. The French established Fort Coligny but were soon assaulted by Portuguese forces, leading Coligny and others to attempt Huguenot outposts elsewhere. Soon he had organized Jean de Ribault's 1562 voyage to La Florida, from which Charlesfort briefly resulted, and Laudonniére's 1564 establishment of Fort Caroline.[4]

There was no doubt that these settlements, like the Brazilian attempts that preceded them, were not simply economic adventures. At their very foundations was a drive to plant a permanent Protestant colony in La Florida from which to evangelize North America's Natives—something Spaniards had failed to do now several times. Ribault himself described how, through such colonization, "a number of savage people, ignorant of Jesus Christ, may, by His grace, come to some knowledge of His holy laws and ordinances."[5] That of course was the worst possible news in Madrid, and King Philip II, having picked up the mantle of the Counter-Reformation from his father, responded forcefully. "Not for him was the path of toleration," wrote one scholar. The Frenchmen squatting in La Florida were not only pirates, but the epitome of blasphemers, and no quarter was to be shown them.[6]

Even though what took place to the south of St. Augustine paled in comparison with the massacre at Mavila, the violence of La Matanza is incomprehensible in light of the relative religious tolerance that we enjoy in the modern-day United States. The two antagonists that would square off against each other in La Florida did so based on what were essentially two different readings of the same bible—both Lutherans and Catholics roll off the tongue in the twentieth century simply as Christians. A level of religious intolerance that would seem completely insane by modern standards, however, was relatively common during the height of Reformation violence, when Catholics would not only have killed Lutherans, but would have burned them at the stake for their heretical beliefs. Even in France, the rise of Huguenots sowed chaos in an already fragile religious and political society, and ultimately culminated in the horrific violence of the 1572 St. Bartholomew's Day Massacre. Coligny himself would lose his life in the uprising, one of the first to die in a bloody, near-hysterical purge of thousands of Huguenots that set the Protestant movement back decades and sent waves of religious violence rippling through France.[7] If Huguenots were a contentious presence even in France, then a colony of them in Spanish territory—where possibly tens of thousands of Native souls were at stake—was completely unacceptable to Catholics in Spain.

As one of Menéndez's chroniclers explained, the fight for the Christian soul of La Florida was not to be taken lightly, and would be fought ferociously. Any "Lutheran" who stood in Menéndez's way "he eliminated, both as a Frenchman and a heretic."[8] Both Philip and Menéndez were aware that allowing Ribault's and Laudonnière's Lutheran messages to run amok in La Florida, spreading their sacrilege, would have dire spiritual consequences. Menéndez's Crown instructions directed the admiral to seek the "salvation" of Native souls, and several clergymen were on hand, among his army, to do just that. As he warned King Philip

II directly, on the other hand, if another nation was to colonize the region first, "forming a friendship, as they will, with the Indians of the land, it will be afterward most difficult to conquer and rule it, especially if the French or English should settle it, as they are Lutheran peoples."[9] The stakes in 1565 could not be higher.

Menéndez's route to La Florida had not been a particularly easy one; after a difficult trip across the Atlantic, with time spent at Puerto Rico repairing his ships and organizing his forces, Menéndez made for La Florida "in order to expel the Lutheran French who are in the said provinces." Having already passed by the French near modern-day Jacksonville and having already exchanged naval fire with them, Menéndez was convinced that the Lutherans would not go quietly. After sailing away from the St. Johns River, he disembarked his army at St. Augustine "with many banners spread, to the sound of trumpets and salutes of artillery." The expedition's chaplain, Francisco López de Mendoza Grajales, had landed the previous night, and he marched out to meet Menéndez's party, carrying a cross and singing hymns. Menéndez approached the cross, he and his men knelt before it, and he embraced it. A group of Natives looking "imitated all they saw done," apparently kneeling and kissing the cross as well. Quite a ceremony and indeed an auspicious beginning to La Florida's first settlement. Not only was St. Augustine the site of America's first church and parish, but it was also evidently both of those things before it was technically even founded as a town, a reflection of the importance everyone, including Menéndez, gave the role of Catholicism in La Florida's future.[10]

Over the next two days Menéndez and his men built a rudimentary fort and offloaded the expedition's supplies. After another quick scare by a French scouting party a small group of soldiers ran across a French prisoner, and from him Menéndez learned that of the hundreds of men at Caroline "one-third were Lutherans, and two priests, who preached the Lutheran doctrine." You can almost feel Menéndez's blood boiling. He held Mass with his men and called another war council. Their endeavor was not only "for the King our Master," he argued, but was "the enterprise of God Our Lord," and as such, they could not falter. They were all Lutherans at Fort Caroline, Menéndez accused, rallying his men. Their Lutheran foe would "prevent our implanting the Holy Gospel in these provinces," and "we seek them because they are Lutherans, in order that they shall not implant their evil and detestable sect in this land, nor teach their belief to the Indians." Therefore, he charged, "the war we have with them, and they with us, cannot be carried on save with fire and blood."[11] The violence that would wipe the French threat from La Florida does not seem so incredible anymore.

Menéndez's plan was to travel overland with the best pick of his soldiers and mount a surprise attack on Fort Caroline. Ribault's sea forces, fighting the current and contrary winds, would not be able to return in time to do anything about it. Either the Frenchmen would leave, or "we shall put them to the sword, everyone."[12] Menéndez and his men set out immediately, and the journey was an epic one. After traveling overland for four days through marshy terrain and often in the rain, the men, near mutiny, still agreed to fight when they finally approached Caroline. The rains "continued as constant and heavy as if the world was to be again overwhelmed with a flood," a surviving Frenchman recounted, giving credit to the Spaniards' determination. In the confusion of their approach there was a scuffle between a lone French sentry, which caused panic. Thinking they had been found out, Menéndez's advance guard began rushing toward the fort. It was in this frenzied moment that Menéndez, himself wearing the Cross of St. James, summoned Santiago. "Santiago! At them! God is helping! Victory! The French are killed! The camp master is inside the fort and has captured it!" To his shouts the men stormed forward and on to an easy victory. As Frenchman Jacques Le Moyne recalled, they attacked "at the double quick in three places at once, penetrated the works without resistance, and, getting possession of the place of arms, drew up their force there."

Several Frenchmen were slain in the rush, while others jumped the walls to flee. Spanish soldiers rushed into the soldiers' quarters, where many were still sleeping, "killing all whom they found, so that awful outcries and groans arose from those who were being slaughtered." The women and young were spared; straggling soldiers who surrendered after originally fleeing into the woods, on the other hand, were almost always finished off. Among them was a companion who Le Moyne encountered while in hiding. After attempting to make it to the coast, the companion, a man by the name of Grandchemin, resolved instead to try his luck at surrendering. That was better than dying of exposure in the woods. "Friend and companion, I pray you, let us not go thither," Le Moyne begged Grandchemin. Nevertheless, the man made himself visible to the Spanish sentries while Le Moyne remained hidden. Immediately, the Spaniards "sent out a party," and Grandchemin "fell on his knees to beg for his life." The soldiers, "however, in a fury cut him to pieces, and carried off the dismembered fragments of his body on the points of their spears and pikes." As not only pirates but infidel they deserved no quarter, and they would be given none. That sort of surrender did not interest Le Moyne at all. Instead, he would flee back to the coast, survive a harrowing return trip to Europe, and live to tell his tale. Thus ended the first of Menéndez's three great victories over the French Lutherans.[13]

After sleeping in French buildings by the fort and enjoying the clothes and provisions they found there, Menéndez got straight to work. After hearing Mass, he raised two crosses "in the places that seemed best to him," marked out a place for a church, and ordered a chapel built "so that mass might be said every day." He ordered a return of most of the men to St. Augustine, who after a walk no less arduous than before, were greeted by the remaining garrison with tremendous fan fair. As soon as Grajales recognized Menéndez, "I had the bells rung," he would recall, "and great rejoicings made in the camp." Four priests led the procession to meet Menéndez, and "holding the cross aloft" and singing hymns, they and the rest of St. Augustine "received the Adelantado with great pleasure and rejoicing, everyone laughing and weeping for joy, praising God for so great a victory." Remarkable was the celebration that followed such barbarity. Tactically, Grajales described, what was gained at the French fort was nothing less of miraculous. The "greatest advantage of this victory is certainly the triumph which our Lord has granted us, and which will be the means of the holy Gospel being introduced into this country, a thing necessary to prevent the loss of many souls."[14] The first strike against the Lutherans had been struck, and for the Spanish, it was a great victory indeed.

The opportunity for more strikes soon appeared. Menéndez learned from nearby Indians and a few surviving French sailors that his main adversary, Jean Ribault, had left Fort Caroline by sea to attack St. Augustine, only to be caught in a storm and shipwrecked farther down the coast. It did not take long to come up with the first group of survivors, marching north to return to Caroline. The men were in dire straits, living on the beach and having gone without food for more than a week. All of them, according to one Frenchman, "were Lutherans." After informing an officer of the group that their fort was sacked and that most of his compatriots were dead, the Frenchmen first tried to negotiate for their salvation. Then they begged for mercy. As they "belonged to the new religion," Menéndez would guarantee them neither. He "held them to be enemies and would wage against them a war of fire and blood, and carry it on with all possible cruelty against those he should find in that land and on that sea." He and his men had come "to implant the Holy Gospel in that land, in order that the Indians might be enlightened and come to the knowledge of the holy Catholic faith of Jesus Christ, Our Lord, as it is preached in the Roman church." Pitiless would be one way to describe the Spanish position. Menéndez's and Philip's previous words of threat, it was becoming clear, had not been idle musings.

The parley went on for some time, with Menéndez standing firm. The French were dying of exposure and could offer little resistance even though they greatly outnumbered the Spaniards. If they surrendered and placed themselves "at his mercy," Menéndez ordered, "they could do so, in order that he might do with them what God should direct him." Over two hundred did, surrendering all of their arms and banners. After systematically separating the prisoners into small groups and hiking them over sand dunes to predetermined locations, away from the rest, he had them all killed with knives and clubs. "Finding they were all Lutherans, the captain-general ordered them all to be put to death," described Grajales, who was with Menéndez to witness the action personally. Grajales protested for a moment, but only because he was concerned that some of the men might be Catholics. Menéndez allowed him to investigate, and the priest did come across a few, which he saved. "All the others were executed, because they were Lutherans and enemies of our Holy Catholic Faith." So it was done, "and they were all left there dead," while the Spanish again returned to St. Augustine.[15]

The last massacre took place shortly after when Menéndez learned of a second group of castaways. This one included Ribault himself, and he had them all treated similarly. Dying of thirst and exposure, they had little option but to surrender. They gave up their arms and banners, led by Ribault personally. Menéndez had them separated into small groups and bound, and led them all away, unawares, to their doom. Aside from sparing a few more Catholics and a few musicians, "all the others were put to the knife." Ribault died with a dagger to the chest, according to Le Moyne, and the rest "who had been tied up, by knocking them in the head with clubs and axes, which they proceeded to do without delay, calling them meanwhile Lutherans, and enemies to God and the Virgin Mary." Along with the very few spared, handfuls of women and children taken from Fort Caroline were shipped to Puerto Rico. With another small party of sailors and soldiers hunted down in the area of Cape Canaveral and enticed to surrender, this ended La Matanza, the destruction of the French Huguenot threat in La Florida and the annihilation of Ribault and his men.[16]

Or, to put it another way, this ended the Thanksgiving Day Massacres. While that name hasn't exactly stuck in the history books, La Matanza has. The river, inlet, and stretch of beach that lie to the south of St. Augustine all still bear that name (*matanzas*). That, of course, roughly translated from Spanish and depending on what landmark it refers to, means something in between the massacre and the river of blood.[17] They remain as markers of incredible slaughter, fitting everyday symbols of the religious struggle waged over La Florida. It was a violent, bloody struggle that culminated with the establishment of America's first church—the Catholic Church. With the death of Ribault and the remainder of his men, the Lutheran threat to La Florida was crushed, and the establishment of Catholic La Florida secure.

Notes

1. Schwaller, *The History of the Catholic Church*, 17-20; Lynch, *New Worlds*, 4-6.
2. Carl Truman, "Luther and the Reformation in Germany," in Pettegree, ed., *The Reformation World*, 73-94; Sugden, *Sir Francis Drake*, 10-11.
3. Reid, "France," 211-224; Lyon, *The Enterprise of Florida*, 19; Sugden, *Sir Francis Drake*, 10-11.
4. Jennings, *New Worlds of Violence*, 62-64; Whitehead, *Gaspard de Coligny*, 312-338.
5. French, *Historical Collections*, 159-161.
6. Weber, *The Spanish Frontier*, 62-64; Sugden, *Sir Francis Drake*, 11.
7. Mentzer, "The French Wars of Religion," 323-333.
8. Merás, *Pedro Menéndez de Avilés*, 33.
9. Merás, *Pedro Menéndez de Avilés*, 33; Gannon, "Altar and Hearth," 37-38.
10. Lyon, *The Enterprise of Florida*, 100-119; French, *Historical Collections*, 218-220.
11. Merás, *Pedro Menéndez de Avilés*, 89-92; French, *Historical Collections*, 226-227.
12. Merás, *Pedro Menéndez de Avilés*, 92-93.
13. Merás, *Pedro Menéndez de Avilés*, 95-101; Bennett, ed., *Settlement of Florida*, 113-116; Lyon, *The Enterprise of Florida*, 120-123; Jennings, *New Worlds of Violence*, 73-76. For Avilés as a Knight in the Order of Santiago, see Merás, *Pedro Menéndez de Avilés*, 190; Lowery, *Spanish Settlements*, 120 n1, 384.
14. Merás, *Pedro Menéndez de Avilés*, 105, 108-109; French, *Historical Collections*, 227, 231; Lyon, *The Enterprise of Florida*, 120-124.
15. Merás, *Pedro Menéndez de Avilés*, 111-115; French, *Historical Collections*, 233-234; Lyon, *The Enterprise of Florida*, 124-126.
16. Merás, *Pedro Menéndez de Avilés*, 121-122; Bennett, ed., *Settlement of Florida*, 120; Lyon, *The Enterprise of Florida*, 123, 127-128.
17. Letter dated October 15, 1565, original in *Spanish Borderlands Sourcebooks: Pedro Menéndez de Avilés.* Translated by Eugene Lyon. Accessed digitally at https://earlyfloridalit.net/pedro-menendez-de-aviles-letter-to-king-philip-ii/; Kamen, *Empire*, 249-250; Weber, *The Spanish Frontier*, 60-64; Hoffman, *A New Andalucia*, 229-230; Milanich, *Laboring in the Fields of the Lord*, 84-86; Bushnell, *Situado and Sabana*, 30, 37-38.

4 Enslaved Origins

Esteban, also known as Estevanico, was present for every miserable day of Pánfilo de Narváez's La Florida nightmare. He was there for every day that followed the conquistador's death, too, even though he went unmentioned for most of it. Cabeza de Vaca did not name Esteban during the peninsular-Florida stretch at all, and he did not mention him by name often afterward; most times when he did, it was just as "el negro," no doubt a condescending reference to his servant status. Esteban was, after all, a slave. We can therefore only imagine how his early days on the trail in La Florida were spent.

Esteban would have had nothing to say in Narváez's fateful decision to send the expedition's ships off, for instance, even though he was probably among the men that watched as they sailed away into the Gulf, never to return. He would survive the terrible month of assault in Apalachee and would surely have done his part to build the five rafts on which all the expedition's survivors hoped they would make their escape. Considering by this point there were at most only a few servants left alive—at least two Africans and one Caribbean islander—it can be presumed then that Esteban did far more than his fair share of the hardest labor, cutting down trees, lashing them together into rafts, and fitting them out with sails and oars. It would have been his lot to do so, working much harder than the otherwise unskilled hidalgos who would not have known what they were doing anyway. While they were dropping dead outside of Aute like flies, Esteban was probably running a boatyard.[1]

Esteban's route to those horrible months in Aute was a less remarkable one, at least by sixteenth-century Spanish standards. He was born in Azemmour, Morocco, a region known as Berber even though most Spaniards would have referred to him as a Moor, a general term used to describe a North African Muslim. He was born sometime around the turn of the sixteenth century, putting him in his mid-twenties by the time he set out into La Florida with Pánfilo de Narváez's army. Sometime before then he had been shipped by Portuguese traders north into the Iberian Peninsula as an enslaved person.

How exactly he got that way is unclear. He could have been born a slave, or he could have sold himself into slavery to escape the famine and destitution that gripped the Moroccan coast when the traders arrived. While the latter option would seem strange, voluntarily consigning oneself to slavery was not particularly unordinary at the time and was an acceptable fate in Spanish culture. Although that seems like an awfully drastic step to take voluntarily, it does sound better than dying of starvation. Regardless of just how he got that way, Esteban soon found himself an enslaved person in the south of Spain, a multicultural and multi-ethnic region where his dark complexion would not at all have been a rarity.[2]

Soon Esteban was a baptized Christian and was the property of a Spaniard by the name of Andres Dorantes de Carranza, a resident of the Extremadura region in the southwest of Spain. Extremadura seemed to be at the time one of Spain's premier conquistador breeding grounds, producing Vasco Núñez de Balboa, Hernán Cortés, Francisco Pizarro, and of course Hernándo de Soto, among others. What a place for Esteban to have been. Soon he, in the company of Dorantes de Carranza, was on a boat destined for Hispaniola, arriving in Santo Domingo in 1527. From there the two joined Narváez's expedition, adding their names to one of the most epic disasters in American history.[3]

While it was not unordinary for African men like Esteban to find themselves in the Caribbean and even in La Florida, what transpired after Aute truly was, in every sense of the word, extraordinary. His own raft survived the float past Pensacola and Mobile bays and the treacherous Mississippi Delta. When it did wreck with the others in modern-day Texas, five of the best swimming survivors were chosen to try their way overland to Tampico on the Mexican coast. That was a death sentence, of course, and luckily for Esteban he was not chosen for the mission because he could not swim. By that point, somewhere near 80 percent of the expedition was either dead on a beach or swept out to sea and long gone, as was Narváez himself. It was at this point that de Vaca, with few other people to mention, listed Esteban among the survivors directly as "Estevanico, the Negro." His name would be listed a little more than a half-dozen times as the surviving men, their number dwindling slowly into the double then single digits, wandered the barrier islands of coastal Texas, now the slaves of the regional Natives themselves. "At all times they had been naked and barefoot. This was in summer when that coast burned like fire." Esteban, now the slave of a slave, endured almost unimaginably hostile conditions and the torment of an ever-changing host of new masters. Yet he survived.[4]

Finally, years later, the survivors escaped their captivity near Corpus Christi, Texas, moving inland and heading south over the Rio Grande before turning west into modern-day Mexico. They moved from town to town, offering their services as medicine men and faith healers, gaining notoriety among the Natives for supposedly curing all sorts of maladies. They performed surgery, and Cabeza de Vaca even appeared to raise one man from the dead. Feats like these allowed the survivors to creep through northern Mexico until they were run across by Spaniards and escorted back to Mexico City. By this time, Esteban's celebrity might have exceeded even the others. He spoke several Native tongues, led the way, and shook the rattle of a shaman as he walked. Despite the decidedly second-rate value de Vaca gave him in his writings, according to several historians it is clear that the most unlikely slave of a slave did not just survive but led the rest of the Spaniards to their salvation as well. Once simply an enslaved Moor from Morocco, Esteban was now much more. As a linguist and an interpreter, a shaman, and a scout across the American Gulf South he was, in sum, one of America's first and greatest pioneers.[5]

Enslaved Origins closes the "Origins" section by taking a separate thematic look at the role of captivity and slavery in La Florida's earliest moments. Consider Estevanico, or Esteban, one of La Florida's African trailblazers. He was a slave, as were most of the African men and women that arrived with the Spanish to North America. They would be the craftsmen and servants who would be forced to build La Florida literally from the ground up, as Ayllón attempted to do in Georgia, as de Luna attempted to do in Pensacola, and as Menéndez succeeded in doing at St. Augustine. Every chapter in America's origin story includes such men and women of African origins. Most came unwillingly, as slaves of Spaniards. Some came of their own free will, a nod to the complicated racial dynamic that Spaniards brought with them to the New World, including into what would be the United States of America. If at one time La Florida comprised the modern states of Florida, Georgia, the Carolinas, Tennessee, Alabama, Mississippi, Arkansas, and Texas, then African American history began in La Florida.

Unfortunately, La Florida's history with slavery goes back even further to the very first moments in its European colonization. Native slavery, too, was instrumental in the landing on, naming of, and settlement of North America by Europeans. The very first Spaniards to set eyes on the present-day states of Florida, Georgia, and the Carolinas were not only explorers but slave raiders, who after emptying the northern Caribbean of its Native peoples, sought out new sources of Caribbean labor anywhere they could find them. Together the slave trade and the Spanish *encomienda*, both in operation by the sixteenth century elsewhere in the Spanish Americas, were to be a part of La Florida's future as well. They certainly would have been had men like de León or de Soto succeeded in founding settlements in La Florida as they were supposed to. What would become the African slave trade was originally the Native slave trade; both are part of America's origin story.

Notes

1. Herrick, *Esteban*, 84.
2. Herrick, *Esteban*, 13-20.
3. Herrick, *Esteban*, 20, 47, 67.
4. Herrick, *Esteban*, 92-96.
5. Herrick, *Esteban*, 110-122, 125-129; Smith, "Beyond the Mediation," 267-268.

Caribbean Slavery, La Florida Slavery

Unfree Africans were not the first source of labor in the Spanish New World, and they were not the first source of labor in La Florida. In both cases, Native people were. Almost from the very moment Columbus set eyes on the Caribbean's Natives in 1492, in fact, he began thinking in terms of their labor value, remarking that the people he found there were gentle and peaceful, but also "fitted to be ruled and to be set to work, to cultivate the land and to do all else that may be necessary." At the conclusion of his second voyage Columbus was clearly ready to take the next step, seizing close to 1,500 Arawaks and holding them in pens to await transport back to Spain. The number was reduced to five hundred only because there was not enough room on the Spanish ships to hold more. Hundreds died on this reverse Middle Passage, their bodies thrown overboard.[1] The very first years of Caribbean discovery set the stage for the decades of subjugation and enslavement that followed quickly in their wake.

What Spaniards developed was a mix of illicit slave raiding and eventually the officially sanctioned *encomienda* system (along with its later replacement, the *repartimiento*). The first populated Spanish gold mining operations in Caribbean rivers on islands like Hispaniola and Puerto Rico, and soon did so using the population of nearby islands. The latter became an engine of emigration for countless Spaniards, and the source of subjugation of millions of Natives. An *encomienda* was the grant of local Natives, who the *encomendero* essentially now held in trust for the Crown. The institution was envisioned specifically not as slavery; while he could benefit from their labor and could force them to work, an *encomendero* was also technically supposed to keep those Natives relatively safe and fed and was also supposed to facilitate their instruction in Catholicism.[2]

Wherever Spaniards went in the New World, *encomienda* allotments were not far behind, beginning with Nicholás de Ovando on Hispaniola. Conquistadores and governors alike, including Ovando, Cortés, and Pizarro, perpetuated the system for several reasons. At the core of the *encomienda* system, however, was labor. Prime lands and *encomienda* allotments could be issued by the leaders of conquests to their subordinates as payment for their participation in that conquest. Because conquistadores often footed the cost of the expedition personally, this was an understood condition granted by the Crown and often written into the terms of a *capitulación*. A successful conqueror could divvy up land and divvy up people for the benefit of his faithful soldiers, which is what both Cortés and Pizarro did when the massive empires in Central Mexico and South America fell to them. They were following precedents set earlier by Ovando and Cuéllar in the Caribbean. In these cases, allotments of Natives were given out as enticements and bonuses from the very first days of Spanish conquest and would continue through the failed conquest of La Florida.

Even after the initial waves of conquest and colonization, the *encomienda* endured. For the royal authorities who followed conquistadores into the colonies, *encomiendas* served as an enticement for permanent settlement. Not everyone could expect to become a Cortés or a Pizarro; most Spanish emigrants would not be toppling empires or claiming gold and silver mines for themselves. For most Spaniards who came to the New World, an *encomienda* allotment, in addition to a grant of land, was their ticket to modest financial success. The twin grants of land and Natives formed the foundation of the *hacienda*, for instance, or the rural estate. That grant made an enterprising Spaniard a *hacendado*, a plantation owner, who could use the Native allotment to produce goods for the regional market or for shipment back to Spain. Caribbean *haciendas* produced sugarcane, tobacco, or cacao; Central American *haciendas* could produce corn, wheat, or livestock. An *encomienda* provided the compulsive Native labor Spaniards would need to extract the wealth of the New World.[3]

The *encomienda* was a fully developed and relatively well-regulated institution by the mid–sixteenth century, peaking after the conquests of Central and South America. In the 1540s there were six hundred *encomenderos* in New Spain, and five hundred in Peru. By that time regulations supposedly recognized the basic humanity of Native peoples. *Encomenderos*, who were after all supposed to be holding them in trust, were to provide their Native charges with standard working days, adequate food and shelter while working, and even time off on feast and other holy days. Very little of that happened, of course. The Crown faced incredible pushback from *encomenderos* when it attempted to pass regulations like these, revealing the extent to which what was supposed to be a trust ownership of Christian souls really was, in reality, slavery. When Charles V authorized the 1542 New Laws, which among other things asserted that the ownership of peoples could not be passed down from generation to generation, he faced a popular *encomendero* uprising.

Such a transfer of property in humans would have effectively recreated European feudalism in the New World. From the perspective of the future English, it also would have signified the establishment of chattel slavery in the New World. In the case of the New Laws the Crown stood firm, ushering in a shifting from the *encomienda* to a more controlled *repartimiento* labor draft system. Like the land itself, Native peoples would revert to Crown ownership upon the death of an *encomendero*. This shift by absolutely no means, of course, absolves the Spanish Crown of its complicity in the large-scale exploitation of Native peoples. Though the letter of the law might have been altered, the *encomienda* remained in function, if not in name. Labor in the Spanish Americas was not only wildly exploitative and destructive; it was the very foundation upon which long-term Spanish colonization across the Americas was built.[4]

As exploitative and violent as they were, the *encomienda* and *repartimiento* systems that dominated much of the late sixteenth and seventeenth centuries were unfortunately still a marked improvement on the horrors of the original Caribbean conquest of Hispaniola, Puerto Rico, Cuba, and Jamaica. Even the *encomienda* was new in those first years, and existed in an almost entirely unregulated fashion that had no larger Christian purpose in mind. By the turn of the sixteenth century Columbus was actively using Native slave labor on Hispaniola to pursue his mining and plantation ventures. It was a precedent followed by Ovando in Hispaniola, de León in Puerto Rico, and Cuéllar in Cuba. Native peoples of all ages and sexes were allotted to mining operations that worked them to a quick death. At the center remained Hispaniola, the proverbial "wild west" of the Spanish New World. It was an island administered by the most avaricious of Spaniards, with absolutely no regard given for Native humanity and with very little colonial oversight. It was in the words of one historian, central to "a wide variety of activities, nearly all predatory," the most notorious being the subsequent pillaging of nearby islands for the slave labor that would replace the rapidly diminishing population of Hispaniola's original Native inhabitants.[5] Long before the Crown grew more involved in the humanity and rights of Native peoples, the Caribbean was being depopulated of Natives by Spanish *encomenderos*. This first wave of Spanish conquest, worse than the worst parts of English chattel slavery generations later, devastated the Native Caribbean.

It was the "Lucayos," known now as the Bahamas, that were hit hardest by the inter-Caribbean slave trade that radiated from these islands. Nothing about it resembled an *encomienda*, and at first glance it is unclear how any royal Spanish official—even a regional one—could legitimize enslavement on such a scale. As they had done earlier when making their argument for spiritual conquest, however, Spaniards proved quite inventive with the rationalizations they made for undertaking such raids. First, several Native groups in the Caribbean were considered to be particularly recalcitrant and barbaric in ways that went far beyond simple religious heathenism. Caribs, for instance, were widely perceived by Spanish authorities as particularly vicious fighters. As has already been described, if a Native population rejected the Spaniards' call for political and religious subjugation, then all bets at respectable governance were off. According to the letter of the requirement they could be warred upon and subsequently legally enslaved. This, presumably, took place regularly in the Caribbean, particularly when Spaniards were eyeing a militant and barbarous people that they entertained little hope of "civilizing" anyway. Spanish officials, all the way to the Crown, also viewed Caribs as actual cannibals. Officials did not have to struggle very hard at all with the legality of enslaving such people. Neither did they have to struggle with their faith. It was for reasons like these that even Spanish royalty could accept, in some cases, the destruction and enslavement of people that, as they saw it, more or less had it coming.[6]

Even if royal authorities did want to curb the abuses of men like Ovando or Cuéllar, doing so was a difficult task. For instance, the 1512 Law of Burgos should have put a stop to indiscriminate enslavement in all but the most extreme cases, but as Peter Martyr suggested decades later, laws passed in Spain had little sway over either the minds or the actions of Spaniards in the faraway Caribbean. To suggest regulation was one thing; to enforce it was another altogether. On the other side of the world, on remote islands where one round of correspondence by letter from Seville could take almost an entire year, oversight was nonexistent. "Carried away by love of gold," regional authorities became "ravenous wolves instead of gentle lambs, and heedless of the royal instructions." Any attempt to rebuke or punish a brutal *encomendero* just led to the establishment of others—"the more diligently we seek to cut off the Hydra's heads, the more numerous they spring up."[7]

Such exploitation was not without its detractors. Religious figures like Antonio Montesinos and later Bartolomé de Las Casas pointed out that conquest and colonization were supposed to be associated with religious conversion. The Spaniards "pretended they laboured to propagate religion while influenced by cupidity and avarice," wrote another contemporary.[8] Religious leaders spearheaded attempts to rein in abuses by *encomenderos*, and eventually they gained some successes. But whatever reforms they were able to achieve came far too late to prevent the kind of depopulation that practically emptied the Caribbean basin of its Native peoples. While epidemic disease was responsible for the destruction of the Caribbean's Taino, Arawak, and Carib populations, slavery certainly was as well.

Spanish oversight was nowhere near capable of protecting the isolated Lucayos. Enterprising *encomenderos* and slave traders from Hispaniola, Puerto Rico, and Cuba began to look at the islands as an outside supply of labor to be tapped when necessary. As far as they were concerned, there was very little else to be gained from such barren places. Small and sandy, they held very little potential for wealth extraction on their own, and so few Spaniards made any attempts to colonize them. As the Native populations on the already settled islands plummeted, on the other hand, the Lucayos grew in importance. They had people on them, in other words. As Peter Martyr remarked early in the sixteenth century, they "formerly abounded in various products" and were "very populous, while now they are deserted." The reason? "[L]arge numbers of the wretched islanders were transported to the gold-mines of Hispaniola" and other Caribbean islands after the original Natives on those islands were all "exterminated, exhausted by disease and famine, as well as by excessive labor." Friar Bartolomé de las Casas agreed. "Not a living soul remains today on any of the islands of the Bahamas," he wrote at mid-century. During a relatively brief period from 1509–1512, upward of forty thousand Lucayan Natives were torn from their homes, turning an entire island chain into an uninhabited Caribbean wasteland. Ironically, by the time de León received his commission to investigate "Bimini," as La Florida would become, there was no longer a human presence on the Bahamian island we know now as Bimini.[9]

The slaving that connected the Bahamas to La Florida was in no way confined to Caribbean islands. With Cuba's central location in the Caribbean, Governor Diego Velázquez de Cuéllar quickly turned west, to the Yucatan, in search of labor for that island's plantations. After settling in Peru in 1530 Spaniards raided the Pacific Coast of modern-day Nicaragua relentlessly for slaves, pulling over two hundred thousand humans from that region in the span of a decade.[10] The unfortunate history of the Bahamas is particularly relevant, however, because the relentless raiding of those islands was what eventually brought Spaniards to the shores of La Florida. America's very discovery, in short, was a product of slavery; the first Spaniards to lay eyes on the present-day states of both Florida and South Carolina were, in point of fact, slave raiders.[11]

Possibly the first, Diego Miruelo, sighted what he thought was a northern edge of the Bahamas a few years before Juan Ponce de León. He presumed it to be an extension of the island chain, when in fact it was most likely a part of peninsular Florida, if not one of the northernmost Keys. He did so by accident after being blown north from the Bahamas on a slaving expedition. Slavers soon followed Miruelo's path, seizing Natives from what was the southeastern coast of Florida and returning with them to Santo Domingo, where they disappeared from the records.[12] These first haphazard expeditions to the La Florida coastline were not made for the sake of exploration. They were made for the sake of slavery.

Juan Ponce de León was no doubt similarly interested in human cargo, even though he did not capture any on his own 1513 voyage. As a Puerto Rican *encomendero* who ran profitable mining, ranching, and agricultural enterprises at the expense of Native workers, he would have been just the sort of man to want to investigate such a new source of potential slaves. His ships, moreover, were manned by sailors and pilots familiar with the Bahamas because of their extensive experience raiding it for slaves. Everything about de León's 1513 voyage was wrong, as was what followed. Following de León's discovery, Diego Velázquez de Cuéllar, then the governor of Cuba, issued licenses directly authorizing slavers to target Bimini and whatever else was in the neighborhood. That might perhaps explain why Calusa warriors attacked Juan Ponce de León so viciously when he turned to La Florida in 1521.[13] By the time de León set out on his voyage of colonization, the Natives of southern peninsular Florida had already had their fill of Spaniards. And why not? Every single Spaniard they had seen to that point was probably there to steal them.

Not only was La Florida's discovery a by-product of Caribbean slavery, but its earliest history would have also included both the *encomienda* and the slave trade had de León succeeded in colonizing the region as he intended. This is evident in the 1512 *capitulación* that authorized de León's 1513 voyage of discovery, which included procedures for the "allotment" of Native peoples. Such an allotment would be made "by the person or persons who should be appointed by [the King], and in no other manner." De León was not to divvy up Native peoples himself, the Crown warned, yet there was a clear expectation that not only would he receive such a payment, but so would his men. Of the Indians that de León should find, they should be allotted "in accordance with the persons" that partook in the expedition, "and that this be observed and that the first discoverers be provided for before any other persons; and that all the preference that should conveniently be shown in this be given to them." In the second *capitulación*, the

King further stipulated that a version of the requirement be read. If the Natives rejected it, the solution was clear: "you can make war and seize them and carry them away for slaves."[14] De León was to develop La Florida along the lines of similarly violent Caribbean conquests, these *capitulaciónes* clearly dictated. One is left to wonder what La Florida's early history would have looked like had he repulsed the Calusa assault in 1521 and achieved his goal.

Perhaps the vague slaving licenses issued by Diego Velázquez de Cuéllar also help explain why, in 1514, there were reports of an expedition off the coast of modern-day South Carolina as well. Not only was the modern state of Florida first discovered by slave raiders, but perhaps so was much of the larger southern Atlantic coastline. Peter Martyr certainly thought so: it was slavery that brought Spaniards to "Chicora," or Carolinian stretch of La Florida, and again he drew connections to the pitiful Bahamas. As "anxious as hunters pursuing wild beasts through the mountains and swamps" the Spanish had hunted Natives through the Bahamas until there were literally none left, forcing plans to venture farther, to places not yet seen but certainly in existence. Hopefully, there they might find a few hideaway Caribs or Arawaks for the taking. The captains of the two ships that sailed from Hispaniola separately to do so were Francisco Gordillo and Pedro de Quejo (also spelled Quexo). The two were seasoned slavers on separate expeditions when they ran across each other somewhere near Andros Island. Joining forces, they hopped from island to island "but without finding the plunder, for their neighbours had already explored the archipelago and systematically depopulated it." Fearful of returning to Hispaniola empty handed, the men pressed onward, ultimately making landfall at the Santee River and Winyah Bay.[15] Like peninsular Florida, the history of the Lowcountry, from Georgia to North Carolina, was set into motion by Spaniards whose only goal was contributing to the Caribbean slave trade.

After reconnoitering the coast and finding it loaded with Natives, the two men began what was ostensibly a trading expedition. They enticed scores of Natives aboard the ships before promptly seizing potentially dozens of them. So it was in August of 1521 that "Quejo's ship put into the river at Santo Domingo with a cargo of sixty North American natives," as one historian put it, where they too disappear from the records. Before Ayllón set foot in either South Carolina or Georgia, and long, long before South Carolina was settled by the English as an enslaved outpost of the English Caribbean, South Carolina had already been defined by slavery.[16]

Perhaps it was the place, but perhaps it was the people, that pressed Ayllón to return to Chicora. He successfully lobbied for the rights to the new discovery, receiving a *capitulación* of sorts in 1523. It included rights to a large swath of land, fisheries, and pearl beds; Native trade; and the authorization to build a fort. Probably to Ayllón's dismay, however, it also included a clear moratorium on the allotment of Natives. Evidently the abuses of the early Caribbean *encomienda* system had altered the King's view of it so much by the second decade of the sixteenth century that La Florida would no longer be a place where the spoils of conquest included Native peoples. Only a few years earlier, de León would have enjoyed *encomienda* allotments for himself and his men in peninsular Florida. Ayllón was not to benefit likewise.[17]

Had either de León or Ayllón succeeded in their settlement plans, it is difficult to see how Native slavery—through either the inter-Caribbean slave trade or the *encomienda*—would not have come to define the American Southeast. Thankfully both settlements failed almost as soon as they landed. The exploitation and outright enslavement of Natives still crept across the stretches of La Florida, however, with both Narváez's and de Soto's entradas. Narváez's failures came too quickly for him to truly impose his will on Native Floridians. He did capture slaves outside of Apalachee, though, so it only stands to reason that had he been more successful and had he kept moving through the region, he would have continued to do so. Narváez, with a long and brutal history of Caribbean violence behind him, certainly would have had no qualms abusing Native peoples in La Florida, that much is certain. His counterpart in de Soto, also no stranger to enslavement either in Peru or Nicaragua, brought Native slavery home to the very stretches of La Florida during his entrada, dragging enslaved Natives with him through the entire American Southeast almost two centuries before the English would bring slavery to the colonies of Virginia, the Carolinas, or Georgia. De Soto relied so heavily on Native laborers that it would seem like if the entrada moved an inch at all, it was on the backs of the enslaved. While many times those laborers were given up to him voluntarily, as we will see in future chapters, he had absolutely no problem seizing Natives and enslaving them whenever the approach seemed more convenient.

The lives of those slaves appeared to be, in general, pretty short. Hundreds were enslaved at Napetuca, a community in northern peninsular Florida, after the warriors' unsuccessful bid to rescue their headmen, only to be summarily executed when they rose up again shortly after. Before that time, however, de Soto had them "all put in chains and on the day following were allotted among the Christians for their service," using a familiar Spanish terminology even though what he was doing was absolutely nothing like an *encomienda*. "Allotted" or not, these were slaves. Killing all those potential laborers, however, only created the need for more. Only days after the massacre, several of his cavalry fanned out in a neighboring town and captured scores more in raids that seemed designed particularly for the purpose of procuring slaves. Here, however, his men did not simply capture men. While the fate of Native women as sex slaves will be explored more fully in future chapters, it must be pointed out that what the chroniclers described about this raid in particular is the first direct American description of the sexual exploitation of enslaved women by their captors. One of the more insidious aspects of the Anglo-American institution of slavery in the Southeast—the systematic rape of enslaved women by plantation owners—really began in the Spanish sixteenth century, when de Soto's men stole women like they did in Napetuca "as well as in any other part where forays were made." One of de Soto's captains "selected one or two" for de Soto himself, one chronicler would write, then divvied the rest up among his men.[18]

The general treatment of those captured outside of Napetuca was described in great detail by one of de Soto's chroniclers. The captives were secured in chains and neck collars and were forced to carry the expedition's baggage, prepare food, and do whatever else "so fastened in this manner they could perform." Some, the source mentioned, escaped with their chains when they had the chance, killing whatever Spaniard was with them. Others tried to file the chains down with rocks. Some managed to escape, while those who were caught suffered terribly. They "paid for themselves and for those others, so that on another day they might not dare do likewise." The toll in lives rose quickly. By the time the entrada left Apalachee, months after arriving, most of the enslaved "being naked and in chains, died because of the hard life they suffered during that winter."[19]

De Soto's actions along the entire march seemed to fit this pattern. Far later in the expedition, a large group of bound Natives "whom the Christians were bringing in chains," were freed by the warriors at Mavila upon the outset of the battle. The laborers had carried Spanish equipment into the palisade when Tascalusa sprung his surprise attack. Rather than kill them, the Mavila warriors released the foreign Natives, hoping they would join the battle, which they did. The recently liberated slaves stole the Spanish supplies they had been forced to carry, including weapons, and joined in the assault against the Spaniards, wielding their own swords and lances against them. In their case many had been taken previously in an uprising at Coosa, seized, and "put in chains." A few of the town's leading men had been released on appeal from the Coosa headman, while "of the rest, each man took away as slaves those he had in chains, without allowing them to go to their lands." Some had run away in the night after filing their chains off. Others ran away in their chains. The last of them, alive at Mavila, were quick to take up arms when the opportunity presented itself. They fought alongside Mavila's men and women, strangers to them and possibly even enemies under other circumstances. Instead, most of them fought together and probably died together, Coosa's warriors dying at the hands of their abductors.[20]

The mentioning of such extensive physical restraints reveals that what de Soto had in mind was the most exploitative and abusive kind of slavery that would continue to tarnish the legacy of the American South for centuries. Only rarely in the most extreme gang systems of Anglo-American slavery were enslaved people literally chained together in such ways. According to the chronicles, however, hundreds of people at a time were shackled quite literally in crude iron chains and drug along with the expedition until, apparently, they dropped dead. Another chronicler mentioned an alternative he witnessed in peninsular Florida, at least with the women and young children. As soon as the women and children were far from their homes, hundreds of miles, "having become unmindful, they were taken along unbound, and served in that way, and in a very short time learned the language of the Christians." Clearly, Coosa's warriors had not "become unmindful" later in the entrada when they rose up at Mavila. Why would other Natives not flee as soon as they were loosed? Kidnapped and now isolated in a distant land, with the rest of their family members still in chains, there was no choice but to continue.[21]

While some were freed, far more were chained together permanently, leading one to wonder just how many iron chains de Soto carried with him. Apparently, it was a lot. One account from Georgia illustrates the expedition stopping at a river so broad that the best arm among them could not throw a rock across it. Perhaps that was the Okmulgee, Oconee, or Ogeechee River. The broad but slow-moving waterways would have been possible to cross, but they certainly are imposing. In order to guide rafts across this one, the men "took the chains in which they brought the Indians," joined them together to create one large chain, and were able to stretch it across the river to guide their rafts. Such a chain would have been possibly hundreds of feet long.[22]

The possibility of enslavement in La Florida is not without its own "what-if" alternative history, which came in the Carolina Piedmont. De Soto, always on the move in search of his next silver windfall, never established a settlement in La Florida. The closest he came was at Cofitachequi, where his men were smitten with both the quality of the land and its seemingly endless supply of high-quality freshwater pearls. This moment is the nearest La Florida came to the kind of long-term settlement that would have been based on the allotment of Native peoples—the reason the *encomienda* developed elsewhere. Not only could the land be made to produce exports, but the pearl beds could be worked with Native labor as well, as one of de Soto's chroniclers suggested. If the land was settled and the Natives "allotted in repartimiento," they could be made to produce more, higher-quality pearls, "worth their weight in gold." This would be the same engine of settlement that was populating the Caribbean, New Spain, and Peru with Spanish settlers even after the initial hopes of gold and silver faded. Carving up Cofitachequi could produce fine Spanish *haciendas*—it was perhaps the only way La Florida would generate wealth for the Crown. But pearls were not gold and pearls were not silver, and de Soto, seeking another treasure like "the lord of Peru," had "no wish to content himself with good land or with pearls."[23] With that, the expedition pushed on.

There are a few more intriguing nods to the future worthy of noting in de Soto's entrada. His men were the first Euro-American Southeasterners to exploit the dramatic ethnic diversity of the region to their benefit. By pitting Native peoples against each other, de Soto and his men were pioneering a tactic that would be mastered by the English more than a century later in South Carolina. It would become known as the period of the Indian slave trade, when Charleston merchants shipped tens of thousands of Natives out of the port of Charleston and into the British Caribbean. Where the British merchants used competing Native groups' desire for trade to whip up one ethnic group against another, de Soto used recently enslaved Natives from different regions as slave catchers and even executioners, which is precisely what he did in the Napetuca uprising. When the Napetuca warriors rose up the first time, they quickly scattered and hid in two nearby lakes. De Soto quickly turned to Natives from nearby Paracoxi to hunt them down. Whether the Paracoxi were along with the expedition as voluntary guides or slaves is not mentioned, but they seemed enthusiastic in their new role. They "went in swimming after them and pulled them out by their hair." And later, when the survivors of the first uprising revolted again, de Soto relied on these same Paracoxi warriors as his executioners. According to at least one chronicler, they were the ones to dispatch the recalcitrant Napetucas, shooting them full of arrows in the center of town.[24]

As one historian revealed, this approach to the Native Southeast was not particularly unique; Spanish authorities had previously suggested using such an approach to Native ethnic diversity in San Miguel de Guadalpe, along the

Georgia coast. Although Ayllón was denied *encomendero* status in his 1523 *capitulación*, according to Hoffman he was authorized to trade with Native peoples, a trade that evidently included slaves. He could trade for slaves not only for his Guadalpe settlement, but to be shipped to Hispaniola and either used by him on his own plantation or sold privately. So, while he was not allowed to directly enslave Natives himself, Ayllón's grant revealed that Spaniards were already considering the possibility that Chicora's Native people practiced slavery themselves, and that it was perfectly fine to dispose of a person who had already been legally enslaved or condemned according to local custom. As long as they had been captured and enslaved by other Native peoples, their enslaved status would not be questioned, and they could be bought and sold accordingly. That was certainly the case in the Native Southeast, as Charleston merchants would come to realize late in the seventeenth century. Ayllón obviously failed to develop Guadalpe, the failure of which postponed for more than a century the horrific internecine warfare that would grip the colonial Southeast.[25]

Notes

1. Reséndez, *The Other Slavery*, 13-26; Lantigua, *Infidels and Empires*, 56; Kamen, *Empire*, 43, 83, 85.
2. Elliott, *Empires*, 39-41; Reséndez, *The Other Slavery*, 35-36; Bushnell, *Situado and Sabana*, 30-31; Schwaller, *The History of the Catholic Church*, 39; Adorno, "The Polemics of Possession," 22-23.
3. Elliott, *Empires*, 39-41; Restall, *Seven Myths*, 35.
4. Elliott, *Empires*, 40; Reséndez, *The Other Slavery*, 46-48; Schwaller, *The History of the Catholic Church*, 42-46; Bushnell, *Situado and Sabana*, 30-31; Adorno, "The Polemics of Possession," 34.
5. Reséndez, *The Other Slavery*, 28-39; Turner, "Juan Ponce de León," 4; Kamen, *Empire*, 124.
6. Landers, *Black Society*, 12; Adorno, "The Polemics of Possession," 23; Sale, *The Conquest of Paradise*, 130-136.
7. Martyr, *De Orbe Novo, Volume 2*, 271-272.
8. Martyr, *De Orbe Novo, Volume 2*, 271.
9. Martyr, *De Orbe Novo, Volume 2*, 254-255; Griffin and Pagden, eds., *A Short Account*, 11; Reséndez, *The Other Slavery*, 40-45; Turner, "Juan Ponce de León," 4, 8; Weddle, *Spanish Sea*, 40; Kamen, *Empire*, 124.
10. Weddle, *Spanish Sea*, 55-57; Kamen, *Empire*, 43, 83, 85, 124.
11. As Charles Hudson put it, "the principal impetus for the Spaniards' exploration to the north of their Caribbean colonies was their need for slave labor." See Hudson, *Knights of Spain*, 32; Hoffman, *Florida's Frontiers*, 22.
12. Turner, "Juan Ponce de León," 5.
13. Turner, "Juan Ponce de León," 8, 31.

14. Davis, "Ponce de León's First Voyage," 11; Davis, "Ponce de León's Second Voyage," 54.

15. Martyr, *De Orbe Novo, Volume 2*, 255-256; Hoffman, *A New Andalucia*, 4-9.

16. Hoffman, *A New Andalucia*, 4-9; Kamen, *Empire*, 83, 85, 124; Weber, *The Spanish Frontier*, 35-36.

17. Hoffman, *A New Andalucia*, 34, 36-38.

18. "The Account by a Gentleman from Elvas," in Clayton, Knight, and Moore, eds., *The De Soto Chronicles*, 68-70.

19. "The Account by a Gentleman from Elvas," in Clayton, Knight, and Moore, eds., *The De Soto Chronicles*, 68-70, 74.

20. "The Account by a Gentleman from Elvas," in Clayton, Knight, and Moore, eds., *The De Soto Chronicles*, 93, 100.

21. "The Account by a Gentleman from Elvas," in Clayton, Knight, and Moore, eds., *The De Soto Chronicles*, 70, 74.

22. "Account of the Northern Conquest," in Clayton, Knight, and Moore, eds., *The De Soto Chronicles*, 269.

23. "The Account by a Gentleman from Elvas," in Clayton, Knight, and Moore, eds., *The De Soto Chronicles*, 83-84.

24. "The Account by a Gentleman from Elvas," in Clayton, Knight, and Moore, eds., *The De Soto Chronicles*, 68-69.

25. Hoffman, *A New Andalucia*, 39.

Slaves, Slavers, and Conquistadores

The collapse of the Caribbean's Native populations followed a decades-long process of violence, disease, and exploitation. The initial violence of island conquest gave way to slavery and the *encomienda*, which in turn accelerated the damage caused by epidemic disease. This was all an "incalculable disaster," in the words of one historian, which in turn led to another equally devastating tragedy—the eventual importation of African labor and the beginning of the Atlantic slave trade.[1]

The first Africans crossed unwillingly into the Caribbean as early as with Columbus, yet it was not until later in the first decade of the sixteenth century when Spanish authorities turned to African laborers to replace Native ones. In 1510 Ferdinand authorized slaves to be shipped directly to Hispaniola for that purpose, setting an important precedent, even though, in that moment, there was nothing particularly groundbreaking about such a request. At that time, the slaves were not coming directly from West Africa, but from Spain. Since the fall of the Islamic kingdoms in the Iberian Peninsula at the conclusion of the *Reconquista*, slaves of North African origins were already laboring in Spain, and particularly in the southern portion. Transferring them from there to Spanish possessions in the New World was not a particularly difficult step for the Crown to take. If they were servants in the south of Spain they probably already spoke Spanish, and were probably already Christianized; Ferdinand would not have to worry about their importation challenging the developing Church. Slavery in the Caribbean, at least in its very first years, was simply an extension of a system of servitude to which Spaniards were already accustomed.[2]

That changed dramatically a few years later when Charles V sold a multiyear contract to Genoese Bankers for the regular importation of slaves to the Caribbean. In time it would come to be known as the *asiento*—the foundation of the first Atlantic slave trade. Thousands of enslaved Africans a year were transported to the islands as well as to Mexico, Peru, Panama, and Chile. Competing figures suggest that, by the end of the sixteenth century, anywhere from 75,000 to double that number of enslaved West Africans had been sent to Spanish America. Portuguese traders recently allied to the Spanish Crown in 1580 soon owned the *asiento*, and they greatly enlarged it. As they established trading connections down the west coast of Africa, these traders soon dominated all aspects of the region's commerce, including the slave trade, from massive trading castles like the notorious El Mina castle on the Gold Coast. From there into the Caribbean, they imported over a quarter million more Africans over the next fifty years; by the end of the seventeenth century, the combined Spanish-Portuguese trade resulted in the importation of close to a half million enslaved West Africans into all corners of the Spanish New World.[3]

While the British, French, and Dutch slave trade into the Caribbean would eclipse these numbers, they were all second comers, enlarging upon a trade system pioneered by the Spanish and Portuguese. After all, the Dutch privateers that sold the first Africans to Virginians in 1619 only had them on board because they had just stolen them from a Portuguese slave ship destined for Vera Cruz—a telling glimpse indeed into a thriving slave trade that was, by 1619, well over a century old. By that time Spanish authorities had spread African laborers across the Americas, slowly replacing Native workers as they disappeared. Slaves worked silver mines in Peru and Zacatecas. They were laborers, artisans, and household servants in urban centers like Lima and Mexico City. In some of those cities the percentage of Africans would approach one quarter of the entire population. In the countryside, enslaved Africans ranched on *haciendas*, worked in textile mills, and particularly in the Caribbean, labored on sugarcane, tobacco, and cacao plantations, the first of which were all Spanish.[4]

This aspect of Spanish slavery would be familiar to the British and French sugarcane plantation owners that would eventually dominate the Caribbean—it was slavery in its most exploitative and dehumanizing sense. At the same time, however, the African presence in the New World was also much more complicated than it would be in seventeenth-century Virginia or eighteenth-century South Carolina. One of the fundamental differences between the cultures was the centrality of the Catholic Church in Spanish society, which claimed the souls of Christianized slaves and which at times could serve as a mitigating factor in their servitude. Another was the legal redress slaves were theoretically capable of seeking, even if in practice that was a rarity in the Caribbean or in New Spain. Even as slaves, men and women were also vassals unto the Spanish Crown, and by the colonization of the Americas, the Crown had developed a legal system capable of dealing with such servitude. It, like so many other aspects of Spanish society, was crafted over hundreds of years of the *Reconquista*. The *Siete Partidas*, a thirteenth-century Iberian slave code, was that system, and in theory it guaranteed basic rights to the enslaved, including the right to marry and the right to some sort of property. It protected slaves from an abusive master, and even set forth conditions for the gaining of freedom through purchase or through service. These supposed rights were certainly hard to exercise in the Caribbean countryside or the silver mines of New Spain, and most slaves would never be in any position to act on such theoretical legal maxims. Yet there is plenty of evidence of lawsuits to suggest that many did. Between the Catholic Church and the Crown, there was at least a sliver of wiggle room available to the enslaved to assert their humanity, both of which appear to be the product of a long history of servitude that already existed in the Iberian Peninsula.[5]

Importantly, Afro-Spanish history was also far longer and more complicated than it was for the British, another legacy of the *Reconquista* but also of simple geographic proximity. Spaniards were used to seeing Africans, and Spanish culture had plenty of North African influences. Southern Spanish cities like Jerez, Cádiz, Valencia, or Barcelona were multi-ethnic, multiracial places with high African populations, both slave and free. Many enslaved laborers lived independently of their masters, comingling with lower-class beggars of all colors. Meanwhile, a small black middle class worked port and labor jobs, belonged to their own social and religious orders, and lived in the cities' ethnic enclaves. Whatever their position in society, Africans were a visible part of Spanish life and culture.[6]

That system was transported from the docks of Seville and Cádiz to the Caribbean in the very earliest years of colonization. Africans were present in almost every major Spanish campaign of subjugation in the New World, either as slaves of the conquistadores or as armed participants in conquest who came over as free people. They were with Vasco Núñez de Balboa when he claimed the Pacific Ocean, writes one historian, "with Pedrarias Dávila when he colonized Panama, with Cortés when he marched to Tenochtitlan, with Álvarado when he entered Guatemala." Even when enslaved, many African men filled "armed auxiliary" roles that were at times critical to the success of an expedition, often blurring the lines between free and unfree. That was particularly so in the dangerous and chaotic Caribbean. Spaniards often brought armed African men to assist them with the conquest of island Natives, as Ovando did in Hispaniola, as de León did in Puerto Rico, and as Cuéllar did in Cuba. Many more belonged to local militias in the Caribbean as well as on the mainlands, protecting their settlements from pirates and Native uprisings.[7]

Neither was it uncommon for freed people of color to travel to the New World on their own, hoping that participation in conquest would bring them their own riches. Some rose to the rank of conquistador, and a precious few would earn the title *encomendero*, becoming in essence the owners of Native slaves themselves. In South America there was Juan Valiente, "a hero of the conquest of Chile, who served with Álvarado, Almagro and Valdivia, became an *encomendero* in 1550 and died in battle against the Araucanians in 1553."[8]

The Caribbean had its own African adventurer of this description—Juan Garrido—whose history is intertwined with that of La Florida. According to his short autobiographical sketch, he described himself as "Juan Garrido, black in color," who in 1540 was a resident of Mexico City with a wife and three children. Perhaps he was exceptionally good looking, for his name translated into English would have meant something like "Handsome John." That might have nothing to do with it at all, on the other hand, as there is also an excellent chance Garrido may have come across the Atlantic as the slave of a Pedro Garrido. It was common for enslaved people to take the surname of their masters, and Pedro Garrido's name shows up in the earliest emigration records.

Before that time Garrido, a man of West African birth, somehow made it to Portugal, either doing so freely or having been sold as a slave to Portuguese traders. According to Garrido himself, he was Christianized in Lisbon before making his way west into Castile. He would have done so right after the conclusion of the *Reconquista*, an incredible time to be in the south of Spain, even for a black man. If he was enslaved then, by the time he had left Seville, seven years later, there was a good chance he was free. Either way, departing Seville he made his way to Santo Domingo not long after Ovando's arrival, "where he remained an equal length of time. From there he visited other islands, and then went to San Juan de Puerto Rico, where he spent much time, after which he came to New Spain." According to another version of his story, Garrido "went to discover and pacify" Puerto Rico, and then Cuba. If his intrigues in the Caribbean were not enough, in New Spain, Garrido traveled with Cortés, survived the Noche Triste assault on the Spanish invaders, and partook in the siege and fall of Tenochtitlan. Cortés gave him land in newly founded Mexico City, upon which it is suggested he was the first man in all of New Spain to plant wheat. He followed Cortés to the Baja peninsula before returning to the city. By the time he died mid-century, Garrido had lived quite a life.[9]

For a man of such potentially incredible significance, very little else about Garrido's life has been easy to determine, and particularly the earlier Caribbean portion, which is only paid passing reference. His arrival in Santo Domingo took place sometime in 1502 or 1503. As such he was one of the very first black men to arrive anywhere in the New World, landing at a time before Spaniards had begun importing African slaves to work island plantations. Juan Ponce de León took several armed Africans with him from Hispaniola to Puerto Rico in 1508, and Diego de Velázquez de Cuéllar took more with him to Cuba in 1511. Evidently, Garrido was among both of those expeditions, and according to one account he may have participated in the conquest of and enslavement of Natives in Dominica and Guadalupe as well. As a resident of Hispaniola and Puerto Rico, Garrido had participated in some of the earliest and most violent of Spain's Caribbean conquests.[10]

The most intriguing chapter to Juan Garrido's life is usually described later, in New Spain, which certainly must have been terrifying to behold in all of its blood and horror. For many his most significant contributions to the development of the New World was the wheat. Yet Garrido is also acknowledged as being a member of several of de León's slaving expeditions throughout the Caribbean and is credited with being aboard one of his ships on the 1513 cruise that named La Florida.[11] What is but a side note in a larger career that moved back into Central America is for La Florida a central paragraph in its very origin story. There is a possibility, although we certainly will never know, that one of the very first Old World men to lay eyes on what is now the United States of America—and certainly one of the first to ever set foot on what would be the United States—might very well have been a black man. According to some accounts he was also with de León's 1521 settlement attempt, which if correct meant he definitely would have physically stepped foot in La Florida.[12]

Garrido only moved on to Central Mexico and Cortés after his attempts at La Florida came to an unceremonious end, just as Juan Ponce de León's life had. Just over an entire century before the first Africans set foot in Virginia, consigned as property, an African man with a very different story had his toes in the sand in what would be the United States, and as such can claim a role in both the discovery and naming of Spanish La Florida. More incredible yet, this African man did so not as a slave but as a slaver, and as a seasoned veteran of island conquest. Had de León succeeded in 1521, one of America's founders would have been a black conquistador.

Decades later another man of African descent set new path-finding records in La Florida. In 1536 a small group of Spaniards moving north from modern Mexico happened to run across "a bearded and sunburnt white man," in the words of one historian, "accompanied by a burly black man, in the company of eleven Indians." The overly tanned one was none other than Álvar Núñez Cabeza de Vaca, wandering through the future American Southwest after a very, very long walk. The "burly black man" at his side, of course, was Esteban. He was one of the four men, out of hundreds, that actually survived the Narváez expedition. He walked into Mexico City having come ashore in North America on the southwest coast of Florida almost a decade earlier. Tampa to Mexico City—all one needs do is glance at a map of the North American continent to realize just how long of a walk that is. Over the course of his eight-year trek, wandering the Gulf Coast, Estevanico did much more than struggle to survive in a foreign and hostile land. He crisscrossed five modern Gulf Coast states and was among the first non-Natives to lay eyes on, to say nothing of actually cross, the mighty Mississippi. Just as Juan Garrido might have been the first non-Native to step foot in America, one of its first true explorers was also black. Centuries before Lewis and Clark trekked west, there was Esteban the Moor.[13]

Something very different but no less significant took place in San Miguel de Guadalpe, which as we now know was in modern-day Georgia. Records of the failed settlement are few and far between, but we know with certainty that the Africans taken there by Ayllón from Hispaniola were not free men but slaves, and they were put to work in the new colony, building homes while the Spaniards jostled for power in the wake of Ayllón's death. Natives killed a few Spaniards that strayed too far from the settlement, spreading chaos, and several groups of ambitious Spaniards, competing for leadership, were soon plotting to assassinate each other. When the night arrived on which "they were going to put into effect their bad intentions, it happened that some blacks set fire" to one of the leading men's houses "by their own minds," "on their own," or "of their own accord," depending on the translation. The flames caused even more chaos. A group of disaffected Spaniards put the fires out while the competing leadership groups went back to going about trying to kill each other. Perhaps this was the moment that broke what remained of San Miguel de Guadalpe.[14]

Unfortunately there is literally no other mention of the fire, the uprising, or the fate of the perpetrators, leaving "by their own minds," "on their own," or "of their own accord" to describe what appears to be the first slave rebellion anywhere in what would be the United States of America—more than two centuries before the Stono Rebellion exploded upon Charleston and just under a century before slaves had even landed in the British world at all. What do we know about these revolutionaries? Almost nothing. Considering the raw and exploratory nature of Ayllón's expedition, the slaves in San Miguel de Guadalpe were probably house servants if not skilled tradesmen, rather than unskilled field slaves. There would be no need for the latter kind of laborers until long after the colony was up and running. And they would have been taken to La Florida from the Caribbean, not directly from Africa. Historian Paul Hoffman, whose work on Guadalpe is the most extensive and detailed, suggested that for seasoned slaves like those to rebel in such a way, the situation had to have been pretty bad indeed.[15] That is not difficult to imagine: isolated on an inhospitable Lowcountry coastline the enslaved men would have spent their days building houses in swamps, fighting off lurking Natives, and enduring bickering Spaniards. Perhaps they were aligned with one of the antagonists in the uprising that was already taking place among the Spanish survivors. Perhaps they simply used the chaos of the situation to assert their own autonomy. The lack of evidence means we will never know exactly how the events of that night transpired. It is not difficult to picture, however, Ayllón's unnamed slaves dealing Guadalpe its death blow.

The failure of this La Florida expedition included not only the first slave revolt, but perhaps also the first instances of slave flight and marronage in North America. The slaves that were at Guadalpe were almost certainly still alive at the conclusion of the chaotic stretch of Native attacks, fire, and Spanish intrigue that led to its abandonment. They do not, however, seem to be among those who arrived back on Hispaniola. Instead, they are supposed to have fled into the Georgia woods, where they would have ended up living with the native Guale people. There is of course no direct evidence of any of this either. Nevertheless, the flight of slaves under similar circumstances was already taking place on Caribbean Islands like Hispaniola, Cuba, and Jamaica. Slaves, fleeing into remote wooded regions often still partially controlled by Natives, created what historians have called maroon communities, from the Spanish word *cimarrone*, or runaway. They were partially self-sufficient places where slaves could exert at least some sort of autonomy.[16] The sheer isolation of Guadalpe and the chaos of its collapse certainly would have provided plenty of opportunity for escape, and there was little incentive for the Africans to board boats back to Hispaniola, where they would have at best returned to their lives of servitude and at worst would have been executed for their rebellious actions. Instead, all indications are that Guadalpe's enslaved workers stayed in La Florida, setting into motion North America's long history of slave resistance in the Southeast.

The proceeding entrada years are filled with similar accounts of African auxiliaries, ranging from soldiers to slaves. Their tales are as vague as they are potentially groundbreaking. Narváez brought at least one Christian African man along in his expedition, who walked inland from the expedition with a Greek man, Doroteo Teodoro, and the two were never heard from again.[17] De Soto personally owned over a half-dozen slaves at the time of his death, of both Native and African descent.[18] He brought an undetermined number of Africans with him to La Florida, ranging all the way up in number to fifty. At least one man, Bernaldo, accompanied the expedition as a free man and survived it, mirroring Esteban's harrowing journey of a decade previous. He, too, would walk into Mexico City having traversed almost the entire American Southeast. His story would have been remarkable on its own, in other words, had it not been told already. There were at the very least a half-dozen enslaved Africans in the army as well, because at least that many departed the expedition for one reason or another. A "Negro named Robles" fell ill and was left in the care of the headman of Coosa, although the Spanish made clear he was no deserter. He was "a very good Christian and a good slave," but evidently very sick, and was left with a local chieftain to heal. On the other hand, there was "Gómez, a very shrewd black man," who disappeared when the army moved through the Appalachians. It was rumored that he had a romantic connection with the Lady of Cofitachequi and had assisted in her escape. De la Vega described three other enslaved men as fleeing during the same stretch. "Two were Negroes," meaning of West African origin, and the other was a Berber Moor. The fleeing of the first two "caused surprise because they were regarded as good Christians and friends of their master." The treacherous action of the Berber, on the other hand, was not surprising at all, "but rather confirmed the opinion that they had always had of him, as he was very bad in every respect." Just a bit farther along another "very shrewd black man who was called Joan Vizcaíno," soon went missing.[19]

In the instance of the Appalachian runaways, it appeared to the chronicler Gracilaso de la Vega that the men fled the expedition in order to remain among the Natives, and even more specifically, to remain with the Native women. Gracilaso was by far the most imaginative and free of the chroniclers, to say the least, so it is difficult to take his words literally. To the extent to which de la Vega's suspicions were correct, however, these desertions might be notable for expanding North America's African firsts. At the very least, these are more instances of slave runaways and marronage in what would become the American South. If the men really had absconded because of women, then with their flight also began the long and entangled history of African-Native relations in the slave South that threatened the growth of chattel slavery, confounding contemporaries and fascinating modern historians ever since.

One particularly vibrant subfield in the study of American slavery, indeed, deals specifically with how Natives and the enslaved coexisted and even intermarried, challenging the racial hierarchy that Euro-Americans were constructing in the enslaved South. As it turns out, that history, too, goes back much further than previously thought—all the way back to de Soto, and even perhaps Ayllón.

Years later, Pedro Menéndez de Avilés encountered both African men and women living among the Calusa and Ais in coastal South Florida. The victims of shipwrecks upward of a decade previous, they were taken captive along with surviving Spaniards. A black man by the name of Luis and a black woman by the name of Juanilla helped Menéndez ransom many of the captives, both black and white, and were soon acting officially as interpreters. They were enticed back to the Spanish camp, but that was not always the case. Some of the captives, again both black and white, chose to stay, so intertwined were they in their new Native homes, probably with Native spouses and with Native children. Permanent African American settlement in the southern edges of La Florida, it turns out, predated permanent European settlement there.[20]

The African men on de Soto's entrada were probably slaves and laborers, as they were at Guadalpe. More of them served as craftsmen in the two colonization attempts that followed, both of which appeared to depend on large numbers of African servants. Their presence also demonstrates the complicated racial dynamic that Spaniards brought with them to La Florida. First was the 1558 Tristán de Luna attempt to settle Pensacola. Within the massive enterprise Viceroy Don Luis de Velasco disparaged what he called a "*canaille*" of tagalongs. The word could be directly translated as a pack of dogs and appeared to be an unflattering reference to the dregs, the masses, or the rabble of society. For Velasco they were the huge number of "half breeds, mulattoes, and Indians" that were accompanying the expedition, who "will serve no purpose save to put the camp in confusion and eat up the supplies." Apparently, there were quite a few of them in a contingent of craftsmen and laborers that was almost twice the size of the expedition's soldiery. Along with the five hundred soldiers were eight hundred additional colonists and servants, including "married Spanish women, negro men and women servants, other servants," and Natives. In this case, as was presumed in Guadalpe, the Africans that came in the expedition were almost certainly slaves, and either house servants or craftsmen that would have helped physically build the colony out of nothing.[21] From the earliest days of Spanish expansion into the Caribbean, to the varied attempts made by several would-be colonizers to establish La Florida, African men and women were there from the beginning.

Notes

1. Kamen, *Empire*, 83.

2. Elliott, *Empires*, 99; Hazlewood, *The Queen's Slave Trader*, 40-41.

3. Elliott, *Empires*, 99-102; Kamen, *Empire*, 135-140; Hazlewood, *The Queen's Slave Trader*, 40-45.

4. Elliott, *Empires*, 100-101.

5. Elliott, *Empires*, 106-107; Landers, *Black Society*, 7-8; Landers, "Gracia Real de Santa Teresa de Mose," 11-12; Twinam, *Purchasing Whiteness*, 84-90.

6. Landers, *Black Society*, 8-9.

7. Kamen, *Empire*, 138-139; Restall, "Black Conquistadors," 176; Vinson and Restall, "Black Soldiers, Native Soldiers," 18-19; Elliott, *Empires of the Atlantic World*, 106-109; Wood, *Black Majority*, 4-5.

8. Kamen, *Empire*, 138-139; Gerhard, "A Black Conquistador," 451.

9. Gerhard, "A Black Conquistador," 452; Restall, "Black Conquistadors," 171-178; Vinson and Restall, "Black Soldiers, Native Soldiers," 18-19.

10. Restall, "Black Conquistadors," 176-177.

11. Gerhard, "A Black Conquistador," 452; Restall, "Black Conquistadors," 171-178; Landers, *Black Society*, 10-12; Rivers, *Slavery in Florida*, 2. According to Landers and Rivers, Garrido was not alone on this voyage, as other African men, including one by the name of Juan Gonzalez Ponce de León, were also known to be working with Juan Ponce de León.

12. Landers, *Black Society*, 12.

13. Kamen, *Empire*, 245; Weber, *The Spanish Frontier*, 44.

14. Hoffman, *A New Andalucia*, 78; Landers, "Africans and Native Americans," 54-55. The original reads "siquióse que unos negros pegaron fuego a la casa del Ginés por su propio sesso dessos esclavos." Oviedo, *Historia*, 3: 629. There is a translation in Morris, *Yes, Lord*, 39.

15. Hoffman, *A New Andalucia*, 78; Herrick, *Esteban*, 45; Landers, "Africans and Native Americans," 54-55.

16. See, for instance, Landers, *Black Society*, 13; Wood, *Black Majority*, 4. For related studies of marronage see Helg and Vernaug, *Slave No More*, 43-63.

17. Adorno and Pautz, eds., *The Narrative of Cabeza de Vaca*, 78.

18. "Inventory," in Clayton, Knight, and Moore, eds., *The De Soto Chronicles*, 490-491.

19. Kamen, *Empire*, 138-139; Hudson et al., "The Hernando de Soto Expedition," 75; "Account of the Northern Conquest," in Clayton, Knight, and Moore, eds., *The De Soto Chronicles*, 282, 285; "La Florida," in Clayton, Knight, and Moore, eds., *The De Soto Chronicles*, 2: 315, 326; Corkran, *The Creek Frontier*, 46; Landers, *Black Society*, 13-14.

20. Landers, *Black Society*, 14-15; Landers, "Africans and Native Americans," 55-56; Rivers, *Slavery in Florida*, 3.

21. Priestly, ed., *The Luna Papers*, 1: 55, 285; Clavin, *Aiming for Pensacola*, 11; Weddle, *Spanish Sea*, 262.

PEDRO MENENDEZ DE AVILES.
Natural de Avilés en Asturias, Comendador
de la orden de Santiago, Conquistador de la Flo
rida, nombrado Gral. de la Armada contra Inglaterra.
Murió en Santander A°. 1574. á los 55. de edad.

PHOTO 2.1. Pedro Menéndez de Avilés, Knight of the Order of Santiago This portrait of Pedro Menéndez de Avilés was displayed in the Smithsonian Institution's National Portrait Gallery. In it, the La Florida *adelantado* is displaying the Cross of Santiago prominently.

PEDRO MENÉNDEZ DE AVILÉS / JOSEF CAMARON LO DIBO; FRANCO. DE PAULA MARTI LO GRABO ANO 1791. CONTROL NUMBER 90716344. LIBRARY OF CONGRESS.

PHOTO 2.2. *La Matanza*
This eighteenth-century take on the 1565 *La Matanza* depicts Jean Ribault kneeling before a Spaniard, presumably Pedro Menéndez de Avilés, while Spanish soldiers massacre Ribault's forces in the background.
NAAUKEURIGE VERSAMELING DER GEDENK-WAARDIGSTE ZEE EN LAND-REYSEN NA OOST EN WEST-INDIËN ... RECORD NUMBER 08984-195. JOHN CARTER BROWN LIBRARY—BROWN UNIVERSITY.

PHOTO 2.3. Spanish Slavery in the Caribbean
Among the earliest depictions of New World slavery, Indigenous slaves mine gold and dump gold ore in front of a Spanish conquistador.
"NIGRITAE IN SCRUTANDIS VENIS METALLICIS..." *[AMERICA. PT 5. LATIN] AMERICAE PARS QUINTA NOBILIS & ADMIRATIONE PLENA HIERONYMI BEZONI MEDIOLANENSIS SECUNDAE SETIONIS HISPANORUM* ... RECORD NUMBER 34724-2. JOHN CARTER BROWN LIBRARY—BROWN UNIVERSITY.

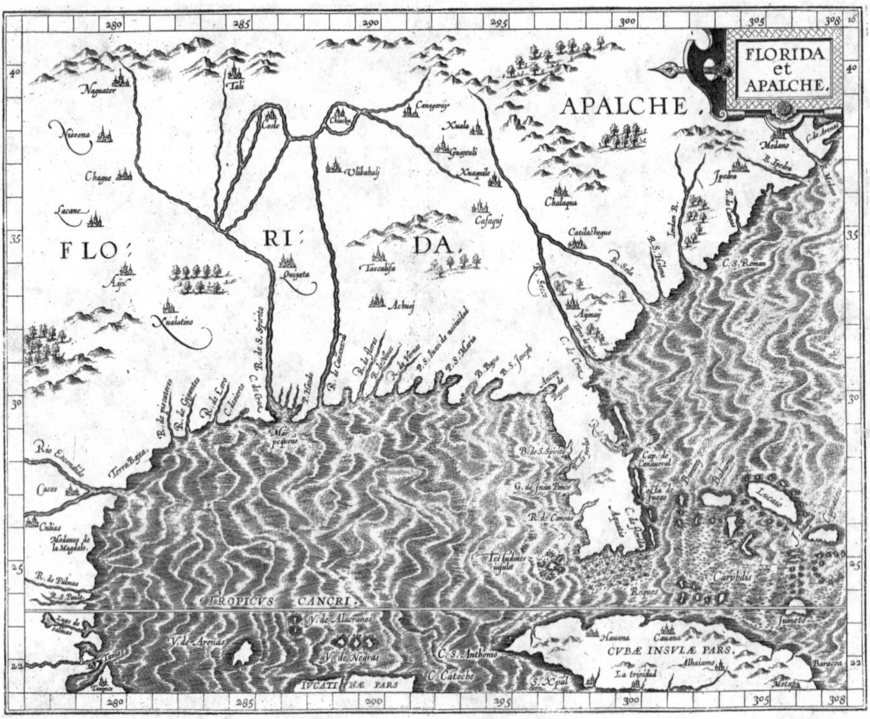

PHOTO 2.4. Florida and the Lucayos

In this 1597 map, the Florida peninsula sits just west of "Biminy," and "Lucayo," demonstrating La Florida's proximity to the modern Bahamas and the reason for its first exploration by Spanish Caribbean slavers.

"FLORIDA ET APALACHE." LOUVAIN, 1597. CALL NUMBER 71 1597. BEINECKE RARE BOOK AND MANUSCRIPT LIBRARY—YALE UNIVERSITY.

III. TRANSFORMATIONS

5 The Mississippian Encounter

Over the course of only a few weeks in 1540 the men of Hernándo de Soto's expedition logged hundreds of miles between the Mississippian chiefdoms of Apalachee, in modern-day Florida, and Cofitachequi, in modern-day South Carolina. It was a fast but otherwise unexceptional trek. It was remarkably peaceful, actually, by the standards of the rest of the expedition. Still, outside of Ochese, de Soto snatched up a group of Native men and women, which his advanced guard, mounted on horses, overtook on the trail. Others plunged into a nearby river in order to escape. Normally, de Soto would keep the prisoners as slaves and march them probably to death, as he had done plenty of times already in the past. This time, however, he interrogated them only about any nearby foodstuffs. His men were starving, and so "they would make this exaction and no other on the road." When the Natives responded plainly that their people would have no problem providing whatever de Soto's men needed, the Spanish tone lightened. It certainly was a more pleasant exchange than had taken place in Apalachee. More important were his men, who badly needed the rest, and the relative peace and quiet they enjoyed in Georgia was welcomed by everyone.

Ochese's chieftain met with de Soto soon after and explained the marvel and fear he shared with many of his people. "Things which seldom happen cause wonder," he explained, and what he and his people were seeing now was definitely a first. "Therefore, what must the sight of your Lordship and your men, whom we have never seen, be to me and mine." Not just Gracilaso de la Vega but several chroniclers made note of this exchange, so perhaps it actually happened this way. While the wording was obviously embellished by the chroniclers, the headman's wonderment is certainly believable. De Soto's men came with "great haste and fury," and "on animals so fierce," referring to the men's horses. Nothing like these strange and terrifying warriors, clad in steel and mounted on huge beasts, had ever been seen before. Neither the horses nor the steel. "It was a thing so new and caused such terror and fear in our minds" that the chief and his men directly rode out to meet the Spaniards, to see things for themselves and offer the town's services. De Soto would face no opposition from these people. Seeing the Natives so cowed continued to put the Spaniards at ease, which boded well for Ochese. "On hearing the reasonable replies of the Indians, the governor, confiding in them and seeing that he could deal with them better by kindness than by force, ordered that they be released immediately and entertained and treated like friends."

Food, laborers, and even women secured, the army enjoyed a downright pleasant march through Ochese. "We spent five or six days passing through this province," went one account, "where we were well served by the Indians, from the little that they had." What little they had, of course, was all of their corn, which the community was built upon and which the chieftain gave freely, as well as whatever wild foods his people had on hand. The same was done at Altamaha, then Ocute, the Cofaqui, and Patofa. Altamaha was "well populated with Indians, and they all served us," both in feeding de Soto's men and producing countless laborers to carry the expedition's gear, all of which de Soto would have forced the chieftain to give had he refused. From there the men marched onward, collecting hundreds more Native laborers from each of the proceeding communities. Leaving Patofa, de Soto racked up more guides and, according to one account, upward of eight hundred more laborers and four days' worth of corn.

Unfortunately for his men, the next stretch, moving through the Savannah River basin and across the modern-day state boundary between Georgia and South Carolina, was much worse. It was a barren stretch of territory without corn or a sizeable community to provide aid, a purposefully constructed frontier designed to separate politically autonomous chiefdoms that were clearly not on friendly terms. This was a politically complex place, which did not bode well either for de Soto and his starving men. For days there the men were "not without great conflict and hardship, and the horses without any food, and they and their owners dying of hunger." The army's supply of corn ran out in the middle of nowhere and de Soto released the Cofaqui and Patofa laborers because his men could not feed them and they could not feed themselves. De Soto ordered his men to butcher some of the pigs they had brought with them to survive, boiling the meat and eating it with nothing else. The slaughter of the pigs, brought along as a last resort, was not a good sign.

With the men near starvation a scouting party returned with the most glorious of news. Scouts had spread out and some of them came back with reports that, nearby, they found a small village of a few hundred Natives. Although it was small, it was loaded with food—another Mississippian chiefdom structured around corn agriculture. There the men swarmed it like locusts, consuming what one chronicler described as several tons of corn, "and many mulberry trees loaded with mulberries, and some other small fruit." The men affectionately named the town "Succor," after the assistance its corn stores provided them in such a time of need. After stripping the town bare, they moved on. Picking up the pace, they made it to Cofitachequi shortly after, ending the harrowing Georgia Stretch and stripping an entire stretch of Mississippian communities of their men, their women, and their food.[1]

This second look at Hernando de Soto's "Georgia Stretch" returns us once more to the earliest days of La Florida contact and colonization to open a new section, "Transformations," which focuses on the impact made by Spaniards on the American Southeast. The Georgia Stretch was in one way rather exceptional, considering how most of the de Soto expedition went. It was way too peaceful. Most of the time relations between Spaniards and their Native hosts were far more confrontational. At the other end of the spectrum of violence were Spanish actions at Napetuca and Mavila, two separate communities on separate ends of the entrada, which were both more or less obliterated by de Soto and his men. If these two sets of experiences mark extremes along a spectrum of violence, then most interactions took place somewhere in between. They were sometimes violent, but also always coercive, exploitative, and ultimately transformative for the Native population.

Even the remarkably peaceful nature of the Georgia Stretch reveals the myriad everyday pressures these earliest days of Spanish colonialism placed on Native communities. De Soto got through Georgia quickly and entered Cofitachequi peacefully; nevertheless, his entrada was still influencing the region's Native peoples in ways that would have lasting—and mostly devastating—consequences. Within a generation of expeditions like de Soto's, many of those places were undergoing dramatic transitions. Almost every one of them would ultimately cease to exist, as de Soto would have seen them anyway. The oldest and most obvious explanation for that destruction was the epidemic disease Spaniards spread as they came in contact with Natives. But epidemic disease cannot account entirely for such demographic reorganization. Other times the causes were more subtle.

The seizure of workers and the systematic theft of a community's food stores weakened already vulnerable agricultural populations, leading to higher mortality rates and weakened immune systems. Those issues would have exacerbated the impact of any diseases and would have lingered long after Spaniards were gone.

To these nutritional woes could be added the almost-daily attacks and outrages to which de Soto and, to a lesser extent Narváez, exposed their Native hosts. The Spaniards did so without knowing or caring, committing insults and distresses of Native communities that influenced the processes of political and social dissolution for years after they were gone. The expeditions sowed political chaos by seizing or disrespecting headmen and could tear at the community's cultural and cosmological fabric by capturing or killing its women. Even in instances where invaders only touched communities briefly, like along the Georgia Stretch, their actions had compounding effects, hastening the death of untold thousands and even ushering in the political collapse of their societies.[2] Epidemic disease was only one among a host of destabilizing day-to-day interactions that all no doubt had roles to play in the horror story that unfolded in the wake of the European discovery of La Florida.

Notes

1. Accounts of this "Georgia" stretch are taken from "The Account by a Gentleman from Elvas," in Clayton, Knight, and Moore, eds., *The De Soto Chronicles*, 76-80; "Relation of the Island of Florida," in Clayton, Knight, and Moore, eds., *The De Soto Chronicles*, 229-230; "Account of the Northern Conquest," in Clayton, Knight, and Moore, eds., *The De Soto Chronicles*, 271-275; "La Florida," in Clayton, Knight, and Moore, eds., *The De Soto Chronicles*, 2: 260-261; Hudson, *Knights of Spain*, 146-172.

2. Kamen, *Empire*, 126-129; Diamond, *Guns, Germs, and Steel*, 197; Smith, "Aboriginal Depopulation," 257-258, 264; Smith, "Aboriginal Population Movements," 3-9; Kelton, *Epidemics and Enslavement*, 81-82; Ethridge, *From Chicaza to Chickasaw*, 60-62; Galloway, "Colonial Period Transformations in the Mississippi Valley," 237-240.

The Word *Pestilence*

In the early 1970s Alfred Crosby coined the term the "Columbian Exchange," forever centering the nonhuman in the story of human history. The Columbian Exchange is the title given to the voluntary and involuntary transfer of goods, peoples, ideas, plants, animals, organisms, etc., that was set in motion by the European "discovery" of the "New World," the Americas, by those of the "Old World," namely, Europe and Africa. The origins of that discovery lay with a chilling of the planet that took place around roughly 28,000 BCE, known as the Pleistocene era, the last of several periods of temperature fluctuation that comprised the last major ice age.

Lower temperatures led to higher levels of oceanic ice, which led to lower water levels, which produced an extended coastline down the modern-day states of Washington, Oregon, and California. It even exposed a land bridge connecting the modern-day regions of Siberia and Alaska. For tens of thousands of years, potentially, migratory waves of nomadic Paleo-Indians made their way down that coastline and across that bridge. In doing so they populated the North and South American continents. That was at least until a warming of the earth around 8,000 BCE led to rising water levels, closing the land bridge and re-isolating the two continents from the rest of the globe. The end of the Pleistocene era had, in effect, created two separate worlds.[1]

From the end of that ice age until Columbus's explorations beginning in 1492, those two worlds evolved in slightly different ecological circumstances. Among those different conditions was the presence in Eurasia and Africa of several species of large, domesticable animals, including horses, cattle, pigs, and sheep, of which North and South America had none, save the llama. Living in increasingly urban spaces and also in the presence of domesticable animals meant living in the presence of the filth they created and the microbes they carried and spread. That led to two separate exposure-generated evolutionary trends. First, diseases like smallpox, measles, influenza, malaria, and typhus, to name only a few, evolved to propagate and spread more rapidly among human hosts. Their evolution created outward symptoms like sores or coughs—vectors through which the maladies could spread—that were then recorded in history. That first evolutionary trend, in short, created highly contagious diseases that presented with visible signs of sickness. Second, humans living in close proximity to each other in urban and many times squalid surroundings naturally got sick. Untold millions died from the maladies while others survived, revealing another evolutionary trend. Over time Old World survivors of these diseases evolved sophisticated immune response mechanisms designed specifically to deal with infection. Neither of these evolutionary trajectories took place in the New World until the moment of contact.[2]

The proliferation of infectious disease and the response by humans to them in Eurasia, and not in North or South America, is the clearest example of the Columbian Exchange's history-shaping nature. A myriad of Old World diseases came over with their explorers, either in the bodies of the first European or African travelers or the animals they brought with them, and spread rapidly through Native communities in what Alfred Crosby termed "virgin soil" epidemics. As Crosby and other scholars originally postulated, their impact on the Caribbean and South America, well documented by watchful Spaniards, was nothing short of apocalyptic. The Native populations of Hispaniola, Cuba, and Puerto Rico were decimated by the combination of exploitation and infection, as were Aztec and Incan populations in Central and South America, respectively.[3]

Even if we accept the idea of "virgin soil" diseases as neatly explaining Native depopulation, the situation in La Florida is a bit more complicated. It is harder to put names to the particular diseases that ravaged the Southeast, their vectors, or their demographic consequences, because there is so little eyewitness evidence of the aftermath of contact. Peoples on the southern coast of peninsular Florida, like the Ais, Tequesta, Calusa, and Tocobaga, or those along the coast of Texas, were in regular contact with other Caribbean Natives. Shipwrecked Spaniards were also commonly in the vicinity, which might also help explain the depopulation trends among their societies. Further inland, where perhaps only de Soto's men had traveled, societies were not contacted again by Europeans for generations. The degree to which disease impacted their civilizations, therefore, can only be imagined. What is left in the archaeological record is of little help. The victims of epidemic disease usually died quickly and were buried haphazardly if they were buried at all, leaving unreliable evidence of massive epidemic infection. Even those suspected of succumbing to disease leave little physical evidence of the sickness on their remains. Smallpox scars are visible on the skin of its victims, not on their bones.[4] For that reason historians and anthropologists have struggled with accurate pre-contact population figures for the American South and have likewise disagreed on the degree of demographic decline that followed Spanish contact.

Following the work of Alfred and others, scholars described the impact of diseases in La Florida in catastrophic terms that were on par with Central and South American experiences. One example is the work of Henry Dobyns, who painted an earth-shattering portrait of European contact in the American Southeast. Waves of diseases swept unremittingly through entire regions, resulting in Native mortality rates that approached 95 percent, rates that extended inland even into the Mississippi River Valley. The physical and cultural impact of these waves of destruction would be difficult for communities to grasp culturally and even cosmologically, leading to the disappearance of entire civilizations. Dobyns placed the Pre-Columbian population of peninsular Florida alone at close to one million and he drew disease connections to Caribbean and South American epidemics. Disease spread to La Florida even before Spaniards landed in North America, leading to almost extinction-level demographic collapse.[5]

According to this approach, diseases spread into La Florida before the actual spread of Spaniards, made possible by the Native connections that already existed between coastal peninsular Florida and the Caribbean basin. Caribbean and Mayan Natives spread diseases as they fled their own homes via large ocean-going canoes and according to traditional trade routes into peninsular Florida, shortly to be followed by Spaniards spreading malaria, smallpox, typhus, and a host of other contagions directly. The distances between the east coast of peninsular Florida and the Bahamas, or from the southwest coast of peninsular Florida to the Keys and from there to Cuba, were short enough to make such travel possible, and de León's 1513 evidence of Native Caribbean trade goods in Calusa territory demonstrates that such travel did evidently happen. As Spanish slavers stripped the Bahamian islands of their human occupants in the early sixteenth century, surviving Tainos abandoned the region, perhaps making their way to peninsular Florida. A disease with "seven-league boots," in the words of Alfred Crosby, the incubation period of smallpox would have allowed those infected to travel long distances before realizing they were sick, and they would have spread it far from the eyes of anyone who could have written about what they were seeing. Refugee contact spread diseases in regions untouched yet by Spaniards. Crosby provided the boldest claim yet for such a theory. Based on these avenues of transmission, smallpox could easily have represented a true pandemic even before de Soto landed in La Florida, ranging from the Great Lakes to the South

American pampa by the 1530s.[6] Waves of different diseases followed with each of the Spanish expeditions that lay foot in La Florida, from de León to Tristán de Luna. Wave after wave of disease, building off of the damage done by the preceding one, killed large percentages of the population and crippled its survivors, leaving those who remained even less likely to survive the next wave.[7]

Scholars have since pushed back against such interpretations, citing the lack of obvious evidence in the historical and archaeological records to support such audacious claims. The work of another historian, Paul Kelton, is representative of that response. He has come to a much smaller number of killed based on more conservative estimations of infection. Only the most direct exposure to very sick Europeans, showing clear symptoms of their disease, could have transmitted the most dangerous pathogens to Natives, and there is little evidence of that happening in the historical records of any of the Spanish entradas. If the Spanish had men that were displaying smallpox symptoms, which is when they would have been most contagious, there would be more evidence of it in the documentary record. In other words, someone would have written about it. Passing Spaniards had little immediate effect on the interior of La Florida, Kelton concluded. Only with the establishment of St. Augustine and the steady stream of Spanish traffic that moved through it did the Southeast start to see steady demographic decline.[8]

The account of a pestilence at Cofitachequi demonstrates the imprecision in the Spanish record that creates such confusion. One of the chronicles mentions a possible plague having passed through Cofitachequi two years before de Soto's arrival, which left bodies stacked up and "uninhabited towns, choked with vegetation" on the outskirts of the province. As Alfred Crosby had suggested elsewhere, the psychological impact of a disease could be enormous, particularly if it was something like smallpox, "an unknown disfiguring disease which strikes swiftly," leaving Natives with horrific oozing wounds, and permanently scarring those who survived. That sort of terror made the abandonment of the Cofitachequi towns easy to understand if it was the result of a plague. There was Spanish contact as well, with the Natives asserting that the coast was only a few days journey. Natives seemed to talk specifically about Ayllón and the failed Guadalpe settlement. De Soto's men even found axes, clothing, and beads that clearly came from Spain. Although Ayllón did not last long and never strayed too far from the coast, Cofitachequi Natives had possibly been on hand to watch the expedition fall apart. At any rate, they certainly brought back what was left of it after the survivors fled.[9]

Still, even in a case of disease as clear as this one seems, the answer is actually not that clear. If the townspeople were anywhere accurate with their two-year time frame for the outbreak, then it took place almost a decade after the failure of San Miguel de Guadalpe and the evacuation of its survivors. That was a period far too long to transmit something as virulent as smallpox directly from the Spaniards to Cofitachequi. Perhaps it was not a disease at all. Despite the use of the terms "plague" and "pestilence," perhaps the townspeople were the victims of a crop failure and the resulting famine. According to one account the "pestilence of the year before" had deprived the Lady of Cofitachequi of "all the provisions" with which the chieftainess otherwise would have entertained de Soto. Such a description would certainly suggest that it was not disease, but starvation, that had created so much chaos in Cofitachequi.[10]

Accounts from the Narváez expedition are just as slippery. There are several mentions of unnamed maladies along the initial stretch of the expedition that could have been any number of infectious agents, or they could have been nothing at all. As the expedition began to fall apart on the outskirts of Aute, de Vaca mentions the painfully slow pace their men made "because neither the horses were sufficient to carry all the sick, nor did we know what remedy to seek because every day they languished, which was a spectacle of very great sorrow and pain."[11] De Vaca did not name any particular symptoms, leaving us to wonder whether the suffering he mentioned was the result of a contagion, or whether the men were simply dying of malnutrition and exposure. Were they wracked with fatigue, fevers, and body aches, the telltale signs of influenza, typhoid, or scarlet fever? Or were they just worn out, starving, roasting under the Florida sun? Either would be equally understandable. Several such reports of vague sicknesses and fevers could be attributable to communicable diseases or to underfed and overdressed Spaniards. Accounts from the de Soto expedition include similarly vague references of disease.[12] The record provides a maddening lack of clear evidence.

Most recent scholarship on the Native Southeast comes down somewhere in between the two poles represented by Dobyns and Kelton. Although far more conservative than Dobyns's early calculations of pandemic-driven demographic collapse, few are willing to admit that disease played only a minor, or passing, role in the collapse of the Mississippian world. Most contend that it was a confluence of several factors, including disease as well as European stresses, which caused such chaos. The lack of clear evidence of epidemic disease "may indicate a lack of documentation and archaeological research rather than the absence of disease," writes one anthropologist. And when there are reliable records later in the seventeenth century there is no shortage of evidence that wherever there was regional contact, there was epidemic disease.[13] Other aggravating factors were certainly also at work, weakening communities both physically and culturally. Nevertheless, disease remains a prime culprit, and it was before anything else in North America, a La Florida phenomenon.

Notes

1. Hudson, *The Southeastern Indians*, 34-44; Diamond, *Guns, Germs, and Steel*, 41-50; Scarry, "Late Prehistoric Southeast," 18.

2. Diamond, *Guns, Germs, and Steel*, 195-214; Dobyns, *Their Number Become Thinned*, 9-10.

3. Crosby, *The Columbian Exchange*, 35-63; Crosby, *Ecological Imperialism*, 200-201; Diamond, *Guns, Germs, and Steel*, 210-213; Dobyns, *Their Number Become Thinned*, 257-259; Smith, "Aboriginal Depopulation," 258.

4. Smith, "Aboriginal Depopulation," 260; Ethridge, *From Chicaza to Chickasaw*, 86-88; Diamond, *Guns, Germs, and Steel*, 77-78; Milanich, *Laboring in the Fields of the Lord*, 159; McEwan, "The Historical Archaeology of Seventeenth-Century La Florida," 505.

5. Dobyns, "The Invasion of Florida," 58-76; Diamond, *Guns, Germs, and Steel*, 77-78, 211-212.

6. Dobyns, *Their Number Become Thinned*, 259-260; Dobyns, "The Invasion of Florida," 58-76; Crosby, *Ecological Imperialism*, 200-201; Diamond, *Guns, Germs, and Steel*, 77-78, 211-212; Turner, "Juan Ponce de León," 4.

7. Dobyns, *Their Number Become Thinned*, 254-271; Crosby, *Ecological Imperialism*, 201.

8. Jones, "Virgin Soils Revisited," xx; Kelton, *Epidemics and Enslavement*, 47-100; Galloway, *Choctaw Genesis*, 134-138.

9. "The Account by a Gentleman from Elvas," in Clayton, Knight, and Moore, eds., *The De Soto Chronicles*, 83; "Relation of the Island of Florida," in Clayton, Knight, and Moore, eds., *The De Soto Chronicles*, 230-231; "Account of the Northern Conquest," in Clayton, Knight, and Moore, eds., *The De Soto Chronicles*, 279-280; Crosby, *The Columbian Exchange*, 56-57.

10. "La Florida," in Clayton, Knight, and Moore, eds., *The De Soto Chronicles*, 2: 286; Kelton, *Epidemics and Enslavement*, 52-56; Hudson, *Knights of Spain*, 179-180; Widmer, "The Structure of Southeastern Chiefdoms," 137-138; DePratter, "The Chiefdom of Cofitachequi," 215-217.

11. Adorno and Pautz, eds., *The Narrative of Cabeza de Vaca*, 70; Dobyns, *Their Number Become Thinned*, 261-262.

12. Dobyns, *Their Number Become Thinned*, 265-266; Kelton, *Epidemics and Enslavement*, 56-58; Galloway, *Choctaw Genesis*, 133-134. For another example, there was a "fever" among the sailors in the failed Barbastro mission to the Calusa, mentioned in Weddle, *Spanish Sea*, 244.

13. This approach can generally be seen in Ethridge, *From Chicaza to Chickasaw*, as well as in Kamen, *Empire*, 126-129; Galloway, *Choctaw Genesis*, 134-138; Smith, "Aboriginal Depopulation," 257-258, 264; Smith, "Aboriginal Population Movements," 3-9; Kelton, *Epidemics and Enslavement*, 81-82; Galloway, "Colonial Period Transformations," 237-240.

The Everyday Theft

The men and animals in both Narváez's and de Soto's expeditions lived off the Native landscape, which meant they stole basically everything they ate. The former, Narváez, did so mostly as a matter of immediate survival. After losing his supply ships off Tampa Bay, he had no other option. Had the situation not gone so poorly, on the other hand, and had his men stayed in La Florida for longer, he probably would have developed the same policy that de Soto later would. De Soto purposefully built his expedition around the idea of Native food stores not of survival, but for practicality. It would be the only sustainable way to support his army as it moved inland, onto wherever the riches of La Florida might lead him, and possibly far away from any source of resupply on the coast. His army marched anywhere from fifteen to twenty miles a day "when going through a peopled region," one chronicler explained, and as far as he could through a depopulated region "in order to avoid the necessity of a lack of maize." That of course is a gentler way of saying de Soto and his men sustained themselves on the corn produced by the Mississippian chiefdoms they passed through, taking by force what was not given to them voluntarily.[1]

In Apalachee, which Narváez's men approached by stealth and entered violently, the men found "a great quantity of maize that was ready to be harvested, as well as much that they had dried and stored," which they presumably then pillaged, having complained to that point of extreme hunger. It did not take long for the Apalachee to grow tired of their guests. After staying less than a month the expedition was driven out of town, and it took more than a week of basically fighting their way out of there to get to the next town, Aute, which they found abandoned and partially burned. The people of Aute had no desire to host the Spanish as their neighbors had. The fields of corn, beans, and squash that were planted around their town, though, were all still there, "all on the point of being ready for harvest."[2] Narváez's men lucked out, albeit to the obvious misfortune of Aute's residents, who would return not only to burned-out homes but to empty fields and ransacked granaries. Worse yet, over the next months, as Narváez's men constructed the rafts that would hopefully take them far away from La Florida, they sustained themselves by continually raiding into Aute for whatever remained.

Whatever the people of Aute rebuilt was torn back down when the men of the de Soto marched through a decade later. A decade is a long time, and Aute did rebuild, but only to be ravaged by a larger army than before. But first, in Ocala, a province inland of peninsular Florida and one of de Soto's first stops, the men found "maize in abundance," and de Soto ordered whatever was ripe enough to be eaten cut down, "which was enough for three months." Moving from there into Apalachee, the omnipresence of corn agriculture was apparent to the men, with "large fields of maize, beans, calabashes, and other vegetables" lining the trail into town on both sides and visible as far as the eye could see. According to another account, "food which seemed sufficient to last over the winter was gathered together" from these outlying Apalachee fields. De Soto's men spent the entire winter of 1539–1540 in Apalachee doing exactly that, and upon leaving, de Soto ordered his men to provide themselves corn for a sixty-league journey—well over 180 miles. A smaller expedition that made its way to the coast found Aute, and again raided its corn stores.[3]

According to Henry Dobyns's early calculations, what Spaniards witnessed on their march into Apalachee was upward of sixteen square miles of cultivation, the equivalent of over ten thousand acres. These estimates were based on cultivation statistics from the Yucatan and used to project what that kind of acreage might typically produce. Based on standard yield figures per acre, those Apalachee fields could have reasonably produced over 4.4 million kilograms, or almost five thousand tons, of shelled corn in one harvest. That was enough, based on standardized dietary needs in calories, to provide for almost seventeen thousand Apalachees, just in corn. If the Spaniards were right in noticing the double or triple cropping of beans and squash in the same fields, then the caloric yield would be significantly higher. If you expand those calculations into larger peninsular Florida, hundreds of square miles of corn agriculture could have supported hundreds of thousands of people.[4]

Naturally, anthropologists and agronomists have since questioned Dobyns's numbers as most likely inflated, yet by doing so they have added incredible complexity to Native farming yield calculations. They have mapped prospective yields comparatively, from Cahokia and the American Bottom to the Lower Mississippi Valley, to modern-day New York. They have postulated yields ranging from ten bushels of corn per acre in the lowest, to fifty and even seventy at the highest, the latter of which would have produced per-acre yield calculations much higher than Dobyns's own math. Doing so, they have demonstrated the varied potentials of Pre-Columbian corn production. They have even considered the comparable quality of arable, productive farmlands in each region, which were at their best in the American Bottom, and not their best at all in the Southeast.

While their calculations present the older work of Dobyns and others as oversimplified, there are some surprises in this new generation of scholarship. Take, for instance, the work of agronomist Jane Mt. Pleasant, who has argued that past Native agricultural techniques and crop yields, like everything else Native, have been historically undervalued by scholars using "unacknowledged European-based values," and "Eurocentric beliefs and assumptions." In other words, western biases, if not downright colonialist thinking. For generations, non-Native scholars dismissed the food-producing technologies and capabilities of many Pre-Columbian peoples and undervalued their farming yields simply because they were of Native, not European, origins. Mt. Pleasant has argued instead that Natives were sophisticated farmers with technologies that have been proven superior to many modern farming practices, and that indigenous cropping systems were permanent and intensive, not temporary and shifting. As another scholar concluded in the American Bottom region, it seems pretty clear that farmers there in all but the worst of times "produced copious amounts of food."[5] What these studies suggest, even if they challenge the early work of scholars like Dobyns, is that the same was true in north peninsular Florida. Native farmers like the Apalachee knew what they were doing, and they knew how to grow an awful lot of corn.

These were the Mississippian chiefdoms de Soto sought for the gold and silver he believed they possessed. While there was no gold or silver, at least de Soto's men were exceptionally well fed. There was lots of corn in north peninsular Florida, true, but only because there were a lot of people living in north peninsular Florida that depended on that corn. Timucuas, Apalachees, and Ocales, to be exact, among others, were the ones who produced and relied on the corn de Soto consumed as he went from community to community, demanding his precious metals. The negative effect of raiding a community's corn stores could be dire indeed: for those Mississippi chiefdoms, small and large, simple and complex, had developed a potentially problematic reliance on corn agriculture for the majority of their sustenance.

Corn agriculture arrived in the Southeast from the Southwest in several phases, with a distinct varietal well suited to the Southeast's climate and soil, spreading not long before de Soto's arrival. Over time that corn became one of the cornerstones of a new societal structure known as Mississippian, which emerged around 1000 CE, around the same time the Spaniards were beginning to turn the tide on their Moorish conquerors back in the Old World. The social structure of even a small, "simple" Mississippian chiefdom was built solidly around corn agriculture by a leadership group that controlled its growth and redistributed it to the rest of the chiefdom's common folk. If a chiefdom grew large enough to control other corn-growing communities, then its leader, now a complex or even a paramount chief, could maintain power through exacting tribute from those small communities in the form of corn and storing it in his own granaries.[6] This was the case in Cofitachequi, where de Soto's men ate corn "which were a deposit" of the headwoman. She had two separate warehouses of corn in that town, which she made clear she had collected to provide for her own people, and potentially tons more located in a nearby village.[7]

While corn provided the stability Natives needed to develop complex societies, an overreliance on corn also had its potential drawbacks. Among them was corn's inadequate nutritional composition. When Mississippian societies began to farm corn extensively, their reliance on other cultivated plants like sunflower, sump weed, amaranth, goosefoot, and others began to decline. The yields for these plant crops were much lower than corn and the harvests harder to dry and store, making them less convenient than corn to grow and harvest on a large scale. Each, however, is higher in necessary starches, proteins, and fats than is corn, which is not a nutritionally complex or even a particularly healthy crop on its own. That left gaping nutritional voids in community diets.[8] Their reliance on beans and squashes, the two other legs of the Mississippian "three sisters" method of cultivation, could only partially augment for the loss of those critical nutrients. Squashes are composed almost entirely of water. While providing vitamin and mineral value they are neither particularly high in calories nor good sources of either protein or starch, save for perhaps the drying and eating of their seeds. A heavy reliance on beans could have righted many of those nutritional deficiencies, but beans came late to the Mississippian diet, and it does not appear that Natives cultivated enough of them to stave off the health problems associated with eating too much corn.[9]

Corn agriculture was the foundational foodstuff of Mississippian communities, even while they continued to hunt and gather. The same studies that argue for permanent and intense Pre-Columbian food cropping traditions, suggest that corn accounted for upward of 75 percent of normal daily diets. Where did the other percentages come from? De Soto's men often took note of the richness of wild products, including tree nuts, which Natives processed into oils. Mulberries and other fruits were spoken of regularly. Venison and other wild game meats were available to his men on occasion, as was various wildfowl and even turkeys. The communities in different regions varied in the degree they supplemented their diets with these wild foods.[10] As communities continued to grow denser the scarcity of those sources of nutrition increased, however, further compounding a community's dietary woes. The sources of wild foods, like white-tailed deer or wild nuts and berries, diminished as competition over them increased. That left communities relying even more heavily on corn agriculture for their daily needs, producing a negative nutritional spiral that actually lowered life expectancies during the Mississippian period. The lack of niacin in an exclusive corn diet could produce the chronic wasting disease pellagra, also known as "corn sickness." The lack of protein produced smaller body masses and the lack of iron left people anemic. Higher rates of anemia left women in particular more vulnerable during pregnancy, which in turn produced higher infant mortality rates. Still worse was widespread anemia, which robs the blood of oxygen, producing systemic negative effects on organ function. That would have left people of all ages lethargic and fatigued, and with suppressed immune systems that were already miserably inadequate.[11]

Corn, in other words, one of the defining characteristics of Mississippian communities, had placed many in the Southeast in a vulnerable situation even before Europeans arrived. While scholars have gone to lengths arguing that Mississippians were excellent growers of corn, their dependence on corn still had its potential drawbacks. That much was visible in Cofitachequi, if the "pestilence" spoken of was indeed a famine. That was a natural disaster that killed hundreds and possibly thousands, led to the abandonment of villages, and had nothing to do with European contact. The lack of wild game and an overreliance on nutrition-deficient corn made sprawling and dense communities potentially unhealthy even during times of feast, and terribly exposed to times of famine. And that was only one of several threats an overreliance on corn might produce. If the finest farmlands were located in alluvial soils, that exposed communities to river flooding. In general, too little rain, or too much, could spoil an entire harvest; that was a catastrophe that would put a community in the direst of straits. Unable to assist tributary communities in their time of crisis or rely on those communities' contributions of corn for their own needs, one bad harvest could collapse a paramount chiefdom. Structural problems like these help explain why

Mississippian communities were already rising and falling by the time de Soto and his men marched through La Florida.[12] One is left to wonder, then, how communities small and large alike were left to fare when hundreds of ravenous Spaniards swept through their fields and granaries like a plague of locusts, moving on, it seemed, only when nothing was left.

Returning to Cofitachequi, de Soto's men so thoroughly depleted that province's already meager corn reserves that one of the primary arguments for leaving it, rather than settling it permanently, was the scarcity of food. If in the past few years, the town had suffered from a famine, it was in no way ready to accommodate hundreds of starving Spaniards. The irony there was apparently lost on de Soto entirely. Accounts describe pretty clearly that what the Lady of Cofitachequi had, she gave almost all of, and that the expedition had consumed almost every kernel of corn left in the province by the time they departed. There was "a very limited amount for the Indians to eat, and we, with the horses and people, used it up very quickly." According to another there was "not food in the whole land for the support of his men for a single month." More surprising yet, de Soto recognized this and concluded that once his men marched out "the Indians would plant their fields and it would be better provided with maize." To him that meant that if things went wrong elsewhere, or he otherwise decided to return, the community's stores would be replenished and available for his men to simply raid again.[13]

Several other examples across the Southeast point to a near systematic depletion of corn supplies wherever Spaniards went. More corn was supplied at the next town on from Cofitachequi, at Chiaha, where de Soto's men ended up staying for an entire month. They no doubt did a number on that chiefdom's corn stores, and whatever wild the countryside might have provided including nuts or berries, fared just as badly. The Spaniards slept in the open under trees and let their horses loose in the fields, where the latter, jaded from the last few months of mountainous travel, "grew fat because of the luxuries of the land."[14] Whatever there was around them there for the Natives to rely on to supplement their corn stores, there certainly was much less of it after de Soto's men and their horses moved through.

De Soto ended up destroying a good deal of whatever was left of Chiaha's cornfields when the town leadership, upset at one of his demands, deserted him. As he demonstrated there, de Soto and his men were willing to use the destruction of cornfields as punishment when they did not get whatever else they wanted, which was of course the community's resources. It was a lose-lose situation.[15] Cases like these were repeated across La Florida. The poor town of "Succor," at the end of the Georgia Stretch, was stripped bare. Then de Soto's army stayed almost an entire month in Coosa. Later, worn out and demoralized from the Mavila debacle, the men arrived at Chicaza and found "it was fertile and abounding in maize, most of this being still in the fields. The amount necessary for passing the winter was gathered."[16] The men would live for months on the corn stores of the outlying lands in a repeat of the Apalachee winter. Apalachee warriors did not appreciate that winter and harassed de Soto's men constantly. Chicaza warriors, ruthless in their night assaults of de Soto's camp, clearly did not either.[17]

Wiping out corn stores, either in aggression or for survival, represented a possibly devastating blow to communities that relied on corn agriculture for the majority of their diets. It was only one blow, however, among many. Perhaps as devastating was the impact Spaniards could have on a Mississippian community's labor pool—the men and women tasked to grow, harvest, and process that corn, as well as hunt or forage for anything wild. Both Narváez and de Soto relied on using Native guides to lead their way, and Native slaves to bear the burden of the march. This too damaged Mississippian communities.

De Soto, moving inland through uncharted and possibly hostile territory, relied on Native guides, interpreters, and burden bearers extensively. The expedition's advance and rear columns could be miles apart. The Spaniards themselves apparently did not carry much, leaving the hard labor of transporting everything from foodstuffs to camp supplies and even the soldiers' weapons to the backs of Native laborers.[18] No doubt linking this work as a logical extension of the *encomienda* and *repartimiento* labor systems of the Caribbean and Central America, Spaniards had no problem using various degrees of coercion to get Natives to do backbreaking manual labor for them. Nevertheless, many such laborers appear to have been given willingly by their headmen, in the hopes of course that their service would be a temporary thing, and once the Spaniards moved on far enough, they would be returned. Somewhere in northern Georgia a smaller chiefdom named Patofa offered guides and laborers in such a way. According to one account, de Soto took seven hundred laborers with him. Although that number seems inflated it was not at all uncommon for a large portion of the expedition to consist of laborers. It was one of the consistent requests de Soto made at almost every community he passed through, and generally they were given willingly by headmen who were not interested in a confrontation.[19]

The men that were taken from Native communities, sometimes by the hundreds, had not simply been doing nothing at home when de Soto found them. Their loss created another potentially compounding stressor on Mississippian societies, regardless of the size of the community. Men filled important roles in communities, including helping women harvest and process potentially tons of corn. They ranged the countryside for the wild game, nuts, and other foods that would supplement their diets. Deer hunts could go on for weeks, meaning that if they were not hunting or farming, they were resting. Men also tended to the town's public and political affairs.[20] A community's men was its labor force in several ways, and the loss of those men, many possibly never to return, could take a terrible toll on what that community could produce. Perhaps their importance explains why there are instances when the laborers did not go with de Soto willingly. At Chicaza de Soto asked for two hundred of them. The headman balked at the request and attacked the Spaniards soon after. After spending the winter living off the community's corn stores, evidently the theft of so many of the workers who would have to replace that food was simply too much to ask.[21]

Many times the Native men and women were given up, the cost of avoiding open confrontation. Outside of Ocale, according to de la Vega, de Soto's men captured one group "whom, with flattery, gifts, and promises, and on the other hand with many threats of cruel death if they refused," agreed to take part as burden bearers through peninsular Florida. Although these laborers probably walked unbound, they were clearly taken against their will.[22] In theory at least, they were relied upon so regularly that one town's men were usually relieved of their obligation as soon as de Soto had entered another province, was greeted by another headmen, and had secured replacement laborers. Forced to participate in what was effectively a rotating labor draft not at all dissimilar to the *repartimiento* system practiced by Spaniards elsewhere, for most the dismissal from their duties might have been the end of the ordeal—an unpleasant but ultimately temporary experience. Yet their service had not at all been voluntary. Now, gone for days or weeks, probably malnourished and no doubt hundreds of miles from their own communities, laborers might have been free, but what now?

Worse yet, chroniclers like Gracilaso de la Vega casually mentioned the mistreatment of so many Native laborers, so often, that it becomes clear that many of the expedition's laborers were not operating under anywhere near the best of circumstances at all. Everywhere along the route are accounts of Natives overtaken by mounted soldiers, ambushed by scouts, or otherwise seized, and then drug along with the expedition in chains. As the chronicler Rodrigo Rangel would later explain, taking so many "burden-bearing Indians" was necessary "in order to have more slaves, and to carry their supplies, and whatever they stole or what they gave them." Some of these laborers died and others fled "or weakened, and thus they had need to renew and take more."[23] As Rangel's account describes, most of the laborers were not well or kindly treated, and would probably be returning to their homes.

These kinds of kidnappings began before de Soto, of course, and go back to Lucas Vázquez de Ayllón and San Miguel de Guadalpe. They continued as a constant through Narváez and to de Soto. When Natives hid from Narváez in the early days of his march, he intentionally set traps for them, in one instance leaving horsemen "behind as an ambush on the road, so that as the Indians passed, they assaulted them and took three or four Indians," which the expedition then used as guides.[24] Later, while the numbers of guides given up by headmen peaceably tended to be larger, de Soto's men captured small groups of unlucky Natives constantly. Captured and enslaved, the untold thousands of men and women snatched from their communities by passing Spanish conquistadores likely disappeared forever. The lines between interpreters and guides, burden bearers and slaves, could be quite blurry in the earliest days of La Florida.

A perhaps far much more destructive kidnapping took place when Spaniards specifically targeted women, which both Narváez and de Soto also did. When Narváez approached Apalachee in 1528, for instance, most of the town's warriors were gone, leaving the Spaniards to capture a number of women and children. It took only days for Apalachee men to realize what had happened and to approach Narváez, asking for their families back. Narváez mostly complied, in a rare compromise, and ended up keeping a headman hostage. Years later, de Soto, in almost the same areas, captured "ten or twelve women," one being the daughter of a local chieftain. Several important Apalachee men approached him soon after and offered a trade for guides and laborers, and to go along with the expedition themselves as hostages. When de Soto refused, they mounted an unsuccessful rescue of the women. The chronicler does not reveal the fate of the women, but there was little doubt they were returned.[25] Why, in these two separate cases, were the warriors and headmen so concerned about the fate of these women?

Women in matrilineal societies, which included most of the Mississippian Southeast, held incredible societal and cosmological power. Their power lay in their clan identity, the real and fictive webs of relations that spread through communities and connected Natives into massive familial groups. Those lineages passed through the female line, a reminder of the incredible life-giving power women controlled. A matrilineal line meant that if a woman was a member of the Bear clan and had children with a man from the Wind clan, the children remained Bears. They would be raised and taught the ways of their clan by their aunts and uncles of the Bear clan, not their father of the Wind clan. That is also why women controlled the planting season and the usage of community property, processed food while men hunted, and even decided the fate of captives. Entire lineages passed through a female's identity, making the survival of a community's women and young girls critical to the community's cultural identity.

These powers explain why men, who did not contribute to their wives' clan lineages, could so easily put themselves in positions of danger, and why women and children were guarded so carefully. Matrilineal power would define Native societies to the chagrin of patriarchal Euro-Americans for generations in the colonial Southeast. They held similar cultural authority when de Soto traveled through the Mississippian world.[26] The historical and cultural power represented by women explains why communities fought so hard to protect and shield them from Spaniards, and why they worked so hard to retrieve them when they were stolen. In the case of the Apalachee women, who were evidently members of the chieftain's clan, their kidnapping would have represented the potential loss of entire future generations of that chieftain's line. What would the damage be to that community if those women did not have those children? This was the kind of damage that could have wide-ranging and devastating consequences.

Consider another attack made by Spaniards, previously in peninsular Florida. Not long after landing, a member of the de Soto expedition was kidnapped by nearby Natives, and a search party was quickly sent out in pursuit of the kidnappers. The warriors had taken the Spaniard to a large canebrake "that the Indians had chosen as a secluded and hidden place where they had their women and children concealed." The mounted Spaniards rushed the canebrake, scattering many but also capturing an unknown but significant number of women and children "who remained in the power of the Spaniards as slaves of him who shortly before had been theirs." Finding their captured compatriot the Spaniards rejoiced, "and gathering up all the people who were in the canebrake, who were women and children, went with them to the army where the governor received them with joy at their having recovered the Spaniard and, in freeing him, having captured so many of the enemy."[27]

Gracilaso de la Vega, of course, pontificated the most on what he considered the humorous reversal of fortunes experienced by the two parties in that moment. "So variable are the events of war and such is the inconstancy of its fortunes," he wrote, "that there is recovered in a moment that which was held to irretrievably lost, and in another is lost that which we believe to be safest."[28] In this case what was lost to the Spaniards and then found was one man, destined either to be ransomed by the Natives or killed—a scary fate indeed. What was thought to be safe to the Natives and now lost, on the other hand, was an entire community's combined cultural past, present, and future, all potentially destroyed by the rushing of the Spaniards into that canebrake. Although the Spaniards would move on from that community leaving it physically intact, there can be no doubt, by dragging their women away in chains, they left it in ruins.

If it was not bad enough for women to be taken from a community, then worse yet was the reason why Spaniards took so many of them. De Soto made clear that women were requested specifically and apart from normal laborers, drawing a distinction between enslaved laborers and enslaved sex workers. When Rodrigo Rangel described how the taking of "burden-bearing Indians" was necessary to carry supplies, he also described how the women, "and these not old nor the most ugly," were taken by the soldiers "for their lewdness and lust." They were taken, in other words, for sex. Perhaps to assuage their guilt the men Christianized these women and girls, baptizing them "more for their carnal intercourse than to instruct them in the faith."[29] Nevertheless there can be no equivocation—the de Soto expedition was one of brutal exploitation, including the systematic sexual exploitation of Native women.

De Soto's capture of women began as soon as he landed in La Florida. In demands surprising in their boldness and depravity, he commonly officially requested women directly from headmen. Although they presumably would be returned after the expedition moved on, these must have been especially insulting demands for a chieftain to take. Many times, in fact, these requests were the cause of confrontation. The situation nearly got violent in Chiaha when, after weeks of excellent treatment, the Natives "went away afterward one Saturday . . . because of a certain thing which the Governor asked them for; and in short, it was that he asked them for women." According to another account, and because of the "importunity of some who wished more than was proper," the number of women was thirty. Chiaha's headman and his "principal men" said they would talk over the idea, but instead deserted the town, with the men fleeing with their wives and children. From the allusion made by the chronicler, describing how the Spaniards "who wished more than was proper," it seems clear the women would not be used as guides or simple laborers. It was an allusion everyone in Chiaha seemed to understand as well. Rather than submit they fled, prompting de Soto to pursue. Eventually a compromise was struck: the headmen agreeing to provide laborers, but not the women he requested, with de Soto himself admitting that "it cost them so dearly to give them to him."[30]

De Soto probably did not understand the power women held in these societies, but such scenes were repeated throughout the Southeast.[31] Sometimes communities were able to reject the demand for their women, but sometimes they did not, and that raises questions about the fates of the countless women who were forced to endure acts of sexual assault at the hands of Spaniards. The stretch from Cofitachequi to Mavila was a particularly difficult stretch in that respect. De Soto took twenty women alone from Coosa, while on the outskirts of Talisi, the headman met his men "and gave what they asked for: laborers, women, and supplies." That was one of two separate towns from which his men took thirty women each on the march to the Tascalusa province.[32]

One wonders what happened to these women when they returned home, if they ever did. Differing circumstances provide starkly different answers. Even before de Soto's journey Peter Martyr, a Spanish historian, recorded legends from the coast of modern-day South Carolina. The Natives there, he explained, "like their women to be chaste. They detest immodesty and are careful to put aside suspicious women." A far more extreme description came from one Spanish friar and a de Soto chronicler who passed through La Florida. He described how regional Natives "greatly abominate those who lie and steal and married women who are bad," by which he meant act adulterously. If a woman was accused of adultery, she and her entire family could be killed. Would a woman forced to endure sexual advances by Spaniards be judged in such a way? The chronicler's fragment does not say. On the other hand were customs in Creek society, which existed later in the Southeast but which had clear cultural connections. Adultery there was still punished with physical violence, bodily mutilation, and possibly even the death of one or both offenders. Unmarried women, however, were free to make their own sexual choices. Furthermore, it was possible for men in influential positions to have multiple wives or concubines, as long as it was authorized by the matrilineage.[33] There is no simple answer, in other words, for what would have happened to such women had they even found their way back home.

The sexual violence subjected upon these women, the loss of them or even the loss of respect for them, is one example of the everyday theft that could have damaged the fabric of the Mississippian world. The theft of women constituted the loss of matrilineages, which represented the loss of both future clan members and past cultural identity. Because matrilineages were ranked and because elite lineages determined the position of headmen, the disruption of those lineages might have complicated the succession of a chiefdom's leadership or even collapsed it. Any of these structural problems, springing from the loss of community women, could have conceivably led to the breakdown of a chiefdom.[34] These were the issues that help us understand a slow but steady collapse of the Mississippian world—a collapse set into motion during the contact era in La Florida. The loss of food, the loss of manpower, and the loss of women were all devastating everyday thefts.

Notes

1. Robertson, "Preface," in Clayton, Knight, and Moore, eds., *The De Soto Chronicles*; "The Account by a Gentleman from Elvas," in Clayton, Knight, and Moore, eds., *The De Soto Chronicles*, 94.

2. Adorno and Pautz, eds., *The Narrative of Cabeza de Vaca*, 64, 67, 69.

3. "The Account by a Gentleman from Elvas," in Clayton, Knight, and Moore, eds., *The De Soto Chronicles*, 65, 72, 74; "La Florida," in Clayton, Knight, and Moore, eds., *The De Soto Chronicles*, 2: 194, 199-200; Hoffman, *Florida's Frontiers*, 35-38.

4. Dobyns, *Their Number Become Thinned*, 138-144.

5. Mt. Pleasant, "A New Paradigm," 374-383, 408-412; Fritz, *Feeding Cahokia*, 114-119.

6. Vanderwarker et al., "Maize and Mississippian Beginnings," 33-57; Smith, *Rivers of Change*, 274-276; Ethridge, *From Chicaza to Chickasaw*, 15-17; Jennings, *New Worlds of Violence*, 16; Ethridge, "Navigating the Mississippian World," 63-64; Hudson, *Southeastern Indians*, 80-82; Hudson, *Knights of Spain*, 13-14, 17; Scarry, "Late Prehistoric Southeast," 21-23, 29-30; Widmer, "The Structure of Southeastern Chiefdoms," 137-140.

7. "Account of the Northern Conquest," in Clayton, Knight, and Moore, eds., *The De Soto Chronicles*, 279; and "La Florida," in Clayton, Knight, and Moore, eds., *The De Soto Chronicles*, 2: 286.

8. Dobyns, *Their Number Become Thinned*, 221-228; Smith, *Rivers of Change*, 267-276; Hudson, *Southeastern Indians*, 82; Hudson, *Knights of Spain*, 14; Scarry, "Late Prehistoric Southeast," 18-20.

9. Dobyns, *Their Number Become Thinned*, 220-221; Briggs, "The Civil Cooking Pot," 323; Kelton, *Epidemics and Enslavement*, 13.

10. Fritz, *Feeding Cahokia*, 116; "The Account by a Gentleman from Elvas," in Clayton, Knight, and Moore, eds., *The De Soto Chronicles*, 87-88; "Relation of the Island of Florida," in Clayton, Knight, and Moore, eds., *The De Soto Chronicles*, 232; Hudson, *Knights of Spain*, 122-123; Halley, "The Chiefdom of Coosa," 231-232.

11. Kelton, *Epidemics and Enslavement*, 11-13; Briggs, "The Civil Cooking Pot," 323; Halley, "The Chiefdom of Coosa," 232-233; Armelagos and Hill, "An Evaluation," 19-37; Anderson, "Stability and Change," 202-207.

12. Hudson, *Knights of Spain*, 24-30; Ethridge, *From Chicaza to Chickasaw*, 17-18.

13. "The Account by a Gentleman from Elvas," in Clayton, Knight, and Moore, eds., *The De Soto Chronicles*, 84-85, 88; "Relation of the Island of Florida," in Clayton, Knight, and Moore, eds., *The De Soto Chronicles*, 228, 231; "La Florida," in Clayton, Knight, and Moore, eds., *The De Soto Chronicles*, 2: 286; Hoffman, *Florida's Frontiers*, 34.

14. "The Account by a Gentleman from Elvas," in Clayton, Knight, and Moore, eds., *The De Soto Chronicles*, 87-88; "Relation of the Island of Florida," in Clayton, Knight, and Moore, eds., *The De Soto Chronicles*, 231-232.

15. "The Account by a Gentleman from Elvas," in Clayton, Knight, and Moore, eds., *The De Soto Chronicles*, 89-91.

16. "The Account by a Gentleman from Elvas," in Clayton, Knight, and Moore, eds., *The De Soto Chronicles*, 94, 105.

17. "The Account by a Gentleman from Elvas," in Clayton, Knight, and Moore, eds., *The De Soto Chronicles*, 89-91; Ethridge, *From Chicaza to Chickasaw*, 38, 42-43.

18. Ethridge, "Navigating the Mississippian World," 72-77.

19. Ethridge, "Navigating the Mississippian World," 72-77. For accounts of Spaniards getting laborers, or "tamemes," see "The Account by a Gentleman from Elvas," in Clayton, Knight, and Moore, eds., *The De Soto Chronicles*, 80, 91, 94-95; "Account of the Northern Conquest," in Clayton, Knight, and Moore, eds., *The De Soto Chronicles*, 281-282.

20. Claassen, "Changing Venue," 68-71; Hudson, *Knights of Spain*, 17.

21. "The Account by a Gentleman from Elvas," in Clayton, Knight, and Moore, eds., *The De Soto Chronicles*, 107.

22. "Relation of the Island of Florida," in Clayton, Knight, and Moore, eds., *The De Soto Chronicles*, 226; "La Florida," in Clayton, Knight, and Moore, eds., *The De Soto Chronicles*, 2: 153.

23. "The Account by a Gentleman from Elvas," in Clayton, Knight, and Moore, eds., *The De Soto Chronicles*, 76; "Account of the Northern Conquest," in Clayton, Knight, and Moore, eds., *The De Soto Chronicles*, 288-289.

24. Adorno and Pautz, eds., *The Narrative of Cabeza de Vaca*, 63.

25. Adorno and Pautz, eds., *The Narrative of Cabeza de Vaca*, 66; "Relation of the Island of Florida," in Clayton, Knight, and Moore, eds., *The De Soto Chronicles*, 226; "Account of the Northern Conquest," in Clayton, Knight, and Moore, eds., *The De Soto Chronicles*, 263.

26. Hudson, *The Southeastern Indians*, 185-198; Jennings, *New Worlds of Violence*, 6-7; Widmer, "The Structure of Southeastern Chiefdoms," 128-133.

27. "La Florida," in Clayton, Knight, and Moore, eds., *The De Soto Chronicles*, 2: 122-123.

28. "La Florida," in Clayton, Knight, and Moore, eds., *The De Soto Chronicles*, 2: 123.

29. "Account of the Northern Conquest," in Clayton, Knight, and Moore, eds., *The De Soto Chronicles*, 288-289.

30. "The Account by a Gentleman from Elvas," in Clayton, Knight, and Moore, eds., *The De Soto Chronicles*, 59, 89; "Account of the Northern Conquest," in Clayton, Knight, and Moore, eds., *The De Soto Chronicles*, 266, 282.

31. "Relation of the Island of Florida," in Clayton, Knight, and Moore, eds., *The De Soto Chronicles*, 238.

32. "Account of the Northern Conquest," in Clayton, Knight, and Moore, eds., *The De Soto Chronicles*, 285.

33. Martyr, *De Orbe Novo, Volume 2*, 265-266; "The Canete Fragment," in Clayton, Knight, and Moore, eds., *The De Soto Chronicles*, 309; Hudson, *The Southeastern Indians*, 198-201.

34. Anderson, "Stability and Change," 202.

Caciques and Conquistadores

The easiest way for the Spanish to gain foodstuffs, laborers and guides, women, and, of course, safe passage from their Mississippian hosts was to capture a community's headman and essentially hold him ransom. Both Narváez and de Soto utilized the tactic frequently. Narváez held a headman in Apalachee and probably would have continued to do similarly had he continued into the Southeast.[1] De Soto, his successor, captured headmen almost wherever he went. The location of the next province and who the most powerful chieftain in it were, in fact, two of the most important questions he normally asked, at least right after he asked about gold. Upon leaving Cofitachequi he "asked the Indians whether they had heard of any great lord farther on." When they answered they did, in Chiaha, that was precisely where he went next. At Chiaha, the answer was Chisca, and so forth and so on. De Soto made his way from one side of La Florida to the next, one chiefdom at a time, one chieftain at a time.[2]

Leading by capturing was standard operating procedure as far as conquistadores were concerned and was spoken of by de Soto as if it was merely a formality. He was "accustomed to place a guard over" headmen to secure guides and laborers, so that "the others, their subjects, would be quiet and not obstruct their thefts and prevent what they might wish to do in their land." If everything went to plan everyone was usually released, including the headman and the laborers, as soon as the expedition made its way to the next chiefdom. Doing so was a tried and true tool of conquest. De Soto picked up the technique in Peru, where the capture of Atahualpa paralyzed Incan society and ended up making everyone filthy rich. If you could control the leader of a centralized community that worshipped him like a god then, naturally, you could control the people.[3]

To a degree, de Soto was right. Seizing a headman in La Florida was much the same as elsewhere, because headmen even in smaller, simple chiefdoms sat at the very top of well-defined hierarchies that combined social, political, and religious authority. While they were not necessarily autocratic rulers in a contemporary European sense, in many ways their power was even more complete.

They were extremely powerful men and sometimes women who belonged to the highest, most prestigious lineages in highly ranked societies where lineages basically meant everything. They received tribute in corn and prestige goods like furs and gems from smaller communities and controlled the distribution of the corn to their people. Those forms of tribute not only supported the political hierarchy upon which these rulers sat, but also served as signs of devotion and deference to powerful leaders. Chieftains were civil and war leaders who both governed in times of peace, and who were the first into battle in times of struggle.

Perhaps more important, Mississippian chieftains claimed spiritual authorization for their power, which they reinforced through religious iconography and sacred ritual. All of this they controlled through esoteric cosmological knowledge passed down through their lineage. In the most extreme cases they recognized themselves as direct kin of deities like the sun, as did the Natchez chieftain the "Great Sun." They frequently rode on litters and when their communities had distinct mound architecture, their homes could be found on the highest, most central one. For these reasons chieftains were treated with extreme veneration and reverence. Seizing such a person ground a community to a political, social, and spiritual halt almost immediately, which was exactly what de Soto wanted. Doing so in Peru allowed Pizarro and his men to consolidate their forces and legitimize themselves, setting the tone for the larger Incan conquest. That was a method de Soto was keen to reproduce in La Florida.[4]

Captivity did not end well for Atahualpa, who was killed despite doing for Pizarro everything of which he was asked. That might have been the case in La Florida had de Soto decided to stay and attempt colonization. He did not, and most headmen survived their capture. Nevertheless, these chieftains were still forced to submit to demands they would have never considered before, to accept a level of disrespect from de Soto that moments before would have seemed unimaginable. An outsider marching into a community, forcing a godlike leader into submission and perhaps roughing him up a bit in the process, might have produced all sorts of negative consequences for a community, ranging from bitter acquiescence to outright war. Even in the most peaceful circumstances, like during the Georgia Stretch, de Soto entered into and directly challenged a very rigid hierarchy that ordered the lives of thousands of people. When he departed, it is not difficult to assume that many people were left wondering about the structure of the world in which they lived, questions their headmen would have difficulty answering.

At one end of the spectrum lay those headmen along the Georgia Stretch. Several chiefs in quick succession approached de Soto at Ochese, Altamaha,

Ocute, and Cofaqui, and did so largely without incident. When the army stayed longer and asked of more from their guests, the situation was usually different. Soon after the Georgia Stretch, de Soto not only held the Lady of Cofitachequi against her will but decided to take her along as they moved onward to Chiaha. Although the people of Cofitachequi had treated his men extraordinarily well, de Soto suspected that the chieftainess would slip away without providing him the guides or laborers he had requested. He "ordered a guard to be placed over her and took her along with him," surprising even one of the chroniclers, who remarked that he was not "giving her such good treatment as she deserved for the good will she had shown him and the welcome she had given him." He paraded her through her own territory for days in an effort to keep subordinate communities in check and provide his men with food. Although she was allowed to take servants with her and was otherwise treated well, she evidently did not appreciate the experience. With the help of her servants, she was able to slip away from the expedition and despite de Soto's efforts to find her, she made her escape.[5]

In these exceptional cases community leaders displayed incredible poise and patience for men and women who were otherwise used to extreme reverence. Most other times they did not handle de Soto's formality so well, generating at best bitterness and at worst confrontation and open hostility. The Coosa chieftain, one of the most powerful men to have endured sustained captivity, was allowed to leave once de Soto made it out of the Coosa province and to Talisi, a chiefdom on the frontier of the Tascalusa province. There the next headman had just agreed to de Soto's terms for laborers, women, and supplies, freeing up the Coosa laborers. With the subjugation of the next chiefdom secured, de Soto released his Coosa prisoner according to the plan, "so that he might return to his land," presumably with his people. Things could have gone worse for the chieftain, of course. He was alive, after all, and had endured his captivity with very little violence. Still, "very angry and tearful" at the end of the ordeal, the chief offered his Spanish captors little by way of parting thanks. There were several reasons for this anger. Not only was de Soto continuing to disrespect him by holding more Coosa captive, including his own sister, but they also had "brought him so far from his land."[6] Forced to endure the indignity of captivity, marched hundreds of miles from his own home and to the frontier of a competing and probably unfriendly chiefdom, and then left there, the Coosa headman's treatment was not only insulting, but potentially fatal. Left there and left behind in the records, it is unclear whether he ever made it back to his people, or if he was welcomed back when he arrived.

The release of the Coosa headman was still exceptional because his seizure had originally generated the potential for so much more violence. Warriors were willing to fight and die to protect these men and women, which they frequently did. At the moment he was initially taken, in Coosa, many in the surrounding communities "thought ill of it and revolted," deserting the town, refusing to assist the expedition, and threatening violence. Doing what he did best, de Soto immediately escalated the situation, sending cavalry out after the hiding townspeople. He "seized many Indians, men and women, who were put in chains," and he used their seizure to coerce the rest of the chiefdom into submission. The plan worked. "Upon seeing the harm they received and how little they gained from absenting themselves, they came, saying that they wished to serve in whatever might be commanded them." Ultimately it was the chieftain that diffused the situation by submitting to de Soto's demands, agreeing to his own captivity, and agreeing to supply de Soto's men with food, laborers, and even women. The respect his men had for his wishes was clear; the damage de Soto was doing to the chief's reputation was equally clear.[7]

De Soto still managed to avoid an all-out war in Coosa, which was exactly what he got in other areas where he followed the same approach. If seizing headmen was designed to cow communities into submission, it definitely did not work in Apalachee, neither for Narváez nor de Soto, the latter of which endured withering assaults by warriors after capturing an Apalachee headman by the name of Capafi.[8] Then again, quite the opposite took place just before de Soto approached Apalachee. At Ocale, in central peninsular La Florida, de Soto "made an agreement" with the Ocale headman to build a bridge across a river. It would be built using Native labor, of course. Warriors soon appeared, however, and showered de Soto and the headman with arrows. When de Soto asked his counterpart how his warriors could show a leader so much disrespect, the chieftain replied that his men, "seeing him inclined to the friendship and service of the Spaniards, had refused him obedience and lost respect for him," and now both their lives were being threatened.[9]

This confrontation might seem surprising, given the amount of structural power headmen wielded. Yet the response by his own warriors against the Ocale headman also revealed one of the pillars of Native American politics in the Southeast that would continue to evolve from its roots in the Mississippian period. Even though Mississippian chieftains claimed to rule through various means, including family lineages, access to prestige goods, the redistribution of corn, sacred authority, and coercion, all of those things apparently had their limits. Rule by consent, persuasion, and respect was also the qualities of a community leader, and the ones that would define civic leaders even more so later in the Southeast. Chieftains mediated sources of conflict and maintained community harmony. They were the qualities of "micos," who rose to prominence in their communities not because of threats or even spiritual guidance, but sound judgment and respect. Although community governance would come to define Native politics in the eighteenth and nineteenth centuries, many of those same qualities still had their place in the Mississippian world. That was a respect the Ocale headman was losing by acquiescing to de Soto's demands. Ultimately, de Soto's men built their own bridge, and the Ocale headman went his own way.[10]

The Ocale episode is admittedly one of the very few to describe a situation where warriors rose up in such a defiant way against their own community leadership. If the story was accurate, they actually tried to kill their own chief. The army continued on its way without much more violence, but behind him was a headman left to mend a very damaged relationship with his own community, which raises important questions indeed about the political wreckage that de Soto was capable of leaving in his wake, even when outwardly the community survived without much violence. While Apalachee warriors rose up in defense of their chief, those in nearby Ocale felt entirely differently, and we will never know what happened to the Coosa or Cofitachequi chieftains. Almost every headman was treated similarly, or worse, by de Soto. If the foundations of a chieftain's authority were undercut in similar ways, did it produce similar challenges to his or her authority? Was de Soto weakening the Mississippian world politically, just by moving through it?

This might have happened in one last important way. De Soto was not only challenging the political and religious authority of chieftains. He was also changing power relationships between competing chiefdoms. As the iconography and physical structure of Mississippian chiefdoms bear out plainly, warfare was everywhere in the Mississippian world. It resulted from a myriad of influences, like competition for resources, ideologies, or the consolidation of chiefly power. Nearby chiefdoms fought constantly, paramount chiefs rose and fell with their ability to subjugate smaller polities, and even smaller or intermediate chiefdoms could struggle from internal dissention among the elite. As generations of anthropologists have come to recognize, the Mississippian world entered into by the Spanish was a violent and competitive place.[11]

By moving from one chiefdom to the next, De Soto's men plunged themselves into a contested, fluid, and violent political landscape, the complexities of which they did not understand. Clear buffer zones encountered by his army between chiefdoms, which existed between Cofaqui and Cofitachequi or between Coosa and Tascalusa, would have alerted de Soto to such a dynamic had he been looking.[12] Nevertheless, the military advantages de Soto possessed were not only wielded against confrontational headmen, but he was also known to support friendly chieftains against their rivals, potentially altering the region's political landscape. Coosa and Tascaloosa were not on good terms, for instance, and quarreled over the province of Talisi, which lay in between the two. "Although the two were not openly at war, Tascalusa was a haughty and belligerent man, very cunning and deceitful," and had stirred Talisi "to disobedience to its lord," the Coosa headman.[13] Perhaps that contributed to the Coosa chieftain's bitter response to be left by de Soto where he was, in a dangerous place far from his own center of authority.

Earlier in the expedition, passing through Ocute and Cofaqui at the end of the Georgia Stretch, headmen offered to lead de Soto's men directly up to Coosa rather than to his intended destination, Cofitachequi. There was no easy route to the latter chiefdom, the headman explained, "since they had no dealings with one another because they were at war." In this case, the frontier in between the two was more than simply a buffer zone. It was a strong natural barrier between two chiefdoms that were clearly not on good terms. Smitten by accounts of gold, however, de Soto made it clear he was getting to Cofitachequi one way or another, and the Cofaqui headman, "having seen our determination," changed his tone. Perhaps he saw a military opportunity of his own develop. If the Spaniards "wished to go to make war on the lady of [Cofitachique], they would give us all that we might want for the journey." From several different accounts, de Soto's men got the men, the guides, the food, whatever they wanted and more.[14]

Even with all that help, the journey through the Savannah River basin was treacherous, and de Soto sent many of the laborers back because he could not feed them. However, according to one account, several of the Cofaqui warriors and laborers were still with de Soto's army when they made it through the frontier to the town they would later name "Succor." While de Soto's men ate and rested, the warriors snuck off, sacking a nearby village, robbing the temples and burial grounds, killing everyone they found "without sparing sex or age," and taking their scalps for trophies. They did so without de Soto's knowledge, and "as it was learned later," the town was a part of the Cofitachequi chiefdom. Cofaqui warriors were taking advantage of de Soto's presence to settle scores, apparently, which continued all week. While the Spanish convalesced, their Native counterparts raided small outlying Cofitachequi towns. "In short, they left nothing undone that they could think of to harm their enemies and avenge themselves."

De Soto wanted to enter Cofitachequi as peacefully as possible, so he and his Native allies thanked each other, exchanged gifts, then parted ways. Although he attempted to distance himself from their actions, it was still his march to Cofitachequi that emboldened the Cofaqui raiders to mount their campaign. The chieftainess of Cofitachequi seemed to be struggling against unruly tributary headmen who were not only refusing her tribute but were ransacking her villages. The retaliation was impressive, surprising the departing Spaniards. Moving up the river toward Cofitachequi, the army traveled for days "without meeting a single live Indian," but found plenty dead ones with their scalps missing. Cofaqui's warriors, with Spanish help, had exacted a brutal revenge.[15]

An even more complicated political drama played out with the help of de Soto's men closer to the end of the expedition, after they crossed the Mississippi River. It involved the warring chiefdoms of Casqui and Pacaha, two chiefdoms of unequal size and strength. Although the headman of the smaller chiefdom, Casqui, treated de Soto's men peacefully and fulfilled the Spaniards' requests for laborers and supplies eagerly, he soon made a request of his own. He wanted the Spanish to assist in battling neighboring Pacaha, whose headman had been submitting Casqui's smaller chiefdom to his will for some time. Pacaha's "more-powerful lords of lands and vassals, had hemmed in Casqui, and were continuing to do so, having almost overcome him." Casqui hoped the Spanish could help him even the field, and he was right.[16]

With Spanish cavalry marching behind Casqui's own army the two set out, and upon entering the fortified central town of Pacaha, the Spaniards watched as Casqui warriors set about pillaging. Their slow approach left time for many of the residents to flee, but the invaders took their time killing whoever remained and collecting scalps as trophies. Then they really went to work, razing the town and demonstrating "well the hatred and rancor that they felt against its inhabitants." They sacked the chieftain's home and seized portions of his family who had been left behind in the hasty retreat, including two of his wives. Then they moved to the community's temple, which de la Vega understood was "the most esteemed and venerated possession that these Indians of La Florida have." They thoroughly desecrated it, committing "all the ignominious and offensive affronts that they could, because they pillaged everything that the temple contained in the way of riches, ornaments, spoils, and trophies that had been gathered at the expense, evidently," of Casqui.[17]

All of this was presumably in the center of the town, and probably on a mound structure. It would be seen by everyone. Desecrating a headman's home, its sacred spaces and the ancestors who were interred there, was typical but a powerful Mississippian weapon, "the ultimate insult" in the words of one anthropologist. Chieftains supported the religious foundations of their authority through the interment of their ancestors in their temple spaces, what has been referred to as "ancestor worship." The presence of past religious leaders in the same places as the current living one was a physical representation of the continuity of that religious power. An attack on that temple and on the ancestors who remained there was an attack on the religious foundation of a chiefdom's authority itself. This was clear to the Casqui warriors. They pulled bones from their resting places and threw them to the floor. They removed the displayed heads of their killed townspeople, "placed on the points of lances at the doors of the temple as a sign of triumph and victory," and replaced them with the severed heads of Pacaha's own recently slaughtered inhabitants. "In short, nothing they could think of was left undone."[18]

Not content with wrecking Pacaha's spiritual center, the Casqui warriors fanned out into the town's cornfields, "laying waste and destroying everything they encountered," as well as freeing their own enslaved people. The headman summoned canoes to assault the Pacaha refugees that had fortified themselves on a nearby island. The combined army made an amphibious assault on the fortified refugees, causing groups of women and children to flee in canoes farther upriver. What began as another route, however, was soon much more complicated. When the Pacaha warriors rallied, they rattled the Casqui invaders, who "as a frightened people often defeated on other occasions," not only stopped their assault but totally lost their nerve, according to the chroniclers. They turned their backs and ran for the canoes. They deserted their headman, deserted their Spanish counterparts, and even attempted to seize the Spaniards' canoes in the resultant panic. Casqui warriors had taken advantage of the Spanish allies in planning an assault they never could have dreamed of pulling off on their own. Now, however, even with the advantage of Spanish arms, it looked like they had bit off more than they could chew.[19]

As chroniclers related things, de Soto and his men looked on the retreat as an embarrassing show of cowardice, which de Soto used to attempt his hand at diplomacy. He made peace with the remaining Pacaha and then attempted to broker one between the two warring neighbors. That was to the great displeasure of the Casqui headman, who wished instead that de Soto help him strike the decisive blow. The headman in particular hoped that his Pacaha counterpart "would have preserved in his obstinacy" so that Casqui warriors "could have taken revenge on him and destroyed him with the Castilians' help." But the Casqui warriors had squandered their opportunity, and instead de Soto escorted the Pacaha chieftain back to his sacked village, where the stoic headman toured his ruined temple. "As he went inside and saw the destruction done, he concealed his feelings and lifted up from the ground with his own hands the bones and dead bodies of his ancestors," kissed them, and returned them to their former resting places. If the relationship between Pacaha and Casqui had already been bad for generations, there was absolutely no chance of seeing it mended now, regardless of what de Soto said or did. He did try, inviting the men to a banquet and overseeing their conversing together. At his behest the two embraced, in an ostensible act of reconciliation. The expressions on their faces, however, "and their looks at one another were not those of true friendship."[20]

De Soto moved on shortly after, leaving the two competing chieftains to hash out their differences far from observant Spanish chroniclers. Although we will never know what happened, de Soto's peace efforts probably did little to keep the Pacaha warriors from avenging the destruction of their temple, the humiliation of their chieftain, and the murder of their people. In all likelihood, Casqui ceased to exist not long after de Soto's departure. If his men looked back hard enough, they probably could have seen the smoke rising from its ashes as they continued moving west.

The Pacaha-Casqui dynamic certainly would have represented the worst transformative violence done by de Soto and his men in the Mississippian Southeast, but it was not the only place his actions sowed political, religious, and cultural chaos. De Soto's men entered a dynamic and complicated world, turned it upside down, and then left.

Notes

1. Adorno and Pautz, eds., *The Narrative of Cabeza de Vaca*, 66.

2. "The Account by a Gentleman from Elvas," in Clayton, Knight, and Moore, eds., *The De Soto Chronicles*, 76-78, 80, 84-85, 89-90.

3. "The Account by a Gentleman from Elvas," in Clayton, Knight, and Moore, eds., *The De Soto Chronicles*, 93; "Account of the Northern Conquest," in Clayton, Knight, and Moore, eds., *The De Soto Chronicles*, 289; Hudson, *Knights of Spain*, 14.

4. Ethridge, *From Chicaza to Chickasaw*, 12-15; Hudson, *Knights of Spain*, 17; Hudson, *The Southeastern Indians*, 203-210; Scarry, "Late Prehistoric Southeast," 30-31; Widmer, "The Structure of Southeastern Chiefdoms," 139-140, 146-152; Anderson, "Stability and Change," 196-199.

5. "The Account by a Gentleman from Elvas," in Clayton, Knight, and Moore, eds., *The De Soto Chronicles*, 85-87; Hudson, *Knights of Spain*, 191-192.

6. "Account of the Northern Conquest," in Clayton, Knight, and Moore, eds., *The De Soto Chronicles*, 288; "The Account by a Gentleman from Elvas," in Clayton, Knight, and Moore, eds., *The De Soto Chronicles*, 93-95.

7. "The Account by a Gentleman from Elvas," in Clayton, Knight, and Moore, eds., *The De Soto Chronicles*, 93, 95; "Account of the Northern Conquest," in Clayton, Knight, and Moore, eds., *The De Soto Chronicles*, 285.

8. Adorno and Pautz, eds., *The Narrative of Cabeza de Vaca*, 64, 66-67, 69; "La Florida," in Clayton, Knight, and Moore, eds., *The De Soto Chronicles*, 2: 189-199, 211-216; Hudson, *Knights of Spain*, 138-144.

9. "La Florida," in Clayton, Knight, and Moore, eds., *The De Soto Chronicles*, 2: 148.

10. "La Florida," in Clayton, Knight, and Moore, eds., *The De Soto Chronicles*, 2: 152; Ethridge, *From Chicaza to Chickasaw*, 15-16; Hudson, *The Southeastern Indians*, 223; Widmer, "The Structure of Southeastern Chiefdoms," 140.

11. Ethridge, *From Chicaza to Chickasaw*, 16; Jennings, *New Worlds of Violence*, 11-28; Widmer, "The Structure of Southeastern Chiefdoms," 143-146; Dye and King, "Desecrating the Sacred Ancestor Temples," 160-181; Anderson, "Stability and Change," 192, 202-207.

12. Anderson, "Stability and Change," 203-205.

13. "La Florida," in Clayton, Knight, and Moore, eds., *The De Soto Chronicles*, 2: 325-326.

14. "Relation of the Island of Florida," in Clayton, Knight, and Moore, eds., *The De Soto Chronicles*, 229; "La Florida," in Clayton, Knight, and Moore, eds., *The De Soto Chronicles*, 2: 272, 282; Hudson, *Knights of Spain*, 164-166. For the "cycling" of the Savannah River basin and its buffer zone, see Anderson, "Stability and Change," 207-211.

15. "La Florida," in Clayton, Knight, and Moore, eds., *The De Soto Chronicles*, 2: 280-283; Hudson, *Knights of Spain*, 180.

16. "La Florida," in Clayton, Knight, and Moore, eds., *The De Soto Chronicles*, 2: 394.

17. "La Florida," in Clayton, Knight, and Moore, eds., *The De Soto Chronicles*, 2: 397-398.

18. "La Florida," in Clayton, Knight, and Moore, eds., *The De Soto Chronicles*, 2: 397-398; Ethridge, *From Chicaza to Chickasaw*, 51-53; Widmer, "The Structure of Southeastern Chiefdoms," 147; Anderson, "Stability and Change," 197.

19. "La Florida," in Clayton, Knight, and Moore, eds., *The De Soto Chronicles*, 2: 400-403.

20. "La Florida," in Clayton, Knight, and Moore, eds., *The De Soto Chronicles*, 2: 402-403, 405.

Two Towns Destroyed

While the everyday theft of people and food could have a devastating impact on communities across the Southeast, their fates can only be suggested. Even the fate of Casqui can only be imagined. The destruction of two towns, Napetuca and Mavila, however, do not have to be imagined, and they demonstrate the raw destructive power of de Soto's men when things took a turn for the worse. Although each ended with the utter annihilation of the entire community, each began with the familiar threads of stealing food, stealing women, and stealing headmen. Each also brings back into focus the power of the Columbian Exchange, although this time it was not disease but technology that led to destruction.

The military technology Spaniards wielded against Natives had the potential to upend and even destroy entire Native communities. First was the steel armor and weaponry utilized by most Spanish warriors. Native archers, Spaniards were quick to admit, were exceptionally good with their bows, which were often described by the chroniclers in great detail. "If the arrow does not find armor, it penetrates as deeply as a crossbow," one described. That usually did not happen, however, because Spaniards of all rank were usually clad in some sort of steel armor that could handle all but a perfectly placed shot. If a Spaniard was only wearing woven chain mail armor, then the arrows, which were made of large reeds, could split and penetrate. If impacting on plated armor, however, they usually broke where the arrowhead attached to the shaft and shattered.[1] Only a head, neck, or even a groin hit usually proved fatal. In general arrows might have been painful but were largely ineffective.

Mississippian warriors also usually carried heavy war clubs designed to inflict blunt-force trauma at close quarters. While these war clubs were capable of doing incredible damage, again, their capabilities were limited against a strongly armored Spanish foot soldier with a shield. That foot soldier also had at least a sword, while cavalrymen usually carried long, thrusting lances. Natives not only did not have a similar type of armor; they wore almost nothing into battle at all, leaving their bodies basically entirely exposed. While the impact of Native weaponry on steel could be incapacitating, the impact of the Spaniards' steel weapons on exposed flesh was, naturally, devastating. At Mavila, according to one chronicler, during one Spanish attack, "we killed them all, some with the fire, others with the swords, others with the lances."[2] Even though they were widely acknowledged to be skilled fighters, there was little Natives could do to protect themselves from Spanish weapons, a vulnerability not necessarily shared by the Spanish. Bladed Spanish weapons could easily wound or kill unprotected Natives, while Natives had to get lucky with amazing shots or with multiple crushing blows with their war clubs to defeat Spanish armor. The effect of military technology, even without horses, was a tremendous Spanish advantage.

Horses greatly magnified that tactical advantage. Horses had not inhabited North America since the end of the last ice age. In Spain, however, equestrian skills and the ownership of a horse were powerful markers of social position among the Spanish hidalgos that made up many of de Soto's cavalrymen. Spaniards bred horses of North African origin, like strong and durable Barb and Arabian breeds, and respected and revered them. The men rode in a flexed style that gave them not only agility and control over their horse but control over the lance they carried, which from their elevated position they could spear down at Natives with devastating effect. Of one engagement a Spanish chronicler casually mentioned that in one charge alone made by his mounted men "thirty or forty Indians were lanced." The cavalryman was the epitome of the Spanish military edge in La Florida. Heavily armored and mounted on armored horses, the violence only a handful of cavalrymen could inflict on a community could be tremendous. During the Napetuca uprising, for example, Luis de Moscoso "struck his legs to his horse" shouting to Santiago to rally his men, "and thus, all of a sudden, the people on horseback went lancing many Indians," beginning what was a quick rout for the Spaniards of a carefully planned and well-executed surprise attack by the Natives.[3]

Mounted cavalry was the backbone of the Spanish entrada, and the loss of horses was a loss keenly felt. If the battle of Mavila sapped Spanish morale, for instance, then the logistical end of the expedition came at Chicaza, when warriors succeeded in taking out most of the expedition's horses. Dozens of horses were burned to death in the attack as well as most of the cavalry gear, meaning that even the surviving horses would be of little use. "We were so poorly supplied that although we still had some horses, we have neither saddle, nor lance, nor shield, because all had burned." Without cavalry, the technological advantage de Soto's men had over their Native counterparts was greatly diminished, and his army was much less of a threat.[4]

All of this destructive power was brought to bear in all its gore in the destruction of Napetuca and Mavila. The destruction first took place in the earliest days of the expedition, well before de Soto and his men had grown bitter over their failure to find gold. It began while the expedition was still in peninsular Florida, and not yet even to Apalachee. De Soto seized a headman named by one account Vitachuco, the chieftain of a smaller town by the name of Caliquen, north of modern-day Ocala. His men left with Vitachuco in addition to countless more of the townspeople as they moved toward Apalachee. Incensed by the theft, the town's warriors shadowed de Soto, pleading with him every day for almost a week to secure Vitachuco's release. This Mississippian chieftain was evidently highly revered, as the stubbornness of Caliquen's warriors revealed. Another headman from a neighboring town, apparently kin, also personally pleaded for his return. "They asked the governor to free the cacique, but he refused to free him, for he feared lest they revolt and refuse to give him guides and from day to day he dismissed them." In other words, what de Soto had done to that point was nothing particularly special. As more principal headmen and warriors grew increasingly belligerent, however, it was clear that the seizure of Vitachuco was beginning to cause problems.

On the road toward Napetuca, the chieftain himself grew angrier, threatening to have the Spaniards killed if he was not released, exerting his spiritual authority to claim he would have the earth eat the Spaniards up. By the time de Soto reached Napetuca, the warriors trailing him were also done asking. They confronted de Soto's men with hundreds of warriors, sending two emissaries to demand the return of their chief. The Spaniards "handsomely equipped, armed, and in battle array," and most importantly having been forewarned, responded with a surprise attack. It was in this attack that the power of mounted cavalry could be utilized to de Soto's terrific advantage. De Soto, "one of the four best lances that have passed to or are now in the West Indies," according to one chronicler, led one of the first charges.

The battle was an absolute rout. It was "laughable," de la Vega wrote, "although bloody and cruel for the poor Indians." With de Soto at the lead of such a well-executed charge the Natives, "unable to resist the impetus of three hundred horses together, as they had no pikes, turned and ran," without putting up much of a fight at all. Instead "their greatest thought was where they could escape." The cavalry was quick to take the offensive. Scores of warriors were lanced, and many more fled either into the woods or into two nearby lakes. Spaniards surrounded the smaller lake, setting off a nightlong game of hide-and-seek where under the cover of darkness, Natives tried to slip out of the water to escape. Pursuing Spaniards, aided no doubt by their dogs, dashed in to grab them. Most of the warriors were captured this way, drug out and chained up until the rest surrendered. According to de la Vega close to one thousand Natives were captured and divvied up among the men "to act as their servants and to be held as such, as a penalty and punishment for the treason they had committed.

Among the captured masses Vitachuco again made plans to rise up, spreading word that at a precise time they should "be ready to kill the Spaniard who had fallen to his lot as master; at the same hour he himself would kill the governor." At the moment of revolt, in the middle of a meal, Vitachuco rose up and struck de Soto in the face so hard he was spitting blood from his mouth. All of the Spaniards around de Soto took their weapons and hacked the headman to pieces. He died "blaspheming the heavens and the earth of not having succeeded in his evil purpose." The revolt still spread rapidly, with the Natives hitting at the Spaniards with everything they had. "One Indian gave his master a blow on the head with a firebrand and laid him at his feet, and then knocked him senseless with two or three other blows. The Spaniards, in retaliation, "lost patience and began to kill and wreak vengeance upon them," turning the meal into a bloodbath. Scores of remaining warriors were subdued a second time, but only the youngest were kept alive. The rest, even those that had not outwardly rebelled, were handed over to a group of Natives from another community who had also been taken along as laborers and guides. Along with the Spaniards these Natives, from Paracoxi, fastened the condemned to poles in the middle of the town and executed them all.[5]

The chroniclers claimed that hundreds, perhaps thousands, were killed. Thousands seems extreme if the size of Napetuca was comparable to surrounding chiefdoms. While we will never know the true death toll at Napetuca, there was little left when de Soto moved on. The town's entire political structure was wiped out, and most of its population was dead or enslaved. When a small group of his cavalry rode through on their way back to the coast for provisioning, they worried about resistance they might find there, and so they approached it with caution. Upon their arrival, however, "they lost all their anxiety because they found it entirely burned and destroyed and the walls leveled to the ground." The town had been abandoned, and hastily. The bodies of the dead lay in heaps, having gone unburied. As was later described, the town's survivors abandoned it "because it was founded on an unlucky and unfortunate site," and that the tragedy that had befell the town "had been caused more by the unluckiness of the place and the ill-fortune of the dead" than by Spanish weaponry. The passerby Spaniards, without understanding Native culture or caring to, were not too far off. The death of so many of its townspeople and the destruction of its temples left a harmonic tear in the community's cultural and religious fabric that simply could not be mended. By the time the men passed by Napetuca a second time on their return to Apalachee, they had very appropriately given it the name "La Matanza," translated as the massacre.[6]

The surrounding countryside fared no better. De Soto's men were attacked relentlessly in the outlying cornfields on their way out of the province. The Spaniards responded by killing everyone they saw: they "speared them without sparing anyone; they took very few prisoners." As a result, the next town they entered was abandoned, "for because of the news which the Indians had of the massacre of Napeteca they dared not remain." The community wanted absolutely nothing to do with de Soto or his men and risked abandoning their town and fleeing into the woods to escape them. That only left their fields vulnerable, and in town the men found the community's food stores rich in corn, beans, and squashes, "and on which the Christians lived there."[7] Two of de Soto's men were tasked with hunting the townspeople down anyway for slaves, and returned with one hundred of them, all of whom were clapped in chains. These, a source makes clear, included plenty of the town's women and children, who were led away with the expedition as it moved on.[8]

These attacks, over the course of only a few days, demonstrated all of the destructive power that could be wielded, knowingly and unknowingly, by de Soto and his men. The theft of food, the kidnapping of labor, and the abuse of chieftains. The destructive power of Spanish weaponry. The vulnerability of Native food sources. The fragile and competitive religious and political worlds the headmen controlled. Everything seemed to come to a head at Napetuca, and the results were devastating. By the time de Soto moved out of the region and into Apalachee, he and his men had more or less wiped an entire town off the map and forced the dislocation or dissolution of neighboring communities. And all within a few months of landing in La Florida.

For all of the carnage of those first months, however, the destruction of Napetuca still paled in comparison to the bodies de Soto's men stacked up around the town of Mavila. That struggle began much the same, with the same formalities de Soto had counted on in the past. After taking laborers and men from Coosa and then Talisi, de Soto's army marched to Tascalusa, where the chieftain of the same name resided. Tascalusa, who met de Soto in a powerful show of pomp and celebration, was a man "very tall of body, large limbed, lean, and well built." His presence was imposing, as was his demeanor. "He was greatly feared by his neighbors and vassals. He was lord of many lands and many people. In his aspect he was very dignified." Most likely a paramount chief, Tascalusa represented the epitome of the Mississippian world. After a few short ceremonial exchanges de Soto began the march onward, and of course he took Tascalusa with him. Different accounts give different dispositions, but most paint the march in tense, irritated terms. "Afterward we asked him to give us Indians to carry the burdens, and he responded that he was not accustomed to serving anyone, rather that all served him before," went one. As was the case with the Lady of Cofitachequi, it seems de Soto tried to strike a balance between keeping the chieftain captive while simultaneously trying to keep him comfortable and even entertained. If that approach only succeeded partially with the Lady of Cofitachequi, it completely failed with Tascalusa.[9]

By the time the army reached Mavila, Tascalusa had dispensed with the pleasantries altogether and was actively plotting his revenge. He left de Soto's party once in town and refused to budge when de Soto planned to march on. If the Spanish wanted to leave peacefully, he warned, then they needed to leave immediately, "and should not insist on trying to take him out of his lands and dominion by force." According to another account, he was already in that moment actively planning an uprising. Whether Tascalusa was actually scheming or just sulking, naturally, de Soto escalated the situation. Accounts about the attack that started the uprising differ from account to account. Tascalusa was holed up in a central building when a man by the name of Baltasar de Gallegos entered to force him out. Instead, he found the room stacked with warriors, poised to strike. Gallegos shouted an alarm and grabbed at the nearest headman by his marten-skin coat, only to have the chieftain slip it off "over his head and left it in his hands."

It is unclear from the several accounts whether this was Tascalusa or one of his war chiefs. At that moment "all the Indians straightway rose in revolt," presumably with Tascalusa at their lead, and Gallegos slashed the chief who had affronted him with his sword, "which opened up his back." By another account the slash evidently lopped his whole arm off, while according to a third it went basically through the entire side of his body, and "as he wore no defensive armor nor even any clothing except the mantle," it "laid open his whole side." Whether this was or was not Tascalusa is uncertain. Regardless, Gallegos's gash set off the battle of Mavila.[10]

According to other accounts, reconnoitering Spaniards discovered countless Native warriors concealed in the houses, both within the palisade and around it, right before violence broke out. Either way, armed resistance had been in the works for some time. Everyone was armed and there were stores of extra arms staged in nearby houses. Apparently, warriors from the entire province were there, and they were waiting for the right moment to pour out.[11] At the first alarms they did exactly that, and so quickly and violently that de Soto's advanced guard, inside the town, was quickly forced out. With his rear guard still on the way into town de Soto dismounted many of his cavalry and prepared them to enter by force, while other mounted cavalrymen surrounded the palisade. The attack that followed, with Spaniards attempting to gain control of the town, raged all day.

"The Indians fought with so great spirit that they drove us outside again and again." Spanish soldiers, exhausted from the struggle, attempted to drink water from a nearby pond only to find it stained red with blood. Finally, in one of their advances into the palisade the men succeeded in setting the town on fire. Natives fled the flames inside the palisade only to be cut down by the cavalry, and "after the Christians had come among them cutting with the sword, seeing that they were assailed beyond repair, many fled into the burning houses, where, piled up one on top of the other, they were suffocated and burned to death."[12]

Gracilaso de la Vega spent entire chapters recounting the battle of Mavila. Of the several chroniclers to write of de Soto's entrada, he was by far the most vociferous, the most colorful, and certainly the most prone to exaggeration. While his accounts should be read with extreme caution, there can be little doubt that the battle of Mavila was fierce. If his writings are to be believed, there were hints at the incredible military prowess of Tascalusa's Native defenders. There is also, unfortunately, plenty of evidence to suggest that such prowess was not enough to stave off a slaughter. In the very first moments of the attack, for example, Baltasar de Gallegos was assaulted by a young warrior, supposed to be kin to one of the slain headmen, who "shot six or seven arrows at him with great fury and swiftness" at extremely close range. His abilities were impressive, no doubt, but because Gallegos was so heavily armored, none of the arrows found their mark. Realizing the ineffectiveness of the quiver the young warrior closed the distance between the two men quickly, bashing Gallegos over the head with his bow as if it was a war club. Gallegos was stunned from the blows and bleeding, but again because of his armor—this time his helmet—was still able to retaliate, and "very hastily stabbed him twice in the breast, and with this his enemy fell." Nothing the warrior was able to do, despite being in close quarters, acting fearlessly and by all accounts being an excellent shot, gave him the advantage against Gallegos.

Then there was Don Carlos Enriquez, who a Native archer did manage to kill while the Spaniard was trying to remove an arrow from his horse. With his body stretched down the horse's neck, trying to grab the arrow, his throat was left exposed by gaps in his armor. At that exact moment of vulnerability, a flint-tipped arrow struck exactly where it needed to, "in the small part of the throat that was unprotected and without armor, for all the rest of his body was well armored," dropping him from his horse and killing him.[13] If it was purposeful, the shot that killed Enriquez required great skill and perfect timing in a split second of vulnerability. If it was luck, then apparently only luck could kill a mounted Spaniard. Either way, the odds were not with the Natives. Enriquez's death, together with Gallegos's assault, demonstrated just how difficult it was to kill a well-armored soldier.

Again, horses created for Spaniards an insurmountable advantage, even when in the rush of the first outbreak of violence, they lost several horses. Many of the advanced guard within the palisade had brought their horses with them but had dismounted and walked them in. In their immediate retreat many of the cavalrymen did not have time to remount and were forced to leave their horses. The Natives, recognizing the animals' importance, wasted no time shooting them full of arrows, "with extreme satisfaction and rejoicing." They also seized whatever armor and weaponry the Spaniards left inside by the men. Actions like these momentarily leveled the playing field, but only momentarily. Whatever the Natives gained by grabbing a few bladed weapons and killing a few horses, far too much remained in Spanish hands. Hundreds of cavalrymen remained, more than enough to mount charges that decimated Native warriors.

It did not take long at all for more mounted men to arrive outside the gate and begin forming a plan of attack. When they pursued Natives too close to the palisade, warriors lobbed arrows down on them. Very soon the horsemen had developed a strategy to use the open landscape surrounding the town to begin setting traps. Groups of cavalries would charge toward the walls and then retreat, purposefully yielding "more ground than the Indians forced them to lose." The ploy drew warriors out of the walls and into the open plain where the cavalry would have the advantage, and "where they could charge them with lances." Only after hours of this tactic, feigning retreat only to turn and charge, did the Natives catch on, realizing "they were getting the worst of the battle on an open field because of the damage that the horses were doing them." To counter the advantage, they retreated into the palisade altogether, forcing the Spaniards to enter on foot.[14]

Groups of warriors had also climbed the walls of the densely packed town and fled out into the cornfields. By using cover to their advantage, these warriors were able to fight the Spaniards in ways most suited to them—by ambushing quickly and stealthily from cover and fighting hand to hand in close quarters with war clubs. Even this advantage, however, was short lived. The warriors "soon recognized that their plan was ill-advised, because if their lightness gave them an advantage over the Spanish infantry, those on horseback were their superiors and speared them in the field entirely at their pleasure." Ambush tactics were no match for heavily armored cavalrymen with lances, and Natives had no knowledge of anti-cavalry tactics or the weaponry that they would need to defeat the horsemen. Natives might have fashioned pikes from nearby trees, for instance, that could have blunted the Spanish charges, but how could Natives have known how to do that? Without experience against armored horsemen these men and women stood little chance, and "thus a great many of them died on the field, ill-advised in their ferocity and vain presumption," wrote a pompous Gracilaso de la Vega.[15]

Native casualty numbers were certainly exaggerated by de la Vega and the others, but it had to have been in the hundreds, if not thousands. Dozens of Spaniards were killed and almost every survivor wounded in several places, a testament to the brutality of the fighting. The town lay in ruins and the dead and wounded were scattered for miles around. "It was pitiful to hear them groaning in the woods, entirely helpless."[16] When Spaniards asked if there were any warriors planning any retaliation, a Native they had captured assured them that was impossible—"that inasmuch as the bravest, noblest, and richest men of that province had perished in the recent battle, no one remained in it who could take up arms." Along with its dead and dislocated men and women, the paramount chief and all of the town's leading men were gone, either dead or on the run. Whatever the Spaniards found to feed themselves while they recovered, they took and burned the rest. The Tascalusa chiefdom would endure the battle of Mavila, but Mavila was rendered a political, cultural, and spiritual wreck.[17] The battle of Mavila, like the massacre at Napetuca, demonstrated the most terrific consequences of the Mississippian encounter.

Notes

1. "The Account by a Gentleman from Elvas," in Clayton, Knight, and Moore, eds., *The De Soto Chronicles*, 59; Hudson, *Knights of Spain*, 17-20; Hudson, *Southeastern Indians*, 244-247.

2. "The Account by a Gentleman from Elvas," in Clayton, Knight, and Moore, eds., *The De Soto Chronicles*, 68; "Relation of the Island of Florida," in Clayton, Knight, and Moore, eds., *The De Soto Chronicles*, 235; Hudson, *Southeastern Indians*, 244-247.

3. "Account of the Northern Conquest," in Clayton, Knight, and Moore, eds., *The De Soto Chronicles*, 265; Crosby, *The Columbian Exchange*, 79-81; Hudson, *Knights of Spain*, 72-74.

4. "Relation of the Island of Florida," in Clayton, Knight, and Moore, eds., *The De Soto Chronicles*, 236-237.

5. This account of the assault is taken from "The Account by a Gentleman from Elvas," in Clayton, Knight, and Moore, eds., *The De Soto Chronicles*, 67-69; "Relation of the Island of Florida," in Clayton, Knight, and Moore, eds., *The De Soto Chronicles*, 226; "Account of the Northern Conquest," in Clayton, Knight, and Moore, eds., *The De Soto Chronicles*, 262-266. The attack is also recounted at length in "La Florida," in Clayton, Knight, and Moore, eds., *The De Soto Chronicles*, 2: 166-175, 178-183; and Hudson, *Knights of Spain*, 108-115.

6. "La Florida," in Clayton, Knight, and Moore, eds., *The De Soto Chronicles*, 2: 207-208, 237; Anderson, "Stability and Change," 197.

7. "La Florida," in Clayton, Knight, and Moore, eds., *The De Soto Chronicles*, 2: 183-185; "The Account by a Gentleman from Elvas," in Clayton, Knight, and Moore, eds., *The De Soto Chronicles*, 70.

8. "The Account by a Gentleman from Elvas," in Clayton, Knight, and Moore, eds., *The De Soto Chronicles*, 69-70; "Account of the Northern Conquest," in Clayton, Knight, and Moore, eds., *The De Soto Chronicles*, 266; "La Florida," in Clayton, Knight, and Moore, eds., *The De Soto Chronicles*, 2: 184-185.

9. "The Account by a Gentleman from Elvas," in Clayton, Knight, and Moore, eds., *The De Soto Chronicles*, 95-99; "Relation of the Island of Florida," in Clayton, Knight, and Moore, eds., *The De Soto Chronicles*, 232; "La Florida," in Clayton, Knight, and Moore, eds., *The De Soto Chronicles*, 2: 327-328. Gracilaso de la Vega gave the contradicting report that Tascalusa asked to accompany the expedition, although he would later write that it started to appear to the Spaniards that he was feigning friendship in anticipation of the attack. See "La Florida," in Clayton, Knight, and Moore, eds., *The De Soto Chronicles*, 2: 328-329.

10. "The Account by a Gentleman from Elvas," in Clayton, Knight, and Moore, eds., *The De Soto Chronicles*, 98-99; "Relation of the Island of Florida," in Clayton, Knight, and Moore, eds., *The De Soto Chronicles*, 232-235; "Account of the Northern Conquest," in Clayton, Knight, and Moore, eds., *The De Soto Chronicles*, 292; "La Florida," in Clayton, Knight, and Moore, eds., *The De Soto Chronicles*, 2: 335. The most extensive account of Tascalusa and the battle of Mavila comes from "La Florida," in Clayton, Knight, and Moore, eds., *The De Soto Chronicles*, 2: 327-354.

11. "La Florida," in Clayton, Knight, and Moore, eds., *The De Soto Chronicles*, 2: 331-333.

12. "The Account by a Gentleman from Elvas," in Clayton, Knight, and Moore, eds., *The De Soto Chronicles*, 99-104; "La Florida," in Clayton, Knight, and Moore, eds., *The De Soto Chronicles*, 2: 337-346.

13. "La Florida," in Clayton, Knight, and Moore, eds., *The De Soto Chronicles*, 2: 336, 339.

14. "La Florida," in Clayton, Knight, and Moore, eds., *The De Soto Chronicles*, 2: 336-339.

15. "La Florida," in Clayton, Knight, and Moore, eds., *The De Soto Chronicles*, 2: 344-345; Hudson, *Knights of Spain*, 23-24; Ethridge, *From Chicaza to Chickasaw*, 51-52.

16. "The Account by a Gentleman from Elvas," in Clayton, Knight, and Moore, eds., *The De Soto Chronicles*, 104; "La Florida," in Clayton, Knight, and Moore, eds., *The De Soto Chronicles*, 2: 352.

17. "Account of the Northern Conquest," in Clayton, Knight, and Moore, eds., *The De Soto Chronicles*, 294; "La Florida," in Clayton, Knight, and Moore, eds., *The De Soto Chronicles*, 2: 342-343, 352, 355; Ethridge, *From Chicaza to Chickasaw*, 28, 66-67.

6 Spanish-American Places

In 1695 St. Augustine, La Florida's largest colonial settlement, was abuzz with drama. Local authorities were pursuing a criminal investigation into two young Apalachee men whom they accused of running a counterfeiting ring. It all began in May of that year, with Crispin de Tapia working at a local St. Augustine grocery. De Tapia was a "free pardo," meaning he was a man of African descent but not a slave. He was also apparently a military officer. As de Tapia described the incident, a boy walked into the shop and bought a Spanish real's worth of rosquetes, small, sweet cakes "made in a spiral shape." He paid with two small silver half-real coins and left, only to return soon after for another order. He purchased more pastries with two more half-real coins and departed again, this time for good.

De Tapia, finding all this perfectly ordinary, put the four coins away. Later that day, however, another servant boy working for resident María de Reina came in to purchase some flour and other provisions. He paid with a real coin, and for change, de Tapia issued him one of the half-reals he had received earlier. The boy went on his way but returned not long after, "saying that the half-real piece that he had been given was not silver," but rather "of tin or pewter." In other words, it was fake. In fact, all four of the half-reals were fake. De Tapia put all four coins aside and waited for the perpetrators to return. Low and behold, one did. Soon, another Apalachee boy appeared, looking for more pastries. De Tapia immediately grabbed this one and made his way to the governor, Laureano de Torres y Ayala, to make sense of the case. The Apalachee boy was soon in jail, and a full investigation was on.

When pressed about the coins, the boy pleaded his innocence convincingly. He pointed the finger instead to an "Andrés de Escavedo," himself a Native laborer who served Patricio de Monson, a soldier in the town's garrison. It was de Escavedo who had given him the coins, this boy claimed. His story was soon corroborated when another victim stepped forward, Isavel de los Rios, who told a strikingly similar story. Isavel de los Rios was "a free morena," meaning she too was African American but not a slave. She was also a store worker, and an Apalachee boy also swindled her out of two reals' worth of rosquetes using the same fake coins, which "she accepted because they seemed to be of silver." She admitted briefly to trying to pass the coins off herself, but to no luck. Instead, more showed up the next day with another Native servant of the same Patricio de Monson, who tried to buy sugar syrup from de los Rios. A strange coincidence indeed. Instead of giving up the syrup, Rios seized the coins, beat the boy with a stick, and "threw him out the door." When later confronted, this kid likewise pled complete ignorance, and also named Andrés de Escavedo as the source of his trouble. Escavedo, mentioned twice now by two separate witnesses, was quickly emerging as the prime suspect.

There was no doubt that these two young boys, who could not even speak Spanish, had clearly been used. The one de Tapia caught, Santiago, was about fifteen years old and served Sergeant Major Francisco de Sigaroa of the garrison, who also owned a ranch outside of town. He described how Escavedo had given him the coins and told him to buy the pastries, and that was all there was to it. When he was seized, he did not even know why, but he did notice that when de Tapia drug him out into the street, Escavedo was watching and immediately ran away. It was clear this poor kid was no counterfeiter. The second boy, even younger, was even more clueless, and "on their showing him the real that he said that he brought, he recognized it and said that it was the same one" that Andrés de Escavedo had given him to buy the sugar syrup. Neither did he have any idea what was going on. And how could he have? A young Native boy like that had held few silver pieces in his lifetime.

The two boys' depositions made this an open-and-closed case. Andrés de Escavedo was the real perpetrator here, who was taking advantage of young and naïve Apalachee boys to launder his counterfeit reals. But the gig was now up; the young boys were ordered released and a warrant issued for de Escavedo's arrest. De Escavedo's master, Patricio de Monson, immediately delivered up the fugitive, who was soon being interrogated. Although at first he denied any knowledge of the incident and the evidence, Escavedo quickly cracked. A twenty-three-year-old Apalachee man who had "no other trade than to render service in what he was ordered to," de Escavedo must have realized he was in over his head.

De Escavedo described finding a tin plate in town and taking it back to de Monson's place. There he and another Apalachee man by the name of Cosme melted the tin down to make buttons. It was a harmless enough experiment, but when their button project was done and the two still had some metal left over, they decided to try their hand at making reals. They made a coin mold out of some wood and used knives to make the coins' characteristic cross engravings. He and Cosme made nine in all, de Escavedo admitted, and had used them all. Hopefully, the men enjoyed their sweet cakes, because they were now caught and they were in deep trouble.

De Escavedo's confession led to a warrant for Cosme, who was soon apprehended and interrogated as well. In contrast to the first defendant, Cosme denied the allegations vehemently, which drew the story out a bit. In the end, however, the evidence was more than sufficient to put these two Apalachees' shenanigans to an end, even without Cosme's confession. Justice was swift. Both were given a short trial, found guilty, and sentenced to work "as forced laborers in the royal works." One of them was also sentenced to a whipping, although it was unclear who that was. Justice meted out, St. Augustine went on its way, and the case of the counterfeit reals was closed.[1]

The Apalachee counterfeiting opens this next chapter on transformations by showing a bit of the creolization of St. Augustine and, to a lesser extent, La Florida. The case makes for an entertaining, almost humorous, early American crime drama. It also offers a tantalizing peek into everyday life in St. Augustine and seventeenth-century La Florida. Consider the actors. First was the cast of royal authorities who conducted the investigation and recorded the depositions. They were led by Governor Laureano de Torres y Ayala, who was described as a *señor don* and a "knight of the order of Santiago."[2] Not only was this man governor and captain-general, but he was a hidalgo of the highest class, who was legally entitled to wear the same Cross of Santiago as Menéndez or de Soto before him. Next down the list were the masters of the Native Apalachee workers involved in the crimes: Patricio de Monson, Francisco de Sigaroa, and María de Reina. They were all members of St. Augustine's military and civilian community, and the men and women who controlled the labor of those much further down the social ladder: the two Andrés, Santiago, and Cosme. They were all Apalachee boys and young men, and worked either as farm laborers, ranch hands, or house servants. Not quite slaves, but certainly not entirely free. Lastly were Crispin de Tapia and Isavel de los Rios, the immediate victims of the counterfeiting. Neither were they slaves; they were free blacks, and one was evidently a soldier. There were all sorts of people living in this tiny corner of the Spanish colonial world, people of all walks of life. Because of the case of the counterfeit coins and stolen pastries, they all made their way into La Florida's story.

St. Augustine, if one is to believe the Apalachee counterfeiting case, was a pretty multicultural place. For all of La Florida's neglect, and for all of St. Augustine's supposed loneliness and misery, this frontier town was still very much a Spanish colonial one, both in design and social composition. It was a Catholic community and a military establishment. It was a port town with a familiar colonial layout. It was a multi-ethnic and multicultural place by seventeenth-century standards, reminiscent almost of a smaller eighteenth-century New Orleans. St. Augustine might have been an unimpressive one, but it is America's first community, and it was a surprisingly cosmopolitan one at that.

Notes

1. Hann, "Apalachee Counterfeiters in St. Augustine," 52-68.
2. Hann, "Apalachee Counterfeiters in St. Augustine," 53.

From Martyrs to Models

La Florida's church history actually predates its settlement history, considering a friar landed at the site of St. Augustine before Pedro Menéndez de Avilés. That marked the end of generations of unsuccessful religious colonization attempts in the region, proselytizing campaigns that had been profoundly unkind to the Dominicans and Jesuits that had attempted them in Spain's least understood colonial possession. Religious men were with Ayllón in South Carolina, and possibly with de León before that. They traveled with Narváez and de Soto. Fray Luis Cáncer de Barbastro and several of his companions died on the beach in southwest peninsular Florida in 1549. Dominicans came and went with Tristán de Luna in 1559, probably to both Pensacola and Santa Elena.[1] In these earliest years religious proselytizing in La Florida did not just fail; it usually meant death.

Father Francisco López de Mendoza Grajales somewhat changed that history when he was already on hand to greet Menéndez as he came onto shore in 1565. Yet the change did not come quickly. While Grajales successfully established the first American church there, Nombre de Dios, not much else worked out. Menéndez oversaw the construction of several fortified missions in peninsular Florida and in modern-day Virginia, all of which included some sort of religious presence. Each one of them was soon gone, and more clergymen were dead. That included Ajacán, in Virginia, which Powhatan Natives wiped out in 1571.[2] For another wave of Catholic missionaries, La Florida represented for the Catholic Church an irresistible challenge. It would also come to represent an almost certain death.

How different things were only a century later. By the late seventeenth century, missions stretched from St. Augustine west across peninsular Florida, almost into modern-day Alabama, and up the Atlantic Coast almost to South Carolina, with circuit-riding friars making their rounds among La Florida's tens of thousands of Native peoples. By that time, it would appear as if the Catholic Church had finally gained the La Florida presence that had eluded it for so long.

The friars that would see to this evangelistic revolution were not Jesuits, who were long gone by the time La Florida missions were actually gaining converts. The disappointing collapse of the coastal missions in the 1560s and the destruction of the entire Ajacán mission in Virginia in 1571 were more than enough for the brothers of the Society of Jesus to wash their hands of La Florida. Their withdrawal threatened to end Menéndez's plans for Florida, both spiritually and strategically. The saving of souls mattered for the Church, of course, but as was the case elsewhere in the Spanish New World, the Church also played a critical role in securing the Native labor that would be necessary to build and defend La Florida. The collapse of the Jesuit missions required a remedy, which Menéndez sought from Crown authorities immediately. Spanish officials quickly obliged, authorizing almost two dozen Franciscans to sail for La Florida in 1573, not only a year or two after the dust had settled at Ajacán.

The field for this next wave of missionaries was the coastline between St. Augustine and Santa Elena, among the Mocama, Guale, and Orista Natives of present-day coastal Georgia and South Carolina. Perhaps, the Franciscan leadership thought, the Guale might prove more receptive to Christianity than their southerly neighbors had been. The land also seemed more appealing for large-scale European-style farming. Consequently, the first three Franciscans to arrive in La Florida immediately headed north. And despite what seemed to be early conversion victories nearby, all three were gone by 1575. Not a good start, but also not surprising. More recognizable yet, if the situation was dicey while they were around, then things only got worse after they left. Within the next year soldiers from Santa Elena had provoked a full-on rebellion that would last for years.

The uprising began with the killing of dozens of Spanish soldiers and ended with the retaliatory burning of Guale and Orista settlements along most of modern coastal Georgia. Santa Elena was briefly besieged and temporarily abandoned. The stretch of coastline from Santa Elena to St. Augustine was in chaos for almost an entire decade, costing the lives of scores of Spaniards and Natives and leaving little room for mission work. The next decade, from 1585 to 1595, brought less violence but more disappointment. Even though more than two dozen Franciscans came and went through the colony, the number of active missionaries always seemed to hover right around zero. Coastal Georgia was a mess, the region around Santa Elena was deadly, and soon Santa Elena itself was no more.[3]

Another dozen friars arrived in 1595 and after a tantalizing stretch of mission expansions up the Georgia coast, more of them were killed in another large Guale uprising that began in 1597. A Guale headman set the rebellion off by murdering Father Pedro de Corpa, who attended to the Nuestra Señora de Guadalupe de Tolomato mission on the Georgia coastline. After bludgeoning him to death with a stone axe the young chieftain decapitated Father Corpa, placed his severed head on display in the town, then moved on to spread the rebellion down the coast. Corpa was the first of a half-dozen clergy to fall in the uprising. Whatever the hopeful Franciscans accomplished in the two years after their arrival along coastal north Florida and Georgia, they had to build again starting in 1600. It took that long for relations to normalize between Spaniards and the Guale after this second violent revolt, and after an even more violent retaliation.[4]

While the Jesuit Order surrendered La Florida after only a few years of failed work and less than a dozen lost clergy, the Franciscans proved much more determined. Not only did the order not abandon Guale after the uprising; it sent over fifty more friars and mission workers to St. Augustine from 1605 to 1620, many of whom went from there to work up the coast. It was this group that finally began making headway for the church, and the La Florida mission district began to expand. By the middle of the 1700s, seven missions along the Georgia coast served the Guale people. Closer to St. Augustine were more missions among the Mocama and Timucua groups along the modern-day Florida-Georgia state line, at places like Amelia and Cumberland Islands. Never again would the friars cross into South Carolina or attempt mission efforts among the Orista. Despite those permanent losses, Franciscan missions slowly but surely expanded along the Atlantic coastline.[5] By the time Protestant Pilgrims landed in Plymouth in 1619, the Catholic Church was well established on the southeastern coast of what would be the United States of America.

Some of those among the same influx of missionaries also began to stretch a Catholic frontier west into north-central Florida. Wary chieftains, lured by Spanish trade goods, agreed to accept the friars, and soon mission districts in St. Augustine, Guale, Mocama, and Timucua expanded to include Potano and Agua Dulce, the latter two extending west near the present-day location of Alachua. By moving into the Florida panhandle the friars edged closer to Apalachee territory, the region that had been the stuff of Spanish legend since the days of Pánfilo de Narváez. What a surprise it must have been when a delegation of Apalachees, hailing from some of the same communities that had squared off against de Soto only generations earlier, met Father Martin Prieto and his Timucua companions in peace in 1608. The celebration, which by the Spanish accounts included tens of thousands of Natives, was enormous. What an unbelievable reversal of La Florida history that moment represented. Franciscans entered triumphantly into a region named entirely after Native ferocity against Spanish expansionism in the past. This was the biggest, clearest victory for the Catholic Church yet in La Florida.[6]

Although it took a few more years to realize, Prieto's gamble had paved the way for the Franciscan proselytizing of Apalachee itself. Fathers Francisco Martínez and Pedro Muñoz followed those first 1608 encounters with the establishment of missions in the early 1630s, kicking off a wave of Apalachee expansion which friars would consolidate near mid-century. This was more than just a reversal of the violence of the past. Apalachee was a Mississippian Complex Chiefdom and existed in the early seventeenth century much the same as when de Soto last marched through it generations earlier. Disease might have already affected it, certainly, but in 1635 the population still stood in the tens of thousands, and the Mississippian social, religious, and economic structures appeared as strong as they ever had been. This provided Catholic missionaries with an opportunity to attempt the widespread, top-down societal conversion of an entire Native society. That was something Catholics had succeeded in doing in Central Mexico, but something which had eluded the church for decades thus far in La Florida.[7]

Much of that conversion would take place in frontier religious outposts, dotting a road that moved through the panhandle of modern Florida. The exact locations of many of these enclaves, which did not house resident clergy permanently, have been difficult to uncover. Known as *visitas*, most were basic sites constructed for baptisms, Masses, etc., and friars and laypeople only passed through them temporarily. They were positioned more or less within a day's ride of each other along a public road, the Camino Real, making for dependable access for a friar on horseback. Hundreds of years before the Second Great Awakening, when circuit-riding Presbyterian, Baptist, and Methodist preachers visited far-flung American settlements, Catholic friars made the very same trek into La Florida in what one historian called "flying missions."[8] These were the first European evangelizers in what would be the United States of America.

Many of the pioneers of Florida and Southeastern Native archaeology, men and women like John Goggin, Kathleen Deagan, Bonnie McEwan, and Brent Weisman, made their academic bones hunting down and revealing these small and isolated chapels. Rudimentary structures made of pine and palmetto, it is not hard to imagine the Florida landscape reclaiming them not long after their abandonment. San Martin de Ayacuto, one such chapel located on the St. Johns River, featured a small half-roofed pavilion, which would have contained little more than an altar and some religious objects. The structure was not much, but it was more than enough for the small community around it and was consistent with other mission chapels elsewhere in the Spanish New World.

Much larger was San Luís de Talimali, which at the end of the seventeenth century was the jewel in the crown of Franciscan La Florida. As friars and other mission workers made their way into Apalachee country the road took them far from St. Augustine, too far to rely on the town for supplies and far too isolated for any hope of safety. For that reason, Governor Mendez de Canço first stationed soldiers in the area of present-day Tallahassee in 1638. A deputy governor, Claudio Luís de Florência, was soon living in the neighborhood. All of this would be the foundation for the sprawling San Luís de Talimali mission complex, complete with a fortification and permanent military garrison of its own, all of which was established by mid-century. Eventually it would also contain a Spanish village that would cater to the soldiers and their families, making San Luís de Talimali one of America's first creole communities.

The establishment and growth of San Luís de Talimali marked the apogee of Franciscan evangelism in La Florida. It was a substantial *doctrina* placed at the center of a significant Mississippian population, a massive complex with sprawling Apalachee communities dotting the countryside around it. The immediate mission community alone boasted a population of more than a thousand residents at its height late in the seventeenth century, while thousands of Apalachees were baptized and living under the mission bell. Just to the south, at the present-day town of St. Marks, authorities constructed a small port and later a fortification, San Marcos de Apalachee. From there the Spaniards could more easily supply the mission and its people, and regional ranches and farms could export their goods without taking them all the way to St. Augustine. The export of ranch and mission products—legally and illegally—opened the center of the Florida panhandle to trade with the outside world. If St. Augustine was the Southeast's first multicultural, multiracial society, then San Luís de Talimali was not far behind it.[9]

By the late seventeenth century, the missions were so successful for the Franciscan Order that when colonial authorities once again considered shuttering St. Augustine, it was the friars that stepped up to voice their objections. The town was the logistical center of an impressive string of missions, reaching up the coast of modern-day Georgia and through the panhandle of modern-day Florida. Overlooking the violent history of disease, exploitation, and uprising attached to those missions, of course, the friars were able to point to thousands of souls already saved, and to tens of thousands more in the waiting. When it came to permanent royal support, the missions and their circuit-riding friars were now an important consideration.[10]

While St. Augustine was always the center of religious activity in the colony, San Luís de Talimali would be the point from which new western Timucua and Apalachee missions, like San Martin de Ayacuto, were created. At its center, as with the other mission compounds in La Florida, was always a church, signifying its importance in the day-to-day life of both the Spanish and the Apalachee. The church at San Luís de Talimali, at over one hundred feet long and fifty feet wide, would have been an impressive structure even by modern standards. In a backwater colony like La Florida, in the seventeenth century, it would have been epic in scale. Most churches were considerably smaller and not nearly as elaborate. Some might have been fully enclosed but others might have had only three sides, creating an open nave. Completely open-air pavilions also existed in the smaller, more far-flung missions. Construction depended on the site, the size of the church, and the building materials at hand. Roofing was almost always thatched palm or palmetto. Flooring would have ranged from dirt to clay to raised wood, while the walls might have been boards secured with nails for a sizeable church, or wattle-and-daub construction for a smaller, more isolated chapel. Most would have contained a sanctuary with an altar and would have been lined with religious carvings, paintings, and artifacts.[11]

While the church was always the main feature, in the larger mission compounds it was only one of several important structures. Conventos where the friars stayed, kitchens, and other outbuildings were also commonly built around the compound's plaza, projecting a European lifestyle that the clergymen impressed upon their Native charges. For many of these friars it was not good enough for Natives to simply rattle back Catholic doctrine when required. In the best traditions of conversion, which would be followed by Europeans elsewhere in Colonial America, Natives had to look and act like good Catholics as well as sound like them. Clergymen introduced Natives to European tools, foods, and farming techniques. Among the new European foods introduced in settings like these were fruits like watermelons, peaches, figs, and oranges; grains like wheat; and animals like pigs and chickens. Chiefs were bribed into accepting and supporting the missions with European clothing and prestige items that projected their privileged status. Meanwhile commoners were taught literacy—to better read and understand Christian doctrines, of course—and a good Catholic lifestyle. By the time a second or third generation of La Florida Natives was growing up among these mission towns, religious scholars argue, they were no more or less Christian than were Spanish settlers in nearby St. Augustine.[12]

This access to European material culture was an important consideration in the bargain that was struck between Natives and the friars. Mission work was complicated, often forceful, and fundamentally exploitative, and the Catholic Church functioned in La Florida the same as elsewhere in the Spanish colonies: it was one of the primary engines of Spanish colonialism. Missions were positioned in the villages of leading headmen only after they had rendered obedience and paid homage to both Spain and the Catholic Church. If the first Jesuit missionaries had been too demanding, too overbearing, or too culturally insensitive in their efforts, then so, too, could be the Franciscans who replaced them. Their proselytization constituted an all-out assault on Native culture. Christian names replaced Native ones. The Spanish language was taught not simply so converts could read, but so they could better learn their catechisms and other Christian liturgy. Corporal punishment was administered to those who neglected their studies, and those who fled in the face of a beating were treated even worse. The virtue of marriage and monogamy was impressed. Native religious practices and superstitions were heavily disparaged, which put friars and Native shamans in direct competition with each other.[13] In the immediate vicinity of the missions Franciscans were clearly fighting both a religious and a cultural war. It was heavily contested and often a violent struggle.

Compounding the issue were the work requirements placed on all Native participants in the communities that surrounded the missions. The larger missions in La Florida were *doctrinas*, just as Spanish missions had always been, beginning on Hispaniola. While the *doctrina* was above all else designed for religious instruction, its close secondary function was to provide structure for the labor requirements made by La Florida's religious and civil-military figures.[14] In that respect what took place in La Florida was hardly unique. Although there was no *encomienda* system of the type that devastated Native communities in the Caribbean and Central and South America, there were certainly *repartimiento* requirements that put immense pressure on Native economies and social structures, and which sometimes fomented violence.

It was Native labor that built and maintained the missions, and Native labor that provided the food for its clergy and any nearby soldiers. Although La Florida was a much smaller and less prosperous mission district than say New Spain, it was not so different in function. None of the missions, and certainly not St. Augustine, would have survived without both Native labor and Native food.

Instruction in European farming techniques was not done simply for the benefit of Native farmers, or to advance European culture. Plows, draft animals, etc., were introduced as farming techniques and were taught in order to get Native farmers to increase crop yields, much of which would then be utilized by the missions or processed and exported out of the mission districts.

The pressure for Natives to produce foodstuffs for Spaniards cannot be better illustrated than by the existence, if only for a short time, of Floridian wheat farms. Wheat, of course, is not indigenous to North America, but wheat bread was as central to a classic European diet as communion wafers were central to Catholicism. For both reasons local Spanish authorities, always hopeful that they might replace heathen corn with civilized wheat, never gave up the hope of developing a local source of wheat. So, they pushed, for decades, for the development of wheat plantations in both Timucua and Apalachee territory. Although these farms did produce the occasional wheat crop, it was never enough to break Spaniards of their need to import wheat at great cost. All this painful experimenting was done, of course, using Native labor.[15]

Increased demand to produce Spanish foodstuffs, like wheat, is an excellent example of the tremendous stress Spanish colonialism placed on Native communities. While widespread systems of exploitation, like *encomiendas* or *repartimientos*, did not develop in La Florida as they had in the Caribbean or elsewhere in the Americas, it was not for a lack of effort on the part of Spaniards. They certainly tried, and their efforts often pushed Native communities to the breaking point, and sometimes over it. First, of course, were the Guale and Orista revolts late in the sixteenth century. A major Apalachee uprising touched off in 1647, after just over a decade of sustained Catholic presence in the region. Spanish soldiers from St. Augustine and Cuba put the rebellion down, eventually, but not before it had at one time included thousands of Apalachees, and not before it destroyed almost every Spanish mission in the province. The fallout revealed how effectively the Spanish had finally extended colonization into La Florida. A separate rebellion coursed through Timucua territory not ten years later, with Timucua headmen rising up for largely the same reasons, and Spanish officials responding with similar violence.[16] Both rebellions were desperate, violent affairs, revealing the toll of Spanish colonization on the Native population. It was a colonization largely overseen by Franciscan Friars.

To say that this mission system was unbelievably culturally insensitive and overbearing by modern sensibilities would be to put it mildly. Yet La Florida's Franciscans were still theoretically committed to a more immersive and inclusive approach to Native communities than had been their Jesuit predecessors, at least by seventeenth-century standards. Their demands created incredible friction, and occasionally fomented violence. They also produced a foothold in La Florida that lasted generations.[17] Friars exerted influence over townspeople with Spanish tools and technology. Banquets and prestige items pleased Native chiefs, supporting their traditional roles. Although it must have been revolting for them to do so, friars also made at least a few efforts to meet Natives in their own spaces. That was true at the most basic level of communication—language. Where previous Jesuits worked through guides and interpreters, the Franciscans were determined to learn the language and better understand the culture as the means to evangelize more successfully. When Father Baltasár López began the Franciscan expansion westward from St. Augustine he evidently already spoke the Timucua language. Fathers Martínez and Muñoz, leading the Franciscan advance into Apalachee territory, learned the language as well.[18]

At the community level and particularly at a large model mission like San Luís de Talimali, physical markers of both Spanish and Native cultural and political comingling were also apparent. A massive reconstructed Native council house stands at the San Luis mission in present-day Tallahassee, evidence that the Spanish did seem inclined at least at times to follow Native diplomatic and political protocols. And while they mounted relentless attacks on Native cultural traditions that they considered incompatible with Christianity, the friars also turned a blind eye to others that might have been questionable, but endurable. Such was the case with the massive plaza that would have also been visible in the center of the mission community. Plazas were central meeting and ceremonial places in Mississippian communities and continued to be so at mission San Luis. There was also the ball game, the massive lacrosse-like athletic spectacle that mixed intense competition and inter-community rivalry with religious ritual. It generated a partying and gambling atmosphere that Spanish soldiers watched, and that Franciscan friars disparaged but for the most part tolerated. Even when friars appeared to get it officially banned from Apalachee, the ball game most likely endured in less visible ways, and would continue serving important social and political functions across the colonial period into the post-Removal West.[19]

Among the most notable of Franciscans to pass through La Florida was Father Francisco Pareja. Pareja arrived in St. Augustine in the great 1595 push and might be considered North America's first professional ethnographer. More specifically, his work translating the Timucua language was a powerful colonial first with a complicated legacy. On the one hand it certainly demonstrates the Franciscans' dedication to their work, while also illustrating the great lengths Franciscans were willing to go to replace Native traditions with Catholic ones. What Pareja produced, in other words, is a fascinating glimpse into the Native cultural traditions Catholic missionaries wanted to better understand, if only to eradicate them more effectively. By 1613 Pareja had not only learned Timucua but translated a catechism and confessional guide into the Timucua language. One published edition includes the same questions posed in Castilian Spanish above its Timucua translation. Pareja designed his questionnaire around the Ten Commandments and the seven deadly sins, and there was no doubt in his mind that most of his Native charges were guilty of just about every one of them.[20]

A glimpse into the opening section of Pareja's guide leads the reader through questions about the spirituality in everyday Timucuan lives, from the meaning of birds chirping to the sight of barn owls and snakes. He also questioned them on customs and ceremonies that righted wrongs or ensured successful growing seasons. Believing in any of this spirituality, according to Pareja, was idolatrous, for it was all in clear violation of the First Commandment:

> *Have you believed that lighting a new separate fire will cure illness?*
>
> *¿has cries que hacienda candela nueva aparte sanará el enfermo?*
>
> *Ano, iqilabamabuetaleqe, tacachaleca, arecota na, baluhabelemanta bohobicho?*
>
> *Have you consented to be cured by some herbalist by praying with words to the Devil?*
>
> *¿Has consentido te cure algun herbolario rezándote con palabras del Demonio?*
>
> *Isucuma chorobonima, hiti hebuata ituhuta choroboqena tema nibicho?*
>
> *When encountering any snake in the road, field, or in the house have you believed it to be a prognostication and omen of evil?*
>
> *¿Encontrando alguna culebra en el camino campo, o en casa, la has creído ser aguero y presagio de mal?*
>
> *Yyolaco pahaco puenotaheco ayaco ali hotaqe nacaquinoleheco maha ynininco nahyqe enenoleheco mosima yabisacatala manda bohobicho?*

If a Native answered in the affirmative, the admonition was stern (only the English translation is presented):

> *Son, from now on do not do these things or consent to them, only with the herbs and baths cure yourself, because they have virtue in that God gave and created them to heal us, and all other things that you do and pray for are not of benefit, but instead harm us since they are sins.*[21]

So went a very long and very detailed confessional that moved from one commandment to the next, asking all sorts of intrusive questions about the role of Native faith healers and chiefs, about warriors and game players, about women's menstruation, childbirth and abortion, and even about everyday sexual relations and homosexuality.[22] Consider how Pareja would have grilled a man on his sex life:

> Have you gone around with desire for someone?
>
> Have you physically fondled someone?
>
> Speaking with someone and embracing or holding the hand, were you aroused?
>
> Did you kiss someone?
>
> Have you had relations with any married woman?
>
> Or with any single woman?
>
> How many times?
>
> Have you had relations with some young lady?
>
> How many times with each one?
>
> Among these are there any that are kin?
>
> On what way are they kin?
>
> With your kin have you gone around?
>
> Kin in what way?
>
> With some kin of your wife have you carried on?

Kin in what manner?

Have you gone around with two sisters?

Or with mother or with daughter?

Have you had intercourse with your mother-in-law?

Have you gone around with your godmother?

Have you had intercourse with someone contrary to the ordinary manner?[23]

Questions like these, reflecting a very conservative Catholic ideology colliding with a very different and generally much freer set of Native sexual norms, were surely tense ones. Polygamy stood in direct contravention of the bible's seventh commandment against adultery, as well as several of the deadly sins the friars would expect Native charges to understand and revere. Same-sex relationships were obviously abominable, but even almost any physical relationship out of wedlock was highly problematic. Perhaps the same questions, asked demandingly in Spanish by overbearing Jesuit priests in shacks along the coast of La Florida a generation earlier, were the reason Natives rose up and destroyed them. Although the Spanish approach of evangelism had changed, the content had not.

Pareja's guide to confession is so culturally insensitive by modern standards that it can be painful to read. Nevertheless, it was celebrated by the Franciscan Order at the time as a revolutionary approach to mission work and was reprinted and utilized as a guide in missions elsewhere in New Spain. That makes Pareja an important, if not an incredibly problematic, La Florida legacy. By translating the sweeping confessional from Castilian Spanish to the Timucua language, administering it in Timucuan, and recording the answers, Pareja and the priests that followed him into La Florida left for modern anthropologists and historians a treasure trove of information on Mississippian peoples, their customs, and their beliefs. By doing so Pareja was transformed, albeit unwittingly, from a backwater Franciscan friar into perhaps North America's first scholar of Native America.[24] He was also, clearly, a pretty terrible person.

The irony is unbelievable. Francisco Pareja's Timucua language efforts were appallingly misguided. Nevertheless, because of his work and those like him, the academic subjects of Native American linguistics, ethnography, and history have their beginnings in La Florida. What a fitting way to describe America's earliest circuit-riding Catholic priests, as well as their place in America's early religious history. Friars like Pavila, Pareja, and the dozens more that traversed the La Florida countryside dropped "their lamps into the darkness," in the words of one more modern church historian, writing "their names into one of the least known but heroic chapters of American and Catholic history."[25] This twentieth-century scholar's own Euro-centric equating of Native life with "darkness" demonstrates the terribly problematic legacy of the religious work done by men like Francisco Pareja centuries previous. Southeastern Natives both in the past and present certainly would not use that terminology to refer to their faith practices. And as for the work of the friars, whose missions more or less enslaved and indoctrinated thousands of Timucuas and Apalachees over the course of generations, heroic might not be the right word. Invasive, insulting, and abusive might be better synonyms. Still, theirs certainly was an important chapter in Catholic, Native American, and American history, and definitely one of the least known.

NOTES

1. Weddle, *Spanish Sea*, 243-248; 260; Weber, *The Spanish Frontier*, 74; Gannon, "Altar and Hearth," 31-35; O'Daniel, *Dominicans in Early Florida*, 114-115; Hoffman, "Legend, Religious Idealism, and Colonies," 61-63.

2. Lyon, *The Enterprise of Florida*, 170, 201-203; Hahn, *Missions to the Calusa*; Hoffman, *A New Andalucia*, 255, 261-266; Weber, *The Spanish Frontier*, 71-73, 100; Milanich, *Laboring in the Fields of the Lord*, 93-103; Milanich, "Franciscan Missions and Native Peoples in Spanish Florida," 278-279; Bushnell, *Situado and Sabana*, 38-40; Lewis and Loomie, *The Spanish Jesuit Mission in Virginia*.

3. Galgano, *Feast of Souls*, 41-42; Milanich, *Laboring in the Fields of the Lord*, 104-106; Bushnell, *Situado and Sabana*, 42-43.

4. Bushnell, *Situado and Sabana*, 60-70; Milanich, *Laboring in the Fields of the Lord*, 109-114.

5. Hoffman, *Florida's Frontiers*, 101-107; Milanich, *Laboring in the Fields of the Lord*, 114-115; Bushnell, *Situado and Sabana*, 49-50.

6. Hann, *Apalache*, 10-11; Milanich, *Laboring in the Fields of the Lord*, 116-123; Bushnell, *Situado and Sabana*, 70-72.

7. Hann, *Apalachee*, 11-14; Hoffman, *Florida's Frontiers*, 107-110; Milanich, *Laboring in the Fields of the Lord*, 123-126, 130-131.

8. Bushnell, *Situado and Sabana*, 64, 71; Milanich, *Laboring in the Fields of the Lord*, 117.

9. McEwan, "Hispanic Life," 295-297; Hann, *Apalachee*, 14-16, 194-212; Milanich, *Laboring in the Fields of the Lord*, 126.

10. Weber, *The Spanish Frontier*, 75, 88-89; Golgano, *Feast of Souls*, 43-45; Bushnell, *Situado and Sabana*, 66-67.

11. Golgano, *Feast of Souls*, 47-50; Milanich, *Laboring in the Fields of the Lord*, 132-137; Hann, *Apalachee*, 212-217.

12. Milanich, *Laboring in the Fields of the Lord*, 143-146; McEwan, "The Historical Archaeology of Seventeenth-Century La Florida," 500-501; Loucks, "Spanish-Indian Interaction," 201-202; Reitz, "Evidence for Animal Use," 377-394; Hann, *Apalachee*, 237-265; Comer, "North America from 1492 to the Present," 1305, 1307.

13. Golgano, *Feast of* Souls, 43-60; Weber, *The Spanish Frontier*, 81-85; Milanich, *Laboring in the Fields of the Lord*, 144; Bushnell, *Situado and Sabana*, 96; Hann, *Apalachee*, 237-265.

14. Bushnell, *Situado and Sabana*, 21, 23; Chatelain, *The Defenses*, 24.

15. Milanich, *Laboring in the Fields of the Lord*, 106-109, 115-119, 149-153; Bushnell, *Situado and Sabana*, 78-79, 111-117; Ruhl, "Oranges and Wheat," 42-44.

16. Hann, *Apalachee*, 16-19, 22; Hoffman, *Florida's Frontiers*, 122-132; Milanich, *Laboring in the Fields of the Lord*, 126-127, 161-165; Bushnell, *Situado and Sabana*, 128-133.

17. Milanich, *Laboring in the Fields of the Lord*, 104-129; Milanich, "Franciscan Missions and Native Peoples in Spanish Florida," 278-280; Bushnell, *Situado and Sabana*, 49, 60-72.

18. Milanich, *Laboring in the Fields of the Lord*, 117, 124; Elliott, *Empires*, 70, 84.

19. Hoffman, *Florida's Frontiers*, 136; Milanich, *Laboring in the Fields of the Lord*, 142-143; 148-149; Hann, *Apalachee*, 18-20.

20. Weber, *The Spanish Frontier*, 108-110; Bushnell, *Situado and Sabana*, 95; Milanich, "Franciscan Missions and Native Peoples in Spanish Florida," 293-297.

21. Milanich and Sturtevant, eds., *Francisco Pareja's 1613 Confessionario*, 23-25.

22. Milanich and Sturtevant, eds., *Francisco Pareja's 1613 Confessionario*, 23-39.

23. Milanich and Sturtevant, eds., *Francisco Pareja's 1613 Confessionario*, 37-38.

24. Weber, *The Spanish Frontier*, 108-110.

25. Gannon, "Altar and Hearth," 42.

Spanish-American Places

Among common misperceptions about the Spanish presence in the Americas—and this would particularly be the case in what would be the United States of America—one would certainly be that of all the European colonizing powers, the Spanish were the least interested in actually staying in America. Spaniards were only in the New World for plunder, so the story goes, while British colonists like the Pilgrims who celebrated the First Thanksgiving had always intended to build their lives in the New World. Yet, not only is the oldest settlement in what is now the United States Spanish, but every prospective *adelantado*, including de León, de Ayllón, Narváez, de Soto, de Luna, and Menéndez, came with the intent to stay.[1] Not only was St. Augustine founded as a place of permanence, but by the time plans for British settlements in Virginia and New England were just getting off the ground, the capital of La Florida had already gone through generations of ups and downs.

Governance of New World territories all began, at least in the beginning, with the *adelantado*. These men would act not only as conquerors, but as governors and colonizers. They were after all expanding—or "advancing," as *adelantado* translates into English—conquest into places without recognizable European-style governments. It should be noted at this point, of course, that all of the places Spanish conquistadores would go in the Americas already had complex and sometimes-sprawling governments, based on centuries-old political traditions, including in every corner of what was La Florida. But for prospective colonizers like Pedro Menéndez de Avilés, they were not Catholic, and they were not Spanish, so they did not count. And so it was that written into Menéndez's *capitulación* was a requirement not just to establish fortified towns, but to see to the creation of permanent settlements. It was the same requirement that was in most of the *capitulaciónes* issued during the age of Spanish New World colonialism. By positioning men and friars along the coast of La Florida, Menéndez was fulfilling that requirement, at least until they all mutinied or were killed. And when Menéndez caught several of them in the act personally, he flexed his enormous authority as *adelantado*. It was his responsibility to build and govern La Florida, at least in these first years, so "by voice and trumpet," wrote one historian, Menéndez went about proclaiming the first set of ordinances that would order people's lives. In doing so, he established America's first laws of European descent.[2]

In the case of St. Augustine, the punishments to be meted out for disobedience were strict indeed, reflecting the importance Menéndez, as an aspiring *adelantado*, placed in the success of his colony. Time in the stocks, the denial of food rations, hard labor, sentences on work boats, and even execution awaited those who perpetrated acts of civil or religious disobedience. Many of these punishments might come off as a bit harsh, but they were far from unordinary. Even a brief perusing of Jamestown's or Boston's first laws would suggest that they were actually quite typical. Bringing order to the colonial chaos of Spain's New World required a hard hand; this was a tradition begun in Hispaniola with the arrival of Nicholás de Ovando, and it continued to La Florida.[3]

Neither was Menéndez's desire to use the structure of the town to curb the chaos of conquest and colonization particularly unique. While certainly strong and decisive, the *adelantado* was only doing what was expected of him in 1565, and by founding St. Augustine was not only following in the footsteps of previous conquistadores, but he was also continuing several important Hispanic traditions into the New World. All notable conquistadores before him, including Ovando and Cortés, came from a Hispanic culture that cherished an urban lifestyle and respected the civil authority that made it all work. The very first decisions made by these men were for the establishment of those two deeply interconnected things—municipalities and their requisite authorities. When Ovando reestablished civil authority in an anarchical 1502 Hispaniola, he was directed by the Crown to bring an island to heel by settling towns and establishing Hispanic government. Cortés did the very same thing along the New Spain coast, legitimizing his authority by founding Vera Cruz and placing it under his control.

These men were not simply going through the motions; this was how the Spanish world was supposed to be. The Pilgrims of the *Mayflower* would do much the same a century later, electing their governor and officials just as Vera Cruz's officials elected Cortés into his positions of authority.[4] In time the authority of the *adelantado* would give way to an elaborate and highly bureaucratic royal government, overseen by the Crown, the Council of the Indies, and regional *audiencias*. Urbanite Spanish influences on the New World would, as these overlapping institutions ensured, remain constant. The Spanish colonial world would mirror the Iberian Spanish world, through the growth of towns and the administration of municipalities.

The foundation of that government was the *cabildo*, or council, the nerve center of any municipality. The *cabildo* constituted each town's leading men, and comprised the governor, its military leadership, town *alcaldes* (mayors), and other officials like a *contador* (accountant), a *tesorero* (treasurer), and others. The *cabildo* elected various *regidores* (civic officials) and set about codifying the community's laws and ordinances. It was the *cabildo* that essentially ran the colony, acting as its primary governing and bureaucratic body, managing all public responsibilities, lands, laws, militias, community standards, etc. This was the foundation of the Spanish world and if this sounds recognizable, it is. La Florida's first *cabildo* functioned the same as any modern municipal government or city council does in America today.[5] Local American governance began in St. Augustine.

The fact that the community's governing body included civil, military, and religious figures meant that such governance, although it was constructed around a common framework, would have looked nothing like it does today. The lines of authority were blurred at a time when the Church was the state and the military was the state. Again, however, that was no different than with any early American settlement. In the early days of Boston, after all, you had to be a member of the Church to live in Boston, let alone vote.

What did set St. Augustine apart, even from other Spanish colonial settlements of the period, was its relation to the Crown. Where royal officials required other settlements to be self-sufficient and to produce some sort of revenue for the Crown, for its entire existence La Florida would do almost exactly the opposite. St. Augustine served for the Spanish Crown a few very simple, narrow purposes, none of which made money. It established a physical claim to La Florida and the Eastern Seaboard, a claim that otherwise would have existed only on paper. It also established control of the Florida Straits and Bahamian Channel, something that was necessary to keep piracy from getting worse than it already was. One historian described the presence as one of "dynastic prestige," and so St. Augustine was maintained "at a cost out of all proportion to benefits received." Because that was ostensibly its only purpose, La Florida was a "perennial military frontier," which never truly grew out of the shadow of fortified St. Augustine.

In this unique situation, La Florida's governors, all of whom were military men, received their orders directly from the King. Colonial affairs were not accountable to the regional Spanish governments either in Santo Domingo or Mexico City, a loophole that seemed to bother neither of those governing bodies.

La Florida was too undeveloped and unserviceable for any outside authorities to want to deal with it anyway. Not only was the colony isolated, but it contained nothing of obvious value, a problem that hurt its prospective residents as much as anyone else, creating a nasty feedback loop that guaranteed that nothing would change. With no functioning *encomienda* labor system, Spaniards could not make money by producing exports the old-fashioned way, which is to say by forcing Natives to produce them. Without exports, the local government had no tax base. Indian trade goods were difficult to come by because Spaniards had nothing to trade for them. Imports were ridiculously expensive because Spanish merchants had no incentive to send ships there. In short and economically speaking, La Florida was useless. Perhaps one of the reasons why St. Augustine regularly eludes discussions of American foundations is because it always seemed so pathetic, teetering on the edge of the Atlantic world and always seemingly in danger of not existing at all.[6]

Instead, La Florida survived because of direct Crown support in the form of cash payments made through the government of New Spain, making St. Augustine a singular place in the Hispanic New World. This was called the *situado* and included funds for every aspect of the colony's operation, from Indian trade goods to religious paraphernalia to soldiers' wages. It all arrived once a year in a massive payment of cash, which might have made things simple if it was reliable. The fund never seemed to be enough, was constantly late coming from New Spain, and sometimes never arrived at all. Usually when it did arrive, much of it went directly to third-party creditors, who billed St. Augustinians exorbitant rates for goods because they did not have cash, again because of the *situado*.[7] Another La Florida feedback loop that guaranteed that St. Augustine was destined to go nowhere.

While La Florida never came close to a thriving Spanish colony, St. Augustine's residents did not exactly resign themselves to lives of complete privation. Difficult conditions that were out of their control forced residents to do what they had to do to make ends meet, and a unique La Florida paradox emerged. For a colony that was notoriously dependent, La Florida could also be a surprisingly independent place, at least when it came to keeping food on the table. As the saying goes, necessity is the mother of invention. St. Augustine's residents in 1650 would begrudgingly agree. The town's garrison and residents relied on what was locally available, which could be plenty when the circumstances were right and if proud Spaniards could bring themselves to eat Native foods. A more recognizable fare of pigs and cattle did well in the area if they could be kept safe, but wild meats like turkey, venison, and fish could always be had if relations with local Natives were friendly. Spanish settlers succeeded in importing fruits and vegetables like chili peppers, melons, peaches, and peas, and grew them in the town commons, while Natives produced wild nuts and berries.

If growing wheat was where Hispanic dreams met La Florida realities, then it was Native corn that kept Spaniards alive in the American Southeast. Compulsory corn agriculture was part of *repartimiento* work in La Florida, but it also flowed naturally as tribute through a preexisting Native system called the *sabana*, which had Mississippian precedents. Native hierarchies and bureaucracies were what enterprising Spaniards so appreciated because they made exploitation simple. Because Natives in the Southeast were already farming large amounts of corn to produce community tribute, St. Augustine officials simply set themselves up as another chieftain to which Natives would pay that tribute. Corn grown by Native men and processed by Native women traveled south along the coast in Guale canoes while Timucua, Potano, and Apalachee Natives shipped it east. St. Augustine residents, the proud Spanish colonizers they surely considered themselves, ate an awful lot of corn.[8]

When the *sabana* system was working properly and Native foodstuffs were abundant, St. Augustinians were well fed. Authorities could never seem to build up reserves adequate to weather the colony's downturns, however, and there were plenty of downturns. Whenever rebellions, disease, or sieges disrupted the flow of corn the entire town faced scarcity, and that happened far too many times in the seventeenth century alone to make even the most prosperous St. Augustine residents confident of anything. This was a feast-or-famine town.[9] Residents were forced by the uncertain nature of the *situado* to run a self-reliant colony and they did, but while St. Augustine always seemed to endure, it never prospered.

To say La Florida's first generation was rough would be putting things mildly. St. Augustine's location shifted back and forth from the mainland side of the Matanzas River just north of the present town, across the river to Anastasia Island in 1566, then back to the mainland in 1572, where it now stands. Within the next decade the French retaliated for their losses at Fort Caroline by massacring all the Spaniards stationed at that same post on the St. Johns River. Menéndez's soldiers mutinied constantly. Several forts were built, abandoned, or demolished, and then rebuilt. Hostile Timucua lurked and Guale Natives rose up in rebellion several times by the turn of the century. There was little reason for anyone to take this place seriously. As one historian summed it up, "harassed by poverty" in a place with no obvious source of wealth, restricted by Spanish laws that made it difficult to trade, own land, or even graze cattle, "beset not only by the natural foes of the wilderness" but by Natives, the French, and pirates, it would appear as if St. Augustine was basically the worst place on earth. And that was all before Sir Francis Drake arrived.[10]

Drake's 1586 raid was not without an interesting but still obligatory La Florida first. In the process of destroying the town Drake's men drew up their approach, creating the first extant map of an American city. That is a technical first, and the map is well engraved and quite beautiful to behold. Still, it depicted St. Augustine buildings that soon would no longer exist. Drake's men burned it all to the ground. There were 250 houses in the town, went one British report, "but we left not one of them standing." To continue to maintain the place, wrote one clearly disillusioned Havana official, "is merely to incur expense because it is and has been entirely unprofitable, nor can it sustain its own population."[11]

Refugees from the abandoned Santa Elena settlement flooded in, making St. Augustine's dependency problem even greater. Everyone went to work rebuilding the place only to see much of it burn again in 1599, this time by accident. Then a hurricane hit. Then it flooded. Not only is it understandable that the town never thrived, but it's also a miracle St. Augustine existed at all as the seventeenth century dawned. The Crown considered abandoning the outpost in the early years of the seventeenth century and almost did. If anything else bad had happened it probably would have, and if it weren't for the Crown's continued support St. Augustine would certainly have gone the way of Roanoke, Popham, or Cape Fear. Instead, Jamestown happened, making a presence in La Florida more important than ever, and making St. Augustine worth its astronomical price tag. So, while seventeenth-century St. Augustine was no paradise, it was fated to endure.[12]

Despite its limitations, St. Augustine was classically Hispanic in design. Although small, this was a Spanish town, a symbol of permanence and stability and the foundation upon which future expansion was built. Among the ranks of its residents were its *dons*, hidalgos who operated at the highest echelons of Spanish colonial society. They were *peninsulares*, who were born in Spain, and most of the colony's highest offices were reserved to them. Just below them were Florida creoles, known as Floridians or *Floridanos*. These were the colonially born descendants of *peninsulares*. Despite their lineage they still maintained a lower social position simply by virtue of being born in the New World, but many of them did rise to attain prominent military and civil positions within the colony. Despite the outrageous hardships of life in La Florida, their number did grow, proof that despite all its trials and tribulations, Spaniards built St. Augustine to stay.

The town's citizenry, whether peninsular Spanish or Florida creole, were foremost *vecinos*, or householders, and their primary residence was in town on a plot of land issued to them by the local government. That city residence was the foundation of Spanish colonial society, just as was the municipality that issued the land. Next to it was the rural estate, a *hacienda* or an *estancia*, a more commercial property that spread out into the countryside and exploited the labor of the Native population through *encomienda* allotments. This, and not the desire for a quaint city life, was what brought countless Spaniards to the New World. Yet you could not have one without the other. Prospective *encomenderos* had to invest in their municipality to gain lands and Native allotments. They had to agree to reside in town for the better part of a decade, proving they were there to stay. Married men had to bring their wives and children over and single men were expected to marry. City residence started it all, even for a man like Cortés, who began his conquistador career with a residency on Hispaniola. If this pattern again sounds familiar, it was the way seventeenth-century Puritan New Englanders wanted things as well. They, too, had to be community members as well as church members. They, too, had to have economic connections to the colony, and they, too, had to contribute to its growth and success. They, too, were *vecinos*, just English Protestant ones.[13]

Haciendas and *estancias* would take decades to develop in La Florida and even then, they were rare compared to in other colonies. First, life in St. Augustine had to improve enough for prospective *vecinos* to consider taking a gamble on the place. Take, for instance, the makeup of St. Augustine's first homes. In the town's earliest years, a well-to-do *Floridano* would have lived in only the most basic home, and would have displayed his family's wealth and prestige in movable goods like furnishings, silver, and fine fabrics. These were things he and his family could pack up and carry into the woods on short notice, like say when the town burned or was attacked by pirates. Who would want to invest in a proper home if that was what the future held?

As life and prospects began to stabilize early in the seventeenth century, that began to change. With years having gone by without some sort of catastrophe, St. Augustinians' outlook improved to the point where many of them began considering more permanent ties. Maybe they should build real houses. According to extensive archaeological work done in the city's center, many St. Augustine *vecinos* did exactly that, and some of them were apparently quite nice. They were considered large and relatively expansive for the period and ranged from wattle-and-daub construction with palm-thatched roofs to boarded homes with shingled roofs. Two-story buildings with balconies in the front and patios and arcades in the back were not uncommon. Most featured fenced or walled-in grounds with gardens as well as barrel wells and garbage pits.[14] Although small, St. Augustine featured classic European homes along walkways and thoroughfares that Spaniards would have found familiar and perhaps even pretty.

That urban scene stretched out into the streets and onto the same roads that tourists can walk today. Spanish colonial cities were the first to expand in the form of classic European squares and rectangles, with commons and spaces for parks. The rules for city construction, codified by Philip II in 1573, made for America's first urban landscapes. At the center of the town was its main plaza, the *plaza mayor*, which for St. Augustine was and remains the Plaza de Armas. It is, as one architectural historian describes it, "an urban space that even today is the undisputed center of town." This was where a particularly well-off *vecino* might buy a prime lot; if he did, his family would be in excellent company. It was upon the central plaza where the governor's mansion, public buildings, and the church were placed. Late in the sixteenth century incoming Governor Gonzalo Méndez de Canço used his own funds to build a new home on the main plaza complete with a fenced-in field. On his way out in 1603 de Canço sold his property to the Crown, creating America's first modern capitol building and executive mansion. From there the town spread out in a "grid-iron" plan, in the words of one historian, which made for easy and orderly expansion. Paralleling and intersecting streets created tidy city blocks, which could be divvied out to prospective *vecinos*. On the outskirts of town were the commons, communal fields and pastures that could be planted by all residents and used to graze animals.[15]

As one scholar wrote, a visitor to St. Augustine in the present can still see the remnants of this growth in the "regularity of the streets, the pleasant plazas or centrally located public squares, the beautiful patios or gardens, often hidden away behind high garden walls, the impressive churches and cathedrals, and the comfortable homes." While such a description evokes images of Charleston or Savannah, St. Augustine came first. The nearby English did take notice of the seventeenth-century Spanish design and referenced its functionality when considering their expansion. This was the orderly plan the Virginia Company referenced in 1622 when trying to save a badly struggling Jamestown. The community needed to be built much closer together as would "make if not handsome towns, yet compact and orderly villages," as "the example of the Spaniards in the West Indies doth fully instance." Future English towns like Charleston, Savannah, and even Philadelphia, which expanded out in an orderly grid fashion, followed the same guidelines.[16] Had members of the Virginia Company looked a bit closer to home they would have found another tightly knit community slowly spreading out in just such a fashion. St. Augustine, undersized and constantly in some sort of trouble, was by the seventeenth century still a classic Spanish colonial town in every essence of its structure.

Perhaps the colony would have struggled less if Spain was not always mired in some sort of conflict, each of which left St. Augustine open to pillage. The French threatened in the 1560s, as did the English from that point basically through the turn of the seventeenth century. The lightly defended St. Augustine stood no chance against Drake when he came knocking in 1586. In all fairness, very few of Spain's colonial outposts could have withstood Drake's flotilla of two dozen warships and two thousand men. If neither Santo Domingo nor Cartagena could resist, what chance did St. Augustine have? The place was so pitiful that Drake seriously considered whether it was even worth his time. By the time his soldiers approached, only a small log fort with a dozen or so small pieces defended the city. It did not even have a defensive wall.

After a brief respite, war broke out with the Dutch and lasted from 1621 to 1648, and widespread Caribbean piracy tormented all colonial Spaniards. When Piet Heyn captured Spain's entire 1628 treasure fleet, the King withheld La Florida's *situado* altogether. Whatever growth was planned in St. Augustine for that year clearly did not take place. Instead, the city's residents faced hardship once more, reminding many that despite the calm of the last few years, in the end they still lived in La Florida. Over time, news of English gains with Jamaica and Carolina only added to the danger. Then King William's War and Queen Anne's War broke out across the turn of the eighteenth century. La Florida was the most isolated and underfunded colony in a Spanish empire that seemed forever under siege.[17]

Drake's invasion crippled La Florida, but afterward the town managed to escape invasion for decades. Meanwhile, the colony grew. Mission work expanded west into the peninsula and entered its most prosperous era. To the east, merchant ships continued to go down in the Florida Straits and the Bahamian Channel. Literally dozens of ships went down along that stretch from the late sixteenth century through the turn of the eighteenth. Several were recorded as carrying large amounts of bullion that were then salvaged, presumably using crews from St. Augustine, and several resulted in survivors that made their way north to the town for safety. In 1632, for instance, Governor Luis de Horruytiner wrote to Havana that upon hearing word of one such wreck he dispatched soldiers to guard it, and "in one day's time we recovered the 100,000 pesos in bullion and specie which the ship had been carrying as registered cargo and we took this treasure to my fort at St. Augustine."[18] The reasons for St. Augustine's existence did not go away, and so neither did it.

Although *Floridanos* escaped physical confrontation for the first half of the seventeenth century, they could not escape disease. The various contagions that spread through the region did not only wreak havoc on Native communities but Euro-American ones as well, revealing the harsh reality of life in the early American South. Oppressive heat combined with swampy environs and constant natural disasters to make life miserable, while biting insects brought diseases like malaria and yellow fever, which often made life short. Epidemics began early in the seventeenth century and came in waves through mid-century, claiming chunks of the St. Augustine population each time. Yellow fever was followed directly by smallpox from 1649 to 1651, sweeping through the colony and sparing neither rich nor poor. Governor Salazar Vallecilla, Treasurer Francisco Menéndez Marquez, military officers, and several friars all died. For those that survived, famine soon followed. Those same diseases crippled Apalachee and Timucua communities, reducing *sabana* production practically to nothing. Increased pressure to produce then led both Native peoples to rise in two separate rebellions, wrecking the mission districts and completely upending La Florida's food supply. Jamestown's "starving time" was a few months' stretch over the course of one winter. St. Augustine's starving time was the entire middle of the seventeenth century.[19]

Just as the fear of epidemic disease began to fade into memory in 1668 and relationships with the remaining Apalachee and Timucua normalized, English buccaneer Robert Searles departed the infamous pirate haunt of Port Royal and ended up in St. Augustine harbor. He seized supply ships and used them to cover his approach, a ruse that worked so well that Spanish soldiers did not even know the town was under attack until Searles's men were already in the streets. Although the fortress was never overrun, Searles's men did a number on the town itself. The raid was more humiliation than strategic loss, yet it still laid bare the complete defenselessness of a town that was, above all else, supposed to be defensive in nature. In just one night the worst of Spain's piracy problems arrived in St. Augustine, another blow in a tremendously bad generation for Spanish colonial officials across the Caribbean. Yet, if there was a silver lining to buccaneer Searles's visit, his attack finally convinced Spanish authorities that if St. Augustine was going to stay, it needed to be taken seriously. The massive stone castles, or *castillos*, that still overlook ports in Havana, Vera Cruz, Cartagena, Portobelo, and San Juan, are a few of the modern legacies of that decision. The imposing Castillo de San Marcos, the last of nine separate forts Spaniards built to protect St. Augustine, is also one of them. It still overlooks the harbor, and probably always will.[20]

Not long after Searles's raid, the Crown ordered a sweeping funding package of guaranteed money to improve St. Augustine's defense and enlarge its garrison. Money arrived from New Spain to make good on years of missing *situado* payments. The *situado* itself increased, as did the number of soldiers in the fort's garrison. At the center of the deal, of course, was the castillo, the construction of which was bankrolled by a guaranteed stream of yearly funding that in the end amounted to more than 100,000 pesos. That was more money than had been spent on anything in the colony in a long, long time. A royal engineer worked with the governor to design a structure that would dominate the harbor and would be built of unique La Florida materials. While certainly European in its design, the fortress was not constructed of granite, but huge coquina bricks that were mined from deposits on nearby Anastasia Island. A softer, almost spongy kind of rock made of naturally cemented seashells, coquina turned out to be the perfect building material. Even expertly placed artillery fire did not crack or splinter the rock. The cannonballs just sank right in, as one contemporary Englishman wrote, "as though you would stick a knife into cheese." Perhaps that was why no European and then American invaders were ever able to take the fort, even though they tried regularly all the way into the nineteenth century.[21]

St. Augustine authorities knew about the coquina deposits for generations, but never had the money to properly mine them until the castillo project. Various native shell middens up and down the coast provided all the mortar the engineers would need—all they had to do was burn piles of the shells to create lime. Resources had never been the problem. Money was, and now St. Augustine seemed to have plenty of it. Sleepy old St. Augustine, wrote one historian, "was stirred to new life." For almost two decades, from 1677 to 1695, the castillo construction project poured money into St. Augustine, creating a boom period that had several consequences. Cash flowed through the colony to pay artisans' wages, as well as the increased number of soldiers and their families. That drove up the price of trade foodstuffs, making *Floridano* traders and ranchers consistently profitable for the first time probably in their existence. On the other hand, hundreds of Native laborers at a time labored on the castillo or in the coquina quarries. While their presence and their needs contributed to the town's market community, governors increased demands on Natives both in amounts of food grown for St. Augustine consumption, and on *repartimiento* labor, stressing already heavily stressed communities and speeding up the demographic collapse of the mission districts.[22]

The modernization of St. Augustine was long, protracted, and costly, the price of which of course irritated Crown communities with each passing year. Yet once finished the imposing Castillo de San Marcos and the maze of walls, ditches, and redoubts that surrounded it would clarify to any passerby that St. Augustine was, indeed, first and foremost a defensive military establishment. The town sported several lines of defenses to the north that would give pause to any South Carolinian considering an invasion by land, and the castillo that now commanded the harbor would have tested even Drake.[23] Even by twenty-first-century standards the fort remains impressive. While colonial authorities always considered St. Augustine a position of immense strategic military and political value, by the turn of the seventeenth century it was finally starting to look like it.

Colonial stability increased across the turn of the eighteenth century. Soldiers raided north into South Carolina in 1686 to check the southern expansion of the English, which had led to increasing acts of piracy. After Governor Juan Marquez Cabrera authorized the attacks on Edisto Island and Port Royal, the threat diminished greatly.[24] The influx of soldiers led to a spike in marriages and home building. Coquina was available from the royal mine on Anastasia Island and there were plenty of tradesmen knowledgeable in using it, all of which led to the rise of stone construction in the town. Soldiers turned to coquina for their own houses as well as for city projects like a sea wall. They never finished the wall, but traces of the original coquina homes still stand. Governor Diego de Quiroga y Losada remodeled the executive mansion in coquina and ordered it used in the construction of other royal buildings. While no buildings remain from this period of St. Augustine's existence, it was clear that for those who survived these tumultuous years, the end of the century was not such a terrible time to be alive and living in La Florida.[25]

St. Augustine had been the lone La Florida presidio since the 1587 abandonment of Santa Elena, in modern-day South Carolina. A small garrison was stationed at San Luis de Talimali at mid-century, which in time featured a small but stable Spanish population of soldiers and their families. There was also the small fort on the coast, San Marcos de Apalachee, yet both of these were mostly dependent garrisons. The next freestanding La Florida presidio was Pensacola, which New Spain authorities added in 1698. That development finally created a string of settlements that stretched through the panhandle of the modern state of Florida. The Gulf Coast had gone neglected since Tristán de Luna's 1549 attempt, but international developments made a new presidio there a necessity. The French had recently descended the Mississippi River and were starting to establish small, fortified positions along the coastline, at places like Mobile and later New Orleans. Relations between the French and the Spanish were far too volatile to allow that kind of territorial expansion to go unchecked, and so Spanish authorities established Presidio Santa María de Galve as a buffer zone between French Louisiana and St. Augustine.[26]

These two La Florida presidios, St. Augustine and Pensacola, were the only settlements left standing after the British raids of the early eighteenth century, which are the subject of a future chapter. South Carolinian James Moore's early eighteenth-century invasions devastated St. Augustine; they are among the main reasons there are no remaining seventeenth-century structures in the town, leaving one architectural historian to comment that any evidence "of actual building" from the founding of St. Augustine to Moore's invasion is now "strictly archaeological." The town's layout does still harken back to the very first days of La Florida, however, and Moore could not topple the newly constructed Castillo de San Marcos. While the mission districts were swept away, both Spanish enclaves endured, fated to carry on as undersized, isolated, and neglected outposts in a region Spain cared very little about.[27]

Despite being neglected, rundown, and burned down, both Pensacola and St. Augustine would endure until Spain gave up on them in 1763. While nothing remains of the town previous to Moore's 1702 invasion except the layout, several buildings and gardens in town date to the remainder of the first Spanish period. Among these, for example, is the governor's house, which was rebuilt beginning in 1706 and included impressive gardens. As one 1743 report detailed, there were three hundred houses and three churches in town, "all built of stone." William Bartram, a British traveler important in future chapters, described several "good houses after the Spanish fashion, all or most with pleasant, covered balconies," when he visited shortly after the 1763 evacuation. Some even included the finer things, like glazed windows. St. Augustine's tourists can still enjoy some of these first Spanish-period houses, their original eighteenth-century coquina and tabby walls forming the foundations of modern restaurants and museums.[28]

By the time Spaniards gave up on St. Augustine, according to these reports, it was not such a bad place to live. Yet, most Spaniards evacuated both St. Augustine and Pensacola at the conclusion of the French and Indian War. They did so only to move back in at the conclusion of the American Revolution, only to move back out a few decades later. Because of their beginnings, both represented Spanish communities that just so happened to be America's first communities.

Notes

1. Elliott, *Empires*, 9; Kamen, *Empire*, 250; Weber, *The Spanish Frontier*, 124; Bushnell, *Situado and Sabana*, 82.

2. Bushnell, *King's Coffer*, 2-3; Lyon, *The Enterprise of Florida*, 170.

3. Lyon, *The Enterprise of Florida*, 171.

4. Elliott, *Empires*, 35-39; Altman, "Towns and the Forging of the Spanish Caribbean," 23; Chatelain, *The Defenses*, 27-29.

5. Elliott, *Empires*, 38-39; Lyon, *The Enterprise of Florida*, 171; Bushnell, *King's Coffer*, 1, 107-113; Chatelain, *The Defenses*, 27-29.

6. Bushnell, *The King's Coffer*, 4, 6-10; Bushnell, *Situado and Sabana*, 36; Chatelain, *The Defenses*, 14; Childers, "The Presidio System," 25-26; Halbirt, "La Ciudad de San Agustin," 33.

7. Parker, "St. Augustine in the Seventeenth-Century," 557-560; Bushnell, *The King's Coffer*, 9-11, 24-25, 63-74; Bushnell, *Situado and Sabana*, 43-48; Chatelain, *The Defenses*, 21-23.

8. Bushnell, *Situado and Sabana*, 111-112; Bushnell, *The King's Coffer*, 11-12, 98-99; McEwan, "The Historical Archaeology of Seventeenth-Century La Florida," 515-517; Ruhl, "Oranges and Wheat," 38-39, 42-45.

9. Bushnell, *The King's Coffer*, 12-14.

10. Jennings, *New Worlds of Violence*, 77-79; Chatelain, *The Defenses*, 50-51; Childers, "The Presidio System," 26.

11. Jennings, *New Worlds of Violence*, 77-78; Quinn, *The Roanoke Voyages*, 1: 305; Document 45, in Wright, *Further English Voyages*, 187.

12. Chatelain, *The Defenses*, 50-51, 54; Deagan, "The Historical Archaeology of Sixteenth-Century La Florida," 360; McEwan, "The Historical Archaeology of Seventeenth-Century La Florida," 491; Parker, "St. Augustine in the Seventeenth-Century," 555, 557; Bushnell, *Situado and Sabana*, 88.

13. Bushnell, *The King's Coffer*, 31; Elliott, *Empires*, 38-41.

14. Bushnell, *The King's Coffer*, 19-20; Chatelain, *The Defenses*, 30-31; Halbirt, "La Ciudad de San Agustin," 41-42; Parker, "St. Augustine in the Seventeenth-Century," 555-556; Deagan, "The Historical Archaeology of Sixteenth-Century La Florida," 363-364; McEwan, "The Historical Archaeology of Seventeenth-Century La Florida," 512-513.

15. Kornwolf, *Architecture and Town Planning*, 1: 86; Deagan, *America's Ancient City*, 9; Bushnell, *The King's Coffer*, 113; Parker, "St. Augustine in the Seventeenth-Century," 556-557; McEwan, "The Historical Archaeology of Seventeenth-Century La Florida," 506-507; Chatelain, *The Defenses*, 30, 46.

16. Chatelain, *The Defenses*, 46; Elliott, *Empires*, 41-43.

17. Bushnell, *The King's Coffer*, 13; Roberts and Beamish, "Venturing Out," 51-52.

18. Bushnell, *The King's Coffer*, 92-96; Marx, *Shipwrecks*, 197-206.

19. Parker, "St. Augustine in the Seventeenth-Century," 564-566.

20. Bushnell, *Situado and Sabana*, 136; Riegelsperger, "Pirate, Priest, and Slave," 577-590; Parker, "St. Augustine in the Seventeenth-Century," 566-567; Chatelain, *The Defenses*, 41-43, 46-48, 54-55, 59-64.

21. Chatelain, *The Defenses*, 67-68; McEwan, "The Historical Archaeology of Seventeenth-Century La Florida," 509-510; Bushnell, *Situado and Sabana*, 136-142.

22. Bushnell, *Situado and Sabana*, 136-142; Bushnell, *The King's Coffer*, 23; Parker, "St. Augustine in the Seventeenth-Century," 572-574; Chatelain, *The Defenses*, 59-75; Halbirt, "La Ciudad de San Agustin," 35-36.

23. Chatelain, *The Defenses*, 46-47, 76-94; Halbirt, "La Ciudad de San Agustin," 37-41.

24. Parker, "St. Augustine in the Seventeenth-Century," 569-572; Worth, *The Struggle*, 146-171; Bushnell, *Situado and Sabana*, 166-170.

25. Kornwolf, *Architecture and Town Planning*, 1: 79-96; Parker, "St. Augustine in the Seventeenth-Century," 574-576; Chatelain, *The Defenses*, 30-31.

26. Bense, *Presidios of Spanish West Florida*, 18-119; Bense, "Presidio Santa María de Galve," 47; Childers, "The Presidio System," 28-30.

27. Bushnell, *Situado and Sabana*, 89; Kornwolf, *Architecture and Town Planning*, 1: 79-96.

28. Kornwolf, *Architecture and Town Planning*, 1: 86-90.

Creole-American Places

By the end of the seventeenth century St. Augustine was small, but it was still an established Spanish colonial town, built of stone homes with small courtyards that lined orderly streets. The nearby stone fortress, just recently constructed, reflected at least a semblance of care on behalf of the Spanish government. It was also classically Spanish in its ethnic makeup and social structure, making it not only America's first permanent community, but its first truly multicultural community.

Unlike their English counterparts, even the most elitist Spaniards had few qualms living among different ethnic groups and social classes, all of whom they considered inferior. Multi-ethnic Iberian urban places like Seville translated to New World urban places like Santo Domingo, Havana, Mexico City, or Lima. Iberian urbanity was a multicultural structure, as would be the New World experience. Just as Spaniards lived in close proximity to Jews and Muslims, and Spanish cities had remarkable African populations, so would Spanish colonial cities. The very foundation of Spanish colonialism—the exploitation of Native labor and Native land using *doctrinas* and *haciendas*—was built upon cohabitation with Natives, and increasingly with Africans. Natives forced to *encomiendas* might work in faraway mines and ranches, but they also commonly labored in forts, churches, and private households in communities of all sizes. So did African slaves, whose numbers rose as the number of Natives fell. For places of incredible inequity, Spaniards, Indians, and Africans lived in remarkably close proximity to each other in Spanish colonial communities.[1]

Spanish colonial culture developed in this milieu, and religious and civil authorities alike shared a dire and crucial concern that only Spaniards remain atop colonial societies. That could be difficult to do in such multiracial places, so authorities constructed strict multitiered structures based on Spanish blood, which followed a person throughout their life. The top tiers, containing *peninsulares* and creoles, controlled Spanish society, which a close adherence to the *limpieza de sangre* guaranteed. Spanish-born *peninsulares* sat atop everyone else, including even New World–born *criollos*, or creoles. In La Florida, these men and women were also known as Floridanos. St. Augustine's earliest baptismal records are full of "legitimate" Floridano sons and daughters born of "legitimate" husbands and wives, which benefited from strong sponsorships and a Catholic pedigree. At the other end of the spectrum—at the very bottom of it—were Natives, *indios*, and in between lay a vast middle composed of mixed-race *mestizos* and *castizos*, the mixed-race children of Natives and Spaniards.[2]

While it would always remain a marker of inferiority, *mestizo* blood could be thinned out through good marriages to the point of no longer holding a person too far back in the world. That identity was at least somewhat fluid. On the other hand, one would think that if a child had two *peninsulares* as parents, then they would obviously be a *peninsular* as well. Yet that was not the case anywhere in the New World, including in La Florida. Any child unfortunate enough to enter the universe in a colonial community was a product of that colonial community, regardless of who their parents were. The sheer ungodliness of the New World had robbed that young boy or girl of some seemingly intangible amount of Spanishness that rendered them less than the sum of their parents. They were now creole, nothing was going to change that, and while a creole could aspire to quite a bit, not all doors were open to them. The highest military and civil positions, like a La Florida governorship, would be forever closed to Floridano men. Creoles were close to the top of Spanish societies but they were not at the very tip-top. If being born in heathen, uncivilized New World communities somehow made Spaniards a little bit less, then what did it look like to be a child of the colonial wasteland that was La Florida? As far as the Spanish Crown and Church authorities were probably concerned, Floridanos were the reason the term *criollo* existed.[3]

Peninsulares were always coming and going through the colony as governors and other royal officials. Marriages and births did happen, and a strong Floridano population did emerge. By the time Spaniards abandoned the colony in 1763, the majority of St. Augustine's residents were Floridanos.[4] Behold a complete reversal of the twenty-first-century phenomenon of the "Florida Snowbird." The unflattering term, which refers to Northerners who come south in the winter to live seasonally in Florida only to return north to their first homes every spring, creates a common perception that very few Floridians are actually *from* Florida. As it turns out, before there were South Carolinians, New Englanders, or even Virginians, there were Floridians. Floridians are, thanks to St. Augustine, the first true Euro-American "natives" of any state in the modern United States of America.

Despite being in the lowest social positions possible, Natives were still everywhere in colonial life, even in the same church baptismal records in which Spanish births were recorded—albeit in different books. Several Potano Natives were baptized in St. Augustine's church in 1606, for instance, in the same spaces as the town's richest vecinos. And, obviously, relationships still happened. Single Spanish soldiers in La Florida of less than noble birth often ended up marrying Native women, and their ensuing families led to familiar definitions of *mestizo* and *castizo*, which also show up in the colony's baptismal records. In 1605 Ana was born of Juan de Bran and Augustine, an "Indian his wife," while the next year Juan was born the son of Francisco Dias and "María de la Cruz, Indian." It is uncertain if the fathers of Ana and Juan were Natives themselves. They were probably not, or they would have been described as such. The very next year, for instance, Gaspar was born "son of infidel Indian parents," meaning not only were both parents Natives, but they were both non-Christian.[5]

While La Florida's *mestizo* population was minuscule compared to a much larger and economically successful colony, like New Spain, there were not nearly as many Natives in La Florida as in modern-day Mexico. There were nearly not as many Spaniards, either, and there were certainly not as many settlements where the two groups lived in close proximity. In fact, in most of La Florida's history, there was only one, St. Augustine. For a time, there was Santa Elena, which was gone by the turn of the seventeenth century. A little more than a century later, the establishment of San Luis de Talimali and Pensacola brought the grand total up to three. These were the places where Natives and Spaniards lived together for generations, and so as was the case elsewhere in the Spanish colonial world, these were the places with *mestizo* populations.

The growth of this population re-created in La Florida the classic three-leveled Spanish caste system familiar elsewhere in the Spanish colonial world. The colony contained a recognizable *mestizo* population even in its earliest days, although like most other aspects of life in the colony, things began to pick up after the turn of the seventeenth century. Another spurt of growth came after La Florida stabilized in the wake of James Moore's attack, when surviving Native communities moved much closer to St. Augustine. From 1735 to 1750, for instance, St. Augustine's parish cathedral recorded over three hundred marriages. Seventy percent of the marriages were between Spaniards or Floridanos, while 11 percent were mixed marriages, meaning they included at least one person of Indian or *mestizo* heritage. To the west, Pensacola was even more diverse. Colonial authorities established and peopled the town directly from New Spain. That meant Pensacola, while even worse off than St. Augustine as far as prospects, contained a significant *mestizo* population from its earliest days, and was even more multi-ethnic in nature than its eastern counterpart. According to one 1708 report, 34 percent of the population was creole, and 41 percent were classified as *mestizo*. Many of these were men brought from New Spain either as convicts or conscripted soldiers, giving Pensacola a gritty frontier community feel to it, more reminiscent of the lawlessness of the later American West.[6]

To put these developments into the proper La Florida perspective, Pensacola might have appeared strikingly reminiscent to New Spain in terms of its ethnic diversity, but it was still a frontier town roughly the size of a single small neighborhood in Mexico City. Nowhere in La Florida, in other words, was there a *mestizo* population that could rival in number the population of almost any other Spanish colony, even the Caribbean. Perhaps that is the reason why America's first creole places go so easily overlooked—while they existed, their populations were small and insignificant when compared to elsewhere in the Spanish colonial world. In the end, they faded away anyway. For instance, the highest *mestizo* populations grew when survivors from James Moore's raid resettled very near St. Augustine's defenses. That created the side-by-side living situation known to create a multi-ethnic Spanish society, and after the mid-seventeenth century there were roughly three thousand people living in the town. While that rate of growth was substantial, it all came to a quick end only a decade later when Spain gave up on the colony altogether in 1763. When Spaniards evacuated La Florida much of the Native population left as well, including hundreds of *mestizos* and the few Natives that remained in the town's small mission villages. Whatever *mestizo* population La Florida might have ever had was gone by the time it became the British province of East Florida.[7]

This Spanish experience, although it had a beginning and an end date, nevertheless complicates the continent's earliest Euro-American heritage. How could America be a place where middle-class people went to create a new model world—a "city upon a hill" as John Winthrop put it—if a multigenerational, multi-ethnic Euro-American community was already there by that time? Spanish authorities were building a familiar world in the Caribbean, in Latin America, and in North America, and it was a very different one than the world the British would create generations later.

While these were multi-ethnic places, they were by no means equal places. Racial and ethnic inferiority was baked into Spanish society, and La Florida, like other colonial outposts, was built atop it. The most powerful and the least powerful Floridians might have been baptized in the same church, often by the same friars, but their baptisms were meticulously recorded in different sets of records, designed to separate the groups by caste. The historical and anthropological value of these records has been tremendous, leading historians and anthropologists to reconstruct a small and isolated social world with surprising accuracy. What those records reveal was the *limpieza de sangre* working to full effect, creating perhaps the strictest segregationist policy perhaps in all of American history. What Jim Crow–era segregationists attempted to construct in Florida, Georgia, and Alabama in the wake of Reconstruction—codified second-class citizenship for the African American residents of those states based on race and ancestry—was actually the second time such a system had existed in the American South. Those records would have seemed very familiar to a Native or African American living anywhere in seventeenth- or eighteenth-century La Florida.

Although racial segregation in nineteenth- and twentieth-century America sometimes included Native peoples in certain areas of the South, it was a primarily white-black tension—a system of oppression wielded by those of Euro-American descent against those of African descent. Even when defined in such precise terms, however, that too is a story older than English America. Of the three thousand St. Augustine residents listed in 1760, for instance, over 10 percent of the population—over four hundred in total—were black. Those African Americans were part of multigenerational families that stretched back, by that point, almost two entire centuries.[8] By the time the first slaves were brought ashore in Jamestown in 1619, entire generations of enslaved people had been born, baptized and married, had their own children baptized, and had died in La Florida. The oldest African American traditions anywhere in the current United States of America, it turns out, originated in La Florida.

Coerced or enslaved labor was central to every Spanish colonial operation in the New World. Menéndez secured the right to import hundreds of African slaves into La Florida in his original *capitulación*, and although he never imported nearly that number, African men and women were on the very Spanish ships that founded St. Augustine. Their presence there continued an important trend of African firsts in American history—African slavery was a part of the American story from its very first days. At times Menéndez hoped to gain slave quotas from the King in order to profit from their sale, therefore helping finance the expansion of La Florida, which would have made St. Augustine America's first slaving port. Although Menéndez never realized those ambitions, among the names listed in St. Augustine's earliest records were ones like "Angola," suggesting that the enslaved men and women who ended up in La Florida came directly from West Africa. They were *bozales*, as the Spanish would describe them, rather than Caribbean- or American-born creoles. These were not northern African Moors or African slaves shipped from Spain, in other words; they were Native West Africans captured and sold through the *asiento*. The same Atlantic slave trade that brought African slaves to Spanish Caribbean islands brought African slaves to La Florida.[9]

By the turn of the seventeenth century St. Augustine was near half a century old, and there were entire generations of enslaved Africans living in and around the town. Baptismal records tell the tale. The first slave birth directly listed in the records comes in 1608 with the birth of Augustin, though he was not alone. Prudentio was born in November of that same year, the son of Bartolo, a slave. There was Francisco in 1610, Juan and Mateo in 1611, Francisca in 1612, etc., representing a clear pattern of regular births among the colony's enslaved population. Even if their parents had been brought to St. Augustine directly from West Africa, these births were of Floridians. They were not only America's first enslaved Africans, but they were also America's first generation of African Americans.[10]

Why were slaves in La Florida to begin with? The region offered few commercial prospects, let alone any that private citizens could have exploited using slave labor. The answer lies in the more complicated and multifaceted nature of enslavement that existed in the early colonial world. While enslaved work in the English South eventually shifted to manual labor done in agricultural fields outside of towns, some of the largest enslaved places in the early British colonial world were in cities like Boston and New York, where slaves worked as urban laborers and servants. Native and African slaves in the Spanish Caribbean did much the same. Domestic slavery in the Spanish world was commonplace in the sixteenth century, and many of the largest Spanish colonial cities, like Mexico City and Lima, were heavily enslaved places. While slavery there was every bit as brutal and exploitative as anywhere on earth, in the early colonial world, slavery could also mean many different things.[11]

Colonial St. Augustine was certainly no Mexico City, yet St. Augustine did have a considerable enslaved population that reflected common Spanish traditions. Private individuals and families owned slaves, as well as did the colony's public and military officials. A captain and a lieutenant were listed as slave owners in early seventeenth-century church records. Diego, Yumar, Christobal, Lucrecia, Francisco, and Guiomar were all names of enslaved people owned by

Colonial Treasurer Juan Menéndez de Marques in 1612 and 1613. The same records reveal treasurers, royal accountants, and even governors as owning slaves. Governors Juan Treviño de Guillamas and Juan de Salinas both owned slaves, which appeared in colonial records, in 1615 and 1623, respectively.[12]

Although these slave owners were public officials, their slaves were still private property, and probably lived as servants in and around St. Augustine. That is an important distinction to make because in the Spanish colonial world there were slaves that were *not* private property. St. Augustine's history is full of "royal slaves," who were the property of the Spanish Crown itself, and for which there was almost no English counterpart. Enslaved Africans were an important source of labor for local authorities, who used them to build and maintain colonial infrastructure, particularly when Natives could not. Because St. Augustine was isolated and underfunded, and because Native labor was so unreliable in the region, royal slaves played particularly important roles in the colony's construction. St. Augustine was not only America's first European community, but it was also the first community in North America to be constructed largely by slave labor.

Pedro Menéndez de Avilés was the first to employ royal slaves, sending a group of them north from St. Augustine to Santa Elena to help rebuild in the wake of the Guale revolt. For the second time Africans were in the very heart of the future English "Lowcountry," yet for the second time it was the Spanish who brought them there. Another significant group of royal slaves appeared in the colonial records a decade later, during Drake's 1586 raid. A group of upward of fifty slaves worked hastily to rebuild St. Augustine's lone fortification on the north side of the city in an unsuccessful attempt to stave off Drake's invasion. When not under siege those slaves did various manual labor tasks, like cutting lumber for shipbuilding and repair. They maintained the town's fortifications, public buildings, and roads. When the Castillo project was ongoing, the number of slaves working on the massive stone structure rose dozens at a time. Some of the enslaved men were laborers, yet some were trained artisans like blacksmiths, loggers, and stonecutters. Without these enslaved laborers, the Castillo de San Marcos likely would not exist. Neither would many of St. Augustine's stone buildings.[13]

Because royal slaves were visible in the colony throughout its history, so too are their lives visible in seventeenth-century church records. They might have come from elsewhere but these men and women still lived their lives in St. Augustine, lives that included growing families. Early in the seventeenth century Antonio was born, the son of Pedro, a royal slave. The 1615 sponsor of newborn

Juliana, Juan Ximenes, was "a slave of His Majesty." So was Juan Angola, who served as sponsor of newborn Sebastian in 1617.[14]

These same records also hint at the complexity of African slavery in La Florida. In the 1695 counterfeiting case, both witnesses to the Apalachee boys' shenanigans were Africans, listed as a *pardo* man and a *morena* woman. Birth and baptism records are full of such descriptions. Diego was born in 1612, the son of Yumar, a *mulatto* slave. Christobal, another slave described as *mulatto*, served as the child's sponsor. Then there was María, who was born in 1614 of the *morena* slave of a private resident. That same year Manuel was born a *moreno* boy. Common in Spanish colonial records everywhere are terms like *mulatto*, *moreno*, *pardo*, and *zambo*, all of which were used during the time to denote levels of mixed-African ancestry. The first three referred to mixed-race children of Africans and Hispanic whites, and the last referred to children of African and Native parents, demonstrating that the multi-ethnic nature of the Spanish colonial world was not limited to the children of Spaniards and Natives.[15]

St. Augustine's population always contained a high percentage of mixed-race African Americans, yet as the numbers of *mestizos* rose in the eighteenth century, so did those of *mulattos*. In a fifteen-year period from 1735 to 1750, close to 20 percent of recorded marriages involved either *morenos* or *mulattos*. Over a quarter of the town's recorded baptisms were also either *moreno* or *mulatto*. Pensacola's early records tell likewise. The town and its defenses were built by Africans brought in from New Spain and the Caribbean, and a decade later the 1708 census revealed that 21 percent of the population were of mixed African-Spanish ancestry, and 4 percent were of mixed African-Native ancestry.[16]

We can credit church officials for these glimpses into America's first multicultural community, even though such records were only produced to make sure Africans stayed African, and Spaniards stayed Spanish. Thanks, in other words, to the highly oppressive *limpieza de sangre*. Such religious traditions demanded strict record keeping, despite its segregationist end goal. Also, as one historian commented, Catholicism was so central to Spanish identity that even slave owners "saw that their slaves were Christian and the babies legitimate." Both meant that marriage and baptismal records were produced for slaves the same as Spaniards. One of the earliest church mentions of slaves was of a marriage in 1598, between "Simon Negro" and "María Negro."[17] This record might be brief, but in this case is more than enough to establish that an enslaved African population was becoming an African American population in La Florida even by the turn of the seventeenth century.

The distinction between *morenos* and *mulattoes* describes the detail with which Spaniards recorded and relied on the *limpieza de sangre*. Racial categories for mixed-blood African Americans could be just as complicated as it could be with Natives. The title *moreno* commonly referred to someone of pure African descent and dark complexion, while *mulatto* referred to someone of mixed descent and a lighter complexion. As was the case with *mestizos*, the lighter complexion of a *mulatto* was assumed to be the product of more Hispanic blood, which was preferable. *Pardo* was another term used usually to describe a light-skinned man of African American descent. Translated from Spanish to English it simply means brown and was used to describe an individual who was not black, but "colored." The more a familial line got whiter over time, the more their lives might get easier, as was the case with *mestizos*. Nevertheless, these were still highly disparaged caste identities in the Spanish colonial world—the lowest rungs in a complicated social ladder.[18]

Brief descriptions in baptismal records bear out one more important distinction—free versus enslaved. Spanish slaves could be manumitted by owners, could be set free for patriotic work, or they might be able to purchase their freedom. Spanish laws and customs concerning slavery certainly supported the institution, but also established that under the right circumstances, an enslaved African certainly might find freedom.[19] When Prudentio was born in 1608 his sponsors were "Augustino a negro and María negro slave." Why was one listed as a slave and the other not? Perhaps Augustino was not a slave. That might be conjecture, but Spanish records were specific, and descriptions had very important consequences, meaning that if the friar wrote down "negro," rather than "slave," that probably means something. Something clearer happened with María, born in 1623. While María was born a slave, her sponsor was listed as Francisco Desabra, a "free *mulatto*."[20]

Then there were those actors in the Apalachee counterfeiting case. Crispin de Tapia and Isavel de los Rios were the two shopkeepers who uncovered the counterfeiting ring. Both were African American, but de Tapia was a "free *pardo*" and de los Rios a "free *morena*." In this case, the label *pardo* clearly distinguished de Tapia in status from either a *moreno* or a *mulatto*, hinting at the subtle complexities in the Spanish caste system. De Tapia was a free "colored" man, not a free black man, a distinction not to be mistaken. *Pardo* signified a higher class within the *mulatto* community, and the label often assumed the person was free. In Crispin's case he was not only a free black man but a military officer, which in the Spanish colonial world and particularly in La Florida was not uncommon.

Pardos were important members of Spanish colonial militias, an avenue many men took to gain stability, a steady income, and even a bit of respect. For Crispin de Tapia this was an important and hard-earned distinction that placed him up several rungs in St. Augustine's social ladder from other African Americans in town, whether enslaved or free. It was an identity he would have protected jealously.[21]

The story of Isavel de los Rios is not as complicated, yet the free black woman tending a shop in St. Augustine in the seventeenth century stands on its own as pretty remarkable. Two free black shopkeepers manage to appear in the background of one isolated counterfeiting case that also includes young Apalachee laborers. Free and enslaved blacks existed at the very bottom of Spanish colonial society, but their populations were still dynamic, lasting, and in this case, visible. St. Augustine's African American community was small, but apparently not that small. Perhaps La Florida was exceptional. Maybe the colony's pitiable size and constant state of vulnerability meliorated the lives of the lowest Spanish classes. The constant need for providers and defenders probably blurred caste lines at least a little, enabling men like Crispin de Tapia to exercise a degree of autonomy and even community respect that would have been difficult to do in Mexico City. If there ever was a silver lining to the danger and uncertainty to living on the edge of the Spanish world, it was that the necessities of survival sometimes bent the rules, and sometimes in the favor of men like de Tapia and women like de los Rios.[22]

These conditions were, ultimately, all still horrific by modern standards. Even with his freedom and a military career, men like de Tapia still inhabited the lowest rungs in a sprawling colonial society, and few venues of social or economic advancement were open to them. Professional jobs were off limits, as was any public office. The same was the case with Native castes as well. Throughout colonial societies, people of mixed-race were not even allowed to dress like Spaniards.[23] The lives of early enslaved African Americans in and around St. Augustine were of course much worse, and often shorter than that of Crispin de Tapia. Questionable nutrition and a diseased and swampy environment, all under the scorching Florida sun, made mortality high for everyone, yet enslaved workers were certainly not the best fed or the best treated. Add to those conditions the rigors of intense manual labor, mostly outdoors, and La Florida's enslaved people lived particularly precarious lives.

The population of royal slaves at the turn of the seventeenth century, for instance, fluctuated badly. Right at 1600 it was just over two dozen, even though many more dozens had been imported into the colony over the years, building and then rebuilding it. Three years later, in 1603, the number was up to over thirty. In 1606 there were over one hundred Africans in the colony, thirty of which were royal slaves. Yet in 1618 the number of all enslaved Africans stood in the low double-digits, and possibly as low as a single dozen. If that number is to be believed it would constitute a roughly 90 percent mortality rate among La Florida's enslaved population over the course of just one decade. That's almost too catastrophic to be accurate, even for the period. Perhaps these numbers refer only to the ranks of royal slaves. Even if that was the case, the decrease was still tragic. The epidemics that had ravaged Timucua and Potano communities early in the century had done a number on the African American population as well. The same thing happened again decades later with the mid-century measles and smallpox outbreaks, which apparently killed every one of the colony's royal slaves and forced St. Augustine's authorities to request more from Havana. Poorly fed and poorly treated, La Florida's enslaved people faced hardships every bit as intense as what enslaved workers would endure later in English Caribbean colonies.[24]

The resistance of Spanish slaves to their bondage reflects that brutal reality. La Florida was the first place in North America where enslaved Africans rose up in revolt, which happened at San Miguel de Guadalpe. The first runaway slaves fled Hernándo de Soto's entrada years later. Those traditions of resistance continued with the establishment of St. Augustine. Slaves ran away from town and down the east coast into Native Ais territory near present-day Cape Canaveral in the colony's earliest days, fugitives that Spanish authorities struggled mightily to get back. There were mixed reports that slaves might have deserted the region when Drake attacked, and twenty years later, in 1606, there were one hundred enslaved Africans in the colony according to Governor Pedro de Ybarra "who would fight with the enemy for their freedom."[25]

To get the fullest and most complicated picture of Spanish slavery in La Florida, this awful tradition of enslavement and exploitation, flight, and possible uprising must be contrasted with the formation of America's first freestanding and independent African American community, which grew right outside St. Augustine's city gates in the early eighteenth century. Gracia Real de Santa Teresa de Mose, which was the home to La Florida's black militia and their families—perhaps to Crispin de Tapia—was established and supported by the colony's governor and regional Spanish officials early in the eighteenth century. The community was located north of St. Augustine and featured its own fort, its own church, and excellent farming land. This was America's first autonomous African American community, which existed just outside the walls of America's first European-American, slave-holding society. At the same time hundreds of free African Americans called Mose home, royal slaves worked in the city and wealthy residents owned slaves privately. La Florida, North America's first creole-American colony, was a complicated place.

Notes

1. Altman, "Towns and the Forging of the Spanish Caribbean," 31.
2. Shephard, "The Spanish Criollo Majority," 65-68.
3. Shephard, "The Spanish Criollo Majority," 67-69.
4. Shephard, "The Spanish Criollo Majority," 65-67.
5. Elliott, *Empires*, 51, 83-84, 169-172; Parker, "St. Augustine in the Seventeenth-Century," 561-562; Deagan, "The Historical Archaeology of Sixteenth-Century La Florida," 364; *Baptisms, 1594-1763*, 1: 20, 22-25.
6. Deagan, "Mestizaje," 56-61; Deagan, *America's Ancient City*, 102-105; Bense, "Presidio Santa María de Galve," 48.
7. Deagan, "Mestizaje," 56-57, 60.
8. Deagan, "Mestizaje," 60.
9. Lyon, *The Enterprise of Florida*, 136-137; Landers, *Black Society*, 15; Merás, *Pedro Menéndez de Avilés*, 77; *Baptisms, 1594-1763*, 1: 24-25, 57; Landers, "Traditions of African American Freedom," 19-20; Bushnell, *The King's Coffer*, 22; Bushnell, *Situado and Sabana*, 118.
10. *Baptisms, 1594-1763*, 1: 33-35, 38, 41, 45.
11. Elliott, *Empires*, 100-101.
12. *Baptisms, 1594-1763*, 1: 42, 43, 46, 51, 56, 70, 74-75.
13. Landers, "Africans and Native Americans," 56; Covington, "Drake Destroys St. Augustine," 86; Bushnell, *Situado and Sabana*, 31; Landers, *Black Society*, 21-22; Bushnell, *The King's Coffer*, 82-83; Chatelain, *The Defenses*, 68.
14. *Baptisms, 1594-1763*, 1: 33-35, 51, 58.
15. *Baptisms, 1594-1763*, 1: 50; Elliott, *Empires*, 170-172; Borucki, *From Shipmates to Soldiers*, 18-21; Forbes, *Africans and Native Americans*, 115-130, 160-167; Landers, *Black Society*, 5-6.
16. Deagan, "Mestizaje," 59; Bense, "Presidio Santa María de Galve," 48.
17. Bushnell, *The King's Coffer*, 22; Parker, "St. Augustine in the Seventeenth-Century," 562.
18. *Baptisms, 1594-1763*, 1: 42, 46; Landers, *Black Society*, 5; Bushnell, *The King's Coffer*, 22; Borucki, *From Shipmates to Soldiers*, 18-21; Forbes, *Africans and Native Americans*, 1.
19. Elliott, *Empires*, 106-107; Twinam, *Purchasing Whiteness*, 84-90; Landers, *Black Society*, 7-8; Landers, "Traditions of African American Freedom," 21-22.
20. *Baptisms, 1594-1763*, 1: 33, 73.
21. Borucki, *From Shipmates to Soldiers*, 20-21; Landers, *Black Society*, 5-6.
22. Landers, "Traditions of African American Freedom," 23-24; Bushnell, *The King's Coffer*, 20.

23. Twinam, *Purchasing Whiteness*, 100-104.

24. Landers, *Black Society*, 19; Landers, "Traditions of African American Freedom," 20, 56-57; Landers, "The Geopolitics," 482.

25. Landers, *Black Society*, 1-2; Gallay, *Indian Slave Trade*, 345-346; Bushnell, *Situado and Sabana*, 118; Wright, *Further English Voyages*, doc. 54, 206.

7 Native Lasts, Native Firsts

In 1774, years after La Florida became British East Florida, famed British naturalist William Bartram took a tour through the province, just as he and his father had done together a decade previous. On this second journey William enjoyed an extended stay at Cuscowilla, a Seminole town near present-day Gainesville, Florida. He was there to behold the greatness of the Alachua savanna, which he described as "vast & beautiful beyond description." Bartram produced a marvelous, sprawling map of the savanna that documents the birds, deer, and all other manner of incredible fauna he beheld during his extended stay in north-central Florida. It remains a visual reminder of the region's striking natural beauty.

Bartram's hosts at the savanna were a unique lot. They were not Spaniards, Britons, Timucuas, or Apalachees. The Spanish were long gone, as were the region's other missions, *haciendas*, and cattle ranches. The British now technically controlled Florida, yet they were nowhere to be found. The new tenants that had taken possession of the region's pristine savannas and grasslands were the Cowkeeper's Alachua band of Seminoles.[1] Wakapuchasi, or the Cowkeeper, was more of a nickname than a proper Seminole title, and the man's actual name was probably Ahaya. According to Bartram, who met and dined with him personally, the Cowkeeper was "a tall well-made man, very affable and cheerful." At about sixty years old his eyes were "lively and full of fire, his countenance manly and placid, yet ferocious, or what we call savage." The Cowkeeper was an imposing man but clearly also a hospitable one, who welcomed Bartram and allowed him to tour the savanna at his leisure.[2]

Perhaps no other headman is more closely associated with the creation of Seminoles than this man, the Cowkeeper. It is clear what his claim to authority was: cows. The same cows, in fact, that are the product of a future chapter. More specifically, the very same herds that Spaniards established in the La Florida interior generations earlier, when Alachua was La Chua, a Spanish cattle ranching *hacienda*. The cattle that had once belonged to La Chua now roamed Alachua.

Their numbers had swelled in the years since the downfall of the *haciendas*, and now were so feral as to be truly wild. During his visit Bartram could not help but notice the "innumerable droves of cattle" there, "the lordly bull, lowing cow, and sleek capricious heifer. The hills and groves re-echo their cheerful, social voices."[3] Evidently, the Alachua savanna was alive with the sounds of mooing.

On one of his wanders through the savanna Bartram witnessed a cattle drive led by a small group of mounted Seminole cowmen. One of them informed their visitor that these cattle belonged to the Cowkeeper and his people, and that a few of the steers, "as large and fat" as any he'd seen before, were being driven to Cuscowilla for slaughter. Bartram's arrival coincided with a large council, which taken together with his visit was cause for a celebration. Bartram was about to be treated to a gigantic beef barbecue, Seminole style.

First was the business at hand, which the Cowkeeper and other influential Seminoles concluded at the council house in the public square. Regional talks, including some British ones, had to be read and debated. After that business was concluded, however, the "banquet succeeded," and townspeople crowded in a separate corner of the square to partake in the festivities. Ribs and "the choicest fat pieces of the bullocks, excellent well barbecued" were brought out first. So far this barbecue would have made any modern-day Texan pitmaster jealous. Next was stewed beef, which arrived in giant bowls. Last but not least, the pièce de résistance, was a dish Bartram took a few extra lines to describe. This "very singular" dish, "made of the belly or paunch of the beef," was diced "pretty fine, and then made into a thin soup." This, in other words, was tripe stew. Bartram described the dish as being "seasoned well with salt and aromatic herbs," but not seasoned nearly strong enough to hide the fact that he was eating cow stomach, and "not over cleansed of its contents," no less. The dish was "greatly esteemed by the Indians, but is, in my judgment, the least agreeable they have amongst them." Although he was a fan of almost everything else, Bartram was clearly no fan of tripe.

Bartram not only survived his encounter with Seminole tripe stew, but otherwise thoroughly enjoyed the barbecue. Barbecue, consequently, is also dealt with in a future chapter. For now, the Cowkeeper's feast was a hit. Everybody went away satisfied and probably very full, including Bartram, who would continue his Savannah stay for some time longer. If there was more barbecue in store for him on behalf of his Seminole guests, who could blame him?[4]

William Bartram's 1774 trek, which admittedly took place after Spanish La Florida was no more, also took him through Georgia and the Carolinas. There he passed among and described Creek and Cherokee communities, in addition to the constantly changing flora and fauna of the coastal Southeast. In doing so, he produced one of the most enjoyable and academically valuable natural histories of early America. It was his time moving down the St. Johns River in Florida, however, that reads as the most wondrous, at least to Floridians. This patch of writing provides a glimpse of a long-ago era of the state's history, filled with intense tropical beauty, novelty, and even danger—a Florida very few living residents would believe ever existed.

Bartram's stay in Cuscowilla also constitutes one of the scarce few sources to mention Seminoles in any great detail during the pre-Revolution years. It is one of the very, very few to describe their homes or mannerisms, not to mention such a grand barbecue. The Seminoles with whom Bartram dined were living in what scholars now recognize as their pre-Removal halcyon days—when Euro-American pressures on them were the weakest, when their political and economic power was the greatest, and when the bounty of north-central Florida was at its fullest. Yet even here, the legacy of La Florida looms large. Seminoles, after all, were not the first Natives to make the Alachua savanna their home. Neither were Creeks—the Native people in Georgia and Alabama from whom Seminoles originated—the first Natives in those places, either. Their existence represented both the carnage of the Mississippian collapse and the resiliency of its survivors. It represented the dispersal of people, their movement into new places, and their reorganization under new identities.

Most of the direct evidence of this restructuring comes from La Florida's once densely populated coastline. The Native peoples of coastal Florida and Georgia, exposed for decades by epidemic diseases, were by the eighteenth century a very different people than what they had been when Spaniards first arrived. Many of the communities there, affected by waves of epidemic disease and subject to Spanish exploitation, then served as the premier hunting ground for a burgeoning Indian slave trade, which groups of ruthlessly enterprising English merchants operated out of Charleston. By raiding La Florida's missions and stripping them of their populations, these Charleston merchants grew rich while emerging Native groups like Creeks grew powerful. In the process, what had been La Florida was destroyed. Its Spanish footprint, never very large to begin with, was gone, while its Native population, once Mississippian, was transformed.

The destruction and transformation of La Florida's Mississippian communities provide only hints at the larger restructuring of the Native Southeast—a process of political, cultural, and economic change that Spaniards, along with the English, ensured with their permanent presence along the coast. How exactly that took place is still not entirely understood. But what scholars are confident about is that from the regional chaos created by both disease and enslavement—what one historian coined the "Mississippian Shatter Zone"—emerged groups like Cherokees, Choctaws, and Creeks, flexible and multi-ethnic communities composed of pieces and remnants of the previous Mississippian world. These would be the Native peoples who would come to dominate the proceeding century, as Seminoles would do in peninsular Florida. In other words, the Cowkeeper's residence on the Alachua savanna represented not a settling, but a resettling, of La Florida, a place once richly populated in Native peoples, but transformed by disease and by enslavement.

Notes

1. Van Doren, *The Travels of William Bartram*, 163-164.
2. Sattler, "Remnants, Renegades, and Runaways," 48; Porter, "The Founder of the 'Seminole Nation,'" 362-364, 381; Van Doren, *The Travels of William Bartram*, 163-164.
3. Van Doren, *The Travels of William Bartram*, 165.
4. Van Doren, *The Travels of William Bartram*, 165, 179.

Smallpox and Slave Raids

With regular colonial contact in La Florida came disease and, eventually, demographic collapse. Perhaps that began as early as the first generations of Spanish presence in the region. Recall Don Tristán de Luna's 1559 attempt to create a permanent settlement on the Florida Gulf Coast, near present-day Pensacola. When a hurricane swept up the Gulf of Mexico in 1559 and wrecked Santa María de Ochuse, basically right after Tristán arrived, he immediately looked inward. There, according to Spanish maps and Spanish chronicles, of which he would be familiar, he would find the solution to the dire situation in which he now found himself.

Anyone reading de Soto's chronicles, in fact, would have learned at least two things. First, there was no gold to be had in La Florida. Second, there was plenty of corn. The latter was something more than a thousand hungry Spanish settlers now needed, yet when Tristán de Luna's scouts headed north they were somewhat disappointed by what they found. Although what had been there twenty years ago was technically still there, it was not the same. Tristán de Luna's men bore witness to an ongoing transformation of interior modern-day Alabama, part of a larger regional demographic reorganization that would continue for another century. The Native Southeast that Spaniards beheld at the turn of the eighteenth century, when they finally did settle Pensacola, would have been unrecognizable to when de Soto's—or even de Luna's—men passed through there decades earlier.

On their way to Coosa, de Luna's scouts passed through Tascalusa. It too still existed, but it too was not what de Luna would have expected, having read accounts like de Soto's, which painted such places in much different terms. Mavilians survived de Soto's assault, but many seemed to be either leaving the province or had already left. Perhaps they were conquered. Perhaps they incorporated themselves voluntarily into other chiefdoms, like Chicaza or Coosa. While the cause will remain hidden, the result was the same—de Soto's actions had placed Tascalusa on a path of transformation. Generations later, Tascalusa would not exist, but Creeks and Choctaws would.[1]

The chiefdom of Coosa would transform similarly, with much of its population displacing down major watersheds in the modern states of Alabama and Georgia. One of "the largest and most powerful polities of its kind in the Southeastern United States," as Coosa was described by one anthropologist, was not what it once was when de Luna's men laid eyes on it. Chiaha, a chiefdom in the Appalachians, which de Soto's, de Luna's, and Juan Pardo's men would all encounter, would follow suit. So would parts of the Oconee province in central Georgia, also visited by disappointed Spaniards at the turn of the seventeenth century. Perhaps its decline began during de Soto's infamous "Georgia Stretch." Maybe, instead, it was the result of St. Augustine and Santa Elena, which Menéndez founded a few decades later, and from the intermittent Spanish expeditions through the turn of the seventeenth century that originated from the latter outpost. Regardless it too was in decline, as nearby Cofitachequi would be soon enough.[2]

This tale of decline and demographic transformation can be told across the extent of interior La Florida as it was defined even in its broadest territorial terms. The vectors of that decline were not only the Narváez or de Soto entradas, but the increasingly steady presence of Spaniards along the coast, beginning even with de León, Ayllón, and de Luna. Then came permanent settlements, ports of entry, and missions. Juan Pardo traveled inland through modern-day South Carolina from Santa Elena, while coastal missions emanating from St. Augustine and Santa Elena dotted the south from the Gulf Coast to the Chesapeake Bay. Small Spanish expeditions moved north through modern Georgia and one west from Apalachee, penetrating repeatedly into the interior of the Carolinas, Georgia, and Alabama. The English were not far behind, bringing coastal competition to the Spanish first with the establishment of Jamestown, then Charleston. Then there were the French, expanding their influence north and east from the Mississippi and the Gulf Coast. Spaniards responded by establishing Pensacola at the turn of the eighteenth century. Even according to the most conservative Native demographic calculations, it was when Europeans started developing long-term settlements that Native populations really began to suffer.[3] For many Southeastern Mississippians, these settlements marked the beginning of the end of their political world.

Although small and in time only few in number, La Florida outposts were important for setting this demographic shift into motion. For however isolated they were, both Santa Elena and St. Augustine still plugged La Florida into a transatlantic trade system that produced continuous Native-European interaction, none of which boded well for Native populations. So in time would

Apalachee and even Pensacola. Constant shipping into the ports, and trade from those enclaves inland, provided regular vectors for diseases like malaria and smallpox. With a consistent Spanish presence, that trade would have been steady enough to spread and establish the maladies throughout the region. Slaves connected La Florida to the West Coast of Africa, and soon missionaries would arrive as well, driving even deeper into Native communities.[4]

The effect of all of these developments on far-flung settlements like Chiaha and Coosa can only be projected using archaeological data and anthropological techniques, and it can only be suggested that European contact and trade led to depopulation. For Natives who were in much closer contact with Spaniards, which was the case along the Georgia coast and through the Florida panhandle, numbers are more reliable and declines can be modeled from clearer, more direct historical records. The declines reveal two separate trends that ultimately left their populations teetering on the brink of collapse. The first was the steady pressure of Spanish colonialism over the course of generations, which dwindled Native numbers to shadows of their pre-contact numbers. Then, on a much quicker and more destructive scale, slave raiding from communities allied with the English swooped in to wipe many of these communities off the map.

For the Natives of peninsular Florida, the presence of Spanish missions and demands for draft labor took a slow but steady toll on their populations. If a visit by a Spanish conquistador for only a few days had the potential to spread disease or destabilize society, then what could years of constant contact and exploitation do? Both took place in La Florida after Franciscan missionaries expanded into the region. *Repartimiento*-style labor requirements, while not nearly what they were elsewhere in the Spanish colonial world, still existed in La Florida. Guale Natives canoed corn and other supplies south through a string of coastal Georgia missions to St. Augustine, while Timucuas and Apalachees used inland waterways and the Camino Real to move food stores from the missions east. The food they carried along the route was usually on their back. The burden bearing was not only demeaning, even for lower-class laborers, but it was backbreaking work that took men away from their families for months at a time. Manual laborers flowed into St. Augustine along these same routes, bringing Native laborers—peons, really—into town to plant for the town's military garrison, cut lumber, or work on fortifications and infrastructure. Some worked as servants for private townspeople and officers. That left large numbers of underfed and overworked Native men lingering around St. Augustine for months at a time. Many would catch diseases there that might kill scores of people in their communities if it did not kill the carriers before they returned home.[5]

Tribute requirements in corn and labor drafts did not go down when the Native population of a community did, leaving survivors to labor even harder to meet St. Augustine's demands. In the finger-pointing that took place after the Apalachee 1647 uprising, for instance, soldiers blamed friars and friars blamed soldiers for the recent violence. Both were right, and both making accusations was nothing new on either side. The friars forced farming and construction labor from nearby Natives to support their expanding missions, all while mounting an existential assault on the Native way of life. Meanwhile, Native laborers assigned to St. Augustine's *repartimiento* died more often than not. Of the two hundred laborers who went into St. Augustine just recently before the 1647 uprising, only ten survived to return home. The La Florida farming and *repartimiento* labor systems might have been the smallest and the least taxing system of exploitation in the Spanish colonial world, but they were still part of the same system. They whittled away the population of La Florida Natives until there was very little left.[6]

By the mid-seventeenth century there were dozens of missions spread up the Georgia coast and through the Florida panhandle, each one surrounded by potentially thousands of Natives, often clustered closely together in mission towns. Each one of these was a potential demographic disaster waiting to happen. Not only were there friars in many of these far-flung missions but soldiers and their families, the coming and going of any of whom might introduce new and dangerous contagions. Even the chickens and pigs produced sickness that easily could have infected vulnerable Natives. Shipping came and went from both the Gulf and Atlantic coasts, from Pensacola, San Marcos de Apalachee, St. Augustine, or any one of the small missions that dotted Georgia's coastline. Travel along the Camino Real connected La Florida while coastal and river traffic spread contact inland. While Spanish clergymen looked upon La Florida's Christian development with pride, these outposts brought the full force of the Columbian Exchange to La Florida, and the results were devastating.[7]

Outbreaks among the Guale were reported in 1595, almost as soon as missionaries arrived. Between 1613 and 1617 Franciscans described epidemics that wiped out half of their Timucua and Guale mission Indians. Smallpox was suspected in the neighborhood of St. Augustine from 1649 to 1651, years when outbreaks were so bad that they not only killed Natives, but plenty of the town's Spanish residents as well. Another particularly bad outbreak raged from 1654 to 1655, and only years later an incoming Spanish governor reported that another ten thousand Natives had recently died from measles. Epidemics were becoming so routine in the region that by the late seventeenth century local authorities more or less stopped making note of them. Another contagion in the 1670s led to so many Native laborer deaths and slowed work on the Castillo de San Marcos so badly that local officials requested royal slaves from Havana. By that time the population of Apalachee had dwindled by a third, from thirty thousand to ten thousand. Those numbers were encouraging compared to Timucua and Guale mortality figures, each of which hovered right around 90 percent. Timucua numbers were down from 25,000 to 2,000 and Guale numbers even less still. While referred to as the "Golden Age" of Spanish evangelism in La Florida, these decades witnessed the slow, systematic destruction of once-populous Native groups. Smaller peoples, like the Potano or the Mocama, disappeared completely.[8]

The decline in Timucua numbers in particular reveals the cost of sustained contact with Europeans. The position of Timucua groups closest to St. Augustine and also along the Camino Real made them the most exposed and vulnerable of La Florida's Native communities. Everything from working in St. Augustine to hauling corn along the road through the mission district made them prime vectors of communicable diseases, even those with quick incubation times. The distance from St. Augustine to their towns was mere days, meaning laborers could spread anything and everything through several villages before anyone knew anything was wrong. The closer Natives got to European settlements, the Timucua demonstrate, the faster their communities suffered from disease. What took place in Virginia with the Powhatans, or in New England with the Wampanoag, Massachusetts, or Pequot, happened first in La Florida with the Timucua.[9]

The demographic collapse of La Florida's mission districts supports even the most aggressive numbers suggested by historians and anthropologists. What took place farther from that epicenter is obviously much less uncertain, yet at one time or another missions dotted the rim of interior La Florida. If disease accompanied Spanish missionizing, then there are several vectors from which disease could have spread deep into the modern states of Georgia, Alabama, and South Carolina. Juan Pardo's 1570s outposts stretched all the way to the Appalachians. Later, more than a half-dozen separate missions stretched into the interior of southern Georgia. Traffic up the Altamaha and other regional river systems was regular, making even the most seemingly remote Spanish missions along the outer edges of the Native South sources of diseases that easily could have spread inland into communities far in the interior.

Short-lived missions stretched farther into the La Florida interior. Santa Cruz de Cachipile and Santa María de los Angeles de Arapaha were both either in or very near the modern-day state of Georgia, near Valdosta. To the west were a few missions along the Florida-Georgia-Alabama line, including Santa Cruz de Sabacola. Farther to the east were Santiago de Oconi and San Lorenzo de Ibihica, closer to the coast and above the St. Mary's River, the modern-day boundary between Georgia and Florida. Farthest away was Santa Isabel de Utinahica, located deep in modern-day Georgia, at the confluence of the Oconee and Okmulgee Rivers.[10] It is easy to think of these missions as so isolated, so short-lived, that they could not have possibly played a role in the region's disease ecology. Yet they endured for years and several lasted decades—plenty of time for a constant movement of Europeans and their livestock to take its toll. The extent of missionary contact in these corners of La Florida will never be fully understood, yet Guale, Apalachee, and Timucua contact is more understood, and that contact had a devastating impact on Native populations. In La Florida, missionizing was one of the prime vectors of epidemic disease that combined to bring the Mississippian world to a close.

The slow toll of epidemic disease is contrasted by the swiftness of the Indian slave trade, which took its toll on the region rapidly and with shattering consequence. By the late seventeenth century an Atlantic trade was spreading into the American colonies, and English traders in particular—the American South's first true capitalists—arrived in Virginia and Carolina with what we could perhaps call an intense entrepreneurial spirit. Although the proprietors that founded Charleston envisioned other more respectable ways to build their fortunes, they were unable to control local traders, who were soon busily exporting one of South Carolina's first major commodities—human beings. By the turn of the eighteenth century, Charleston merchants were major slave exporters to New England and the Caribbean, and they relied on competing Native groups to procure their product. The Southeast's many and ethnically diverse peoples already shared a retaliatory culture of raiding each other for captives, a shared culture that made them excellent slavers. Neighbors surprised neighbors, captured and bound them, and exchanged them in Charleston for guns and other trade goods, which turned out to be a far more profitable trade than anything else Natives had access to, like animal hides.[11]

While the slave trade ultimately spread to all corners of the Southeast, La Florida suffered some of its worst atrocities, and not simply because of its proximity to South Carolina. The demographics of mission towns made raiding into Florida profitable work. Tightly packed around La Florida's Catholic missions were thousands of potential slaves, making for obvious targets. Then there was a long simmering Anglo-Spanish political rivalry, rising to new levels at the end of the seventeenth century with the establishment of Virginia and then South Carolina, the latter founded on land still claimed by Spain. Imperial rivalry would soon spill over into war, referred to in America as Queen Anne's War. For many enterprising English traders, the coincidence was fantastic. The declaration of war brought legitimacy to almost any violent act the agents of one imperial power, including its auxiliary Native allies, might use against another. Raiding for slaves, a profitable enterprise already, turned out to be an excellent weapon of war, stripping La Florida of the Natives St. Augustine authorities relied on to provide food and labor for the colony, while also generating wealth within South Carolina. Not to be forgotten, time had done little to temper the intolerance and hatred that had, one hundred fifty years previous, led a Catholic Menéndez to massacre a Protestant Ribault on a La Florida beach. The colonial powers of St. Augustine and Charleston now embodied that same religious struggle, which would rage seemingly until one was no more.[12]

Religious, political, and military exigencies, combined with naked economic interests, all drove South Carolinians to strike powerful blows to their neighbors to the south. La Florida, a backwater in the Spanish world standing against a rapidly expanding Carolina frontier, stood no chance in the imperial contest that exploded upon the Southeast late in the seventeenth century. The far-flung Spanish frontier emerged as the prime target of the emerging slave trade, enriching Charleston merchants while crippling La Florida's Native peoples. Among the 50,000 or so Natives presumed to have been captured and enslaved in the entire Southeast over a thirty-year period of the slave trade, upward of 12,000 came from La Florida over the space of a few years alone. More would have been taken, but that was all that was left.[13]

The once-sprawling and once-populous Guale coastline, already wracked by disease and exploitation, was the first to suffer. A stretch of Catholic outposts that originally stretched to Port Royal, shrank first with the abandonment of the Orista province in modern-day South Carolina, leaving only the Guale to suffer a slow and painful demographic decline driven by Spanish societal pressure and epidemic disease. By the mid-seventeenth century less than a half-dozen missions remained, and the population of the Guale people themselves was well under one thousand. The province's largest mission, Santa Catalina de Guale, was still considerable and included a small garrison of Spanish soldiers. Unfortunately, there was not much left for them to protect.[14]

Upon this coastal graveyard sprang the slavers. Westo, who the Spanish referred to as *Chichimeco*, descended the Altamaha River to attack the coastline as early as 1661. The attackers converged on Santo Domingo de Talaje, a small mission at the mouth of the river, forcing its residents to flee to another mission, San Joseph de Sapala, on nearby Sapelo Island. The governor responded by sending troops, dispersing the Westo, saving San Joseph de Sapala and allowing for the Talaje mission to be rebuilt on St. Simon's Island. This small victory was soon followed by another one with the arrival of Yamasee refugees, fleeing the interior of Georgia and South Carolina, presumably because of the same Westo. They hoped the Spanish might offer them protection, and the Spanish, facing dwindling Guale and Timucua numbers, were happy to boost La Florida's population. Soon Yamasee communities were established on St. Simon's, Cumberland, and Amelia Islands, the overlapping frontier of the Guale and Mocama mission districts along the Atlantic Coast of modern-day Georgia and Florida.[15] This single bright spot—an actual rise in the regional Native population—was only an illusion. Westo raiding had just begun.

Much is written about the Westo, and very little is known for certain. As a relatively small group they played a hugely outsized role in the development of the early Southeast; they were among the first Natives in the region to gain access to guns and ammunition. The weapons they wielded from their perch on the Savannah River created a strategic advantage that is almost difficult to fully comprehend. While the muskets were probably less accurate than arrows, they were deadlier when used effectively. They were also terrifying, striking fear into their victims even when the Westo warriors missed their shot. No one else had those weapons, making the Westo a small but incredibly influential group. Refugees themselves from farther north, the Westo were armed by Marylanders and nearby Susquehanna Natives, only to be pushed away by Dutch-backed war parties in the 1650s. They relocated to Virginia and set up trade there before moving farther south still. They were already on the Carolina frontier and spreading regional devastation on behalf of Virginia when Charleston emerged as a trading center operated by basically the most unscrupulous traders in the entire world. Although no doubt alarmed by the power this small Native group possessed, Charleston authorities soon supplanted the Virginias and engaged the Westo south into La Florida.[16]

Another La Florida attack came quickly, this time at St. Simon's Island, against the recently arrived Yamasee, and soon the Westo were again attacking the Santa Catalina mission. Five Spaniards were killed and much of the small mission town was torched. When a larger relief force from St. Augustine arrived, they found the whole place in chaos. Soldiers and friars relocated the nearby Guale and Yamasee farther south to Sapelo Island and the San Joseph de Sapala mission. In the retreat more missions were abandoned, further shrinking the extent of the Guale province.[17] The Carolinians soon eliminated the Westo by turning to nearby "Savannah" Natives (probably Shawnees who had recently arrived from over the Appalachians to the north) when the Westo grew too powerful. By essentially paying the Savannah to destroy the Westo, South Carolinians simply replaced one group of slavers with another, a move that in the end mattered little in the trajectory of La Florida's decline.[18]

Only a few years later a mixed group of English and French pirates raided up the coast, wiping out more missions and killing and scattering whoever was left on several small Sea Islands. Mission towns on Sapelo, St. Simon's, Ft. George, Cumberland, and Amelia Islands were attacked, leading to the deaths of more Guale and causing some of the nearby Yamasee to flee La Florida for South Carolina. Their decision to seek shelter with the Spanish had clearly been a bad one, leading many Yamasee to depart and try their luck with the British. Soon they would return as slave raiders themselves. Meanwhile, the attacks prompted the abandonment or relocation of more than a half-dozen missions. Everything north of Cumberland Island, situated right above the modern-day Florida border, was abandoned. Where Spanish missions once stretched the entirety of the coast of Georgia, by 1685 not a single one remained.[19]

These raids were devastating, yet they paled in comparison to the attacks initiated in 1702 when notorious merchant and slave trader James Moore became governor of South Carolina. By that time Queen Anne's War had broken out, so Moore billed his first invasion not as a slave raid, but as an attack on Spanish power in St. Augustine. It was also a preemptive strike against the French in Louisiana, who were allied with the Spanish and were reportedly drawing up plans to attack South Carolina from the south. Moore argued that his attacks would remove both colonial competitors from the Southeast. This first bid was enticing enough for South Carolina's proprietors to give him official funding, even though they were clearly hesitant. The invasion force contained upward of five hundred South Carolinians, few of which were soldiers and most of which were participating in the hopes of slaves and plunder. With them were hundreds of Natives, including recently arrived Yamasee.[20]

Moore's eventual attempt to fulfill his promises against St. Augustine never amounted to anything; his army never came close to threatening the Castillo de San Marcos. A Spanish flotilla from Havana arrived to force Moore to lift his makeshift siege, and the invaders had to basically walk back to Charleston. The invasion never came close to evicting the Spanish from La Florida, let alone scaring the French away, leading the Carolina proprietors to complain of Moore's colossal waste of money. What the governor did accomplish, however, was the utter ruin of the Guale and Mocama provinces, including the Santa Clara de Tupiqui mission and the recently relocated Santa Catalina de Guale mission. If the proprietors hated his invasion, in other words, his merchant and Native allies probably loved it. Because of them, Guale, one of La Florida's oldest and most significant mission districts, was officially no more.[21]

Simultaneous to these coastal assaults was an ongoing attack on peninsular La Florida's mission districts. There the Timucua missions in north-central Florida and the sprawling Apalachee province in the Florida panhandle comprised La Florida's other two districts. Although the Timucua missions struggled with uprisings and depopulation, Apalachee had been for decades the jewel in the crown for La Florida's Franciscan clergy and one of the most consistent missionizing successes in all of the New World. Near modern-day Tallahassee sat San Luis de Talimali, the massive mission complex that also maintained a sizeable Spanish garrison. It was the centerpiece of a mission trail that extended basically from St. Augustine to Pensacola and cared for tens of thousands of Native souls.

Sensing the danger of the expanding Carolina frontier to this rich region, Spaniards attempted to extend fortified missions to the north in hopes of blunting attacks, but the missions never lasted long. Instead, in 1685, Yamasee raiders, having recently fled the Spanish to the embrace of Charleston traders, penetrated all the way into the Suwanee River in modern-day Florida, raiding the Santa Catalina de Ajohica mission. They burned the mission and convent to the ground, killed more than a dozen Timucua defenders, and snatched up another two dozen slaves before withdrawing to South Carolina. Slave raiding had arrived in the heart of La Florida. Another attack on the Suwanee burned another mission, San Juan de Guacara, in 1691, and another attack in 1702 killed several more Timucuas and a Spanish lieutenant. Spaniards again responded with a retaliatory raid, this time from Apalachee, manned by almost one thousand Native warriors taken from nearby mission towns. The force marched north to chastise the offending party of Creek Indians, known as Apalachicolas, but they were ambushed and crushed by the defenders, whose guns were more than a match for the Apalachees's arrows. Hundreds of Natives were either killed or captured in this supposed counterattack. Soon the Timucua province was reduced to only one mission.[22]

As was the case with Guale, these were all relatively small raids in comparison to the cataclysmic assaults mounted soon after by Carolinians, which peaked from 1704 to 1706. The opening attack was spearheaded by none other than James Moore, who this time did not even try to convince the proprietors that his goal was anything other than the capture of Native slaves. His invasion was only given approval by colonial officials because Moore insisted it would not cost South Carolina a dime, and he was right. To secure fighters he assured bounties of slaves and other spoils, which made it easy to raise a force of fifty Carolinians and one thousand Native invaders. Together the army descended upon La Florida in January 1704 and went right for Apalachee. First they hit La Concepción de Ayubale, defeating the small Spanish force sent to cut them off, burning the church down around its defenders, and then burning a few of them alive for good measure. Even though the sprawling San Luis de Talimali survived, very little else around it did. In all, several missions were destroyed, over one thousand Apalachees returned with the army to South Carolina willingly, and another one thousand were swept away as slaves of the Carolinians and their Native allies.[23]

These campaigns were vicious attacks, marked by mutilations, burnings, and even the skinning alive of a few victims. Neither Friars nor Spanish soldiers were spared. The brutality of the attacks grew legendary, yet the Creek and Yamasee slavers were far from done. More small-scale attacks continued over the course of the next year, convincing the residents of San Luis de Talimali that they were doomed if they stayed. Soon they evacuated the mission town, joining other nearby refugees in making their way to Pensacola. Burning the mission and the garrison, however, only left those who remained in nearby villages even more isolated and vulnerable. Within months San Pedro y San Pablo de Potohiriba, San Matheo de Tolapatafi, and Santa Elena de Machab, all nearby missions, were burned. Neighboring headmen were executed and the villagers enslaved, leaving only the most heavily fortified Apalachee mission towns remaining and nothing in the Timucua province. Noted English trader Thomas Nairne described the carnage. For two years they had "been intirely kniving all the Indian Towns in Florida which were subject to the Spaniards and have even accomplished it."[24]

Over the course of this sustained assault, Native and Carolinian forces destroyed upward of thirty missions. Their destruction not only wiped out the Apalachee and Timucua districts but opened the door for Native raiders to pillage the rest of the peninsula. Soon Tocobaga and Calusa Native communities, far down on the Gulf Coast, were being targeted. Far more isolated than their neighbors to the north, these communities were in no way prepared for the onslaught of the heavily armed Creek and Yamasee slavers that soon arrived in their provinces. A description of one such raid "to go a slave catching" described Thomas Nairne and his allied Yamasee making their way all the way south of modern-day Orlando by canoe, trudging through dense Florida swamps to catch three dozen slaves. Their progress was finally halted by a swarm of Natives who attacked them with harpoons, some of which were tipped with fish bones. Perhaps they were the remnants of the legendary Calusa, who had squared off against Spaniards with much the same weapons almost two centuries earlier. Whoever they were, their shark tooth–tipped arrows were now a poor match for English guns. Refugees were pushed by these raids all the way into the Florida Keys, so that in 1710 one Englishman celebrated that "there remains not now, so much as one Village with ten houses in it, in all of Florida, that is subject to the Spaniards." Nothing was safe if it was farther than shooting distance from the Castillo de San Marcos in St. Augustine, the rest of the region being "continually infested by the perpetual Incursions of the Indians, subject to this Province."[25]

By this point St. Augustine and Pensacola remained, but not much else did. The uselessness of those two fortifications for the purposes of regional protection was demonstrated by the groups of Creek raiders that were able to slip by them without any notice on their way south to the sites of the modern-day cities of Tampa, Fort Myers, and even Miami, in search of slaves. Eventually these raids tapered off as the Native population of Florida sank to almost nothing. By that time more Native slavers also began to question their Carolinian allies. The abuses of the trade were too much to bear for many regional Natives, including the Yamasee, for whom the uprising that ended the slave trade was named. The war, which ravaged the Carolinas from 1715 to 1717, involved many of the Southeast's remaining Native peoples. Very few Guale, Timucua, Apalachee, Ais, Tocobaga, Calusa, or any other Florida Natives participated, however, because there were few of them left.[26] Disease and slave raiding had reduced La Florida to a fraction of its previous population, both in Spaniards and Natives, numbers that would never really recover.

Notes

1. Hudson, *Knights of Spain*, 244-246; Smith, "Aboriginal Population Movements," 22.

2. Halley, "The Chiefdom of Coosa," 227, 249-250; Ethridge, *From Chicaza to Chickasaw*, 62-64, 80-81, 87-88; Mark Williams, "Growth and Decline of the Oconee Province," 191-193; Smith, "Aboriginal Population Movements," 22-27; DePratter, "The Chiefdom of Cofitachequi," 217-221; Galloway, *Choctaw Genesis*, 143-163; Merrell, *The Indians' New World*, 19.

3. See, for instance, Beck, *Chiefdoms, Collapse, and Coalescence*, 151-161; Worth, "Spanish Florida and the Southeastern Indians, 1513-1650," 105-111.

4. Kelton, *Epidemics and Enslavement*, 78-82; Beck, *Chiefdoms, Collapse, and Coalescence*, 92-95, 123-124, 151-161; Waselkov, "Seventeenth-Century Trade," 117-130; Galloway, *Choctaw Genesis*, 177-181; Crosby, *The Columbian Exchange*, 40; Crosby, *Ecological Imperialism*, 200-201.

5. Galgano, *Feast of Souls*, 122-123; Milanich, *Laboring in the Fields of the Lord*, 106-109, 115-119, 149-153; Bushnell, *Situado and Sabana*, 111-128, 138-142.

6. Hann, *Apalachee*, 16-19, 22; Milanich, *Laboring in the Fields of the Lord*, 126-127, 161-165; Bushnell, *Situado and Sabana*, 128-133.

7. Kelton, *Epidemics and Enslavement*, 82-83; Milanich, *Laboring in the Fields of the Lord*, 157-158; Galloway, *Choctaw Genesis*, 133-135.

8. Hann, "Demographic Patterns," 371-392; Milanich, *Laboring in the Fields of the Lord*, 158-161; Hoffman, *Florida's Frontiers*, 105-110, 126-134; Kelton, *Epidemics and Enslavement*, 82-87; Ethridge, *From Chicaza to Chickasaw*, 78-79; Milanich, "Franciscan Missions and Native Peoples in Spanish Florida," 280-282; Bushnell, *Situado and Sabana*, 140; Smith, "Aboriginal Depopulation," 259; Milanich, "The Timucua Indians," 11; Wood, "Changing Population," 51-53.

9. Milanich, *Laboring in the Fields of the Lord*, 160; Milanich, "The Timucua Indians," 20-22.

10. Milanich, *Laboring in the Fields of the Lord*, 122-123; Galloway, *Choctaw Genesis*, 168-169.

11. Gallay, *Indian Slave Trade*, 57-69; Crane, *The Southern Frontier*, 112-114; Kelton, *Epidemics and Enslavement*, 102-104, 126-127, 141; Ethridge, *From Chicaza to Chickasaw*, 232, 238.

12. Gallay, *Indian Slave Trade*, 134-135; Milanich, *Laboring in the Fields of the Lord*, 175-176; Ethridge, *From Chicaza to Chickasaw*, 194-195.

13. Ethridge, *From Chicaza to Chickasaw*, 210-211, 237-238; Milanich, *Laboring in the Fields of the Lord*, 175; Crane, *Southern Frontier*, 24.

14. Milanich, *Laboring in the Fields of the Lord*, 170-171; Bushnell, *Situado and Sabana*, 134-136; Crane, *Southern Frontier*, 8.

15. Bowne, *The Westo Indians*, 75-78; Bossy, "Yamasee Mobility," 205-214; Milanich, *Laboring in the Fields of the Lord*, 168-171; Beck, *Chiefdoms, Collapse, and Coalescence*, 114-119; Gallay, *Indian Slave Trade*, 73-74; Crane, *Southern Frontier*, 24-25; Ethridge, *From Chicaza to Chickasaw*, 99; Kelton, *Epidemics and Enslavement*, 112-113, 127; Bushnell, *Situado and Sabana*, 145-147.

16. Bowne, *The Westo Indians*; Gallay, *Indian Slave Trade*, 40-43, 53-57; Meyers, "The Seventeenth-Century Native-Colonial Borderlands," 193-196; Jennings, "Cutting One Another's Throats," 120-123; Crane, *Southern Frontier*, 12, 17; Kelton, *Epidemics and Enslavement*, 105-106, 112-114, 127; Ethridge, *From Chicaza to Chickasaw*, 92-93, 98.

17. Milanich, *Laboring in the Fields of the Lord*, 171-172; Crane, *Southern Frontier*, 17-18; Kelton, *Epidemics and Enslavement*, 129-130; Bushnell, *Situado and Sabana*, 145-147, 161-170.

18. Bowne, *The Westo Indians*, 89-105; Milanich, *Laboring in the Fields of the Lord*, 172; Crane, *Southern Frontier*, 18-21; Kelton, *Epidemics and Enslavement*, 127-128; Meyers, "The

Seventeenth-Century Native-Colonial Borderlands," 196-200; Jennings, "Cutting One Another's Throats," 120-123; Beck, *Chiefdoms, Collapse, and Coalescence*, 146-150.

19. Milanich, *Laboring in the Fields of the Lord*, 172-174; Gallay, *Indian Slave Trade*, 74-75, 79; Crane, *Southern Frontier*, 24-26, 162; Kelton, *Epidemics and Enslavement*, 130; Ethridge, *From Chicaza to Chickasaw*, 162-163; Bushnell, *Situado and Sabana*, 161-170.

20. Gallay, *Indian Slave Trade*, 93, 135-136; Beck, *Chiefdoms, Collapse, and Coalescence*, 181-184; Jennings, "Cutting One Another's Throats," 124-126; Crane, *Southern Frontier*, 75-77; Milanich, *Laboring in the Fields of the Lord*, 178-182.

21. Milanich, *Laboring in the Fields of the Lord*, 178-182; Ethridge, *From Chicaza to Chickasaw*, 207-209; Gallay, *Indian Slave Trade*, 136-137; Crane, *Southern Frontier*, 76, 78.

22. Gallay, *Indian Slave Trade*, 82; Milanich, *Laboring in the Fields of the Lord*, 183-184; Crane, *Southern Frontier*, 31, 79; Kelton, *Epidemics and Enslavement*, 131, 182; Ethridge, *From Chicaza to Chickasaw*, 163, 206-207.

23. Gallay, *Indian Slave Trade*, 144-149; Jennings, "Cutting One Another's Throats," 124-127; Milanich, *Laboring in the Fields of the Lord*, 184-188; Crane, *Southern Frontier*, 78-80; Kelton, *Epidemics and Enslavement*, 182-183; Bushnell, *Situado and Sabana*, 190-194.

24. Milanich, *Laboring in the Fields of the Lord*, 184-188; Ethridge, *From Chicaza to Chickasaw*, 209-210; Crane, *Southern Frontier*, 80-81; Bushnell, *Situado and Sabana*, 190-194.

25. Crane, *Southern Frontier*, 81; Gallay, *Indian Slave Trade*, 127-128, 147-148; Wood, "Changing Population," 53-54.

26. Crane, *Southern Frontier*, 162-186; Ethridge, *From Chicaza to Chickasaw*, 232-254.

A Southeastern Coalescence

THE COLLAPSE OF THE MISSISSIPPIAN ERA, FOR ALL OF ITS DESTRUCTION, DID not mark the end of the Native Southeast. The waves of diseases characterizing the Columbian Exchange did not permanently "widow" the land, as Henry Dobyns had once put it. Neither did South Carolinians or the Indian slave trade destroy all Native peoples. Instead, the regional disruption caused by these overlapping forces generated what one scholar termed a "Mississippian shatter zone," a period of instability in the North American Southeast that destabilized old societies and led to the formation of new ones. Secondary waves of population movement followed the destabilization and even collapse of old Native polities, often into lands disrupted or possibly even emptied in consequence of that collapse. What Europeans set into motion beginning with La Florida was a sweeping and devastating reorganization, which possibly killed more than it spared, but it was a reorganization, nonetheless. These waves of "coalescence" created the Native societies that dominated the Southeast for centuries afterward, from the time of La Florida to the Removal era and even to the present. The processes of coalescence that created the Cherokee, Chickasaw, Choctaw, Creek, and even Seminole followed the collapse of the Mississippian world. The European settlement of La Florida played an important role in that process.[1]

In the Piedmont region of the Carolinas, populations of smaller Siouan-speaking peoples, including the Cheraw, Congaree, Wateree, Waxhaw, Tutelo, and Saponi, among others, were so thinned by the consequences of European contact—through both disease and trade—that surviving communities began to merge with each other. Eventually English explorers in the Carolinas early in the eighteenth century recognized them as Catawbas.[2] A bit farther to the south, the Savannah River basin was the location of progressive waves of resettlement following the dissolution of the Mississippian settlements there. The Westo arrived from the north, followed by the Shawnee and Yamasee.[3] In modern northeastern Georgia, northwest South Carolina, and eastern Tennessee, the collapse of nearby Mississippian chiefdoms that included Coosa, Chiaha, Chisca, and Xaula, created the possibility for other Natives to move south to form new communities. These Iroquoian- and Illinoian-speaking travelers coalesced into Cherokees, and different groups of immigrants formed different Cherokee regions. In particular, the bands that would become the "Overland" and "Middle Town" Cherokee towns re-inhabited regions formerly settled in the Chiaha and Coosa chiefdoms after the remnants of those chiefdoms displaced to the south.[4]

The Alabama River, which forms at the confluence of the Coosa and Tallapoosa Rivers, was one important point of coalescence for those remnants. Another important confluence lies just to the east, where the Flint and Chattahoochee Rivers combine to create the Apalachicola River. These two regions soon became the loci of reorganization for a people who Europeans would soon know as Creeks. Refugee communities in modern-day Alabama, possibly part of the once-sprawling Tascalusa and Coosa chiefdoms, moved east and southeast to the same river systems. Dispersal from the Oconee region, which included Ocute and Ichisi communities, would have added to those developments. Between de Soto, Santa Elena, St. Augustine, the missions, and then the English, those chiefdoms most likely suffered several violent waves of dispersal, and by relocating to the Alabama and Apalachicola watersheds, they would be recognized by Europeans respectively as "Upper" and "Lower" Creeks, respectively. At least one anthropologist has suggested a direct connection between Ocute and Coweta, a prominent Creek town that rose to regional prominence along the Chattahoochee River.[5] Creeks, one of the most powerful Native people to confront Euro-Americans for the next two centuries, might not have ever existed without the collapse of the Mississippian world.

Likewise, the regions of the Mississippi River Valley wandered through by de Soto's men in the twilight of their expedition, coalesced into Choctaws and Chickasaws.[6] Farther to the west and southwest, communities in west Louisiana, eastern Texas, and southern Arkansas were harassed by the remainder of the de Soto entrada in its final days. Even after de Soto's death the remnants of the expedition continued to influence regional communities in ways that fundamentally transformed the resident Caddoan people. A bit farther to the north in modern-day Arkansas, the Casquin and Pacaha peoples who were struggling against each other when de Soto intervened would be replaced by Native immigrants from the north, near present-day Ohio. These would coalesce into the Quapaw. In every case, Native peoples went through tragic cycles of collapse. Yet that collapse also produced systemic structural changes that in time would give rise to new societies.[7]

Although Mississippian and coalescent peoples were made of "the same basic organizational stock," in the words of one anthropologist, the structure of coalescent societies reflected the violence, chaos, and regeneration of the period. They were more multi-ethnic, politically and socially flexible places that were markedly different from their Mississippian predecessors in several important ways. One of the most obvious examples of this transition was in the shifting of political culture from rigid hierarchy to inclusivity. Chiefdoms became confederacies, as another anthropologist put it. Communities got smaller in size and less hierarchical in structure, much of which can be witnessed in the archaeological record. Mound building, for instance, was long gone by the seventeenth century. If the construction of mounds was the quintessential physical marker of a Mississippian community, projecting both the religious and sociopolitical authority wielded by chieftains in rigidly hierarchical societies, then the disappearance of those mounds marked an important shift. That system was giving way. Neither were chieftains any longer receiving tribute in the form of prestige goods. That, too, began to fade from the archaeological record.[8]

Consider as a counterpoint to Mississippian power the political leadership structure of the Creek society that came to dominate much of the Southeast in the eighteenth century. There, a town's leading civil headmen were referred to as "micos." A smaller community might only have one mico, but a larger community might have several. Below them were almost equally powerful warriors, or "tustunnuggees," followed by several classes of trusted advisors and shamans. Some similarities between this structure and a Mississippian chiefdom are clear. Micos were immensely respected men whose position still reflected a ranked leadership, and oftentimes leaders did claim hereditary lineage. The same could be said about the tustunnuggees and other leaders around them. Micos also took tribute of a kind, mostly in food stores, creating another Mississippian connection.

These traditions demonstrate clear Mississippian continuities, yet adaptations and elaborations on those traditions were also clear. While micos wielded authority, that authority was not entirely based on heredity power or cosmological knowledge, as was the case in the Mississippian world. Neither was that authority coercive, as it had been before. Micos's power was persuasive, and they attained their positions of authority through their actions—their sound judgment, their leadership, and the trust their community's men and women had in them. While their thoughts were important, a town's decision-making was done by consensus and included the voices of micos, warriors, and other leaders with civic titles. The presence of council squares where those discussions took place was the marker of a politically and economically autonomous town and was usually located in the center of that town. Neither was a mico's position of authority a signifier of personal wealth. The corn or food provisions he accumulated were not prestige items. While a mico might have exercised some ability to redistribute those resources, they were not necessarily his to do with as he pleased. He only managed them. They remained the product of the town and the town's common property.

The social, political, and cultural dynamics of a "coalescent" society like Creeks retained Mississippian trappings, certainly, but there were also developments upon them that stressed inclusivity and multi-ethnicity. Clan identity remained central to Native lives, but clan groups were not necessarily ranked in terms of religious power, as they had before. In coalescent societies they functioned more to tie sometimes-disparate peoples together in webs of kinship, creating family networks that spanned communities. Migration stories and other myths stressed population movement and the incorporation of refugees. Community ceremonies like the Busk, or Green Corn, celebrated renewal and rebirth. Sporting events like chunkey or the ball game drew communities together and settled disputes. That was the sort of cultural cohesiveness that bound together independent communities in ways that were remarkably strong at times, but could also create tensions between communities when regional action was required. Together the two formed the foundation of identity: a passing Creek or Cherokee would have described themselves by their clan identity, or their home community, and not necessarily as a Creek or a Cherokee.[9]

Every one of these political or cultural developments signified the bending of Native lives to the harsh realities of Mississippian collapse. As one prominent Creek historian suggested, that sort of bending created a bit of an irony. For all of the horrors that destabilized and upended the Mississippian world, the Creeks who emerged from the carnage emerged favorably disposed to chart their own way forward. By the dawn of the eighteenth century they had weathered the storm of slaving and epidemic diseases. Spaniards along the coast and in the missions were far enough away for them to keep an arm's length, but close enough to benefit from European material culture. Creek social and political structures were strong but also flexible, meaning they could engage with competing colonial powers effectively, something they were able to do for generations. In short, Creeks, like the Southeast's other coalescent peoples, emerged from the collapse of the Mississippian world positioned to prosper, which they did.[10] If La Florida was a force that destroyed, it was also a force that created.

Juxtapose that prosperity with the slow demise of La Florida's missionized Native populations, most namely the Guale, Timucua, and Apalachee. In another irony, Spaniards were largely responsible for the devastation of their own mission system in ways that extended beyond their basic inability to protect their Native wards. This began with the problematic nature of the mission system itself, the foundation upon which Spanish colonialism in the New World was built. Designed to transform Natives into good European Christians, La Florida's Native peoples were assimilated into a Spanish culture based around the church. Nothing that was needed to protect themselves at even the most basic level, like guns, was therefore forthcoming. It was not enough that Spanish trade was never as good as its English competition; Spaniards wanted their Native wards to be farmers and herdsmen, not hunters for the deerskin trade and certainly not hunters for the slave trade. Because of the history of revolts in La Florida, Spanish authorities also did not want nearby Natives too armed for their own safety. Spanish garrisons would provide protection for their friars' Christian flocks, who otherwise would become good Christian farmers. Increasingly, however, it was clear the Spanish could not protect their Natives in even the most basic way, and in their failure neither could the Natives defend themselves. The flock analogy used often by the friars was more accurate than they knew: Guale, Timucua, and Apalachee farmers really were sheep.[11]

Spaniards also propped up remnants of Mississippian societies that were disappearing elsewhere. As they had done across the New World for generations, colonial authorities built their systems of economic exploitation atop preexisting Native hierarchies, which were well suited for doing so. Spanish colonial authorities did not destroy the political systems that undergirded Native societies, which were highly structured and could be exploited to generate labor and wealth. They simply replaced themselves at the top of those social and economic pyramids and reaped the benefits that usually accrued solely to the chiefs. Cortés did that in Mexico City by killing and replacing Montezuma. Pizarro did the same in Peru by killing Atahualpa. La Florida's Mississippian societies had similarly clear hierarchies, which Spanish authorities supported as long as they could benefit from them by, say, growing corn or supporting the colonial infrastructure.

Spanish officials supported Apalachee and Timucua headmen as traditional Mississippian chiefs as long as they provided tribute in corn and labor in the form of their workers. Tribute and agricultural production were already foundational mechanisms of Mississippian chiefdoms, making the contributions relatively easy for the Native elite to make. St. Augustine's population was sustained with Native corn, grown by Native workers, who walked the corn from Apalachee and Timucua missions along a Camino Real that was built and maintained using Native labor. The Castillo de San Marcos was built largely using Native labor. In turn the Spanish supported regional headmen, ensuring—in theory at least—military alliances and the giving of European prestige goods, like ornate clothing. All of this reinforced chiefly power in familiar Mississippian ways. The arrangement allowed headmen to remain atop their chiefdoms as their ancestors had done for generations. Spanish colonialism stabilized Apalachee and Timucua chiefdoms with Spanish alliances supporting traditional Native power and shielding Native communities, at least temporarily, from violence. As one scholar concluded, to be a Christian chief "seemed to mean becoming a more powerful chief."[12]

The story was entirely different in Native societies deeper in the interior, which were farther away from Spanish influence and benefited in the short term from neither the stability nor the protection provided by Spanish colonialism. Many of the Southeast's collapsing Mississippian chiefdoms subsequently reformed into recombinant groups like Creeks, Choctaws, or Chickasaws. They did so in an "armed borderland between competing European powers," according to one historian, where they had to learn how to survive in a rapidly changing world. With the arrival of Westo slave raiders in the 1660s, Charleston in the 1670s, and the expansion of trade and the slave trade in the 1680s, the learning curve was a steep one indeed. Everyone's roles, from chiefs to women to warriors, changed. Ultimately a Native identity emerged in which men were transformed from primarily Mississippian laborers to primarily hunters and killers. While Apalachee men produced corn, Creek women produced corn while Creek men produced deer and, increasingly, slaves.

The difference in the political culture of these two counterpoints was like the difference between night and day. Apalachees were Mississippians, whose rulers still controlled their people through resource distribution and family lineages. Creeks valued leaders who did not maintain chiefly power by controlling growing resources or familial lines. They valued leaders who had been tested in war, and who had earned the respect of their people. While stability in Apalachee might have appeared positive in the short term, clearly in the long term it was not. Through a violent period of social transformation, coalescent societies like Creeks emerged as adaptable and flexible, qualities that made them well suited to exploiting the emerging colonial world. Meanwhile Apalachees, having gone through no such transformation and lacking the means to even protect themselves, went from a feared people to a very weak and increasingly endangered people. Apalachee headmen governed increasingly dysfunctional and failing societies that were propped up by increasingly weak Spaniards. Once unleashed by the English upon La Florida, the destructive forces of conquest and enslavement represented by Creeks and Chickasaws struck quick. Mississippian La Florida was out, and the coalescent Southeast was in.[13]

Notes

1. Ethridge, *From Chicaza to Chickasaw*, 35, 66-69; Ethridge, "Introduction," 1-3; Ethridge, "Differential Responses Across the Southeast to European Incursions," 216-228; Rodning, "Reconstructing the Coalescence," 159; Kowalewski, "Coalescent Societies," 116-120; Hudson, *The Southeastern Indians*, 34, 94; Anderson, "Stability and Change," 187-188.

2. Merrell, *The Indians' New World*, 18-27; Beck, "Catawba Coalescence," 115-141; Davis, "The Cultural Landscape of the North Carolina Piedmont at Contact," 139.

3. Smith, "Aboriginal Population Movements," 17.

4. Rodning, "Reconstructing the Coalescence," 161-163; McLoughlin, *Cherokee Renascence*, 7; Hatley, *The Dividing Paths*, 1-8; Smith, "Aboriginal Depopulation," 265, 272; Smith, "Aboriginal Population Movements," 25-27.

5. Jenkins, "Tracing the Origins," 213-236; Shuck-Hall, "Alabama and Coushatta Diaspora," 250-271; Smith, "Aboriginal Depopulation," 264-267, 270-272; Smith, "Aboriginal Population Movements," 14-16, 27–29; Wood, "Changing Population," 56-57; Ethridge, *From Chicaza to Chickasaw*, 64-74.

6. Smith, "Aboriginal Depopulation," 265-266; Smith, "Aboriginal Population Movements," 16-18; Galloway, "Colonial Period," 240; Galloway, *Choctaw Genesis*, 341-342, 349-360; Ethridge, *From Chicaza to Chickasaw*, 74-78.

7. Perttula, "Social Changes among the Caddo," 251-269; Hoffman, "The Terminal Mississippian Period," 208-226.

8. King, "Historic Period Transformation," 182-184; Kowalewski, "Coalescent Societies," 95, 116-120; Ethridge, *From Chicaza to Chickasaw*, 35, 66-69; Hudson, *The Southeastern Indians*, 34, 94; Anderson, "Stability and Change," 187-188.

9. This discussion of Southeastern Native culture is taken from Ethridge, "A Brief Sketch of Creek Country," 19-35; Piker, *Okfuskee*, 111-134; Saunt, *A New Order of Things*, 11-63; Green, *The Politics of Indian Removal*, 1-16; Hudson, *The Southeastern Indians*, 184-257; King, "Historic Period Transformation," 182-184.

10. Piker, *Okfuskee*, 18-19.

11. Crane, *The Southern Frontier*, 7, 24, 74; Hann, *Apalachee*, 233, 246-247.

12. Worth, "Spanish Missions and the Persistence of Chiefly Power," 39-64; Bushnell, *Situado and Sabana*, 104-110; Milanich, *Laboring in the Fields of the Lord*, 124.

13. Worth, "Spanish Missions and the Persistence of Chiefly Power," 39-64; Worth, "Bridging Prehistory and History," 196-206; Bushnell, "Ruling 'the Republic of Indians,'" 134-150; Saunders, "The Guale Indians," 42-45.

Los Cimarrones

When the Spanish left St. Augustine in 1763, no more than handfuls of Timucuas, Apalachees, and others of the peninsula's Native peoples left with them. These were basically the remainder of La Florida's once-vast Native populations, and with their evacuation to Cuba, that chapter of the Native Southeast basically ended. Yet, the coalescence of Creeks, Cherokees, and other Native groups means that the story of Native La Florida in no way ends there. In fact, by the time the last Spaniards cast off from St. Augustine and the once-sprawling mission districts, new tenants had already begun to take possession. These would be the people later known as Florida's Seminoles.

Perhaps a man colloquially known as the Cowkeeper had already made the Alachua savanna his new home by that point. Ahaya, also known as the Cowkeeper, founded Cuscowilla sometime in the mid-eighteenth century, from which he carried on a generally unfavorable relationship with the nearby Spanish at St. Augustine. Surely a sign of his Creek roots and a continuation of traditions he had no intention of mending. Yet the Cowkeeper only had his Spanish antagonists to thank for the stunning views of the Alachua savanna he now regularly enjoyed. It was the lure of an empty Alachua that brought Cuscowilla into existence—the product of earlier La Florida generations of hunting, ranching, missionizing, and of course, withering Native depopulation. His view, after all, was in all likelihood the same one which the Spanish residents of the La Chua *hacienda* probably enjoyed almost exactly one century earlier.

Seminole men enthusiastically continued a cattle industry once forced on Native cowboys at La Chua generations previous. One only has to look at Ahaya's nickname, the Cowkeeper, to recognize the place of cattle in the history of the Seminole people. These were among America's original cowboys, second only to the other Native groups and enslaved Africans who preceded them in Florida (the subject of a future chapter). When naturalist William Bartram toured Cuscowilla and the Alachua savanna at the height of Seminole power, he marveled not only at the cattle he saw, but the Seminole herdsmen driving them. Packs of "beautiful fleet" Seminole horses roamed the savanna, and Seminoles were apparently excellent horsemen.[1] The best part was that these cattle were ownerless, at least as the Cowkeeper saw it. The Spanish in St. Augustine would probably disagree, but then again what position were they in to assert ownership of anything between Pensacola and St. Augustine? These were now the Cowkeeper's cows, distinguishing a Seminole Indian as one of the largest ranchers at any time in the colonial American Southeast. And just as much as any newly introduced crop or product, cattle changed the cultures of the places in which they arrived, whether in the modern countries of Mexico, Chile, or Argentina. That was no less the same in Florida and Texas, and whether considering African Americans, Euro-Americans, or Natives. In the case of Florida, cattle were central to the very creation of a new Seminole Native identity.[2]

How did the Cowkeeper come to lord over such incredible bounty as what Bartram described? It was under the Cowkeeper's leadership, as the story goes, that the Seminoles slowly began to break away from the Creek communities from which they originated. As Bartram described, the Cowkeeper dressed simply, with his head "trimmed and ornamented in the true Creek mode." Seminoles are direct descendants of Creeks, the very same Creeks that originally devastated La Florida's mission districts and *haciendas* almost exactly where Cuscowilla now stood. It was only a generation previous, in fact, when Creek raiders first swept in and destroyed everything they saw, burning missions and *haciendas* at will and enslaving or killing the various Yamasee, Guale, Timucua, and Apalachee Natives they encountered along the way. Bartram actually claimed to see Yamasee slaves among the Seminoles in Cuscowilla. Perhaps the Cowkeeper knew of Alachua because he was among those who burned La Chua to the ground.[3]

Creek and British raids not only targeted the human population of La Florida, but the physical wealth of the mission districts and the *haciendas* there as well. Creeks, like many other Southeastern Natives, often raided specifically for prizes and booty. That was certainly the case with slaves, but was also so with the missions' farming equipment, corn stores, and whatever horses and livestock the attackers could have led off with them. Much of that booty ended up in Creek territory, laying a foundation for the future development of Creeks as ranchers themselves.[4] La Florida missions, representing the wealth of European culture in the Native Southeast, made for easy and lucrative targets.

The reason why Ahaya was known as the Cowkeeper was clear enough, but scrub cattle alone cannot explain why Cuscowilla was thriving in 1774, or why it was only one of several Seminole communities in La Florida. Cattle were only one example of the riches that Creeks found in a territory that was ripe for resettlement. As one early Seminole scholar elaborated, by the eighteenth century the Florida peninsula had become "that rare sort of vacuum, a habitable environment, recently peopled" but now utterly devoid of anyone. It was La Florida's demographic collapse that set the stage for Seminole "colonization," in the words of another.[5] What Bartram witnessed in Cuscowilla was the Native *re*populating of La Florida.

Not only had Spanish *haciendas* once stood nearby on the edge of the Alachua savanna, so had other Native communities. Bartram noticed one abandoned community and explained how Seminoles "abdicated the ancient Alachua town on the borders of the savanna," and built Cuscowilla nearby instead. Passing by it as he rode the rim of the savanna, Bartram had a chance to reconnoiter the old town, describing "ancient Indian fields, now grown over with forests of stately trees, Orange groves, and luxuriant herbage." This was "the ancient Alachua, the capital of that famous and powerful tribe, who people the hills surrounding the savanna." Perhaps these were the Potano or the Ocale, or another Mississippian people who had succumbed either to conquest or disease in earlier La Florida years. It was clear someone had been there, "as almost every step we take over those fertile heights," Bartram described, "discovers remains and traces of ancient human habitations and cultivation." Perhaps Cowkeeper knew some of that story himself. Regardless, the destruction of the Spanish missions and *haciendas*, and the decline of the region's original Native peoples, had been to him and his own people a windfall. Alachua Seminoles controlled incredible stocks of cattle and prime pasturage and had fine horses to work them. All of this was because of La Florida.[6]

Neither was the Cowkeeper squatting on someone else's land. The Creek communities from which Cowkeeper originated would have claimed this territory in Spanish La Florida by right of their dramatic conquests there. The territory of vanquished or subdued peoples, according to widespread Native traditions in the Southeast, became the territory of the conquerors. This was clarified in several later councils and talks between British colonial authorities and Creek leaders, who viewed the arrival of large numbers of settlers into Georgia and even East Florida as an unacceptable intrusion into some of the Creeks's finest and most productive hunting lands. Creeks declared their determination to drive off any squatters they found in the area, kill their cattle, and possibly kill them. While British East Florida never posed the threat that nearby Georgia did, the Alachua savanna was defended aggressively. As an entire generation of Creeks learned in the wake of the Yamasee War, the British were much more dangerous than were their Spanish counterparts. To men like the Cowkeeper, La

Florida land was therefore doubly enticing. Not only were there vast stocks of cattle there, but there was also plenty of distance between them and their closest neighbors. Euro-American expansion was far away from the Cuscowilla, which was just the way the Cowkeeper and his Alachua Seminoles wanted it.[7]

The same was true with the boundless wildlife that filled north-central Florida. Although deer numbers rebounded after the collapse of the Mississippian world, Native market hunters had taken a toll on Southeastern fauna by the middle of the eighteenth century, and deer numbers dropped again. The sun was beginning to set on the golden age of the deerskin trade and the threat posed by indebtedness was increasing rapidly. As Creek hunters traveled farther and farther for pelts, their extended absences stressed their communities. Their travels also began to put them in territorial danger. If they traveled too far to the north, they risked conflict with Cherokee or Shawnee hunters. Too far west, and they were poaching on Choctaw and Chickasaw lands. But what about to the south? There was no risk hunting into La Florida. The only thing there was a seemingly endless stock of white-tailed deer.[8]

In La Florida, in sum, Seminoles could have it all. Among the first generation of Seminoles were several small waves of immigrants that appeared in both British and Spanish records as early as the fallout from the Yamasee War. Some came on their own, and some were invited by Spaniards. The result was several separate regions of settlement that stretched from Pensacola to Tampa Bay. Groups of Creeks from nearby communities like Coweta moved south among the mission ruins and empty fields of the once mighty Apalachees. They did so after Spanish officer Diego Peña made a trip into Creek territory specifically to entice Creek communities back into La Florida. Spaniards were anxious to repopulate a long-collapsed anti-English buffer zone, and in the wake of the Yamasee War, there were plenty of Creeks that felt the same way Spaniards did about Charleston. Peña's expedition was evidently successful, because by mid-century there were nearly a half-dozen towns spread in the panhandle region of modern-day Florida. Euro-Americans would in time recognize many of these groups as Miccosukees, or Mikasukis. One group of Creek immigrants from Tallassee provided the namesake for Florida's state capital, Tallahassee.[9]

Another group simply moved downriver from already existing Creek communities on the modern-day Flint and Chattahoochee Rivers, including Coweta. The two rivers combine to create the Apalachicola River near the present-day Georgia-Florida border. That confluence, the northern edge of what would have been Apalachee and Timucua territories, was inviting for several Creek bands that would creep south across the modern-day Florida-Georgia border. Euro-Americans would come to know them both as Flint River Creeks, but also as Seminoles.[10]

Last but not least there was Cowkeeper's band, which originally hailed from Oconee and surrounding communities among the Lower Creek. They did not emigrate at the behest of the Spanish and were far more pro-British in their politics. They probably first laid eyes on Alachua during the Moore invasions of the early eighteenth century, and then again during Georgia's assault of La Florida during the 1739–1742 War of Jenkin's Ear. While James Oglethorpe assaulted St. Augustine, allied Creek warriors fanned across the frontier, perpetrating more raids that evidently also enamored them with the La Florida countryside. In time his band, the Alachua band, spread out much farther than just the old boundaries of old La Chua, extending settlements south through the peninsula, along the Suwannee, Santa Fe, Ocklawaha, and Peace Rivers.[11]

Even though the Alachua band had perhaps the rockiest relationship with nearby Spaniards, by the 1770s their looks still reminded outsiders that they definitely lived in Spanish La Florida. As Bartram wrote, Alachuas, like most of the Seminoles he saw, "appear evidently tinctured with Spanish civilization," and they manifested "a predilection for the Spanish customs." Viewing later etchings of Seminole wearing plumes, turbans, and multicolored cotton shawls evokes such imagery. Some also wore crosses and claimed to be baptized Christians, and most of them understood at least a little Spanish.[12] It was actually the Spanish who gave these Creek hunters and herdsmen their new moniker—Seminoles. They were *cimarrones* to the Spanish, which translated more or less to runaways. British authorities, including John Stuart, quickly picked up on the term, describing Seminoles as "wild people" for their breakaway history. Americans would as well, with Indian Agent Wiley Thompson describing in 1835 how Seminole meant "runaway or broken off," which in time Americans applied to all of Florida's Natives because all of them were, essentially, from somewhere else.[13]

The varied composition and motivation of these different immigrant groups is a testament to the fiercely autonomous nature of Native Southeasterners, and of Creeks in particular. All, however, ended up in La Florida for similar reasons, and in time all of these disparate groups would be recognized as Seminoles. In 1757 Georgia Council meeting authorities greeted the Cowkeeper and fifty Seminole travelers, who were there to converse with the governor. While there, however, the headman made it clear that he did not talk for any confederation of Creek communities and had not been in Creek territory for four years. He still considered himself Creek, just one living a bit farther away than normal from the loci of

Creek authority, and therefore a bit more out of touch with the happenings there. Perhaps this was what the term *cimarrone*, or Seminole, meant.[14]

More distance was put between Creeks and Seminoles during a 1765 council and conference held between Creeks and the British at Fort Picolata, on the St. Johns River. There the Cowkeeper, described as the headman of Alachua, did not attend. Instead, he chose to deal with the British personally, traveling to St. Augustine to meet with John Stuart, Governor James Grant, and other British colonial officials regularly. This was the beginning of a remarkably warm relationship shared between the Alachua Seminoles and British St. Augustine, one that would last until the Spanish retook La Florida at the conclusion of the American Revolution. While the British were to be feared elsewhere because of their desire for land, that was not so much the case in the province of East Florida, which never really took off as a colony. Instead, the British depended on Seminole beef and horses, and even warriors, to defend the East Florida colony during the American Revolution. As a result, as the British increasingly recognized, these Alachua Seminoles were putting more distance between themselves and their Creek neighbors to the north. It was during the American Revolution that a new Seminole identity really began to solidify.[15]

Unfortunately for the Seminole people, the halcyon days of La Florida, or even East Florida, did not last. As for the Alachua band, by the time Bartram dined with the Cowkeeper, the latter man was old in life. He lived another decade, dying in 1784, and upon his death control of the Alachua band fell to a man by the name of Payne. As either a nephew or son of the Cowkeeper, Payne would have inherited his kin's position of authority, a part of Seminole culture that flowed from Creek and even Mississippian precedents. Once described by an American as "Mr. Payne, the great Seminole and Lachaway King," he was a strong and capable leader himself. It is his name which the Alachua savanna now bears—Payne's Prairie. The center of the Alachua Seminole world shifted from Cuscowilla to nearby Payne's Town, but not much else changed. In 1793 he was reported to own well over one thousand head of cattle and four hundred head of horses. Payne harbored less Spanish resentment than had the Cowkeeper, and relations between the Seminoles and Spanish grew closer during a turbulent period of American expansionism. He regularly offered the services of his warriors when St. Augustine was threatened, and would actually die in the fighting that resulted when Americans attempted to sack St. Augustine and annex Spanish Florida decades later, in 1812. Although their attempt on St. Augustine was maybe the most pathetic attempt on the fortress yet, American invaders from

Tennessee and Georgia devastated the Alachua savanna, throwing the Seminoles there into chaos.[16]

From there the Alachua leadership position passed to Bowlegs, another of Cowkeeper's direct descendants and probably Payne's brother. Little is known about Bowlegs, except that he took the reins of the Alachua band when Spain was losing what little grip on Florida it had, and when Americans were beginning a furious expansion into Native lands. Under Bowlegs's leadership, the center of the Alachua Seminoles moved west from Payne's Town to Suwannee Old Town, where Bowlegs lived, on the river of the same name. While this position was not as advantageous for cattle as the savanna, Bowlegs still reportedly owned large herds that he both sold and relied on for food. Unfortunately for the band, it was during that time that possibly thousands of Creek refugees, fleeing their own devastating civil war and then fleeing Andrew Jackson, flooded into Florida and into Seminole communities in 1814. Jackson himself was not far behind, mounting a full invasion of Florida in 1817 that was at least partially designed to get Spain to give up on its long-neglected colony. While the Spanish King did eventually do that, the war has come to be known since as the First Seminole War, clear evidence that Jackson was also in Florida to crush the mounting threat posed by the Seminoles to the expanding states of Georgia and Alabama. Americans killed not only Bowlegs during the invasion but the leading Miccosukee headman, Kinache, as well.[17]

Bad times gave way to worse times as Spanish Florida became the American Territory of Florida in 1821, and the removal of all of the Southeast's Native peoples was soon the plan in Washington. The lands Seminoles claimed in north-central Florida were supposed to be some of the best in the entire Southeast, which was not good at all for the various Seminole bands that called it home. By this time the three separate Seminole subgroups were all being called the same thing by American authorities. Finally, they started coordinating their anti-expansionist efforts in response. Alachua Seminole leadership devolved to Micanopy, yet another direct kin of Cowkeeper, who is still memorialized as the namesake of a town just outside Gainesville. Although he was described as a much less capable leader at a very dangerous time, nevertheless Micanopy chose the path of armed resistance to Indian removal when it was forced on the Seminoles from both the territorial and federal levels, sparking the Second Seminole War in 1836. He was captured and removed west two years later with a large contingent of Alachua Seminoles.

That left Billy Bowlegs, "a member of the so-called Seminole ruling family" in the words of one scholar, in charge of the once-Alachua band. While that meant hereditary leadership of the Alachua band stayed in the Cowkeeper line, Billy Bowlegs was soon far from the Alachua savanna. He, like most other Seminoles, had been pushed by the war into the southern tip of the peninsula, where he lived on the Peace River. Still, his leadership represented Alachua continuity, and he held his position from the conclusion of the Second Seminole War in 1842 through a tumultuous period of interwar expansion and then, finally, the Third Seminole War. Eventually he, too, would be removed west at the conclusion of that much smaller and localized struggle, in 1858.[18]

The emigration of Billy Bowlegs west did not mark the end of the Florida Seminoles, even though it did signal the end of the Cowkeeper "dynasty," as one scholar described it. Small groups from all the major bands, including the original Alachua communities, spread themselves so thin in the swamps of extreme South Florida that Americans simply stopped looking for them. While that isolation protected them from capture, the bands were so isolated that any sort of traditional Creek or Seminole power structure that might unite them faded away, and with Billy Bowleg's removal, the Cowkeeper line faded away as well. While his removal, in that sense, put an end to generations of Seminole struggle with Spanish, British, and American authorities, it also punctuated one of the most sustained and effective campaigns of resistance against the forces of colonialism and settler expansion in American history. Every one of those generations, right up until the end of the third war, in 1858, included a man of influence and power whose position flowed hereditarily from one of the first and most powerful Seminole chiefs—Ahaya, the Cowkeeper—whose rule was set into motion with the arrival of Creeks onto the old La Chua savannas over a full century earlier.[19] The Seminole story, spanning generations and enduring into the present, did not just begin in Florida. It began in La Florida.

Notes

1. Calloway, *The American Revolution in Indian Country*, 247; Hallock and Franz, eds., *Travels on the St. Johns River*, 126; Van Doren, *The Travels of William Bartram*, 163-180.

2. Calloway, *The American Revolution in Indian Country*, 248; Jordan, *North American Cattle-Ranching Frontiers*, 108.

3. Mahon, *History of the Second Seminole War*, 3; Porter, "The Cowkeeper Dynasty," 341; Van Doren, *The Travels of William Bartram*, 164; Calloway, *The American Revolution in Indian Country*, 246-247.

4. Jordan, *North American Cattle-Ranching Frontiers*, 108; Sattler, "Cowboys and Indians," 79-99.

5. Calloway, *The American Revolution in Indian Country*, 247; Mahon, *History of the Second Seminole War*, 2-3.

6. Van Doren, *The Travels of William Bartram*, 169, 173; Jordan, *North American Cattle-Ranching Frontiers*, 108; Calloway, *The American Revolution in Indian Country*, 246-247.

7. Mahon, *History of the Second Seminole War*, 6; Sattler, "Remnants, Renegades, and Runaways," 50; Porter, "The Founder of the 'Seminole Nation,'" 377-378; Covington, *The Seminoles of Florida*, 18.

8. Covington, *The Seminoles of Florida*, 11; Hoffman, *Florida Frontiers*, 216; Calloway, *The American Revolution in Indian Country*, 254-255.

9. Sattler, "Remnants, Renegades, and Runaways," 44-48; Weisman, "Nativism, Resistance, and Ethnogenesis," 199-202; Hoffman, *Florida Frontiers*, 215-216; Wright, *Creeks and Seminoles*, 109; Calloway, *The American Revolution in Indian Country*, 249; Mahon, *History of the Second Seminole War*, 3-5; Porter, "The Founder of the 'Seminole Nation,'" 365-366, 368-374; Covington, *The Seminoles of Florida*, 10, 15-16.

10. Sattler, "Remnants, Renegades, and Runaways," 49-50; Weisman, "Nativism, Resistance, and Ethnogenesis," 199-202; Hoffman, *Florida Frontiers*, 215-216.

11. Sattler, "Remnants, Renegades, and Runaways," 44, 48-49; Weisman, "Nativism, Resistance, and Ethnogenesis," 199-202; Hoffman, *Florida Frontiers*, 215-216; Mahon, *History of the Second Seminole War*, 4; Porter, "The Founder of the 'Seminole Nation,'" 362-364, 381; Covington, *The Seminoles of Florida*, 11-12.

12. Van Doren, *The Travels of William Bartram*, 164.

13. Mahon, *History of the Second Seminole War*, 7; Calloway, *The American Revolution in Indian Country*, 248-249; McReynolds, *The Seminoles*, 12; Covington, *The Seminoles of Florida*, 13.

14. Hoffman, *Florida Frontiers*, 211-215; Porter, "The Founder of the 'Seminole Nation,'" 376, 381-383; Calloway, *The American Revolution in Indian Country*, 250-251; Covington, *The Seminoles of Florida*, 16.

15. Calloway, *The American Revolution in Indian Country*, 251-266; Hoffman, *Florida's Frontiers*, 217-230; Kokomoor, "Burning and Destroying," in Mahon, *History of the Second Seminole War*, 7; Porter, "The Founder of the 'Seminole Nation,'" 381-383; Covington, *The Seminoles of Florida*, 16-18.

16. Sattler, "Remnants, Renegades, and Runaways," 51-52; Hoffman, *Florida's Frontiers*, 256-257, 263-264; Covington, *The Seminoles of Florida*, 19-21, 28-33; Calloway, *The American Revolution in Indian Country*, 266-271.

17. Sattler, "Remnants, Renegades, and Runaways," 52-57; Hoffman, *Florida's Frontiers*, 265-266, 274-281; Covington, *The Seminoles of Florida*, 29-50.

18. Covington, *The Seminoles of Florida*, 50-71, 107, 124-126, 141-144; Hoffman, *Florida's Frontiers*, 284-298, 304-316; Porter, "The Founder of the 'Seminole Nation,'" 362-364; Porter, "The Cowkeeper Dynasty," 341-349; Mahon, *History of the Second Seminole War*, 10; Sattler, "Remnants, Renegades, and Runaways," 56-59.

19. Covington, *The Seminoles of Florida*, chapters 8-14; West, *The Enduring Seminoles*; Porter, "The Cowkeeper Dynasty," 349; Mahon, *History of the Second Seminole War*, 10.

PHOTO 3.1. A Mississippian Chieftain and His Wife
A Timucuan Chieftain walking with his wife, followed by attendants who fan them and carry baskets.

"WIE DER KÖNIG UND DIE KÖNIGIN SICH ZU ERLUSTIREN SPASSIREN GEHEN." *[AMERICA. PT 2. GERMAN] DER ANDER THEIL DER NEWLICH ERFUNDENEN LANDTSCHAFFT AMERICAE, VON DREYEN SCHIFFAHRTEN, SO DIE FRANTZOSEN IN FLORIDAM ... GETHAN ...* RECORD NUMBER 08915-44. JOHN CARTER BROWN LIBRARY—BROWN UNIVERSITY.

PHOTO 3.2. Mississippian Agriculture
This depiction of Mississippian agriculture in modern northeast Florida shows Timucua men tilling with hoes, and Timucua women planting.
"WIE SIE IRE ÄCKER BAUWEN UND BESEEN." *[AMERICA. PT 2. GERMAN] DER ANDER THEIL DER NEWLICH ERFUNDENEN LANDTSCHAFFT AMERICAE, VON DREYEN SCHIFFAHRTEN, SO DIE FRANTZOSEN IN FLORIDAM ... GETHAN ...* RECORD NUMBER 08915-26. JOHN CARTER BROWN LIBRARY—BROWN UNIVERSITY.

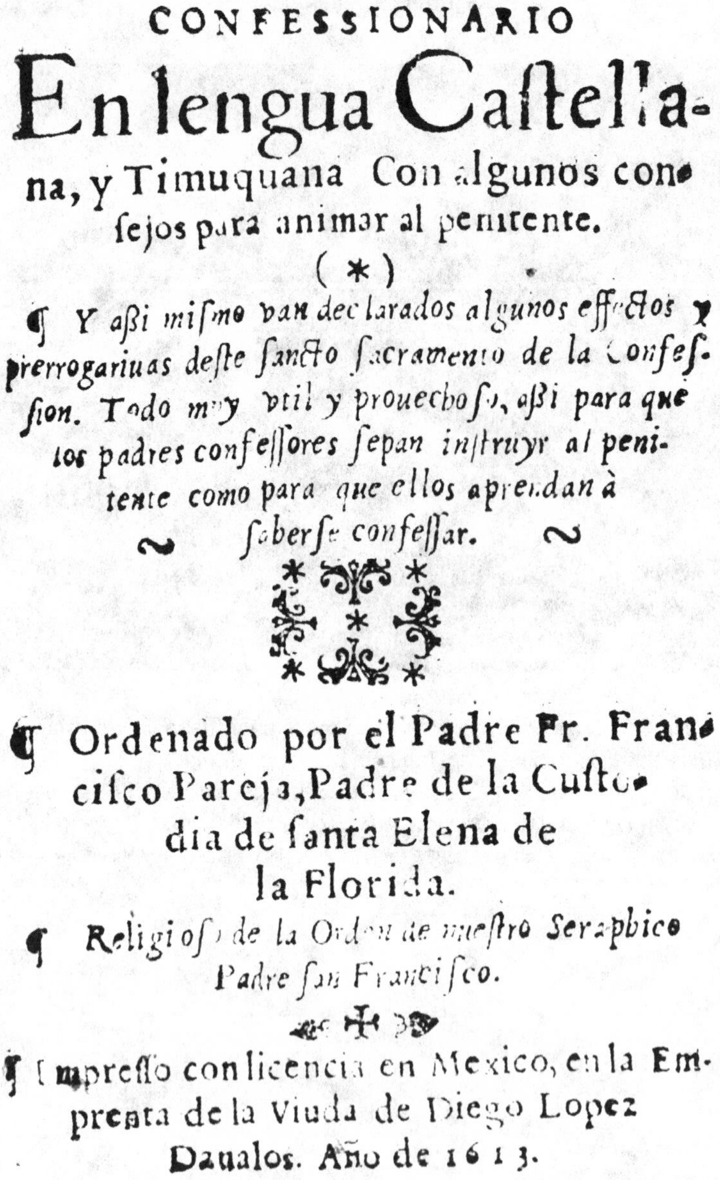
CONFESSIONARIO
En lengua Caſtellana, y Timuquana Con algunos conſejos para animar al penitente.

(*)

¶ Y aßi miſmo van declarados algunos effectos y prerrogariuas deſte ſancto ſacramento de la Confeſſion. Todo muy vtil y prouechoſo, aßi para que los padres confeſſores ſepan inſtruyr al penitente como para que ellos aprendan à ſaberſe confeſſar.

¶ Ordenado por el Padre Fr. Franciſco Pareja, Padre de la Cuſtodia de ſanta Elena de la Florida.

¶ Religioſo de la Orden de nueſtro Seraphico Padre ſan Franciſco.

¶ Impreſſo con licencia en Mexico, en la Emprenta de la Viuda de Diego Lopez Daualos. Año de 1613.

PHOTO 3.3. Pareja's Confessionario
This Timucuan translation of a confessional was created by Franciscan missionary Fray Francisco Pareja, and was used widely as a missionary guide after its publication.
FRAY FRANCISCO PAREJA. CONFESSIONARIO EN LENGUA CASTELLANA, Y TIMUQUANA. MEXICO CITY, 1613. JOHN CARTER BROWN LIBRARY—BROWN UNIVERSITY.

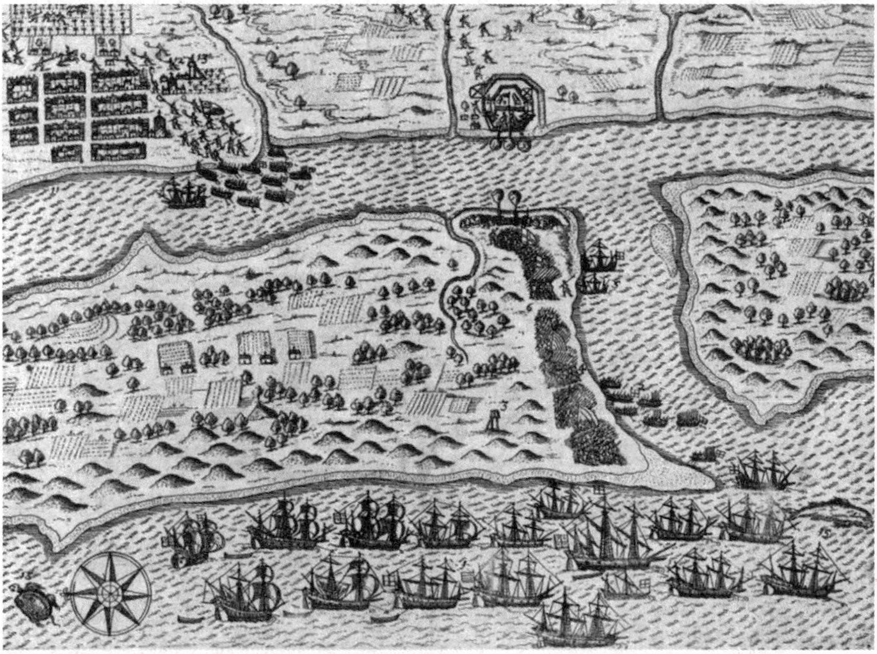

PHOTO 3.4. Drake's 1586 Raid

In this reproduction of Drake's 1586 assault on St. Augustine, English artillery can be seen bombarding one of the *presidio*'s original wooden forts, while troops overrun the town itself.

THE KRAUS COLLECTION OF SIR FRANCIS DRAKE. LIBRARY OF CONGRESS.

PHOTO 3.5. The Presidio of St. Augustine

While this engraving was made of St. Augustine after the Spanish turned it over to the British in 1763, it shows the layout of the town at the center, the Castillo de San Marcos on the north of the town, and the town's defensive wall.

PLAN OF THE TOWN OF ST. AUGUSTINE, THE CAPITAL OF EAST FLORIDA | THE BAY OF ESPIRITU SANTO ON THE WESTERN COAST OF EAST FLORIDA. LONDON: W. FADEN, 1777. JOHN CARTER BROWN LIBRARY—BROWN UNIVERSITY.

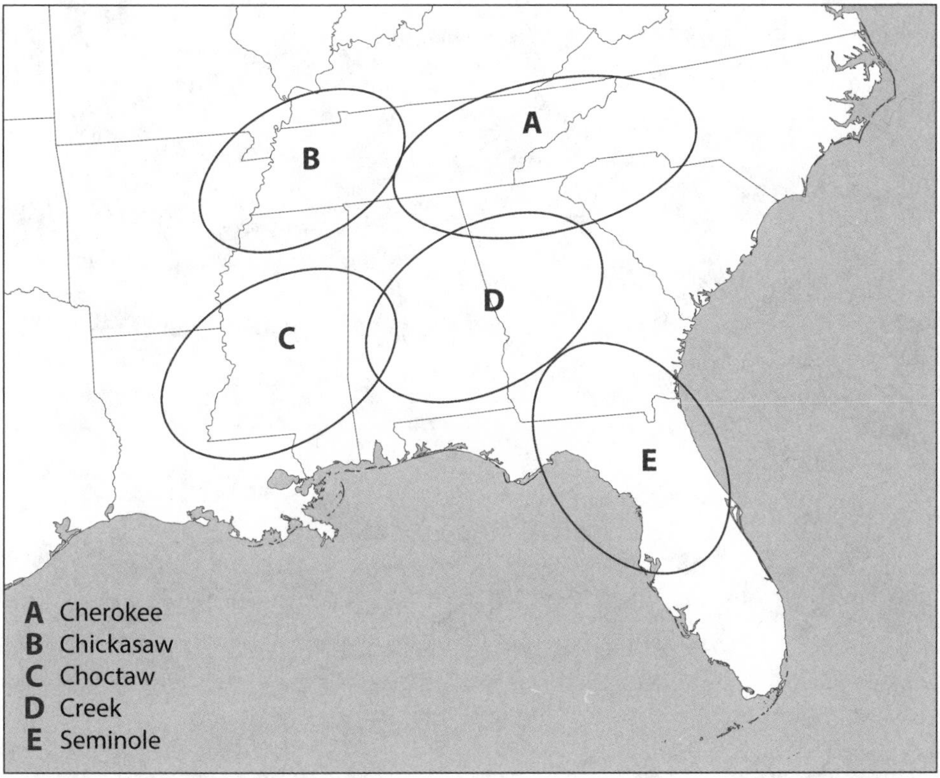

Map 3.1. The Coalescent Southeast

IV. LEGACIES

8 American Saints, American Legends

As a certain well-known American legend goes, a young European man, captured and taken before a Native American chieftain, is about to be ceremoniously executed. Condemned, prostrate before the chief, and about to be dispatched in brutal fashion, things look grim indeed for this young man. Only moments before his execution, however, out charges a commanding young woman, kin to the chieftain. The woman beseeches the headman, her father, to spare the young European's life, "for neither he nor his companions had been to blame for the evil their predecessors had done," and that the young man definitely deserved to be saved, "for his youth absolved him of blame and called for mercy." She may have even thrown herself between the condemned young man and his would-be executioner. The woman's intervention works; the man is saved. Could this be John Smith, about to die at the hands of the Powhatan chief, only to be saved by Pocahontas? No, this was Juan Ortiz, about to die at the hands of Hirrihigua, only to be saved by his wife and daughters. And no, this story did not happen in Virginia. It happened in La Florida, around the vicinity of Tampa Bay. This was not the Pocahontas legend, but the Juan Ortiz legend, the legend that inspired the Pocahontas legend.

The Juan Ortiz legend was related by Gracilaso de la Vega, among other enthusiastic Spanish chroniclers, meaning it very well could be just a legend. According to de la Vega, Juan Ortiz arrived in La Florida as a part of the Pánfilo de Narváez expedition, even though he did not get to partake in much of the expedition at all. Instead, he was lured onto land and captured, along with three others, before Narváez's expedition even really got going. Ortiz's three companions were not as lucky as he—all three were tortured to death by Hirrihigua, a regional chieftain who had suffered previously at the hands of Spaniards and had sworn his revenge. Poor Ortiz had borne witness to this revenge, having overseen the torturous death of the three, shot up with arrows in the town's central plaza. There, "like wild beasts," the townspeople ran them "from one side to the other," and Hirrihigua made sure that "too many arrows were not to be shot at the same time, in order that they should die more slowly, and their torment be greater, and the Indians' celebration and enjoyment longer and more festive." Previous Spaniards had made an impression on Hirrihigua, clearly. Having enjoyed the spectacle so far, Hirrihigua ordered up the last of this captive—the young Juan Ortiz—who "was a youth scarcely eighteen years of age, a native of Sevilla." Ortiz was about to be loosed in the plaza, fated to endure his own death-by-arrow torture, when Hirrihigua's own wife, "accompanied by her three young daughters," stepped in to stop the violence. The women pleaded for Ortiz's release, and "in order to satisfy his wife and daughters," Hirrihigua begrudgingly obliged. This was the first time Native women intervened to save Juan Ortiz's life.

It would not be the last. Although Juan Ortiz survived this first ordeal, he got little else out of Hirrihigua, who proceeded to work the young Spaniard to the bone. Sometimes run to the point of collapse, sometimes beat, sometimes actually tortured, it was clear Hirrihigua was keeping Ortiz alive against his will. Eventually he did dare to finish off his prisoner, ordering Ortiz to be burned alive. And he would have, too, had it not been for the women. Strapped to a giant wooden grill and slowly roasted over flames, things looked worse for Ortiz than they had before. "At the cries that the poor unfortunate gave in the midst of the fire, the wife and daughters of the cacique came," and "begging the husband and even reproaching his cruelty," they again saved him. Twice now, and far more brutally, had this Pocahontas story played out. This time Ortiz had suffered terrible burns, "having blisters . . . as large as half-oranges, some of them broken and bleeding freely, so that it was pitiful to see." Yet again, intervention by the women led to a reprieve.

Ortiz survived his burns only to endure more torment as Hirrihigua's unwanted slave. Even heroically killing a panther that was desecrating the grave of dead clan members, a feat that enamored Ortiz to many in Hirrihigua's province, could not warm the chieftain to the young Spaniard. Ultimately, he once more ordered Ortiz to be killed, declaring that "notwithstanding his bravery, for as an enemy he should be rather abhorred than esteemed." Back to death by arrows. Again, and for the third time, it was Hirrihigua's wife and daughters who secured Ortiz's escape. It was clear to them, and from Hirrihigua's own admission, that nothing would stop the headman from avenging past Spanish wrongs done him by killing every Spaniard he laid his hands on, including Ortiz. It was at this point that his wife and daughters determined to save Ortiz once and for all, even if it meant planning his escape.

It was Hirrihigua's eldest daughter that personally arranged for Ortiz's flight out of the province. She provided not only the guide, but the destination. If he could make it to Mocoso, the headman of a neighboring province, he would be safe. Mocoso "wishes me well and desires to marry me," the daughter confided in Ortiz. Using Mocoso's desire for her as leverage, this young woman set Ortiz on his way. So, for a third time, Native women saved Ortiz. He would make it to Mocoso, who took him under his protection and "treated him like a well-loved brother," as de la Vega described. When Hirrihigua and his kin angrily demanded Ortiz's return, Mocoso denied them, forcefully at times, and even at the cost of his marriage to Hirrihigua's daughter. Instead, Mocoso kept Ortiz "constantly with him, much esteemed and well treated, until Governor Hernándo de Soto entered La Florida."[1]

Saint names are legacies. So are legends. Competing captivity narratives open this last section, "Legacies," by reminiscing—and challenging—some of America's earliest names and legends. At first recounting, the broad outlines of the Ortiz and Smith/Pocahontas legends do appear quite similar. A young European man is about to be killed by a Native chieftain, until a Native woman, the kin of that chieftain, steps in to save him. Yet, John Smith was only supposed to be clubbed to death. Ortiz was going to be shot with arrows, then roasted alive, then shot with arrows again. While Pocahontas supposedly stepped in only once to stop John Smith's death, Hirrihigua's wife and daughters intervened three times. They actively disobeyed their father in spiriting Ortiz to safety. The Juan Ortiz legend, in other words, puts John Smith's Pocahontas tale to shame.

These are, of course, both legends. The best recounting of the Juan Ortiz legend comes from Gracilaso de la Vega, who in no way can be trusted with providing an accurate recounting of anything. Perhaps it happened like that, or perhaps de la Vega, like he was known to do, was embellishing the story. On the other hand, however, scholars seriously doubt whether the John Smith/Pocahontas encounter ever happened at all. This theme runs through several La Florida legends. Nevertheless, when it comes to the Ortiz-Smith debate, not only did one seem more plausible, but as historians have suggested, the Ortiz legend might actually be the reason for the Smith legend even to exist. Did John Smith fabricate his own tale of survival after reading what Juan Ortiz endured generations previous? Perhaps, for those reasons, the legends of Juan Ortiz and John Smith belong in the next chapter, which focuses on such connections. Yet, both are legends; both might have never happened at all. And American Legends is, after all, a chapter on La Florida legends, including the Fountain of Youth legend and the Black Legend.

If these legends represent the legacies of Spanish colonialism in the American Southeast, then so do its Saints. Catholic Saints, more specifically. Many of those Saints can still be seen on modern-day maps of the American Southeast. In older maps, they were the only things that could be seen. The name places of islands, bays, rivers, and other natural landmarks, they represented standard Spanish seafaring traditions. They are the reason that Florida is named Florida. American Saints does not just refer to the naming of European discoveries after Saints. It does a bit more, highlighting in general all of the place names that reflect Spanish origins, going back to a time when Spaniards, and not the English, were the driving force behind exploration and colonization. Names, like legends, are La Florida legacies.

Note

1. "La Florida," in Clayton, Knight, and Moore, eds., *The De Soto Chronicles*, 2: 99-113.

American Saints

By the end of the sixteenth century, decades' worth of conquistadores had passed through La Florida. Countless Catholic friars too. Very little positive had come of those decades, at least as far as Spanish authorities were concerned. All of the conquistadores were dead, as were the majority of their armies, and very little missionizing had taken place. If La Florida had a reputation, it was the place where Spanish dreams of conquest went to die.

Yet, in the process, for Europeans an entire continent was also coming into focus. By de Soto's failure, "the broad outlines" of North America, according to noted borderlands historian David Weber, "had begun to appear on European maps," and all of the east of it was defined in Spanish terms as La Florida. Spanish travels failed to produce an easy route to Asian markets and failed to reveal the sources of fantastic wealth. Nevertheless, for one scholar, during "that interval tenacious Spaniards had not only navigated the shores of North America but had spanned the continent."[1] As Weber suggested, the extent of those Spaniards' travels reveals the impressive scale of early La Florida. While it would be much smaller by the turn of the next century, and basically non-existent by the time Spaniards left St. Augustine in 1763, at one time Spanish exploration into La Florida extended far beyond just the Florida peninsula. It was most of what is now the Eastern United States.

A brief recap from earlier chapters bears out the size and scope of La Florida. Among the sailors, soldiers, and friars in the expeditions of de León, Antón de Alaminos, Francisco de Garay, Álvarez de Pineda, and Pánfilo de Narváez, were Spaniards that floated almost every inch of the American Gulf and Southeast Atlantic coasts. De León's men charted, passed over, and walked along such fabled modern Florida beaches as Palm Coast, Fort Lauderdale and Miami, Naples and Fort Myers, Sarasota, St. Petersburg and Clearwater, and Pensacola—beaches that consistently rank among America's most popular seaside destinations. Alonso Álvarez de Pineda, likely the first Spaniard to connect the western Gulf Coast to the east, cruised past and charted the marshlands and coastlines of

Texas, Louisiana, Alabama, Mississippi, and Florida. Spanish mariners were the American South's first explorers.

Then there was Cabeza de Vaca's torturous marathon of survival, made public as *La Relacion*. Described as "one of the epics of discovery literature" and "a classic of travel lore," de Vaca's account is perhaps North America's first sensationalist travel guide, and much of it covered popular and well-known islands and sand dunes, both then and now. Trudging along Cape San Blas and Destin in Florida, the Gulf Shores of Alabama, and the beaches of Galveston Island, de Vaca painted the Gulf Coast as a desolate, godforsaken place of hunger, thirst, and death. The irony is almost amusing. Centuries later, Americans flock to the very same white sandy beaches for the sole reason of soaking in the very same sun that de Vaca and his doomed compatriots roasted under for years.[2] Their adventures and misadventures demonstrate just how much perceptions of the beach have changed over the centuries. Just as America's wild places came to mean something very different to twentieth-century Americans than they did their Puritan predecessors, so it was with the beach. Americans now love to visit the very same hot, sunny, sandy places Spaniards feared so terribly hundreds of years previous.

The survivors of both the Narváez and de Soto expeditions were also the first Europeans to encounter the mighty Mississippi. To get there those in the Narváez expedition floated past the future ports of Pensacola, Mobile, and afterward, Houston. Those in de Soto's expedition would not only cross the Mississippi but later would float down it, passing the future sites of Vicksburg, Natchez, Baton Rouge, and New Orleans, generations before French explorers descended the river from the Great Lakes and almost a full three centuries before Americans were exporting thousands of tons of cotton from those ports per year.[3] The men of the two combined expeditions had effectively crisscrossed the heart of the Antebellum Deep South, centuries before it was recognizable as such. Generations before sprawling cotton plantations stretched across the states of Alabama, Mississippi, Louisiana, and Texas; before riverboats loaded with cotton would ply the Mississippi River; and before slavery dominated the social, economic, and political world of "King Cotton," Spaniards described it all as La Florida.

Hernándo de Soto's men went much farther, adding the most far-flung additions to the emerging map of North America. If de Soto was specifically targeting the Southeast's Mississippian chiefdoms as the means to his treasure, then he at least did an excellent job finding many of them. Wandering from one edge of the South to the other, his men passed through no less than a half-dozen of the region's largest Native polities. Doing so he crossed the Appalachian Mountains into modern-day Tennessee and into the Tennessee River Valley. After moving south through Alabama, he continued west, following the Arkansas River all the way to the edge of the Great Plains. His men were probably the first Europeans to lay eyes on the American Bison. Before returning east to the Mississippi, his men made it well into the modern-day state of Texas, possibly to the Brazos River. The list of states wandered through by the hundreds of de Soto's men is astounding, connecting several sub-regions of the Antebellum South.

The Atlantic Coast was no different. The Chesapeake Bay hosted Ajacán long before Jamestown, part of an Atlantic Coast that Spain claimed at one time and in theory at least, all the way into Canada. Only one conquistador attempted settlement along the eastern seaboard in La Florida's first years, making his mark on the history of what would become the British "Lowcountry." Lucas Vázquez de Ayllón's failed Guadalpe colony, first in Winyah Bay and then somewhere in coastal Georgia, was established in the center of what would later be British America's rice-producing empire. The very tidal swamps Ayllón and his men found confusing and desolate would in time count among the richest plantation districts in the British colonial world. Because of the intense labor needed to make rice profitable, they would also be the most enslaved in all of colonial and Antebellum America—another first begun when Ayllón brought the first African slaves to the Atlantic Coast. And before all of this, the coastal regions surrounding the rice ports of Georgetown, Charleston, Savannah, and Beaufort, were all charted and explored by Spaniards as the Atlantic coastline of La Florida. When added together the several attempts made by these Spaniards to settle La Florida being into frame not only the entire Antebellum South, from the Chesapeake Tidewater to East Texas, but the mid-Atlantic and the rim of the Great Plains.

These Spanish explorers and would-be colonizers generated the earliest maps of what would become much of the eastern United States of America. But how could anyone, from a casual glance at a map of the Southeast, be able to recognize any of this? American place names followed European explorers and colonizers into North America, including what would become the United States of America. While very few modern place names east of the Mississippi clearly reflect Spanish origins, a close look at Southeastern maps, and particularly coastal ones, reveals the impact of Spanish colonialism dotting what was all at one time claimed as a Spanish possession. Recall that before there was Port Royal or Beaufort, for instance, there was Santa Elena. While the Spanish outpost and one-time capital of La Florida did not make it to the seventeenth century, nearby on a map of coastal South Carolina reads St. Helena Island. Coincidence? Clearly not.

Place names were—and remain—the common markers of colonial ownership, and what Spaniards first discovered in North America for the European world, they were first to name.[4] First, the obvious. Naming and mapping "discoveries" were colonialist processes. Of course, by "discoveries" we mean "European discoveries," because for the Natives throughout what the Spanish called La Florida, none of this was new at all, and these places already had names. Consequently, not everything in what would become the United States of America already had an original Native place-name that was promptly changed to reflect an old town somewhere in Europe. The Rappahannock, Potomac, or Susquehanna Rivers in Virginia and New Jersey, or the Housatonic, Piscataqua, or Pettaquamscutt Rivers in New England, are only a few examples of the innumerable place names of indigenous origins that dot American maps, or at least only slight corruptions of them. Almost everything in eastern Massachusetts is in one way or another named after its Native people, including Massachusetts itself.[5] The names Winyah, Waccamaw, Pee Dee, and Cape Fear, among others, mark the Carolinas. These were clearly Native names that stuck. Natural features, including lakes, rivers, and bays, frequently carry Native place names that harken back to the days of La Florida.

A particularly dense collection of names derived from local or Native sources come from in and around the modern-day state of Florida. Charlotte Harbor, on the southwest coast of Peninsular Florida and the site of present-day Fort Myers, was originally named Bahía de Juan Ponce, after its discoverer. While that name seems to have faded into the past, nearby San Carlos Bay did not. Named after a Calusa headman at the time of Menéndez's founding of St. Augustine, and a host to one of La Florida's original missions, San Carlos Bay's name evokes the very first days of Spanish presence in the American Southeast. Considering the difficult time Spaniards had with the Calusa—they did kill de León, and the Spanish did kill Carlos—it is easy to understand why the bay gained such distinction. Ocala, south of Gainesville, is only a slight variation of the Mississippian Ocale people. Further to the west, Mobile and Tuscaloosa owe their names to the region's harrowing Native defenders, Mavila and Tascalusa. Further up the Atlantic seaboard, nearby names include Edisto, taken from the Orista mission province named by Spanish friars, and Cayagua, a Spanish pronunciation of Kiawah Island. For an even more impressive example of Native resistance, recognizable to anyone in early America even up to the present, one would need to look no further than the Appalachian Mountains. Even though the southern foothills of the Appalachian range begin hundreds of miles away from the Florida panhandle, nevertheless they are named after the Apalachee, whose fierce resistance not only tormented the men in both the Narváez and De Soto entradas, but clearly impressed them and those who followed.[6]

There are also a few nods to the violence that dominated much of this early interaction. A few small mentions of "la matanza," or the massacre, come from de León and de Soto, legacies of their attempted conquests. The first mention was to a beach in southwest Florida where de León first violently encountered and killed a few Calusa warriors. The second referred to the town of Napetuca, in northern central Florida, which some of de Soto's renamed shortly after they massacred almost everyone in it and left it in ruins.[7] While none of these references to a "massacre" remain, the visible legacy of Menéndez's slaughter of Jean Ribault and his men south of St. Augustine certainly does. A traveler on Florida's A1A, driving down the peninsula's east coast, will eventually cross Matanzas inlet by bridge. That is the Atlantic outlet of the Matanzas River, which itself runs up the coast all the way to St. Augustine. The National Park Service operates the Fort Matanzas National Monument, which oversees the Spanish watchtower of the same name. Inland is the Matanzas State Forest. All are named after the notorious 1565 slaughter.

Another glance at a map of the Southeast, particularly of the coast, reflects another source of familiar place names with Spanish origins. Locations with striking natural features were often named by mariners for those features. The region around Cape Canaveral was originally given the name Cabo de Corrientes, or the Cape of Currents, for the strength of the Gulf Stream in that area. It was around that time when Juan Ponce de León lost sight of one of his ships, an experience that seemed to make an impact on he and his men. Doubling back and entering the Gulf of Mexico, de León not only passed along the Keys but made it all the way to the Tortugas. He arrived there in June, the middle of sea turtle nesting season. De León's men quickly snatched well over one hundred of the huge animals and brought them on board to eat them. Perhaps that is the reason the islands, sitting well to the west of Key West, are still named the Tortugas. Perhaps they are even named the "Dry" Tortugas because even though the Spanish found plenty to eat there, they did not find the fresh water they were looking for.[8]

What about place names with clearer European origins? A drive through New England reads like a journey through Old England, after all, and the origins of towns like Charlestown or New Haven seem clear enough. Cartagena and Valladolid, in Colombia and Mexico, respectively, present the same tradition in the Spanish colonial world. Why was this not the case in what was once La Florida? Why are there so few placenames of obvious Spanish origin east of the Mississippi, if it was all at one point claimed by Spain? Had Spaniards stayed in the interior of what is now the American South, perhaps there would be. The multitude of Native names that once filled the interior of La Florida's map were left to wither away as the Native demographics shifted in the wake of contact, and few Spanish settlements replaced them.

If there is one striking legacy to Spanish colonialism in what is now the United States of America, it can be seen in the Catholic references replete on the earliest maps of the country's Gulf and Atlantic seaboards. This too is a clear nod to the earliest days of Spanish maritime exploration. Spaniards, perhaps more than any other Europeans, were noted for naming their finds after religious iconography. According to contemporary Spaniard Gonzalo Fernández de Oviedo y Valdéz, someone browsing any random coastline on a Spanish chart of the period would be reading "a not very well-ordered calendar or catalogue of the saints."[9] Oviedo was making a generalized remark that would make sense for anyone perusing any corner of the Spanish empire. It certainly makes sense when looking at an early Spanish map of Florida, the Gulf Coast, or even the larger Atlantic coastline.

These names usually corresponded with a feast day taken from the Catholic calendar of Saints and feasts. Because most of the sailing was done in the spring and early summer, the window between cold front season and hurricane season, Spanish explorers had only so many Saints to choose from. Accordingly, some place names pop up more than once, a testament to the regularity and popularity of the tradition.[10] It is a tradition that begins with the very first mention of La Florida. As legend goes, Juan Ponce de León named Florida for its lushness. This is only partially true. Even though accounts did note the coastline's vegetation, de León was a seasoned Caribbean explorer used to tropical locales including Puerto Rico, Cuba, and the modern-day Bahamas. The vegetation of the east coast of peninsular Florida probably would have seemed pretty standard, if not a bit disappointing, to de León and his crew. Cruising north from the Bahamas, however, de León first approached what he thought was Bimini on a Sunday, "which was the day of the Feast of the Resurrection," known as *Pascua Florida*, the Feast of Flowers. According to that account, the men named the new place La Florida on the one hand because of its vegetation, "and because, moreover, they discovered it in the time of the Feast of Flowers," and "Juan Ponce wished to conform the name for these two reasons." Perhaps there was something to the lush vegetation, but in the tradition of naming findings after Saints and feasts, the choice for de León was clear.[11]

The same cruise led the ships along the Florida Keys, which Antón de Alaminos named after a Christian martyr, for all the devastation and carnage the coral islands heaped on Spanish shipping. That was in turn reproduced in many of La Florida's first maps, which commonly show wrecked ships strewn about the area.[12] A few notable islands were still given names, like Santa Marta and Santa Pola. Santa Marta was a common place name given by Spaniards in the Caribbean, all of which took their namesake from Martha of Bethany. Florida's Santa Marta is believed to be Key Biscayne. The second, Santa Pola, was a town along the Mediterranean Coast in the Valencia region of Spain, and a derivation of St. Paul the Apostle. It is unknown what Key that is now. Neither name exists in the present.[13]

Several significant features along the Gulf Coast of La Florida were at one time or another christened Espíritu Santo, or the Holy Spirit, after a particularly meaningful feast and celebration in contemporary Portuguese and Spanish Catholicism. Alonso Álvarez de Pineda issued the name at least once in 1519, when he charted the northern Gulf Coast. Although it is possible, he referred to both the Mobile and the Mississippi Rivers as such, only the Mississippi retained the name on his 1519 map, the first to chart a connected Gulf basin that stretched from the modern-day Mexican Coast to the Atlantic. It was on Pentecost Sunday, the Feast Day of Espiritu Santo, that the Mississippi earned the distinction. In 1539 de Soto might have extended the name to either Tampa Bay or Charlotte Harbor, having also sighted land on Pentecost. Early La Florida maps listed Tampa Bay as Espiritu Santo. Ten years previous Narváez named a shallow bay, perhaps Tampa Bay or one to the south like Sarasota Bay, Bahía de la Cruz, or Bay of the Cross, which corresponded to the Feast of the Invention of the Cross.[14]

One should definitely be picking up on a pattern, even if the redundancy and overlap in names starts to get confusing. Farther to the north Tristán de Luna arrived at the future site of Pensacola—Ochuse—writing the King of Spain directly that because the men entered the harbor on the Feast of the Assumption of the Blessed Virgin Mary, and "as we entered on the day I say, I named the bay in your honor as Bahia Filipina del Puerto de Santa María." Santa María de Filipino, the first name for Spaniards' first attempt at Pensacola, did not last long.[15]

Saint names and feast days were not just for mariners. If the most successful attempts at long term colonization in La Florida were made by Franciscan Friars in the mission district, a close look there reflects more religious iconography. The Santa Fe River near present-day Gainesville has roots in the Franciscan mission era. Nearby, both Narváez and de Soto had to negotiate the Suwanee River, but neither cared enough to name it. Generations later, however, nearby San Juan de Guacara mission was pieced together using St. John the Baptist and also the original Native name of the river, Guacara, a common Spanish practice for missions. At one point, according to anthropologist Jerald Milanich, the name was just shortened to San Juan-ee, from which Suwannee developed. Narváez passed over the Ochlockonee River in the Apalachicola National Forest, naming it Río de Magdalena, presumably after Mary Magdalene. After building their ships the men in the Narváez expedition made their way out to sea. On the feast day of St. Michael, they named modern St. George Sound San Miguel Bay as they made their way through it and past Apalachicola.[16] The expedition very quickly fell apart; naturally, very few attempts to name anything followed. Few other saint names were listed on the Gulf Coast until well down the coast of modern-day Mexico. On the 1529 Diego Ribero map only one river, the Río de la Concepción, is visible. It was most likely named after a feast day and its location in Florida would make probably make it the Apalachicola, although no other information exists to corroborate that location.

Expanding back out of modern-day Florida for a bit, one can't help but follow American saints out of the Gulf and all the way up the Atlantic seaboard. The American portion of Diego Ribero's 1529 world map would seem clearly to be the product of English or at least French exploration. The names, however, are of Spanish origin, and reflect the extent of Spanish exploration across a La Florida that was far more than the modern-day state of Florida. Extending from the Florida peninsula to Newfoundland, Ribero defines the territory in the "tierras," or lands, of its discoverers, beginning in the Gulf with Francisco de Garay. Moving up the east coast is the land of Ayllón, a reference to Lucas Vázquez de Ayllón's settlement attempt there. Farther to the north was the land of Estavâo Gomes, who in 1524 began charting north all the way to the Labrador Coast in search for the fabled northern passage.[17]

The discovery and renaming of the eastern seaboard began in earnest even earlier, in 1521, when the first two Spaniards to land in what is now South Carolina named it the "Land of St. John the Baptist," for the feast day on which they first sighted it. Nearby Winyah Bay clearly represents a Native place name, as does one of the primary rivers to feed it, the Santee. Spaniards had other ideas, originally naming the Santee the Jordan, in association with St. John the Baptist and after one of the most important Middle Eastern rivers in the Christian Bible.[18]

Because of Ayllón and Chicora, the Florida–Georgia–South Carolina corridor now recognized as the "Lowcountry" is replete with Catholic iconography. Above Cabo de Corrientes and Cabo de Cañaveral was the first mention of a Cabo de La Cruz, known now as St. Augustine Beach. From there a mariner would have sailed past the St. Johns and St. Marys Rivers to the limits of modern Georgia; both modern rivers have names with clear biblical origins. On Quejo's 1525 reconnoitering voyage he first sited land on May 3, the feast day of the Invention of the Cross. As such, he named the river he found Rio de la Cruz. If his landfall was supposed to have been Tybee Island, then Rio de la Cruz, the River of the Cross, would have been the Savannah River. If Ayllón had chosen to make his settlement attempt there, on one of the most important rivers in the entire Southeast, who knows what would have happened. Georgia, settled there over two centuries later by the British, would look a whole lot different, if it even existed at all.[19] Still other island names nearby reflect Catholic Saints, even though their origins are less known. Among them is Santa Catalina, which would become Saint Catherine Island, as well as nearby St. Simon's Island. Saint names are not only for the modern-day state of Florida, these rivers, islands, and bays reveal.

Recall one more time both Santa Elena and St. Helena. They are the same reference to the mother of Emperor Constantine the Great, and a leading female figure in the early Catholic Church. All sorts of references to Santa Elena are visible in the neighborhood, as capes, bays, and rivers of the coastal Southeast, yet it is not the only Saint reference. Sailing north of Winyah bay in 1525, Quejo named the imposing cape Cabo de San Nicolás according to the feast day. It was soon known however as Cabo de San Román, which serves as the origin of the Anglicized Cape Romain National Wildlife Refuge.[20] For evidence of La Florida's extent well into the Carolinas, all one needs to do is look at a map.

Spanish exploration did not end there, even though any hope of Spanish colonialism largely did. At the apex of the Outer Banks was Cabo de Trafalgar, known now as Cape Hatteras. Farther yet was Cabo de San Juan, Cabo de Santa María, and Rio de Santa María, titles used several times to describe different parts of the larger Chesapeake Bay, which bore the name La Bahia Santa María, or La Bahía de Madre de Dios, the latter being the Bay of the mother of God. Because he entered the Chesapeake on June 24, the feast day of John the Baptist, he named the cape Cabo de San Juan. That would correspond with modern

Ocean City, Maryland.[21] A quick glance into the heart of England's first successful colonial region in the seventeenth century, English counterpoints are evident. Virginia was named after Queen Elizabeth I, "The Virgin Queen," Jamestown was named after King James I, and Maryland was named after the wife of King Charles I. The English certainly had their own naming traditions. All of these places, however, had already been named, and they were all Catholic.

Even the center of future Puritan New England holds similar evidence. Cape Cod was originally named Cabo de las Arenas, or Cape of Sands, presumably after the dunes. To the north were the Bahía de San Antonio, Rio de Buena Madre, and another marker of St. John the Baptist. The Bahía de San Antonio is probably in the same location as the Rio of the same name, which is what Gomes named the Merrimac River in modern-day Maine. Of the most important perhaps was the name that lay between them, just above Cape Cod and just below the Merrimac. On the Ribero map this was named Bahia de San Christobal. That bay was marked near the present-day location of Boston, and might even be a reference to Massachusetts Bay. If that is the case, then Spanish influence in America charts much farther north than La Florida. It was a Spanish explorer who originally named two New England Puritan landmarks—at least one after a Catholic Saint no less—almost an entire century before Pilgrims landed there.[22]

Notes

1. Weber, *The Spanish Frontier*, 55.
2. Hoffman, "Narvaez and Cabeza de Vaca in Florida," 50-73; Weber, *The Spanish Frontier*, 42-45; Hoffman, *Florida's Frontiers*, 31.
3. Weber, *The Spanish Frontier*, 222.
4. Weber, *The Spanish Frontier*, 52-55; Elliott, *Empires*, 34.
5. See, for instance, Douglas-Lithgow, *Native American Place Names of Massachusetts*.
6. Borchard, *Appalachia as Contested Borderland*, 1-12; Hann, *Apalachee*, 5; Swanton, *Indians*, 89-90; Swanton, *The Indian Tribes*, 122-125.
7. Weddle, *Spanish Sea*, 45; "La Florida," in Clayton, Knight, and Moore, eds., *The De Soto Chronicles*, 2: 207-208, 237.
8. Gannon, "First European Contacts," 19-20; Weddle, *Spanish Sea*, 42, 45; Hoffman, *New Andalucia*, 25-27.
9. Elliott, *Empires*, 35.
10. Elliott, *Empires*, 33-34; Milanich, *Laboring in the Fields of the Lord*, 12-13.
11. Worth, *Discovering Florida*, 49-51; "La Florida," in Clayton, Knight, and Moore, eds., *The De Soto Chronicles*, 2: 64; "Ponce de León's First Voyage," 17, 19, 21, 38-39; Weddle, *Spanish Sea*, 42.
12. Weddle, *Spanish Sea*, 43.
13. Worth, *Discovering Florida*, 50-51; Weddle, *Spanish Sea*, 42-43, 46.

14. Gannon, "Altar and Hearth," 20, 23; Weddle, *Spanish Sea*, 100, 187-188, 197-198, 213-214.

15. Gannon, "Altar and Hearth," 32.

16. Weddle, *Spanish Sea*, 191, 193; Milanich, *Laboring in the Fields of the Lord*, 12-13.

17. Weber, *The Spanish Frontier*, 37-39.

18. Hoffman, "The Chicora Legend," 419; Hoffman, *A New Andalucia*, 8, 68.

19. Hoffman, *A New Andalucia*, 25-27; 51-52, 54.

20. Hoffman, *A New Andalucia*, 68-69.

21. Hoffman, *A New Andalucia*, 10, 13, 25-27, 52-53, 68-69.

22. Weber, *The Spanish Frontier*, 37.

American Legends

The Pocahontas legend certainly needs no introduction. Tremendously popular, yet of highly dubious origins. It is one of America's most mythical, apocryphal tales. It is apocryphal because, academically speaking, scholars of all disciplines have cast doubts on the veracity of John Smith's account. As one noted historian of Native North America suggested, for instance, "almost every particular of this familiar story" was "either incorrect or misleading." If something like Smith's capture and almost-execution actually did happen, this critique goes, then according to Native custom at the time, it was probably staged. It was a ceremony designed by Powhatan to absorb the English into his realm as dependents, or at least as allies. John Smith was never in any danger, in other words. He simply did not know what was going on.[1] According to harsher criticisms, Smith made the whole thing up. Worse yet, he copied it from Gracilaso de la Vega, of all people, which would make the Pocahontas tale the plagiarizing of an exaggeration. Smith only described his harrowing Pocahontas account in his second edition of his time in Virginia, not his first. By that time, Gracilaso de la Vega's de Soto chronicle had been published as *La Florida del Inca*, had been translated into English, and was available in London. Only after reading of Ortiz's harrowing captivity and looking to spice up his own already-ostentatious narrative, did Smith transform a La Florida legend into a Virginia legend. The rest, is history.[2]

The state of Florida has its own legend, no less popular, no less apocryphal, than John Smith's Pocahontas tale. Ask any Floridian about their state's foundational origin story and most would not hesitate to describe a mythical "Fountain of Youth," the search for which originally drew Juan Ponce de León to La Florida's shoreline. With roots supposedly in the early sixteenth century, this is perhaps America's first origin story. Absolutely none of it, of course, is true. This legend never was to Spaniards what it has become to modern-day Floridians. It is the myth of a myth, the legend of a legend.

Peter Martyr, one of the first Spanish historians to speak of La Florida, mentioned the fountain in passing in a massive history published first in 1530. He described it as a "spring whose waters restore youth to old men." While there was no evidence that he had read accounts of either de León's 1513 voyage of discovery or his recently failed 1521 expedition, or that de León referenced the legend ever at all, Martyr nevertheless tied the location of the fountain to the unknown Bimini region that lay to the north of the Bahamas, of which de León certainly was interested. Still, unconvinced of the fountain's existence himself, Martyr dismissed the legend as silly and perhaps blasphemous, even as he admitted that it had already made its way through the Spanish Royal Court, "and made such an impression that the entire populace, and even people superior by birth and influence, accepted it as a proven fact."[3] The Fountain of Youth Legend had, already by the mid-sixteenth century, taken on a life of its own. It already had its proponents, and it already had its critics.

Despite this shaky foundation, accounts of de León's supposed search for the fountain endured, creating what has certainly become one of the most stubborn myths in American history. Stubborn because it endures despite every attempt made over the centuries to discount it. That was the case with Martyr, who saw no direct evidence actually connecting de León to the fountain, or river, or any such magical body of water, during the explorer's time plying La Florida's waters. Only indirect suggestions made long after de León's death speak of his supposed interest. There is Hernándo d'Escalante Fontaneda, for example, whose own 1570 shipwreck tale also connects de León to the legend directly. Fontaneda suggested that the conquistador did so based on legends passed along from Natives in Cuba and southern peninsular Florida, who themselves partook of a certain river's rejuvenating qualities, which turned "aged men and women back to their youth." De León was hooked, according to Fontaneda, so that "he might earn greater fame than he already possessed," or "that he might become young from bathing in such a stream." Fontaneda also made it clear he had little more faith in the legend than did Martyr. With unmistakable sarcasm he described how he, while a captive in La Florida for almost twenty years, had enjoyed bathing in plenty of the region's rivers, "but to my misfortune" never did quite make it to that one. Nevertheless, the legend endured, recounted next by none other than Gracilaso de la Vega, who described de León's first voyage to La Florida. Knowing Gracilaso de la Vega's propensity to embellish, it should be no surprise that he picked up the Fountain tale and ran with it. "There, according to fabulous tales of the Indians, was a fountain that rejuvenated the aged. He traveled in search of it for many days, lost, and without finding it."[4]

The Fountain of Youth and de León's search for it remains one of Florida's most enduring foundational myths to this day, despite the waves of more recent historians who point to its factual inaccuracies and its obvious, outlandish nature. It makes no sense, for example, for de León to have been interested in such a thing. He was not that old, at least not old enough to want to expend such a fortune on an expedition just to feel a bit younger.[5] Perhaps modern Americans rally around such a romanticized legend because it sounds far better than the more sinister ambitions that we know de León certainly did have when he shoved off from Puerto Rico in 1513. While de León certainly was in La Florida looking for fame, we know now it wasn't a fountain he was after. It was people. A magical fountain certainly sounds better than conquest, subjugation, and enslavement.

Conquest, subjugation, and enslavement are at the core of a very different legend with La Florida connections: the "Black Legend." While certainly a tale of death and destruction, this legend is a bit misleading—while legend is in its name, it is not much of a legend at all. Its foundation was in the reality of violent colonialism, and its purpose was to anger contemporary Spanish Catholics into intervening in an ongoing but very much failed spiritual conquest in the New World. In other words, very much unlike the Fountain of Youth, there is quite a bit of fact to the Black Legend.

Although it was not referred to as such at the time, the foundations for the Black Legend were laid earlier in the sixteenth century, and possibly in 1511. That was the year when Fray Antonio de Montesinos gave a charged and highly contemptuous lecture in Santo Domingo, condemning the brutality with which Spanish settlers treated the island's Natives. It was a brutality that was effectively wiping the Natives out, bringing what the Spanish were doing in the Caribbean dangerously close to the modern definition of genocide. A "just war," Montesinos argued, was not at all what was being waged in the Caribbean. Ironically, Montesinos would be one of the Dominicans to depart from Hispaniola with Ayllón on the failed Guadalpe expedition, hoping to try his hand at peaceful conversion there. Before that time, however, the complaints of men like him were the reason King Ferdinand instituted the Law of Burgos in 1512, the New World's first comprehensive legislative code, as J. H. Elliott put it. The code was designed to guarantee basic human rights to Native people while upholding the incredibly popular *encomienda* system which was, after all, one of the driving engines of Hispanic settlement. Naturally the laws did nothing and would do nothing. The brutal conquest of New Spain had not even begun yet.[6]

The main progenitor of the Black Legend was not Montesinos but a man by the name of Bartolome de las Casas, whose circuitous route to championing Native humanity followed an extensive history of trampling on it himself. De las Casas was actually on Hispaniola at the same time Montesinos gave his sermon and was by that time a priest himself, although he was not swayed by his fellow clergyman's 1511 pleas. The Seville-born de las Casas arrived on Hispaniola in 1502 with incoming Governor Nicolás de Ovando and he took part in some of the bloodiest moments in the island's conquest, for which Ovando granted him an *encomienda* allotment of island Natives. De las Casas was at the same time working to become an ordained priest, hoping to benefit financially from his control of a *doctrino*, a Catholic parish on the island that was supposed to serve the needs of Natives, but in reality, simply provided another means for Spaniards to squeeze labor from the local population. A crusader for Native humanity de las Casas absolutely was not in 1511.

From Hispaniola de las Casas traveled to Cuba to assist Diego Velásquez de Cuéllar and Pánfilo de Narváez in the almost unimaginably brutal campaign of conquest there, doing so as a chaplain to Cuéllar's men no less. Although he would recall the campaign later in disgust, de las Casas did little to stop it at the time. Instead, he accepted another *encomienda* allotment from Cuéllar. Soon he was using his Native slaves to run a number of profitable island enterprises. He certainly was more conquistador than friar at that point. In fact, "so preoccupied was he with his material interests," wrote one historian, that he shut down a fellow Dominican friar who had arrived on the island to admonish him and those like him about their conduct. Perhaps it was the denial of his own absolution by the visiting friars that prompted de las Casas's 1514 turn to the light, beginning the change of heart for which he would become famous. He renounced his *encomiendas* not long after, traveled to Spain, a began a lifelong campaign for Native human rights.[7]

Although de las Casas fought the good fight for the rest of his life, his crowning achievement was his 1542 *A Short Account of the Destruction of the Indies*, which more than any other text birthed the Black Legend. The account, penned originally as an appeal to the Spanish Crown, was billed as a largely firsthand accounting of the innumerable atrocities committed by conquistadores basically everywhere they went in the New World. To describe the narrative as scathing does it no justice. Downright pornographic in its detail of wanton and gratuitous acts of violence committed against Natives, and even more so with the images later included, *A Short History* turns the stomach.[8]

De las Casas opened his tale on Hispaniola, describing the Natives there "as many and varied as they are, as open and as innocent as can be imagined." They were simple people, "never quarrelsome or belligerent or boisterous," and "the notions of revenge, rancour, and hatred are quite foreign to them." They were also poor, "among the poorest people on the face of the earth," with no material possessions and therefore were "neither ambitious nor greedy," and were "totally uninterested in worldly power." They would have made perfect Christians, he recounted, had they only been given the chance. Instead, it was upon "these gentle lambs" that from the very first day "they clapped eyes on them the Spanish fell like ravening wolves upon the fold," like lions and tigers "who have not eaten meat for days." From these very first lines it was clear de las Casas would be doing his fellow Spaniards no favors. "Purely and simply greed" was the reason his so-called Christian companions "uprooted these pitiful peoples and wiped them from the face of the earth."[9]

Many of the worst atrocities de las Casas cataloged were in the Caribbean in the earliest, headiest, bloodiest days of conquest. That began of course on Hispaniola, "the first to witness the arrival of Europeans and the first to suffer the wholesale slaughter of its people and the devastation and depopulation of its land." Among the many atrocities there de las Casas spoke of the pacification of the Higuey province, of which he personally took part. After the elderly chieftainess was "strung up," presumably crucified, the attackers "burned countless inhabitants alive or hacked them to pieces, or devised novel ways of torturing them to death," enslaving whoever remained. Spaniards "invented so many new methods of murder," at Higuey, he concluded, "that it would be quite impossible to set them all down on paper and, however hard one tried to chronicle them, one could probably never list a thousandth part of what actually took place." That was just one massacre, on just one island.[10]

Bartolome de las Casas spared no corner of Spanish conquest, moving through New Spain and the Yucatan to Tierra Firma and finally La Florida. By the writing of his account, las Casas charged that Spaniards "still do nothing save tear the natives to shreds, murder them and inflict upon them untold misery, suffering and distress, tormenting, harrying and persecuting them mercilessly."[11] La Florida, unfortunately, was no different. Since its discovery, "three tyrannical adventurers," among them no doubt de León and Narváez, had made their way there and acted "in much the same way as have their compatriots in other parts of the new world." At least in these pages de las Casas could take pleasure in celebrating the unceremonious and "sticky" end each of these men met in La Florida, the fortunes they had already squeezed from the New World "by pillage and murder" sunk, and the memory of them "expunged from the face of the earth." It was a fitting condemnation indeed of de León, considering his past in Puerto Rico, and certainly of Narváez, considering his infamy in Cuba. Bartolome de las Casas would have had firsthand knowledge of both. The Lord punished them for their crimes, "cutting them short before they could wreak havoc on a larger scale in these provinces." It was now, he earlier concluded, "as though they had never been born."

Bartolome de las Casas dwelt particularly on de Soto, "a fourth and very determined blackguard," whose expedition coincided with the very publication of *A Short Account*. De Soto had just recently set out on his conquest and so de las Casas only made passing reference at first to the various atrocities he must certainly be committing on "anyone and everyone unlucky enough to cross his path." He was, after all, "a notoriously ruthless and seasoned campaigner and he and his companions-in-arms have been responsible for some of the worst atrocities ever seen in the New World." Oh how right he was. As his writings continue, however, it appears de las Casas had not yet put the finishing touches on his La Florida chapter when the survivors of the expedition wandered back onto the scene. The firebrand author wasted no time adding a few paragraphs to his manuscript. So too had de Soto met his sticky end in La Florida, but only after indulging in a reign of terror that confirmed las Casas's most damning charges. The longer conquistadores spent in the New World, de Soto's account proved, "the more they have become accustomed to the carnage and butchery around them, the more brutal and the more wicked have been the crimes they commit against God and their fellow-men."

Bartolome de las Casas's narrative was designed to outrage. To what extent was it "legend," however, and to what extent was it fact? Parts of it are, without doubt, sensationalized. That being said, moving from one atrocity to the next to the next, not only does a reading of his de Soto section not come off as particularly gratuitous, but parts of it seem downright accurate. He mentions communities giving up hundreds of laborers whose lives de Soto and his men proceeded to make "an utter misery, treating them as so many beasts of burden," lopping the heads from the bodies of the slaves rather than loosening the chains from their necks when they were too exhausted to carry on. While there is not much evidence of de Soto's men decapitating prisoners as a means of removing their chains, there are plenty of references to slaves and to chains, and of the untold number of the former who died in the latter.

Just a few lines later an entire town is put "to the sword, young and old, chiefs and commoners. Not even the children were spared." Perhaps this was Napetuca, or perhaps Mavila. Technically speaking, there were no children at the battle of Mavila, possible evidence of the sensationalism written into de las Casas's works. Nevertheless, the point is made, and there is little doubt that, had he been at Napetuca or Mavila, the carnage there would have given even Bartoleme de las Casas pause. Neither do any of his other charges, while too vague to put towns to, seem particularly farfetched. Natives treated de Soto with kindness and in return he had their towns pillaged and their leaders lanced, sparing one group after having the "noses, lips and chins sliced from their faces," sending them away "in unspeakable agony and all running with blood." Acts of gratuitous violence abound, yet they do not seem particularly out of place considering what de Soto's own chroniclers so frequently, and so leisurely, described. Ultimately, de las Casas got the closure he desired. De Soto too died in La Florida; a death no less righteous than any of the others. "Their wretched leader died a wretched death without benefit of confession, and there can be no doubt that he is now in the depths of Hell enjoying the wages of his wickedness."[12]

Hernando de Soto's entrada and the rest of the La Florida horrors were part of a comparatively small chapter of Bartoleme de la Casas's *A Short Account*, but they definitely belong there. These were the accounts that formed the foundation of the infamous *La Leyenda Negra*, the Black Legend of Spanish conquest, which, as it was, is only partially a legend. De las Casas's *Short Account* was a moralizing tale constructed partly of fiction, no doubt, but also containing more than a few shreds of fact. Although it was certainly not his intent, the impact of de las Casas's *Short Account* on the common view of Spanish colonialism proved transformative as it traveled across Europe in whispers, and then in translations.

Widespread dissemination of *A Short Account* began in the mid-sixteenth century. One English translation was available in London by the early 1580s, right about the time the English first pushed off for Roanoke. There was no doubt that men like Walter Raleigh and Richard Hakluyt, men who were keen to weave condemnation of Spanish abuses on Natives into their own colonization propaganda, had copies on their shelves. There was a conflicted and even tortured view with which many Englishmen viewed their Spanish counterparts, what one historian labeled the "specter of Spain." Successful and rich colonizers—too successful and too rich—the Spanish needed to be taken down a notch, however possible. Piracy was one way to do that, as we will see in the next chapter. Moralizing certainly was another. Even the most economically motivated, enterprising boosters, like Hakluyt, Raleigh, and Gilbert, jumped at the opportunity to integrate the violence and inhumanity of Spanish colonialism into their arguments. For these men, de Las Casas's *Short Account* was worth its weight in gold.[13]

The best example comes in Richard Hakluyt's *Discourse Concerning Western Planting*, one of the most famous pieces of British colonizing propaganda, and one with direct ties to Roanoke. An entire chapter was dedicated to Spanish atrocities, beginning "That the Spaniards have exercised most outrageous and more than Turkishe cruelties in all of the West Indies." So many "and so monstrous" were the "Spanish cruelties, such strange slaughters and murders" of the New World's peoples, Hakluyt wrote, "together with the spoils of towns, provinces, and kingdoms," that if he was to try to describe them all, it would take another entire book. Hakluyt made sure not just to criticize the violence of Spaniards' initial conquest, but to assure his readers that the English would do things differently.[14]

So much for the Fountain of Youth! This is how Spain's colonial competition cultivated and propagated the Black Legend. Once in the hands of men like Hakluyt, it is no wonder the Black Legend made its way around the world. Of all the American legends, the Back Legend has cast the longest shadow, a legacy of violence that tarnished the Spanish Catholic image for centuries and has endured, in one way or another, even to the present day. Of the three American legends, from Pocahontas to the Fountain of Youth, this La Florida legend unfortunately is also the most accurate.

Notes

1. Richter, *Facing East*, 69-72; Figueredo, *Revolvers and Pistolas*, 28-29.

2. Figueredo, *Revolvers and Pistolas*, 28-29; Voigt, *Writing Captivity in the Early Modern Atlantic*, 304-310; Young, "Pocahontas," 13-21.

3. Martyr, *De Orbe Novo*, 1: 274; Worth, *Discovering Florida*, 54, 60-62.

4. Worth, *Discovering Florida*, 202-203; "La Florida," in Clayton, Knight, and Moore, eds., *The De Soto Chronicles*, 2: 64.

5. Francis, "Juan Ponce de León and the Fountain of Youth," 127-132; Davis, "Ponce de León's First Voyage," 25; Arana, "The Exploration of Florida," 4-5; Weber, *The Spanish Frontier*, 33; Weddle, *Spanish Sea*, 38-39.

6. Elliott, *Empires*, 67; Griffin and Pagden, eds., *A Short Account*, xx-xxx; Schwaller, *The History of the Catholic Church*, 43-44; Lynch, *New Worlds*, 33.

7. Elliott, *Empires*, 67-68; Lynch, *New Worlds*, 33-38; Schwaller, *The History of the Catholic Church*, 44-45; Griffin and Pagden, eds., *A Short Account*, xviii-xxx; "Introduction," in Clayton and Lantigua, eds., *Bartolemé de las Casas*, 3-27; Giménez Fernández, "Fray Bartolomé," 67-70, 72-74. De las Casas's extensive history as an advocate for Native rights is covered in Giménez Fernández, "Fray Bartolomé," 74-125.

8. Griffin and Pagden, eds., *A Short Account*, xiii-xvii.
9. Griffin and Pagden, eds., *A Short Account*, 9-13.
10. Griffin and Pagden, eds., *A Short Account*, 22-23.
11. Griffin and Pagden, eds., *A Short Account*, 11.
12. Griffin and Pagden, eds., *A Short Account*, 102-104.
13. Milton, *Big Chief Elizabeth*, 49-51; Restall, *Seven Myths*, 118-120; Williamson, *Powhatan Lords*, 18-22; Elliott, *Empires*, 72-78; Kamen, *Empire*, 125-126; Sanchez, *The Spanish Black Legend.*
14. Hakluyt, *A Discourse Concerning Western Planting*, 7-9, 71.

9 An Anglo-American Counterpoint

September 9, 1739, was a Sunday, so many of the white residents of the Stono River, which ran between Port Royal and Charleston, were most likely in church. Sunday was also a day that plantation owners often left their slaves to tend to their own gardens and activities, leaving them more or less on their own. Perhaps those were the reasons why a large number of slaves, mostly if not all men, were able to meet near a bridge over the Stono and begin their march to freedom in St. Augustine. There they set into motion what would become known as the Stono Rebellion.

The slaves had no intention of making the long march to La Florida quietly, as their first stop soon attested. At a nearby trade store that was stocked up with guns and ammunition the rebels, numbering somewhere around twenty, overwhelmed and killed the two white men inside. They "cut their heads off and set them on the stairs," a particularly gory first stroke that set the tone for the rest of the day. The gang quickly looted the store and moved down the road, the main thoroughfare "through Georgia to Augustine," which would take them by several nearby rice plantations.

Heavily armed and well liquored up, the rebels made quick work of the Godfrey household, killing Mr. Godfrey along with his wife and child. This was the first of several entire families to die at the hands of Stono's former slaves. Moving south "in a daring manner out of the province," the marchers left a trail of dead bodies and burned-out homes for miles in their wake. The only exception was a nearby tavern keeper, who was spared because he evidently was a nice guy with a reputation for not abusing nearby slaves. Soon after, however, the marchers picked up where they left off, killing the nearby Lemy family and marching on.

Word spread quickly and soon untold numbers of nearby slaves were joining in, swelling the march to anywhere from a few dozen to over one hundred. The runaways and rebels soon formed an army that filled the small dirt road, which they marched along "calling out Liberty," flying banners, beating drums, and "pursuing all the white people they met with, and killing Man Woman and

Child when they could come up to them." Plantations fell in quick succession. "They burnt Colonel Hext's house and killed his overseer and his wife," went one account. "They then burnt Mr. Sprye's house, then Mr. Sacheverell's, and then Mr. Nash's house," killing anyone they found and leading credibility to another account that described how "the country thereabout was full of flames."

It was around this time, however, in an almost unbelievable stroke of bad luck for the revolutionaries, that South Carolina's very own Lieutenant Governor, William Bull, just happened to be riding north on his way to Charleston up that very same road. He trotted within sight of the marchers and, no doubt alarmed by what he had run across, turned and galloped away as quickly as he could. He "was pursued, and with much difficulty escaped," riding back to the nearest town and perhaps right into the church house, where most of the white population was at the time, spreading the alarm. This unluckiest of all coincidences immediately complicated the largest slave uprising yet in the British American colonies and the first major one in the south, guaranteeing the Stono rebels would have to fight their way into La Florida.

The army of former slaves did themselves no favors by marching as slowly and deliberately as they did. They took an extended break in a field and set out congratulating themselves on their accomplishments thus far, drinking and singing, "thinking they were now victorious over the whole Province, having marched ten miles & burnt all before them without opposition." Unbeknownst to them a posse of planters was already in pursuit. The militia, mounted on horses and no doubt highly motivated by the sight of so much smoke in the air, caught up to the rebels in practically no time at all. They "with great briskness pursued them and when they came up, dismounting; charged them on foot."

In that epic moment of confrontation one particularly bold enslaved man recognized his former master from among the approaching militiamen, which makes sense because many were either local plantation owners or overseers. Armed with a pistol and almost certainly emboldened by a strong dose of liquid courage, the former slave walked up fearlessly to confront his former oppressor. When the white man asked his slave "if he wanted to kill him" the Stono rebel replied yes, raised his pistol, and pulled the trigger. It "snapped," however, meaning it misfired. Another stroke of the worst luck. The rebel, nowhere close to La Florida, was promptly shot in the face.

Much of the rest of the Stono Rebellion went the same way. According to different accounts the slaves, many of whom were by that point probably drunk, either scattered immediately or made a few ineffective volleys of gunfire, "without any damage." The militia responded with a much more accurate return fire, dropping by one report more than a dozen rebels in the first few moments of the skirmish. From there the affair quickly became a route, which few of the slaves escaped. Some fled from the field and apparently back to their plantations, hoping that they might be able to conceal their involvement in the now-failed uprising. Most of them were hunted down and summarily executed. "Such as were taken in the field also, after being examined," were "shot on the spot." Pursuing the rest, the militia cut the heads off many of the slain rebels "and set them up at every mile post they came to."[1] Just as violently as the Stono Rebellion began, it ended.

The majority of Stono, as it has since been referred to in short, was over in a matter of hours. Those hours of carnage, however, cast a long shadow over the British Lowcountry, changing the trajectory of South Carolina history and the development of slavery in the larger Southeast. For those reasons it carries important weight for historians, despite a maddening lack of primary sources that make it difficult to describe the uprising with any accuracy. Scholars have explained Stono as a natural result of the increasingly brutal institution of slavery as it was being constructed in South Carolina. It was perhaps the product of the martial, gendered virtues of its enslaved actors. It even had origins in wars along the West Coast of Africa, the region from which most of South Carolina's enslaved people were stolen.[2] But clearly the Stono Rebellion also took place because of La Florida, as many of the enslaved rebels, everyone who witnessed their actions, or heard anything about it from afar, were all quick to claim. Stono represented the threat La Florida posed to rice culture and the development of slavery in the Lowcountry. St. Augustine was, in this one instance, the foil of the Lowcountry, with its existence influencing the laws that white South Carolinians created to control their own world. That makes it an excellent example of a La Florida legacy.

If Floridanos struggled to build themselves a place in the seventeenth century Spanish world, the eighteenth century proved even more difficult. From James Moore's destructive raids to the surrender of La Florida to the British in 1763, Spain's once-sprawling American holding had shrunk to no more than a few isolated colonial outposts in the present-day state of Florida. Long gone were the days of Spanish claims to the Atlantic seacoast, or even the Gulf coast. The British and the French now claimed those spaces as well, and the influence of the first of the two rivals—Great Britain—was expanding rapidly across seemingly all of it. No more were the missions and the *haciendas*, the places that had given

La Florida meaning in the Spanish empire and the Catholic Church. La Florida was, in this light, a failed colony. Yet as small and as isolated as it now stood, La Florida was still not irrelevant. Far from it, as the Stono rebels saw things.

This chapter continues "Legacies" by considering how La Florida and the larger empire of Spain influenced the minds and actions of the British beyond the colony's limits, both geographic and temporal. La Florida was at times very much a thorn in Britain's side, as Stono clearly demonstrated. Even before there was Carolina there was Virginia, the first English colony planted in North America. In the arc of the American story, Virginia is considered the infinitely-more successful counterpoint to St. Augustine, which in terms of its growth, it clearly was. But what if one would not have existed without the other? What if the British movers and thinkers who founded the first British colony in North America did so out of jealousy towards the Spanish, who were already there, and who used the waters off of La Florida to transport all of their wealth back to Europe? What if those British movers and thinkers were little more than pirates, who established Roanoke only to prey on Spanish shipping in the Florida Straits?

Lastly, in somewhat of a reversal of La Florida's Native misfortune in the era of the Indian slave trade, the Spanish were able to rehabilitate the colony at least partially after the end of the Yamasee War. That war, which ranged from 1715 to 1717 put an abrupt and very violent end to the slave raiding which had once defined the Charleston trade. English merchants, who replaced Native slaves with deerskins, were forced once again to deal with an old foe: their Spanish neighbors to the south. Yet neither Spaniards nor the British, you could argue, were the true winners in this struggle. Regional Natives were; more specifically, Creeks. It was a Spanish imperial counterpart to the English that provided for one of the Southeast's most defining periods—the period of play-off diplomacy, which would dominate regional politics in the region for the next two generations.

Emerging Native groups like Creek Indians, spread through the border between the English south and La Florida, were able to use Spanish authorities to drive down English trade prices and force the latter merchants, even though they provided the far superior trade, to act competitively. That sprawling period of Native American history, in which Native societies wielded the most economic authority and political power they ever would have, would not have been possible without La Florida. Although by the eighteenth century the Spanish colony had shrunk from a sprawling frontier to just a few fortified settlements, these examples of legacies suggest that Spain still cast a long shadow in an American Southeast, even though it was no longer La Florida.

Notes

1. Smith, ed., *Stono*, 4, 7-10, 12, 14-17.
2. See the collected essays in Smith, ed., *Stono*, 59-123.

The Lost Pirate Colony of Roanoke

THE "LOST COLONY" OF ROANOKE CASTS A TREMENDOUS SHADOW OVER EARLY American history, even though in the end the ultimate fate of the colonists who were left along the coast of North Carolina in 1587 can be presumed easily enough. They all either starved to death, died at the hands of the local Natives, or melted into the landscape, becoming Natives themselves. Every aspect of the expedition has been heavily scrutinized by generations of scholars, and so the basics are well understood, even if the ending is not.

A group of English adventurers backed by Walter Raleigh and led by Richard Grenville and Ralph Lane made their first attempt at the colony in 1585. It was a short-lived attempt that lasted only a year or so before it was abandoned in the face of rising Native animosity. Francis Drake evacuated the colony, and the few men left behind were the first to disappear into the wilderness, although there is little doubt, they were all killed by Natives. Undeterred, some of Roanoke's first investors mounted a second attempt not long after, in 1587. It is this attempt, led by John White, which has left historians and archaeologists scratching their heads ever since. After establishing his colony, Governor White sailed away from Roanoke in 1587, intending to return as soon as possible with more supplies and recruits. Instead, he was swept up in the Anglo-Spanish war, which broke out the next year, leaving the Roanoke colonists forsaken for three entire years. When White did finally return in 1590 everyone was gone—more than one hundred colonists seemingly wiped from the face of the earth.[1]

While these colonists represent some of English America's firsts, including the first English birth in North America, to Spaniards they represented something else altogether. Roanoke settlers were squatters and they were pirates, and in thinking that the Spanish were not wrong. Many of the primary boosters and actors in the English attempt at Roanoke, including Grenville and Lane, just happen to be among the most notorious pillagers of the Spanish Main. If they had gotten their way, Roanoke would have been the premiere piracy base in North America, a fortified military outpost purpose-built to encourage and safeguard British privateers. From it, the English could sweep forth into the Gulf Stream and prey on passing treasure galleons at will. Almost its entire existence, in short, was predicated on the Spanish trade route that ran along the coast of La Florida. "Roanoke was intended to be parasitic," wrote one prominent Virginia historian; "its reason for existence was the Spanish treasure fleet."[2] Considering this was widely known in both England and in Spain, then as far as La Florida Governor Pedro Menéndez Marques was concerned, then goodbye and good riddance to Roanoke—the Lost Pirate Colony.

This version of Roanoke begins with one of the most popular English seagoing pastimes of the late sixteenth century: privateering. First, to the Spanish there was no such thing as privateering. The term did not even exist at the time, and the men who attacked Spanish merchant shipping did so during peacetime with no other goal than to make money. Nothing about that was legal as far as the Spanish were concerned—these men were simply pirates. To the English there was much more gray area in the law, for they held official letters of "marque" issued them by royal authorities that allowed them to prey on Spanish shipping on behalf of England. Because they considered themselves legitimate agents of English authorities, to them everything was legal. The line between piracy and privateering was a murky one indeed. The ultimate high-risk, high-reward profession, privateering was wildly popular in England among the merchant class, and the legality of the profession is still debated among historians. Doing economic battle with Catholic Spain certainly had a positive moralistic vibe to it at the time, and since England had no other navy at the time, Crown officials were more than happy to look the other way if not sign privateering commissions officially. Some have even referred to these men affectionately as Queen Elizabeth's "Sea Dogs," seeing as how they proliferated during her rule and considering how more than a few of them, including Walter Raleigh, were her friends.[3]

Elizabeth's unleashing of the Sea Dogs followed a slow deterioration of relations between the English and Spanish in the mid-sixteenth century that had never really been that good at their best. Even when Mary was on the throne and married to Spanish King Philip II, English pirates preyed on Spanish ships in the vicinity of the English Channel and there was little Mary could do about it even if she wanted to. What was already a contentious Anglo-Spanish relationship during Mary's time only declined further when the Protestant Elizabeth assumed the throne in 1558 and picked up the mantle of the Reformation once raised by her father, Henry VIII. Between that clear antagonism and the aggressive expansionist policies Spanish kings were pursuing in Europe, tensions continued to rise until confrontation seemed inevitable.[4]

Privateering was also not entirely political. English merchants might undertake what they considered a legitimate attack on Spanish interests if they could prove they were prosecuting a "reprisal" raid. That meant that the booty they might gain in such an expedition was supposed to right some financial wrong originally done to them by the Spanish, which the Spanish refused to remedy themselves. In other words, it was payback. Because English merchants were beginning to creep illegally into the Caribbean, the conditions there were ripe for payback, even when things seemed peaceful in Europe. Spaniards might capture English ships they accused of smuggling, which English merchants would retaliate against with reprisal cruises, and so on and so forth. This too however grew shady very quickly, since what soon developed from the reprisal concept was a black market in reprisal authorizations that proliferated along the English coast and were no way anchored in the truth. A prospective privateer simply had to conjure up some sort of vague story about a financial insult they or someone in their employ sustained at the hands of any Spanish official anywhere on earth. From there it took very little to gain the necessary paperwork from corrupt local English authorities who would share in the winnings of a reprisal cruise. All this did was create a sham legal procedure used to justify what was clearly piracy. It too was a high-risk and high-reward venture, and it too was a popular one.[5]

These conditions created waves of reprisals that eventually erupted into a de facto state of war, the 1585 Anglo-Spanish war, which would not end officially until 1604. This freed Elizabeth to unleash the full force of the Sea Dogs against Spanish shipping wherever they might encounter it. According to one Spanish 1585 report to Philip II, for instance, the Queen had been giving away letters of marque to basically anyone that asked, having "issued more than seventy letters of marque to merchants," under which authorization they sailed "for the purpose of plundering your majesty's subjects everywhere." The pirates left from so many different ports at different times and with different destinations that it was impossible to even figure out how many of these "unusual pirates" were on their way to the Indies at any one time. In all close to 150 privateering ships made dedicated cruises in the two decades of the Anglo-Spanish war, raiding coastal settlements along the Caribbean repeatedly and capturing an untold number of Spanish prizes.[6]

Among the notable commissions issued by Elizabeth to these Sea Dogs were the ones that Francis Drake used on his legendary raiding adventure of 1585–1586.

By the time Drake returned to England he had cast a trail of destruction across the Atlantic and Caribbean, capturing and then ransoming Santo Domingo and Cartagena, and departing St. Augustine in smoldering ruins.[7] While Drake has gone down in history as the meanest, most successful of Elizabeth's Sea Dogs, he was not the only privateer of American importance to make a name for himself during the war of reprisals. A familiar cast of merchant-pirates made their rounds during these years, names recognizable to students of Virginia history. Sir Humphrey Gilbert's 1577 "Discourse how her Majesty may Annoy the King of Spain" was a not-so-thinly-veiled plan for wrecking the Spanish and Portuguese fishing fleets off Newfoundland, very à-la Drake. However much Gilbert extolled the virtues of the American northeast and planned a settlement there, privateering was also certainly on his mind.[8]

Another of England's most influential Sea Dogs was Sir Walter Raleigh, who was on the Gilbert expedition and afterward "went in search of Spanish treasure-ships," according to one old account, "and had a severe fight off the Cape Verde Islands." Richard Grenville began his career as a Sea Dog around the same time. William Parker, from Plymouth, gained notoriety raiding Spanish Tierra Firme around the turn of the seventeenth century, sacking Puerto de Caballos in Honduras, Campeche on the coast of New Spain, and then finally Portobelo in 1603. Three years later he was among the founding members of the Virginia Company.[9]

Then there was Christopher Newport, the namesake of Newport, Virginia, a prototypical merchant-privateer and an incredibly successful one at that. Born in 1560, Newport made his first recorded sail to the New World twenty years later, from London to Brazil. A well-trained seaman by 1587, he was sailing on a ship owned by noted privateer John Watts, and also partook in Drake's legendary raid on Cádiz, after which Newport continued to cruise the Spanish coast. He rose rapidly through the ranks of privateer, so that by 1590 he was captaining one of Watts's ships in the 1590 cruise that finally carried John White back to Roanoke. Watts himself would not make it to Virginia; in a fight off Cuba against two small New Spain Flota ships he lost an arm, an understandable reason to cut that privateering season short. He would soon return. Despite having only one arm Newport was seemingly everywhere in the Caribbean through the last decade of century, holding one Hispaniola settlement ransom and burning another in 1592, only to leave and raid the Honduran settlement of Puerto de Caballos. Four years later he commanded a formidable ship by the name of *Neptune*, which he in part owned, and which he used to raid the Caribbean relentlessly. His list of piratical accolades rambles on and on, stretching across the turn of the seventeenth century. There truly was no one quite equal to him, which explains why the members of the Virginia Company tapped him to lead their Jamestown expedition in 1606. His excellent training, tested leadership, and extensive experience in the region, built of several decades of privateering, were all no doubt influential in the success of the Jamestown expedition, even though he left the enterprise in 1611.[10]

It is no coincidence, in short, that American colonization emerged right at the very height of the 1580s "sea war," another term for the 1585 Anglo-Spanish war. So connected was Virginia with piracy that, according to one scholar, "no satisfactory history of either can be written without some account of the other." Virginian settlements were envisioned, planned, and manned by Sea Dogs, bases from which privateers would continually harass Spanish interests from Newfoundland to New Spain.[11] It was this line of thinking which led to Roanoke. Had the settlement been successful in these early years, Roanoke would not only have produced an English stronghold on the American coast, but would have ushered in a new era of New World piracy. All of this was because of the Spanish treasure fleets, and all of this was because of the location of the American east coast on the Gulf Stream. Without Spanish treasure, what point was there to Roanoke?

Richard Hakluyt the Younger emerged during the period as one of England's loudest and most determined advocates for Virginia, and not just for the natural bounty of the land. Probably the most widely read piece of literature he produced in his attempt to convince English Queen Elizabeth I of the importance of "western planting," aka colonization, was aptly titled *A Discourse Concerning Western Planting*. He published it in 1584, one year after Sir Humphrey Gilbert's attempt at Newfoundland, the same year Arthur Barlowe first scouted the Outer Banks, and one year before Richard Grenville set out on the first attempt to settle Roanoke. What is abundantly clear from his writing is that Hakluyt, like so many other ambitious upper-class Englishmen, was a very jealous man. He complained of the "the riches that the Indian treasure wrought in time of Charles the late Emperor father to the Spanish king," which had catapulted Spain to world power and was wreaking havoc on European politics, an "unrecoverable annoy of this realm, whereof already we have had very dangerous experience."[12] Considering the sea war would break the very next year, he was not wrong.

Central to taking Philip down "from his high throne," as Hakluyt put it, was a North American colony or two. In what would be "a great bridle to the Indies of the king of Spaine," he proposed establishing two or three "strong fortes" along the east coast, on the Gulf Stream, from which the English could pick off passing

Spanish shipping, including Newfoundland fishing ships to the north and treasure galleons from the south—hundreds of them a year, he claimed. From such a perch, armed ships could also raid into the Caribbean and threaten even New Spain itself. As another booster wrote Elizabeth, doing so would put her "near upon every event, to possess King Philip's purse." The Gulf Stream traveled up not only the modern states of Florida but Georgia and the Carolinas as well, clear on to the Chesapeake Bay. Spanish shipping was "carried by the current north and northwest towards the coast which we propose, God willing, to inhabit," Hakluyt wrote. Raleigh was of the same mind. A settlement in the Outer Banks-Chesapeake region was far enough away from St. Augustine to provide safety, but still close enough to the route of the treasure fleets to give them real trouble. This would be the place for an English counterpoint to St. Augustine. Where the Spanish outpost guarded the Gulf Stream and therefore the treasure fleets, however, an English position nearby would prey on it all.[13]

As soon as Raleigh received Gilbert's old patent for colonization, he dispatched Arthur Barlowe and Philip Amadas on their reconnoitering mission to the Outer Banks in 1584. At that same time Hakluyt was busy putting the finishing touches on his *Discourse*. It did its job, convincing the Queen of Virginia's importance and connecting Hakluyt with Raleigh, Grenville, Sir Francis Walsingham, and Sir George Carey, all of whom were seasoned privateers and all of whom would play a role in Virginia's earliest days. The interconnectivity of it all simply cannot be denied. "In the period up to 1590 nearly all the English privateering visits to the Caribbean were connected with the Virginia enterprise," concluded one historian. "Western planting" and privateering were "two manifestations of the same dynamic," a product of the past two decades of growing trade hopes and deteriorating politics. Richard Grenville cast off for Virginia around the same time another privateer headed off to Newfoundland to round up Spanish and Portuguese fishing ships, and the same year Drake set off for his Caribbean cruise. "In these circumstances privateering was the natural and inevitable accompaniment of every Virginia voyage."[14] The first Roanoke voyage not only pushed off amidst the flood tide of privateering raids that originated in 1585, but it was also a part of them.

Grenville's actions on the way to the La Florida coast made clear that Virginia and privateering were one and the same word to him. A smaller ship called a pinnace, associated with Grenville's *Tiger*, was sunk in a storm during his Atlantic crossing. Because such smaller ships were commonly used to catch prizes as well as make shallow-water explorations, Grenville waited on a small island off Puerto Rico while his men literally built another from the keel up. Grenville had no intention of just going to Virginia; he would raid his way there and raid his way back, and several exchanges of gunfire with Spanish soldiers near his encampment made it clear the Spanish probably knew what he was up to as well. Having built their newest ship, the Englishmen promptly went about cruising their way west through the Caribbean basin, and succeeded in capturing several prizes in the passage between the islands of Puerto Rico and Hispaniola. Soon after they made their way north to the Outer Banks and into Pamlico Sound, beginning the next phase of the expedition only after a quick but successful phase one—a privateering cruise. It would be the first of many to involve the would-be pirate base of Roanoke.[15]

More successful yet was Grenville's cruise back home. Roanoke Island turned out to be a bad choice because of the poor quality of the harbor, but its location on the return leg of the treasure route could not be denied when Grenville successfully assaulted and seized the *Santa María de Vincente* shortly after his departure. He caught up to it off Bermuda, overtook it, renamed it the *Galleon Dudley*, and sailed it triumphantly home. It was "the flag-ship of the Santo Domingo fleet," wrote an enraged Spanish Admiral Álvaro de Bazán, one of Spain's Treasure Fleet commanders, and on board was "an abundance of gold, silver, pearls, cochineal, sugar, ivory and hides," worth tens of thousands of British pounds. Grenville's seizure of the much larger and richly laden galleon made him an instant celebrity in England and provided all the proof in the world that Roanoke could not only work, but could pay for the expenses of Virginia colonization through privateering and make its investors a lot of money. In fact, after the abandonment of the first Roanoke, which had cost Raleigh and the other investors a fortune to plan and provision, it was only the seizure of the *Santa María de Vincinte* that gave the men hope that a second attempt was worth the cost. That one prize basically recouped all of their other losses. If more prizes like that were in its future, then Roanoke definitely deserved another shot.[16]

If Grenville's 1585 prize run through Roanoke proved to the English that piracy could work in Virginia, it was not news at all to Spanish authorities. For a long time now, they had suspected that something nefarious was afoot on the northern edges of La Florida. Reports made note of Grenville's stir in the neighborhood of Puerto Rico and Hispaniola. Although he scored only two small prizes, the ease of Grenville's cruise had officials in the Council of the Indies bemoaning the "great damage and plundering" which such corsairs continually carried out on Spanish trade, a damage that was growing every day and guaranteed to continue should the Englishmen succeed in their planting. Something had to be done to better protect Spain's Caribbean interests, a protection that extended to La Florida, "where it may be presumed that the corsairs . . . have gone to establish themselves."[17]

Admiral Álvaro de Bazán and others were quick to chime in once reports of the cruise spread. Aside Grenville were assuredly countless other pirates, which were "known to have left England for the Indies." There was no doubt "that their chief aim is a special effort to secure a foothold there." If they succeeded in doing so "help in the form of further settlers and ships will be readily forthcoming, and all this will contribute to increase their power on land and sea." He was not wrong, for not only was Drake making his way north from the Caribbean but Raleigh was on his way from England with supplies, shortly to be followed up by Grenville and a small fleet, all of whom would reach Roanoke in 1586. That meant that by 1587 Spanish fears were even graver, for by that time it would have seemed certain that several English voyages would have reinforced the outpost of unknown location, somewhere in La Florida. "If they make themselves masters of this position," went one account, "it will be a very severe blow to this crown" and would necessitate an immediate response against them, "so as to avoid leaving the Peruvian and New Spanish fleets exposed to so manifest a danger in their usual passage through that strait."[18]

Unbeknownst to Spanish authorities, Drake's 1586 arrival was the only one of any consequence, and it was upon his ships that most of the original Roanoke settlers evacuated. Drake knew about Roanoke and purposely made a call at the port, and when he realized the extent of the colony's woes he was fully prepared to offer Governor Ralph Lane provisions and men to reinforce it. A strong storm however, and possibly a hurricane, changed those plans, striking right as Drake was anchored off the Outer Banks. An entire ship packed with provisions and men meant for Lane was lost, and although Drake offered more help, for the beleaguered colonists it was clearly time to go. Instead of helping to build Roanoke back up, Drake's men helped tear it down. When Raleigh and Grenville arrived shortly after, they found a ghost colony.[19]

Spanish fears of a thriving pirate outpost turned out to be quite unfounded, but having Drake of all people call at Roanoke was an obvious and ominous sign of why exactly the English were trying to build a fortified military colony on the outskirts of La Florida. The fear of piracy had long influenced Spanish plans for La Florida, which had long proved worthless for any other economic or religious purpose. Drake embarrassed the Spanish and revealed the weaknesses of frontier outposts like St. Augustine and Santa Elena, which led to the abandonment of the latter garrison. As perhaps the smallest and most isolated of any official Spanish garrison anywhere in the Caribbean, St. Augustine's defensive capabilities were comical, and now it was the only one in La Florida. Still, it did serve valuable strategic goals. It asserted Spain's continued claim of La Florida and at least in theory protected the Gulf Stream, and Spanish authorities had no intention of relinquishing either of those things to a bunch of pirates.[20]

Plans for the re-settlement of Roanoke were soon in motion, creating fresh alarms. Another unnamed English expedition took a sugar-laden Spanish ship upon its departure, and it has been suggested that this was the expedition of Sir George Carey, who was on his way to begin the second Roanoke attempt in 1587. This time John White and more settlers were also in tow; White made port in Roanoke, setting into motion the Lost Colony mystery. This attempt, although occasioned by the presence of more civilian settlers and with a long-term civilian settlement in mind, was simply the vanguard. It would lead the way for a larger set of settlements which would produce, in the words of David Quinn, "a more or less self-contained supply depot, heavily defended, where ships could be stationed and revictualled for the continuing struggle in the Caribbean and against the Europe-bound Spanish fleets." White had aimed for the Chesapeake but was forced to land in the Outer Banks after his ship captain, anxious to begin the lucrative privateering phase of his own cruise, cut his reconnoitering voyage short. It was only for privateering, then, that the second failed Roanoke colony would share the same location of the first failed colony.[21]

Spanish authorities also tried to get to the bottom of things, but neither did they get very far. Philip II personally revoked the official leave he had previously granted the governor of La Florida, Pedro Menéndez Marqués, ordering him instead to stay in La Florida and help repulse such any English squatters that might show themselves. Small Spanish scouting expeditions soon made their way north on at least two separate occasions, searching the coast for signs of the rumored English outpost. Had they found it they most certainly would have finished it off, but they never found much. On their second voyage a detachment originally passed over the Outer Banks to enter the Chesapeake Bay. On the return south however, the ships entered inland from the Outer Banks and may have even found the abandoned Roanoke settlement, but there was not much left by that point. Spanish officials continued to bemoan some unknown privateering base into 1588 and 1589 even though it was, to history, somewhere in the process of disappearing.[22]

Meanwhile with the Anglo-Spanish war heating up, all merchant ships were ordered into the English navy in preparation for a Spanish assault, which materialized in the famous Spanish Armada engagement of 1588. While the battle was a massive success for the English, it came at the price of the abandonment of Roanoke and the settlers there. Men like White, Raleigh, and Watts tried to get relief ships across the ocean several times up to 1590, but they never quite materialized. One expedition was forced to turn back when the captain spent too much time privateering, and even when two small unrelated privateering fleets did make it to the Caribbean and up the east coast, for some reason they did not think to stop in Virginia. By that point it might have been too late anyway.[23]

The destruction of the Spanish armada in 1588 broke Spain's naval superiority and opened the privateering floodgates. One of the most intriguing ironies to the Lost Colony mystery, then, is that if help had come, or if the settlers somehow had been able to hold on until 1590, Roanoke almost certainly would have flourished; as far as piracy was concerned, the future looked bright indeed for Virginia. Drake and Hawkins both talked of calling at Virginia on their way to Newfoundland to deal the Spanish fishing fleets a crushing blow there, which if they timed it right they might "capture so many ships and Spaniards that they will not recover the loss for years." In the end, however, a relief voyage had to wait all the way into 1590, when White pushed off as a part of Watts's Caribbean expedition. After an electrifying privateering cruise, White finally returned to Roanoke only to behold the emptiness of Roanoke Island and the cryptic symbols that still lead historians and anthropologists searching coastal Virginia for evidence of the lost colony.[24] By that time the outpost was long gone; whoever was alive had melted into the Virginia wilderness.

While men like White or Raleigh rued the fate of the Roanoke settlers, the privateering war was only heating up in the 1590s, leaving enterprising gentry-pirates little time to search for bones in Virginia. That expedition was dead and gone, while many of the actors continued on. Watts and Raleigh were both back in the Caribbean in 1591 on another massive and massively successful Watts-led privateering cruise. It was rumored that Raleigh was intent on returning to Roanoke to continue searching it out, but it was unclear whether he did so. Legendary privateer Christopher Newport was a member of the 1585 expedition, and Spaniards would surely have named a saint day after his death had he been among the disappeared. To their chagrin he was not. Instead, he would haunt the Caribbean for another two decades and return to Virginia as a member of the Jamestown expedition.[25]

Like all good things, the glory days of the sea war did eventually end. James I assumed the throne in 1603 and pursued a more peaceful relationship with Spain. Virginia's future would be in natural resources and land speculation and no longer piracy, at least for the time.[26] As privateering faded into the distance, so did the Lost Pirate Colony of Roanoke.

Notes

1. General histories of the colony can be taken from Horn, *A Kingdom Strange*; Quinn, *Set Fair for Roanoke*; and Kupperman, *Roanoke*.

2. Kupperman, *Roanoke*, 15.

3. Pringle, *Jolly Roger*, 34-36; Andrews, *Elizabethan Privateering*, 5, 22-32; Horn, *A Kingdom Strange*, 11-15; Milton, *Big Chief Elizabeth*, 37-43.

4. Bradley, *British Maritime Enterprise*, 84-88; Rankin, *The Golden Age of Piracy*, 3; Andrews, *Elizabethan Privateering*, 6-10; Pringle, *Jolly Roger*, 26-27; Horn, *A Kingdom Strange*, 56-60; Hazlewood, *The Queen's Slave Trader*, 84-89; Quinn, *Set Fair for Roanoke*, 14-16.

5. Andrews, *Elizabethan Privateering*, 3-5, 10-15, 22-32; Pringle, *Jolly Roger*, 27-33.

6. Bernardo de Mendoza to Philip II, n. 134, in Quinn, ed., *The Roanoke Voyages*, 2: 758; Rankin, *The Golden Age of Piracy*, 3-4; Andrews, *Elizabethan Privateering*, 175-186.

7. Drake's Caribbean cruise is well documented, including Bradley, *British Maritime Enterprise*, 65-74, 91-101; Milton, *Big Chief Elizabeth*, 140-148; Hakluyt, *A Discourse Concerning Western Planting*, 64-67; Kamen, *Empire*, 88. For "Drago," see "Rumours of Drake in Florida," n. 130, in Quinn, ed., *The Roanoke Voyages*, 2: 752.

8. Andrews, *Elizabethan Privateering*, 18, 190-191; Horn, *A Kingdom Strange*, 27; Burrage, ed., *Early English and French Voyages*, 225.

9. Andrews, *Elizabethan Privateering*, 18, 18, 83-84; Horn, *A Kingdom Strange*, 15-16; Burrage, ed., *Early English and French Voyages*, 225.

10. Andrews, *Elizabethan Privateering*, 84-86, 88, 170, 172, 177-178, 180-181, 185-186; Bradley, *British Maritime Enterprise*, 108-110, 129-130; Elliott, *Empires*, 7-8; Kamen, *Empire*, 260-261; Weber, *The Spanish Frontier*, 87-88.

11. Andrews, *Elizabethan Privateering*, 187; Horn, *A Kingdom Strange*, 35-37.

12. Quinn, ed., *The Roanoke Voyages*, 1: 118; Horn, *A Kingdom Strange*, 62-64; Hakluyt, *A Discourse Concerning Western Planting*, 50; Hoffman, *A New Andalucia*, 291-293, 298-299; Merrell, *The Indian's New World*, 11; Sugden, *Sir Francis Drake*, 12-17.

13. Hakluyt, *A Discourse Concerning Western Planting*, 45, 64, 66; Elliott, *Empires*, 6-7, 9; Milton, *Big Chief Elizabeth*, 18, 71; Williamson, *Powhatan Lords*, 18; [Herle?] to Queen Elizabeth, n. 40, in Quinn, ed., *The Roanoke Voyages*, 1: 225.

14. Andrews, *Elizabethan Privateering*, 163, 191; Milton, *Big Chief Elizabeth*, 71-73, 76-82; Bradley, *British Maritime Enterprise*, 270-271; Horn, *A Kingdom Strange*, 63-64; Quinn, *Set Fair for Roanoke*, 40-41; Quinn, ed., *The Roanoke Voyages*, 1: 119-120.

15. Quinn, ed., *The Roanoke Voyages*, 1: 159-166; Quinn, *Set Fair for Roanoke*, 57-60; Kupperman, *Roanoke*, 20; Milton, *Big Chief Elizabeth*, 90-99; Horn, *A Kingdom Strange*, 64-70.

16. Quinn, ed., *The Roanoke Voyages*, 1: 169-170; Alvaro de Bazan, Marquis of Santa Cruz, to Philip II, n. 131, in Quinn, ed., *The Roanoke Voyages*, 2: 753; Bernardo de Mendoza to Philip II, n. 134, in Quinn, ed., *The Roanoke Voyages*, 2: 757-758; Quinn, *Set Fair for Roanoke*, 242; Andrews, *Elizabethan Privateering*, 192; Horn, *A Kingdom Strange*, 83-86; Kupperman, *Roanoke*, 26-27; Bradley, *British Maritime Enterprise*, 272.

17. The Relation of Hernando de Altamirano, n. 121, in Quinn, ed., *The Roanoke Voyages*, 2: 740-743; Council of the Indies to Philip II, n. 124, in Quinn, ed., *The Roanoke Voyages*, 2: 744; Rodrigo de Junco to the President of the Council of the Indies, n. 125, in Quinn, ed., *The Roanoke Voyages*, 2: 746-747.

18. Rodrigo de Junco to the President of the Council of the Indies, n. 125, in Quinn, ed., *The Roanoke Voyages*, 2: 746-747; Alvaro de Bazan, Marquis of Santa Cruz, to Philip II, n. 131, in Quinn, ed., *The Roanoke Voyages*, 2: 753-754; Hieronimo Lippomani to the Doge and Senate of Venice, n. 141, in Quinn, ed., *The Roanoke Voyages*, 2: 768.

19. Kupperman, *Roanoke*, 88-95; Milton, *Big Chief Elizabeth*, 148-151, 168-172; Bradley, *British Maritime Enterprise*, 273-274; Quinn, *Set Fair for Roanoke*, 130-149.

20. Andrews, *Elizabethan Privateering*, 187-188; Quinn, *Set Fair for Roanoke*, 62-63.

21. Miguel de Oquendo to Andres de Alva, n. 143, in Quinn, ed., *The Roanoke Voyages*, 2: 769-770; Quinn, *Set Fair for Roanoke*, 295-314 (quote on 297); Andrews, *Elizabethan Privateering*, 193-194; Bradley, *British Maritime Enterprise*, 274-275.

22. Quinn, ed., *The Roanoke Voyages*, 2: 772-775; Pedro Menendez Marques to Philip II, n. 146, in Quinn, ed., *The Roanoke Voyages*, 2: 778-781; Philip II to Pedro Menendez Marques, n. 126, in Quinn, ed., *The Roanoke Voyages*, 2: 748-749; Kupperman, *Roanoke*, 135-137; Quinn, *Set Fair for Roanoke*, 297-298.

23. Andrews, *Elizabethan Privateering*, 194; Quinn, *Set Fair for Roanoke*, 334-338.

24. Notation 2 in Gabriel de Luxan to Philip II, n. 140, in Quinn, ed., *The Roanoke Voyages*, 2: 767; Kupperman, *Roanoke*, 122-128; Bradley, *British Maritime Enterprise*, 276-277; Quinn, *Set Fair for Roanoke*, 315-334.

25. Andrews, *Elizabethan Privateering*, 164-167.

26. Bradley, *British Maritime Enterprise*, 312-314.

America's First Underground Railroad

THE STORY OF SOUTH CAROLINA REALLY BEGINS WITH THE STORY OF BARBADOS. A tiny island originally discovered and "pacified" by Spanish conquistadores at the turn of the sixteenth century, Barbados was one of the many relatively small Caribbean spits of land soon going ignored in the Spanish empire. Keen to focus on building up their holdings in the mineral-rich and already well-settled Viceroyalties of New Spain and Peru, colonial authorities focused their Caribbean efforts on Puerto Rico, Hispaniola, and Cuba. As they retreated from the rest, French, Dutch, and mostly English colonists slowly replaced them. England eventually gained an important prize in 1627 when settlers landed unopposed on Barbados.

English settlement there was originally overwhelmingly white. After enterprising planters discovered the island's suitability for sugar production around the middle of the seventeenth century, however, its population dynamic began to change rapidly. Economies of scale dominated sugar production—plantations grew in size and landholders shrunk in number as the successful ones quickly enlarged and consolidated their holdings. All of this, of course, was done increasingly on the backs of African slaves, and the British Caribbean, centered in Barbados and Jamaica, was soon the engine of the second Atlantic slave trade. By the second generation of Barbados's English colonial history, the island had an enslaved majority working massive plantations owned by a small colonial elite. When the opportunity for small land holders and new emigrants vanished, they looked elsewhere. As the island's governor wrote in 1680, people "no longer come to Barbados," and many of its inhabitants had departed for other places, "in hope of settling the land which they cannot obtain here." For many, the answer lay in the Carolinas. It was, essentially, Barbados's overflow colony.[1]

By that time Charles II had successfully reclaimed the English throne. A group of wealthy planters and merchants approached him not long after, hoping to cash in on their past loyalty to his father, Charles I. Men with familiar names to South Carolinians, including John and Peter Colleton, John Berkeley, George Carteret, and Anthony Ashley Cooper, were among the eight "Lords Proprietors" that Charles II rewarded with Carolina's original 1663 charter. A passerby would recognize such names across South Carolina, and particularly in the neighborhood of Charleston. Very early in its trajectory however it was the Barbadian contingent, led by the Colletons, Berkeleys, and their friends, who eyed the potential of the Carolina coast from the perspective of the overpopulated and under-provisioned Caribbean. It was for this reason historians have long referred to South Carolina as the "Colony of a Colony," a reference to its close connection to the Caribbean, and particularly to Barbados.[2]

The first attempts to make money in South Carolina came from the deerskin trade, timbering, and the ranching of feral hogs and cattle. Eventually it would become rice. At all steps the desire was to use Carolina's natural resources to produce goods for export, either to Europe or back to the Caribbean. Carolina's settlers, wrote historian Alan Gallay, "shared no common purpose but to accumulate riches," and without markets for their goods elsewhere in the English empire, Carolina probably never would have existed.[3]

Because South Carolina was always tied to Barbados, all of these money-making endeavors would naturally be tied to slavery and the Atlantic slave trade. Even before Charleston the earliest and unsuccessful attempts to entice planters to the Cape Fear River, near present-day Wilmington, included land grants for every slave transported from the Caribbean. The successful landing of British colonists at the site of Charleston in 1670 was also accompanied by enslaved Africans, who arrived with the very first waves of settlers. Within the first two years of Charleston's existence there were hundreds of slaves in the colony, amounting to upward of a third of all arrivals. South Carolina always was destined to be, to borrow a term coined by the renowned historian of slavery Ira Berlin, a "slave society"—a place where slavery would be the foundation upon which everything else was built.[4]

Only a few hundred miles down the coast was St. Augustine, where Spanish authorities were not ignorant of any of these troubling English developments. Charleston existed only miles up the shore from Santa Elena, which was one of the original targets for settlement by South Carolina's Proprietors and which, of course, had once been the very capital of La Florida itself. Although the proprietors settled on Charleston there were soon small English and Scottish settlements popping up to the south, and even near Santa Elena, which the English referred to as Port Royal. That was not only an affront to Spanish claims to La Florida but also dangerously close to the coastal Spanish missions that still existed on the coast of present-day Georgia.[5] Carolina was, in short, a squatter colony, and a dangerous one at that, and local Spanish authorities in St. Augustine recognized it as such. The Governor of La Florida made a few early attempts at breaking up the squatters, blockading Charleston and raiding the small plantations to the south, including the infamous 1686 Edisto Island raid. While the small outlying settlements suffered repeated attacks Charleston endured, a constant thorn in the Spanish side that St. Augustine's governors never seemed capable of destroying altogether.[6]

Beginning in the late 1680s, however, fate presented Diego de Quiroga, one of those governors, the opportunity to undercut the development of the Carolina colony in a uniquely La Florida way. The opportunity arrived in the form of a group of runaway slaves who showed up at St. Augustine's defenses in 1687 in a stolen canoe. Among them were eight men, two women, and a small child. Quiroga faced a dilemma. The slaves clearly came from South Carolina and their owners would certainly be wanting them back. On the other hand, the fugitives were requesting Catholic instruction and baptism, perhaps recognizing that by doing so they might gain their freedom. If that was the case then their gamble paid off. Quiroga obliged them, overseeing their baptism and even the marriage of some of them. He also put them to work. The men were soon working in the Castillo de San Marcos and the women were working as domestic servants in the Governor's own home. They worked not as enslaved people but were paid wages that were comparable to the wages Indian laborers were being paid for the same services. These were the first runaways to have nominally gained freedom by fleeing slavery in English South Carolina and finding their way to La Florida.[7]

The precedent set by the first eleven enslaved runaways and the response by Diego de Quiroga was a powerful one in the history of the Lowcountry, which as one historian explained "would shape the geopolitics of the Southeast and the Caribbean for years to come." When the emissary from South Carolina did arrive, as predicted, Quiroga declined to return the fugitives. They were now Christians, after all, and no longer slaves. He did offer to pay their worth in Spanish currency, a deal the English emissary was forced to accept. Yet that was not the end of things. In the next three years more runaways followed suit, fleeing to St. Augustine, and receiving freedom in return for Catholic instruction and service to the Crown. They grew so common that Quiroga requested a clarification on his developing policy from the Crown, which he received in 1693. By royal proclamation the Spanish King, ironically now also named Charles II, officially gave liberty to the fleeing slaves, "so that by their example and by my liberality others will do the same."[8] The order was as clear as day, generating a watershed moment in the Southeast that opened up what was, in effect, America's first Underground Railroad. It headed south, to La Florida.

Over the course of the next few decades a steady stream of runaway Carolina slaves arrived at the gates of St. Augustine. Although in a few instances they were sold to Spanish residents or even returned in acts of appeasement, those seemed to be the exception, and even then, seldom did such agreements work out to the Carolinians' satisfaction. The response by South Carolina legislators can be seen in the increasingly restrictive and brutal slave codes they passed. Three, in 1712, 1714, and 1722, reflected a critical period, right as the colony was transitioning to rice cultivation, the enslaved population was exploding, and the number of runaways to Florida was rising to alarming levels. Each of the three enlarged on the colony's original 1690 slave code, imported from Barbados, in ways that dealt specifically with the Lowcountry issues Carolinian authorities were being forced to address.[9]

Both the 1712 and 1722 laws, for instance, created controls on the movement of slaves, which included mandating them to carry passes or "tickets" in order to move among plantations. It allowed any white person to "beat, maim, or assault," or even kill a slave "who shall refuse to show his ticket, or by running away or resistance, shall avoid being apprehended or taken." Slave patrols were also authorized to ride down and capture runaways or any slave away from a plantation without such permission. On the one hand, slaves often left plantations for short periods of time for personal reasons, an irritating habit that slave owners still often tolerated, unofficially at least, in the interest of maintaining the status quo. It seems clear that these provisions in the 1712 and 1722 laws were meant to address instead the more alarming habit of running away in which slaves had no intention of returning, and which increasingly led them to La Florida.[10]

The 1712 law also codified increasingly brutal punishments which masters were required to administer to slaves guilty of attempting to run away, a sign that the problem was a significant one. An apathetic owner might even face financial penalties for failing to punish runaways in a swift-enough manner and could ultimately lose ownership of a particularly notorious runaway who had not, apparently, been dealt with harshly or quickly enough. For the slaves themselves that harshness intensified for a male with each unsuccessful attempt, from whipping for the first offense, to whipping and branding for the second offense, to whipping and having an ear cut off a third offense. Finally, for a fourth offense, the last before death, the guilty runaway was ordered to be "gelded." In other words, he would be castrated.[11]

As one historian suggested, castration was not only an unusually shocking punishment to be codified in the way South Carolina legislators ordered it. It was actually quite rare to see castration in writing anywhere. Not even in Jamaica or Barbados—the latter colony being the one that gifted South Carolina its first slave code—was "gelding" formally listed as a legitimate punishment in the law, even though plantation owners did on occasion castrate slaves accused of planning or orchestrating rebellions. While their punishment had been ad hoc in nature and usually wielded in moments of crisis, in South Carolina "gelding" was the law of the land.[12]

Worse yet, this violence was unique in the way it mirrored one of the colony's original industries—cattle ranching. Thousands of cattle roamed the Lowcountry scrub unattended until cattlemen, mostly enslaved African men, rounded them up from time to time, branded them to assert ownership, and castrated many of the young bulls. "Gelding," it turns out, was something enslaved African men had not only probably heard of, but a ranching act in which they regularly participated. By threatening prospective runaways with that exact same gruesome treatment, plantation owners were not simply animalizing slaves by comparing them to cattle. They threatened the men with a punishment that "would have been immediately recognizable and terrifying," as one historian wrote.[13]

But why would South Carolina's slave owning elite proscribe such a violent and often-deadly punishment for a crime that would not seem particularly dangerous? What about running away, even repeatedly, deserved castration? The severity of the punishment, perhaps, reflected the anxiety that runaways were causing Carolinians at a pivotal time in the colony's growth, threatening to undermine the institution of chattel slavery just as it was beginning to define labor in the region. As the number of runaways continued rising across the turn of the century, and La Florida authorities increasingly refused to return them or even pay for them, South Carolina legislators turned to increasingly brutal punishments for their deterrent factor, a familiar trend in English slave codes.[14] Drastic times called for drastic measures. South Carolina authorities also made it clear that the punishment did not just exist theoretically on paper, either. The first three enslaved men to be castrated in accordance with the law were done so within a year of the 1712 ordinance, and a slave owner was later reimbursed for one of the men, named Cyrus, which meant he was either killed in the act or so seriously maimed by it that he was no longer functional. The three men that were punished so severely had been caught attempting to escape to St. Augustine.[15]

Such acts of deterrence did not achieve their objective, creating instead more desperate and violent attempts at flight. Runaways not only increased, but so did incidents of armed resistance, which were reported in 1711, 1714, and then during the Yamasee War, when groups of slaves joined in the Native uprising that almost wiped Charleston off the map. These fears seemed to peak in 1720 when a particularly dangerous conspiracy was uncovered outside of Charleston. Accounts referenced slaves "rising with a design to destroy all the white people in the country and then to take the town in full body." At least some of the slaves declared they were trying to make their way directly to St. Augustine.[16] Only a year after the dust of that uprising had settled, Carolina legislators passed the 1722 slave code, which included expanded and hardened rules that it would seem came as a direct result of the chaos of the past decade.

Both the 1712 and 1722 laws dealt with the increasing likelihood of slaves wielding weapons against their masters; yet the second act, coming on the heels of the 1720 uprising, was considerably more detailed. Slave patrols were allowed to seize any weapon a slave might have on them if they did not also have express written permission for carrying that weapon for some legitimate reason, for the purpose of say hunting. Patrols could also enter any plantation they wanted, and forcefully enter and search whatever slave cabins they wanted, in the search for illegal or unaccounted-for weapons, from hunting rifles to swords and knives. In order to ensure that weapons did not accidentally fall into the hands of slaves, "every master or head of any family" was required to keep "all his guns and other arms, when out of use, in a room locked up," and could be charged with neglect if they did not.

While whippings and brandings were authorized for lesser crimes, the more "heinous or grievous" felony crimes like murder, robbery, or arson were to be dealt with immediately. Added to this in both the 1712 and 1722 ordinances were any slaves that "shall make mutiny or insurrection or rise in rebellion against the authority and government of this Province." Planning any such uprising by collecting "arms, powder, bullets, or offensive weapons, in order to carry on such mutiny or insurrection," was to be dealt with similarly, as was holding "any confederacy or conspiracy for raising such mutiny, insurrection or rebellion." All of these charges demanded an immediate trial and, upon a guilty verdict, immediate execution "by the common or any other executioner, in such manner as they shall think fit; the kind of death to be inflicted to be left to their judgment and discretion."[17] By creating open-ended death sentences, the laws certainly left slaves guilty of insurrection vulnerable to gruesome, public displays of violence, no doubt orchestrated to terrify others and, hopefully, dissuade future attempts. Of the 1720 conspirators, "many of them taken prisoners and some burnt some hang'd and some banish'd." More were being held in a nearby settlement and would be "executed as soon as they came down," no doubt in a similarly public and brutal fashion.[18]

The reason for such draconian and barbaric laws continued to be—partially, at least—the threat posed by La Florida. "Of the various sources of outside agitation," wrote noted historian Peter Wood, "none seemed so continually threatening" as St. Augustine. That was particularly so after the first major slave uprising in 1720, in which slaves directly referenced the Catholic sanctuary as their motivation. Spaniards were using South Carolina's most dangerous weaknesses—a majority population of slaves in the colony and those slaves' natural resistance to their bondage—against their English foe, and it was working. Each slave lost to South Carolina planters constituted not only a loss of property; news of that loss threatened to spread to surrounding plantations like a virus, inspiring more fugitives to flee and now apparently even fomenting insurrection.[19] La Florida was the engine that drove South Carolina planters mad with fear of violent uprising, and with rage against the Spanish for setting their enslaved population against them.

None of the increasingly elaborate and violent systems of control concocted in Charleston, however, seemed to matter as the Underground Railroad into La Florida sped up. Multiple complaints about runaways were made in 1722, the same year the colonial assembly passed the most comprehensive and brutal slave code yet. Two years later Yamasee Indians guided another ten slaves to St. Augustine, who upon questioning made it clear they had heard of the Spanish offer of freedom in exchange for Catholic instruction. Fourteen more fled from the area of Stono and four more from the neighborhood of Port Royal, both in 1726. A year later another group escaped from near Hilton Head, and they apparently carried English prisoners with them to St. Augustine. Carolina authorities had responded by offering higher bounties for finding runaways. Militias and slave patrols were increased. Still, more slaves ran.[20]

Not only did Charleston's responses to St. Augustine disappoint in the 1720s, but in 1733 royal Spanish authorities answered back, with Charles II issuing a second royal proclamation even stronger than the first. Although it would take years for Spanish authorities to fully implement the new edict and spread it throughout the colony, in no uncertain terms it continued the trend begun in 1693, freeing runaways and ordering Governors to refuse compensation to their English owners.[21] By continuing to offer freedom to Carolina's slaves, royal authorities at all levels were doubling down on their controversial approach to Charleston, undermining the developing institution of slavery in South Carolina as it became, by the 1730s, one of the most enslaved places in the English colonies.

What was already a terrible situation for Carolinians only continued to deteriorate with the expansion of St. Augustine's black militia and the establishment of Fort Mose. Mixed militia units were part of Spanish colonial custom on every corner of the New World, a tradition that continued into La Florida. That tradition went as far back as the founding of St. Augustine, when Africans served as auxiliaries in Spanish and Native units. Not only were some of America's first militias a mix of Spaniards and Natives, but they also included Africans. In 1683 a group of African men were organized into a militia, which three years later was involved in the raiding of Edisto Island and the plantations south of Charleston when it was reported that "one hundred fifty-three [Spaniards], Indians and Mulattos" had "fallen upon the out skirts of our settlement and burnt and plundered some houses." They affected the escape of more than a dozen slaves as well. Decades later, by the 1720s, runaways were returning north as part of that same Spanish militia, many times working in concert with Spanish-aligned Native warriors and even sometimes with Spanish soldiers. They sacked plantations and pulled away more of Carolina's slaves. "They have found a new way of sending our own slaves against us," South Carolina Governor Arthur Middleton wrote, "to rob and plunder us."[22]

The empowering of runaway slaves was the best example of what one historian considered a La Florida version of the Spanish policy of *repoblación*, the act of protecting territory threatened by a competing foreign power by populating it with armed settlers. Spanish governors had already instituted similar policies using slaves elsewhere in the Caribbean. On Hispaniola, authorities established freed slaves from St. Dominique—the French half of the same island—in an autonomous village on the outskirts of Santo Domingo. On Trinidad they set up a haven for regional runaways, declaring that "all blacks who came seeking faith from whichever of the foreign nations that occupy the lands of this Kingdom must enjoy freedom." Runaways from across the Caribbean basin were likewise integrated into Puerto Rico, Cuba, Guatemala, and Venezuela. What Quiroga set in motion in St. Augustine, it turns out, was a tried-and-true tactic of using fugitive slaves to undermine nearby colonial rivals.[23]

All of these havens were based at least ostensibly on Catholic conversion and Christian civilization. While Church officials would have looked approvingly upon the saving of such souls, St. Augustine's governors, like those elsewhere in the Caribbean, also had clear strategic plans for the runaways. They had no problem arming and organizing fugitive slaves defensively into militia units; for the chronically understaffed St. Augustine garrison, such service was not just helpful, but indispensable. And for the recently freed slaves, the opportunity to defend their newly found freedom by force of arms was something most would probably embrace passionately, and indeed, African militiamen served honorably in the defense of St. Augustine and its surroundings during several English invasions. Using freed slaves defensively turned out to be one of the most mutually beneficial arrangements ever made in the Spanish colonial world, and nowhere was that more obvious than in La Florida.

As South Carolinians soon disparaged, many times these men and women also acted offensively. They were encouraged to return north to cause whatever trouble they could, sacking plantations and bringing away more runaways. They knew the contours of the swampy Lowcountry as good as the local Natives. They probably spoke English and soon might speak Spanish and would be able to spread the word about St. Augustine through South Carolina's plantations. Nothing could be more insulting and threatening to English planters than to have recently freed slaves lurking about their plantations, enticing more of their laborers to flee.[24]

While St. Augustine's black militia bad been a thorn in Charleston's side since the late seventeenth century, the threat of it expanded rapidly in 1738 when the new Spanish proclamation of freedom was finally operating in full effect. That year a group of runaways petitioned La Florida's newest governor, Manuel de Montiano, for land, which he eventually granted. This would be the basis for Gracia Real de Santa Teresa de Mose, known simply as Fort Mose, a heavily fortified free African community just to the north of St. Augustine. The center of the settlement was a small but traditional contemporary fort, which was built with royal engineering. Montiano fed the town's residents while the fortifications were built and while the first crops were being sown. Because of the town's favorable location in hardwood stands and along a saltwater creek, however, it did not take long for Mose to develop into a prosperous and largely self-sufficient community, complete with a Catholic friar who lived in the settlement and provided ongoing religious services to its people.[25]

While certainly designed to be a permanent free settlement, Mose was above all else defensive in nature. The community was positioned along the road that approached St. Augustine from the north, designating its small fortification as one of St. Augustine's several lines of defense. While one of many free black communities in the Spanish New World, Mose was perhaps the best example anywhere of *repoblación*, and royal Spanish officials approved of Montiano's actions. The town was home to many of the members of St. Augustine's black militia, and almost every single person that lived had at one point been enslaved in South Carolina. Not only did Mose contribute to the defense of St. Augustine, it served as a beacon of freedom that made life terrible for South Carolina's slave owners. Although the number of residents in the town was never too large, usually hovering near one hundred, the impact it had on the region was tremendous.[26]

The same year the fortification of Mose was under construction a group of twenty-three slaves fled Port Royal and made it to St. Augustine, while another large group ran from St. Helena Parish, south of Charleston. Despite strenuous complaints lodged by their owners the runaways were not returned, and instead most likely restarted their lives at Mose. Early the next year another four slaves, thought to be cattlemen, fled on stolen horses, evidently killing a white overseer and wounding another in the process. Although Carolinians again remonstrated to Montiano, they got nowhere. Spanish policy by that time had been set in stone, leading Lieutenant Governor William Bull to complain that the runaways were causing tremendous anxiety among the planters, who found "their property now become so very precarious and uncertain," and South Carolina's government was basically powerless to do anything about it.

As Bull described it, the source of that misery was clearly La Florida. The edict "having been published at St. Augustine declaring freedom to all Negroes, and other slaves, that shall desert from the English Colonies, has occasioned several parties to desert from this Province by both Land and Water," and despite every effort to track them down, they "have been able to make their escape." In response the South Carolina legislature increased bounties for runaways, including for their scalps. Evidently the return of a runaway was now just as good dead as alive. Around that same time authorities also had two recently apprehended runaways made example of in town. One man was publicly whipped and another publicly executed in the center of Charleston and in front of a group of other slaves. The condemned man gave a speech to the assembled group "exhorting them to be just, honest, and virtuous, and to take warning by his unhappy Example." After his execution his body was "hung in chains" on the river as a show of deterrence, "in sight of all Negroes passing and repassing by water."[27]

As with before, however, this well-orchestrated show of violence and terror deterred no one. Fort Mose was having exactly the effect Spanish authorities had hoped it would. All of these disturbing trends appeared to come to a head late in 1739 in what would become known as the Stono Rebellion. One of English America's first major slave insurrections, it ended in the death of over twenty whites and more than double that number of slaves. It was also the product of La Florida.

In the weeks leading up to the revolt, rumblings of conspiracy ranged up the Carolina coast all the way to Winyah Bay, well north of Charleston. Smallpox and Yellow Fever were sowing chaos in the colony and there were reports that slave owners, in response to the increasing frequency of runaways, were acting even more brutally towards their slaves in an attempt to scare them away from running. Anxiety and conspiracy were rampant, and as it turned out, well-founded.[28] Although most of the bloodshed was over in one day the failure of the rebellion was not immediately apparent to anyone in the region. Dozens of suspected rebels were snatched up by militia units in the following days and immediately and sometimes brutally killed, "some shot, some hang'd and some Gibbeted alive," the last punishment referring to the act of caging up and leaving the condemned hanging in very visible places to slowly die of exposure. A punishment usually reserved for pirates, the gibbeting of the accused rebels along the road continued the habit of making executions as public and terrifying as possible. Still, militiamen did not catch up to the remaining insurgents for several more days, at which point a second pitched battle took place. Even that seemingly conclusive victory, however, brought the white residents of the Lowcountry little comfort. Alarms continued to spread through the region for weeks and even months. Straggling runaways were captured, tried, and summarily executed. Militia units continued their patrols and owners removed their families from exposed plantations. Every whisper, in the shadow of Stono, stoked regional fears.[29]

These years, for white Carolinians, proved transformative. While on the one hand Stono enticed legislators to pull back a bit from some of the harshest provisions of previous slave codes, it also contributed to the sweeping Negro Act of 1740, which would set the conditions for the growth of slavery in the Lowcountry for another century. While the new code had been under debate for some time, it took the crisis of Stono to unite legislators around many of its new provisions, which dealt specifically with the freedoms many slaves had enjoyed in unofficial but still very real ways. No longer would slaves be able to assemble amongst themselves freely, hunt or grow their own food, earn their own money, or even learn English. Slave autonomy, in short, was at an end. The new codes also effectively ended manumission, ending the threat of freedmen in the midst of slavery, requiring individual legislative acts to authorize the granting of freedom to a slave. On the heels of Stono these changes constituted a watershed moment in the hardening of slavery in early British America.[30]

To the extent Stono had been inspired by St. Augustine, then so was everything that came in its wake. "It is hoped these measures will prevent any Negroes from getting down to the Spaniards," one man wrote, referring to all the militia patrols and other security measures regional authorities had implemented in the wake of the uprising. Less a revolution and more a particularly violent effort to leave the province in force—one massive, armed, and ultimately unsuccessful runaway attempt—Stono was the culmination of a half-century's worth of carefully orchestrated Spanish policies designed to weaken South Carolina. South Carolinians were quick to blame Spaniards for Stono just as they had blamed them for all the runaways that preceded it. "I hope our government will order effectual methods for the taking of St. Augustine from the Spaniards which is now become a great detriment to this province by the encouragement & protection given by them to our negroes that run away there," one complain went, lodged only weeks afterward Stono. "An insurrection" had just happened, the man continued, "in order to their going there." A larger and more official report made years later told the same tale, that "the Negroes would not have made this Insurrection had they not depended on St. Augustine for a Place of Reception afterward was very certain; and that the Spaniards had a Hand in promoting them to this particular Action there was but little room to doubt."[31]

Harsh reprisals followed, from both South Carolina and from Spain's newest English neighbor to the north, Georgia. Those reprisals coincided with the outbreak of war between England and Spain, prompting more fear. "If such an attempt is made in a time of peace," William Bull asked, referring again to Stono, "what might be expected if an Enemy Should appear upon our Frontier with a design to invade us?" Those worries provided all the authority Georgia's Proprietor and military commander, General James Oglethorpe, needed to launch a full-scale invasion of La Florida in 1740. After capturing the nearby frontier posts, Oglethorpe set his eyes on the Castillo de San Marcos and went through Fort Mose to get to it. Although his men did capture Mose, they lost it soon after in a Spanish counterattack led largely by the black militia that used to live there. The battle was a brutal one and a decisive victory for the Spanish, collapsing Oglethorpe's siege and earning the black militiamen of Fort Mose praise from Governor Montiano for their bravery.[32]

When Montiano mounted his own counterassault, he envisioned the black militia playing an even more important role, ranging the English plantations, arming slaves, and hopefully fomenting widespread slave insurrection. His superior in Cuba even added the offer of land to those slaves who would rise up and assist in the Spanish invasion. It was an ambitious plan that would certainly have resulted in the real carnage William Bull feared, had Montiano had the opportunity to implement it. Instead, Oglethorpe routed the Spanish assault force sent north to take Santa Elena, stopping them in their tracks on St. Simon's Island on the coast of Georgia. The loss was demoralizing, putting a halt to Montiano's plans for the black militia as it put a halt to the entire invasion. Eventually English and Spanish forces in the region settled into a local stalemate, and the war of which their fighting was a part, the War of Jenkin's Ear, moved out of the region.[33]

Despite its gallant defense Fort Mose, like St. Augustine's other outlying forts, was left by the end of the war in bad repair. The town's residents were relocated into St. Augustine where they lived for more than a decade. In the meantime, runaways began to arrive again. Unfortunately for the Mose refugees, who enjoyed their time within the city walls, St. Augustine's leadership was not interested in that kind of cultural development and determined that Mose should be rebuilt and the black families moved back outside the city. This was ordered by Governor Fulgencio García de Solís in the early 1750s and accepted the black settlers only under threat of violence. Although they had grown accustomed to living in the city and were not at all interested in the move, Mose's inhabitants had no choice but to serve once more as St. Augustine's last line of defense, which they did. Fort Mose was rebuilt and a community was reestablished in its midst. Once again, a fugitive community existed on the frontier of the Lowcountry; although it would be a stretch to say it flourished, not much else in La Florida did either. Yet Mose, like St. Augustine, endured for another decade.[34]

Mose was only broken up permanently in 1763 with the rest of St. Augustine. At the conclusion of the French and Indian War Spain traded La Florida for the return of the far more coveted island of Cuba, which had fallen to the British late in the war. In response to the evacuation order, Melchor Feliú, La Florida's last Spanish governor for twenty years, transported Mose's residents to Cuba for resettlement along with the rest of St. Augustine's near three thousand residents. That departure finally ended more than two decades of America's first free black community, and over seventy-five years of America's original Underground Railroad, both of which were in La Florida.[35]

Notes

1. Wood, *Black Majority*, 6-9; Navin, *The Grim Years*, 16-44, 70-71; Roberts and Beamish, "Venturing Out," 49-72.

2. Crane, *The Southern Frontier*, 4-5; Navin, *The Grim Years*, 45-57.

3. Wood, *Black Majority*, 28-34; Gallay, *Indian Slave Trade*, 3, 5.

4. Wood, *Black Majority*, 15-17, 20-25; Navin, *The Grim Years*, 50-57; Berlin, *Many Thousands Gone*, 8.

5. Crane, *The Southern Frontier*, 3-8.

6. Gallay, *Indian Slave Trade*, 71-72, 82-84; Landers, *Black Society*, 23; Landers, "Gracia Real de Santa Teresa de Mose," 13; Crane, *The Southern Frontier*, 9-10; Navin, *The Grim Years*, 54.

7. Landers, *Black Society*, 24-25; Landers, "Gracia Real de Santa Teresa de Mose," 14; Landers, "Africans and Native Americans," 58.

8. Landers, *Black Society*, 25; Gallay, *Indian Slave Trade*, 86-87.

9. Landers, *Black Society*, 26-27; Navin, *The Grim Years*, 97-105; Jennings, "Cutting One Another's Throats," 129-133.

10. These laws are laid out in *Statutes*, 7: 352-375; Berlin, *Many Thousands Gone*, 67-71; Jennings, "Cutting One Another's Throats," 129-133.

11. McCord, *The Statutes at Large of South Carolina*, 7: 360; Navin, *The Grim Years*, 113-115; Jennings, "Cutting One Another's Throats," 129-131.

12. Rugemer, *Slave Law*, 71-73; Woodard, *The Republic of Pirates*, 58-59.

13. Rugemer, *Slave Law*, 71-73; Helg and Vernaug, *Slave No More*, 53; Berlin, *Many Thousands Gone*, 67-68.

14. The sparsely settled, swampy mazes of the Lowcountry made it relatively easy to run away. Perhaps slave owners should have provided slaves with more autonomy in an effort to keep them from rolling the dice on St. Augustine. Instead local authorities moved in the other direction and quickly, mandating harsher and harsher punishments as the means to maintain order. Berlin, *Many Thousands Gone*, 67-70.

15. Rugemer, *Slave Law*, 73; Landers, "Gracia Real de Santa Teresa de Mose," 15.

16. Wood, *Black Majority*, 298-299; Navin, *The Grim Years*, 111-112; Landers, "Africans and Native Americans," 59.

17. McCord, *The Statutes at Large of South Carolina*, 7: 352-375. All of the relevant codes can be seen in *Statutes*, 7: 343-375.

18. Wood, *Black Majority*, 298-299.

19. Landers, *Black Society*, 25-26.

20. Wood, *Black Majority*, 304-306; Landers, *Black Society*, 26-27; Landers, "Africans and Native Americans," 59-60; Crane, *Southern Frontier*, 244-245.

21. Wood, *Black Majority*, 306; Landers, *Black Society*, 27-28; Berlin, *Many Thousands Gone*, 73.

22. *Records in the British Public Record Office*, 2: 184; *Records in the British Public Record Office*, 4: 89; Landers, *Black Society*, 22-24; Landers, "Gracia Real de Santa Teresa de Mose," 13-14; Landers, "Africans and Native Americans," 58; Crane, *The Southern Frontier*, 31-32; Berlin, *Many Thousands Gone*, 65; Rivers, *Slavery in Florida*, 3; Halbirt, "La Ciudad de San Agustin," 40-41.

23. Landers, *Black Society*, 25-26; Helg and Vernaug, *Slave No More*, 57-58.

24. Landers, *Black Society*, 25-26; Vinson and Restall, "Black Soldiers, Native Soldiers," 22-25; Landers, "Gracia Real de Santa Teresa de Mose," 10-12, 15; Berlin, *Many Thousands Gone*, 72; Helg and Vernaug, *Slave No More*, 57; Rivers, *Slavery in Florida*, 3-4.

25. Landers, *Black Society*, 29-32; Landers, "Gracia Real de Santa Teresa de Mose," 17-18; Landers, "Africans and Native Americans," 60; Siebert, "Slavery and White Servitude," 3-4.

26. Landers, *Black Society*, 30-31; Landers, "Gracia Real de Santa Teresa de Mose," 11, 18; Wood, *Black Majority*, 310-311; Berlin, *Many Thousands Gone*, 74.

27. Landers, *Black Society*, 33-34; Landers, "Gracia Real de Santa Teresa de Mose," 19; Smith, ed., *Stono*, 13-14; Wood, *Black Majority*, 284, 311-312; Siebert, "Slavery and White Servitude," 4.

28. Wood, *Black Majority*, 311-314.

29. Wood, *Black Majority*, 318-323; Smith, ed., *Stono*, 12, 19.

30. Wood, *Black Majority*, 324; Berlin, *Many Thousands Gone*, 73-74; Helg and Vernaug, *Slave No More*, 59-60; Smith, ed., *Stono*, 20-27; Jennings, "Cutting One Another's Throats," 132-133.

31. Smith, ed., *Stono*, 9, 15, 28-29.

32. Smith, ed., *Stono*, 17; Berlin, *Many Thousands Gone*, 74; Landers, *Black Society*, 35-38; Landers, "Gracia Real de Santa Teresa de Mose," 19-20.

33. Landers, *Black Society*, 38-39; Landers, "Gracia Real de Santa Teresa de Mose," 21-22; Landers, "Africans and Native Americans," 61-62; Mulroy, *Freedom on the Border*, 8-10.

34. Landers, *Black Society*, 45-53; Landers, "Gracia Real de Santa Teresa de Mose," 23-30.

35. Landers, *Black Society*, 56-60; Siebert, "Slavery and White Servitude," 5.

Deerskin Diplomacy

THE CLOSE OF THE YAMASEE WAR IN 1717 LEFT THE SOUTHEAST IN RUINS. THE conflict, largely the product of unscrupulous English traders and a slave-raiding system they built, had exploded upon the Southeast in 1715. Two years of attacks and counterattacks devastated Native communities in the Carolinas. It left countless Carolina traders dead, and the backcountry abandoned. Far worse, however, was the situation to the south, where the war marked the end of a decades-long assault on Spanish La Florida that had effectively rendered it an uninhabited wasteland. The Spanish mission system was gone and thousands of Natives captured, freighted out of the province, and sold into slavery. The Native Southeast stood utterly transformed. Communities of all sorts—Native and Euro-American, were left to pick up the pieces of their collapsed worlds and try to reassert their influence.[1]

After the collapse of the slave trade, English merchants reverted back to what had made them money in the past—animal skins. Although European merchants would pay something for almost any animal pelt, the white-tailed deer was far and away the most popular. If processed correctly, quality deer leather had a luxurious feel that closely resembled suede. Natives knew how to produce skins in such ways for themselves, fashioning skirts, leggings, bedding, and other clothing or household products that their people had relied on for generations. Europeans not only also appreciated the soft and supple texture of the finished product, but depended upon deerskins when cow hides were not so easy to come by. One of those moments of shortage arrived, ironically enough, right before the Yamasee War. A terrible plague spread through European cattle herds, prompting European countries like England to closely control and even ban the production of cow leather altogether.[2] The situation after the close of the Yamasee War was, it turns out, perfect for the reintroduction of the large-scale deerskin trade.

Previously, Mississippian hunters harvested deer to supplement their otherwise corn-based diets. As the Mississippian world expanded and the population density of the Southeast increased, resource competition and overhunting drove white-tailed deer to scarcity. Naturally, with the collapse of the Mississippian world, overhunting was no longer a problem. As Native hunters disappeared, white-tail numbers rebounded, again filling Southeastern forests. By the time Europeans introduced a market for deerskins a century later, there was no shortage in the Colonial Southeast.[3] With eager merchants and ambitious traders willing to reenter Creek communities and reestablish trading relationships, the conditions for a thriving deerskin trade were set. Economics drove diplomacy, business, and even life in the Southeast, and largely in terms of white-tailed deer.[4] From the turn of the eighteenth century to the outbreak of the war in 1715, South Carolina merchants exported over fifty thousand dressed deerskins annually. With a war against the producers of the trade raging, naturally the market on skins fell apart. With peace in 1717 it quickly rebounded, however, bringing tremendous returns for merchants. Native hunters ranged the Southeast and returned to the coast with 160,000 deerskins in 1748 alone. As British agent John Stuart approximated later in the century, the total number was much higher—close to one million pounds of deerskins were produced annually by Native hunters from the entirety of the Southeast.[5]

Far more consequential than the production of fine leather for the London market were the European tools gained by Natives in the barter. Traders from English, Spanish, and even French merchants traveled into Native communities packed down with everything from shoes, clothing, and thick blankets; to metal farm implements, knives, and cooking utensils; to hunting rifles, powder, and munitions. Last but certainly not least, there was also rum. The transformative impact of these wares is almost impossible to comprehend by modern-day sensibilities. No longer would Natives dress in buckskins, hunt with bows and arrows, eat in clay pots, or cut with stone tools. They would dress in lighter, cooler cotton clothing. They hunted with guns, and prepared and ate food with knives and metal tools. As British agent John Stuart would explain only a generation later, "a modern Indian cannot subsist without Europeans; And would handle a Flint Ax or any other rude utensil used by his ancestors very awkwardly; So that what was only Conveniency at first is now become Necessity."[6]

Unfortunately for Native communities, Stuart was not kidding when he referred to the trade in the 1760s as a "necessity." Dressed deer skins were never equal in worth to what Natives wanted for them. A smoothbore musket, one of the pricier items in the trade but no less a critical one, cost a hunter a tall stack of deer skins, something which might take an entire season to procure. The resulting drive for animal pelts, basically the only thing Natives were able to produce for the Atlantic market, took a toll on their culture and the environment in several ways that built over time with devastating effect. From a diplomatic perspective, as Stuart had recognized, the trade left Natives dependent on Europeans for the goods they got used to having but could not produce themselves. It was a dependency Europeans were keen to weaponize. If a community did anything that angered colonial officials, either legitimately or illegitimately, officials could simply cut off the town's trade. Halting the flow of gunpowder and lead ball alone could cripple a community, leaving hunters without any ability to support or even defend themselves. Such a stoppage put incredible pressure on communities that usually produced quick results for colonial officials; Native communities had no other choice but to acquiesce to their trading partners, even though they often saw such acts as acts of war. The relationship was clearly not one of equality, as many Native peoples had hoped to frame the trade.

Far more troubling, the astronomical number of deerskins needed to fuel the trade led to unsustainable hunting practices that quickly pushed white-tailed deer once more towards disappearance. Most hunters bought European trade items on credit, and when they went farther from home for extended periods of time and still came back with insufficient numbers of pelts to satisfy those debts, they found themselves on the wrong side of merchants' ledgers. The trade not only made Native people dependent on goods they could not manufacture themselves, but it saddled them in cycles of debt they could never hope to repay. That reversal led one scholar of Creek history to recall ironically how the deerskin trade "propelled the people through a time of riches and power unparalleled in their history" to end up "in a dependence so debilitating" that it basically meant the end of them. Although it would take generations, there would come a time when Creeks could not defend themselves against Euro-American expansionists when they began demanding land cessions to satisfy trade debts. Eventually, removal was the end result.[7]

Although these systemic trade inequalities would ultimately devastate most of the Southeast's Native communities, most of that decline would take place far later in the eighteenth century, two full generations or more after traders brought the market hunting of white-tailed deer to the region. Until that point it was the "time of riches and power unparalleled in their history"—the glory days of the deerskin trade—which made Native peoples like Creeks powerful political and economic players that helped shape the Colonial Southeast for generations. Yet this was only possible because the British were not the only Europeans in the

Southeast. This was also a time of La Florida resurgence, setting into motion a dramatic period of Native autonomy known as play-off diplomacy.[8]

For Native groups like Creeks, play-off diplomacy was all about options. With at least two separate imperial powers competing with each other for Creek trade and alliances, communities had choices. If an individual Creek community had the ability to turn away from one European trader when the relationship grew unfair and be welcomed and courted generously by a direct competitor, then no one imperial power would be able to corner that community diplomatically to establish hegemony. Meanwhile, competition for Creek hunters drove the price of the trade down and kept English merchants in check. In other words, traders could never abuse their Native trading partners too badly if their Native trading partners could simply walk away; as long as the Spanish remained in La Florida, Creeks could always threaten to walk away from their British allies.[9]

Creeks were only one of the several strong Native groups in the Southeast to produce deerskins for the market and benefit for decades from play-off diplomacy. Choctaws lived a bit farther to the west and Chickasaws to the northwest. Both of the latter groups benefited from French competition in ways that allowed them to articulate their own neutrality policy for decades. France was also involved in Creek diplomacy from New Orleans, Mobile, and Fort Toulouse, yet in this story it was the Spanish in La Florida that provided the strongest check on the expanding British, making the play-off system work for Creeks and forestalling dependency for decades.[10]

Up to the point of the Yamasee War, Creeks had traded exclusively with the British, to the detriment of La Florida and the eventual destruction of its Native peoples. The attempt by Spaniards to extend the mission system north in the 1680s and resulting Creek antagonism prompted the large-scale relocation of many Creek communities from the Chattahoochee River valley north, towards Carolina, a pivotal move in the abandonment of the Spanish. It was a disastrous diplomatic move away from La Florida that chilled Creek-Spanish relations for decades and played a critical role in the slave trade. Eventually, however, many of those same Creeks saw the downside in their unilateral dependence on increasingly abusive British traders, who were quick to turn on and even enslave their debtors. It was only when Creek communities ultimately backed away from the Yamasee War, when a regional peace was possible.[11]

Despite peace with Carolinians in 1717, Creek eyes had been opened. The past generation of trade abuses and violence had shaped them in ways that would make them forever wary of the British, even if they still favored their trade goods over their Spanish or French competitors. Never again would Creek communities be pawns in a larger geopolitical game over which they had no control. Several of these headmen, led by a Creek leader by the name of Brims, soon approached Spanish authorities in La Florida, hoping to renew old alliances. That seemed clearly to be the desire when many of the same Creeks that had picked up their homes after the Spanish attacks in 1685 and moved closer to South Carolina, soon moved back. As many Creek headmen had come to realize, the British were no bargain either. That enticed the leaders of many of the same communities to St. Augustine who, only a few decades earlier, had been instrumental in burning the entire La Florida Spanish mission system to the ground. By pulling themselves away from Charleston and bringing their communities back to the frontier of La Florida and into the Spanish orbit, these headmen initiated a power shift that instantly made La Florida relevant again.[12]

That renewed Spanish counterpoint, however unequal St. Augustine would always be to Charleston or Pensacola to Savannah, was still enough for a play-off system to emerge and even flourish. For Creeks like Brims, all they had to do was utter the word Spain, and their bargaining power with the British improved almost instantly. And if Spaniards could use Creeks to undermine English growth in the Southeast, then so be it, and so Spanish authorities welcomed Creek peace envoys with open arms and with generous supplies of trade goods. As early as 1715, in fact, right at the outbreak of violence, Creek and Yamasee ambassadors traveled to St. Augustine to meet with the governor. A year later a Creek diplomatic envoy again traveled to St. Augustine, inviting Spaniards north to broker a new friendship. When Governor Don Pedro de Olivera y Fullano obliged them and sent a Spanish officer and four soldiers north up the Chattahoochee River in a diplomatic mission, it was the first time a Spanish officer had done so in two decades. Creek people began appearing at Pensacola as well, looking for trade goods and, perhaps, peace.[13]

Coalescent societies like Creeks were constructed well for playing this sort of game. While Creeks represented a tightly knit people who shared strong cultural and social connections, individual communities could still look, sound, and act quite different. Again, in the case of the Creek people, their communities were spread in two distinct clusters of "Upper" and "Lower" communities along the Alabama and Apalachicola River sheds, respectively. Traveling among the two a visitor might hear a half-dozen different Native languages. Politically, economically, and even socially, Creek society was a patchwork of self-governing communities that operated independent of each other in all but the most pressing of crises. One Creek community, like Coweta, might chart a diplomatic or economic course that could be radically different from a neighbor like Oakfuskee, a tradition that could be confusing, but also extremely advantageous when playing one European power off another.[14]

This flexibility confounded Europeans. Even though they tried, neither South Carolina's nor La Florida's governors were able to secure anything close to a unilateral peace accord that would have drawn all Creeks away from their rivals. While a powerful headman like Brims of Coweta fostered consistently close ties with St. Augustine, he could do little to sway his neighbors away from Charleston, no matter how hard he tried. At the same time, however, Spaniards could never compete with the English colonies when it came to trade, by far the most important Creek consideration, and the true driver of community loyalty. Spanish authorities were not driven by the same market forces that enticed English traders into the region, and La Florida had no entrepreneurial equivalent of private English trade outfits. Spanish governors simply could not provide either the quantity or the quality of trade goods that private English traders could, and which Creeks came to expect. Not until the Spanish government partnered with private interests after the American Revolution did they ever make a dent in the Creek trade. That relationship was a long way away from 1715, leaving the Spanish trade to languish a far, far distant second behind the English.[15]

In 1716, for instance, when the Spanish ascended the Chattahoochee, Creek women resisted calls for the unilateral alliance with St. Augustine and Pensacola that was being suggested by prominent headmen. By that time, because of the disruption of the Yamasee War, the women had gone far too long without the spinning and weaving supplies that they needed to turn cotton or wool into clothing—to provide for their own communities. While women did not have much direct say in political matters, they did have plenty of say in how their communities functioned. It was widely known that what these women wanted was better, cheaper, and more reliable trade good, which they got from the English rather than the Spanish. That led them to protest against an exclusive alliance with the Spanish which, if only for the prospect of shirts and britches, was not in their peoples' best interest.[16]

While Spaniards would forever lag far behind their British competitors in matters of trade, they had a few critical goals that they shared with almost every single Creek man, woman, or child: an interest in frustrating British plans for regional hegemony. What even the most enthusiastic Anglophile among Creek communities saw when they traveled to Charleston was alarming. It was a very different place than St. Augustine or Pensacola. The latter two outposts were basically the only ones that remained of La Florida, "atrophied colonies" in the words of one historian, which few Creek diplomats would have considered dangerous. There was no long-term threat to land or sovereignty coming from that direction.[17] What they saw in South Carolina on the other hand was a colony growing, growing fast, and growing into Native hunting lands. By the end of the Yamasee War, Carolina authorities were hard at work rebuilding abandoned fortifications and erecting new ones deep into the frontier, places that would project British sovereignty as well as provide trade goods. Meanwhile, rice cultivation was transforming the Lowcountry.[18] What was once just Charleston, in other words, was now much more. Creeks and Spaniards had clear territorial reasons to be good friends, if only to check Carolina expansion.

What evolved was a dance that was entertaining to watch Creeks perform, if not a convoluted and at times dangerous one to try and follow. At the same time a group of Creek leaders traveled to a fort near what is now Augusta to make peace and renew trade relationships with the English, for instance, another group was boarding a ship in Pensacola that was bound for Vera Cruz. There a seven-man Creek delegation would make its way to Mexico City and meet personally with the Viceroy of New Spain, Baltasar de Zúñiga y Guzmán, Marquis de Valero. One of the headmen would be baptized and the Viceroy proclaimed his godfather. At almost the very same time another Creek delegation arrived in St. Augustine at the head of a group of over 150 headmen and warriors, hoping to receive gifts and renew their communities' friendship. The leaders of the procession put on quite a show. They dressed in Spanish clothes, wore sombreros, and held canes, all of which evoked the imagery of Spanish hidalgos. Their stay was marked with several elaborate ceremonies that went on for days. The headmen offered the acting Governor a head dress, a gesture the Spaniard reciprocated with an embrace and a toast. More importantly, on their way out the headmen managed to squeeze from the gift-strapped governor a Spanish musket for seemingly every member of their party—154 in total—in addition to a generous supply of powder and ball.[19] Such a bestowing, the equivalent of more than one thousand deerskins, no doubt sent a powerful message to the Creek diplomats. The Spanish, although they lagged behind the English in terms of trade, still had plenty to offer.

Rather than return to Carolina "as pawns of the British empire," in the words of one historian, Creek community leaders sought to "cultivate a multilateral—and competitive—political environment" built on overlapping arrangements between the English, Spanish, and even the French. By the second decade of the eighteenth century, it was clear they were succeeding in bringing all their European competitors to the table, and on their own terms. Follow-up talks were held on the Savannah River then in Charleston, as well as both Pensacola and St. Augustine, throughout 1717. The next year the Mexico City travelers would return, setting off more waves of Spanish visits just as more Charleston visits were taking place.[20] This play-off system suited Creeks well for generations.

It was during this period of Creek courtship that Pensacola, for almost a generation an even smaller and more pathetic colonial backwater than St. Augustine, gained new importance. Far closer to Creek communities than St. Augustine, Pensacola's military leadership began hosting more Native visitors during the Yamasee War period and afterward, as they came in to court Spanish friendship and gain Spanish trade goods. The guests soon asked for the reestablishment of San Marcos de Apalachee, which had sat burned and abandoned for almost a generation. The Creek guests rightly understood that the location of the fort in the panhandle was ideal for an easy intercourse with Havana, making it easier to secure Spanish trade. The location near the Apalachicola River made for a relatively easy journey directly into the heart of Creek Country. The spot was, in short, perfect to build a strong Spanish relationship. In the 1718 flurry of diplomatic inroads made by all actors in this diplomatic game, the Spanish seemed to be gaining the upper hand. That was the year Captain José Primo de Ribera arrived to begin construction of the new fort at Apalachee.[21]

The development of those post-war years peaked in 1718 when community headmen from across Creek Country met in one council to discuss how they might best approach the competing imperial powers. What they came up with was a neutrality policy termed the "Coweta Resolution," so named after the Creek town in which the headmen convened. According to one scholar the moment should be considered one of "Southern history's decisive turning points," for the generation of regional diplomacy it created. Spanish vs. English competition was what drove the resulting period of play-off diplomacy in much of the eighteenth century, with one the critical players being the Spaniards anchored in the small, but still very relevant, La Florida.[22] The Coweta Resolution was the product of individual Creek communities charting their own political and economic paths with different European powers, generating confidence that their communities were in control of their own destinies. It was also the product of a complicated Colonial Southeast, crowded now with Euro-American actors, to which the reemergence of La Florida contributed.

For the Native players of this diplomatic game, the stakes were high. Creek politics and play-off diplomacy could generate intense competition among communities that at times grew chaotic and violent, exacerbating the divisive tendencies inherent in coalescent societies. Playing one European power off another was definitely not what suited Europeans the best, after all, and both British and Spanish authorities stubbornly pushed Creeks to do their exclusive bidding, contributing to their own defensive networks and economic interests. Shortly after the Coweta Resolution, for instance, Carolina officials demanded Yamasees return to the English sphere of influence. When the Yamasee chose instead to stick close to St. Augustine, Charleston officials turned to Creek communities, pushing them to either force their Yamasee neighbors into submission or destroy them. That pressure succeeded in inducing small-scale Creek raiding in the 1720s, in some instances attacking Yamasees right outside of the Spanish forts at Apalachee and St. Augustine. That in turn led Creeks aligned with pro-Spanish leaders like Brims, and at times including Brims, to travel to St. Augustine, Pensacola, and Apalachee to apologize to their so-called friends and to reassert their allegiance.[23]

Far more dangerous than the Yamasee split was the ongoing conflict Creeks were waging against Cherokees, their neighbors to the north, a struggle the play-off system was also exacerbating. The Yamasee were a fragment of the people they used to be before the war named after them, and were only safe when living directly under the guns of their Spanish protectors. The Cherokee, on the other hand, were a much larger and more dangerous people, fully capable of bringing terror and devastation into Creek communities. Cherokees were much farther from St. Augustine than Charleston, and close to new British post-Yamasee outposts, like forts Moore and Congaree, built specifically to stabilize the deerskin trade. Cherokees had, overall, proven far firmer allies with the Carolinians than their Creek counterparts and had been since the Yamasee War, when they massacred a Creek delegation sent there to create an anti-Carolina coalition in 1716. Animosity still ran deep a decade later, producing a simmering Native conflict that had generated a steady stream of reprisal raiding for years. These attacks produced significant casualties and spread division among the Creek communities in the north that bore the brunt of Cherokee assaults.[24]

Back among Creeks, some of the strongest Spanish partisans were among the Lower Towns along the Flint and Chattahoochee Rivers, which were physically very close to what remained of La Florida. One of the major British trade paths, however, also went directly through those same towns. The situation was much the same to the northwest, in the Upper Town cluster. While trade paths and easy-traversable waterways still connected them to Pensacola and Mobile, a major British trade path moved from the Carolinas through there as well, and these towns, like Oakfuskee and Tallassee, were also closer to their Choctaw and Cherokee rivals. These communities were more exposed to the violence that might result from the diplomatic game they played. Creeks' position, while flexible, could also be confusing, and many times overlapping colonial pressures put the leaders of those groups into conflict with each other. Eventually, this era of Creek politics brought several of their communities the closest to a civil war they had been since perhaps their coalescence. Their Choctaw neighbors, farther to the west, did actually erupt into civil war, having been similarly torn between the French and British. Neutrality, it turns out, was a much easier policy to articulate than enforce.[25]

For Creeks, the confusing and violent actions of a three-year stretch from 1726 to 1728 were representative of this alarming escalation. In 1726, while a group of Creeks were in St. Augustine meeting with the Governor, a large party of Cherokees and Chickasaws marched into Creek territory flying a British flag. Spanish-backed Creeks, mostly from Cusseta, ambushed the march and killed dozens of them. Harsh Cherokee reprisals followed, and soon Creek delegates were in Charleston attempting to broker a peace with both Carolina and the Cherokee, which Charleston authorities supported. Very soon after, however, a group of allied Yamasees and Creeks raided the frontier of modern-day Georgia on the Altamaha River, killing a well-known trader and five others, pilfering their trade store, and taking several other settlers prisoner. A separate group of Yamasees raided directly into South Carolina, killing even more settlers. Carolinian authorities responded by invading La Florida, annihilating what was left of the Yamasees right outside of St. Augustine. It was a crushing blow that scattered what was left of the Yamasee, knocking out La Florida's most reliable Native allies and laying Spanish defensive capabilities bare to Creeks. The Yamasee communities destroyed by the Carolinians were right within view of the Castillo de San Marcos.[26] Spaniards could have done much more, perhaps, had regional authorities dumped more money into their Creek partners. Yet that could be said about La Florida in general.

Through several decades of the eighteenth century, in short, the Spanish continued to play second fiddle to their English competitors in every way when it came to Native relations, and were prone to humiliation at times. The destruction of the Yamasee communities right outside the walls of St. Augustine was embarrassing and would inspire little confidence in Creek allies that their Spanish friends could protect them. Meanwhile, the Creek trade itself languished as did the entire backwater colony. The post at Apalachee never developed as a trade hub like it should have, depriving Creeks of a more stable trade and leaving them feeling betrayed by unfulfilled Spanish promises.[27] If there was ever any suggestion that the Spanish were equivalent to the British when it came to Native politics and economics, the stagnation of these years makes it clear they were not.

Nevertheless, the Spanish did not necessarily have to be equivalent to get what they needed geopolitically. Their role as spoiler was still all that was needed for a vibrant play-off system to emerge, and Spanish authorities played the role well for decades. English colonial officials were so convinced of a Spanish threat that they enthusiastically backed the establishment of Georgia in 1733, basically as a buffer colony between South Carolina and La Florida. With the broad and slow-moving Savannah River connecting the towns of Savannah and Augusta, merchants from the young colony also immediately thrust themselves into the Native trade, providing another source of competition with which the Spanish, already lagging in a distant second place, would have to compete. Yet Augusta traders would also increasingly compete with Charleston traders, further complicating the play-off system and keeping it vibrant for another entire generation.[28]

A small group of outcast Creeks made the original agreement with James Oglethorpe in 1733, the agreement which birthed Georgia. In 1739 a second treaty was signed in Coweta, just a bit over two decades after the Resolution in 1718 which codified the play-off system. While the 1739 treaty was a peaceful one, as nearby Creeks soon discovered, Georgia represented an even bigger expansionist threat than did Carolina, and more pro-Spanish and pro-French partisans quickly rose to power, like the Mortar and the Gun Merchant, both from a Creek community in the Upper Towns called Ockhai. As a counterweight to British expansion, La Florida took on even more importance to these worried Creeks. With British settlers expanding past the limits of the Ogeechee River and with new sets of traders committing all the same old abuses, the positivity of Oglethorpe and the first few years of Georgia's existence had soon worn off entirely, and Creek play-off diplomacy intensified.[29]

While one group of Creeks under the direction of a local leader named Tomochichi met with the British in 1734, for instance, another group of over twenty-three Creeks from the Lower Towns met with Álvaro Lopez de Toledo, the commander of the recently rehabilitated San Marcos de Apalachee. While one group of Creeks traveled with Oglethorpe to mark out the southern limits of

Georgia, which would draw raids from both the English and Spanish, another set of Creeks soon arrived from a trip to St. Augustine, where they had a pleasant meeting with the incoming Governor, Francisco de Moral Sánchez. Not only were the Spanish responsive to their Creek allies, but sloppy and aggressive actions taken by the new British Creek agent, appointed by Oglethorpe, soon drove more Creeks to St. Augustine. As the overbearing British agent disparaged, the Creeks were "overawed by that silly place in possession of the French called Fort Toulouse and by Saint Marks," the latter referring to San Marcos de Apalachee. Creek informants, in fact, were who regularly kept the commanders at San Marcos and St. Augustine apprised of British machinations as Anglo-Spanish antagonism intensified in the run-up to war.[30]

As Anglo-Spanish rivalry heated up, so did Spanish efforts to draw Creeks into their orbit. San Marcos, for instance, was generally a disappointment for Creeks when it came to trade, but still turned out to have tremendous strategic value for the Spanish, which the British would recognize after the transfer of La Florida in 1763. In 1738 the governor of Cuba sent a trade ship, heavily laden with everything from ceremonial jackets to food, tobacco, and liquor, to the fort to woo Creeks into a Spanish alliance he hoped would keep them from joining the British in what was quickly becoming a real war, the War of Jenkin's Ear. Even though Creeks—possibly the same Creeks—soon appeared in Savannah, the Spanish ceremony was a success, bringing the largest delegation of Creeks to La Florida in a decade and demonstrating that the Spanish remained important players in the play-off game. Who knows how the Southeast would have developed had the Spaniards been able to maintain such demonstrations of good will.[31]

All of this animosity would simmer over only a few years later as the War of Jenkin's Ear brought colonial fighting to the Southeast. In an otherwise international competition between two worldwide imperial actors, it was the Georgia-Florida border that would be the seat of the North American struggle that pitted Spanish and British empires against each other. As British and Spanish authorities both were sure, Natives would play a significant role in the struggle. When it came to the war's actual fighting, which took place in both Georgia and La Florida, this turned out to be only partially the case. Handfuls of Creeks were with the Spanish in their invasion of coastal Georgia just as they had been with Oglethorpe in his invasion of La Florida, numbers what were far more disappointing to Georgia's Oglethorpe than to La Florida's Manuel de Montiano. Even in the instance of Creeks joining in with the Georgia assault force, they spent most of their time on their own, hunting up horses, livestock, or scalps as prizes rather than contributing to the failed siege of St. Augustine.[32]

In the wake of Jenkin's Ear, which had fizzled out in the Southeast entirely by 1743, Spanish and British authorities settled into a sort of a détente, and the Creek play-off system thrived for almost another generation. The deerskin trade peaked, Georgia expanded into the southwest, and its coastline transformed into a proto-South Carolinian rice frontier. Regional Spanish and British authorities continued to vie with each other for Creek loyalties until the conversation again shifted to war—this time the much larger and more transformative French and Indian War. Although Spaniards eventually backed the French and would pay dearly for it by losing La Florida, none of the war actually involved La Florida. For Creeks, the play-off system would endure for a few more years, until the American Revolution changed the regional dynamic entirely. That meant that the play-off system, anchored at least partially in La Florida, shaped frontier diplomacy for the better part of a half-century.

Notes

1. For the war, see Crane, *The Southern Frontier*; Gallay, *Indian Slave Trade*; Oatis, *A Colonial Complex*; and Ramsey, *The Yamasee War.*
2. Braund, *Deerskins & Duffels*, 42-43, 68, 71; Hahn, *The Invention*, 163; Kelton, *Epidemics and Enslavement*, 103; Krech, *The Ecological Indian*, 156-157.
3. Braund, *Deerskins & Duffels*, 61; White, *Roots of Dependency*, 32-34.
4. Braund, *Deerskins & Duffels*, chapter 3, particularly 43-49; Crane, *The Southern Frontier*, 110.
5. Crane, *The Southern Frontier*, 110-112; Braund, *Deerskins & Duffels*, 69-71; Krech, *The Ecological Indian*, 159-161.
6. Braund, *Deerskins & Duffels*, 30, 121-138; Krech, *The Ecological Indian*, 157-158; Green, *Politics*, 18-23; Kelton, *Epidemics and Enslavement*, 104-106.
7. Crane, *Southern Frontier*, 117; Braund, *Deerskins & Duffels*, 71-72; Green, *The Politics of Indian Removal*, 18-19. For excellent regional studies of those processes, see White, *Roots of Dependency*, 1-146; and Krech, *The Ecological Indian*, 151-171.
8. White, *Roots of Dependency*, 34-68; Green, *The Politics of Indian Removal*, 21-23.
9. Krech, *The Ecological Indian*, 158.
10. For the influence of Fort Toulouse on the region, see Crane, *The Southern Frontier*; and Corkran, *The Creek Frontier*.
11. Hahn, *The Invention*, 81-84; Green, *The Politics of Indian Removal*, 20; Crane, *The Southern Frontier*, 169-170.
12. Braund, *Deerskins & Duffels*, 35; Corkran, *The Creek Frontier*, 60; Green, *The Politics of Indian Removal*, 20; Milanich, *Laboring in the Fields of the Lord*, 190; Sweet, *Negotiating for Georgia*, 19-20; Crane, *The Southern Frontier*, 184-185.

13. Hahn, *The Invention*, 84-86, 90-93; Boyd, "Diego Pena's Expedition," 1-27; Corkran, *The Creek Frontier*, 62; Galloway, *Choctaw Genesis*, 199-202; Bushnell, *Situado and Sabana*, 195.

14. Hahn, *The Invention*, 91-92, 95.

15. Crane, *The Southern Frontier*, 23, 115.

16. Hahn, *The Invention*, 93-95, 143; Braund, *Deerskins & Duffels*, 36.

17. Hahn, *The Invention*, 108-109; Green, *The Politics of Indian Removal*, 20-21.

18. Hahn, *The Invention*, 108-109; Corkran, *The Creek Frontier*, 187-191.

19. Hahn, *The Invention*, 96-100; Corkran, *The Creek Frontier*, 60, 62.

20. Hahn, *The Invention*, 101-103, 109-111; Corkran, *The Creek Frontier*, 62-65; Green, *The Politics of Indian Removal*, 22-23.

21. Hahn, *The Invention*, 96, 101, 115, 118; Milanich, *Laboring in the Fields of the Lord*, 191.

22. Hahn, *The Invention*, 116-120.

23. Hahn, *The Invention*, 122-124, 145-148.

24. Hahn, *The Invention*, 123, 126-129, 135-136; Sweet, *Negotiating for Georgia*, 20; Corkran, *The Creek Frontier*, 68-78, 180-186; Bushnell, *Situado and Sabana*, 196.

25. For evidence of civil strife in Choctaw country, see White, *Roots of Dependency*, 60-65.

26. Hahn, *The Invention*, 142-145; Corkran, *The Creek Frontier*, 73-78.

27. Hahn, *The Invention*, 142-145; Bushnell, *Situado and Sabana*, 196-198.

28. Braund, *Deerskins & Duffels*, 41-42; Gallay, *Indian Slave Trade*, 72; Green, *The Politics of Indian Removal*, 23-24; Sweet, *Negotiating for Georgia*, 99-105.

29. Green, *The Politics of Indian Removal*, 24-28; Sweet, *Negotiating for Georgia*, 114-127.

30. Hahn, *The Invention*, 164-169, 176-177; Sweet, *Negotiating for Georgia*, 107-113.

31. Hahn, *The Invention*, 176-179.

32. Green, *The Politics of Indian Removal*, 24; Hahn, *The Invention*, 179-184; Sweet, *Negotiating for Georgia*, 140-158.

10 La Florida Foodways

MIGHT SMOKED MULLET BE AMERICA'S TRUEST BARBECUE TRADITION? IT MOST certainly could be the state of Florida's, an intriguing contribution to America's culinary history. The first meats Spaniards usually saw smoking in the New World were fish, which makes sense because all the coastal societies where Spaniards first went in the New World were built upon the natural wealth of the surrounding waters. In other words, fish. That reliance is not so different from the Pacific Northwest, where Native peoples still view salmon less as simply a food source and more as an entire way of life.[1] Salmon's rich and oily flesh stands up well to a smoke cure. The same is true of mullet, a saltwater fish with a practically timeless history of consumption in the coastal Southeast. In the state of Florida smoked mullet remains a delicacy in the present, often prepared as a dip or a spread.

The largest harvests come when vast schools of ocean mullet run along the coasts seasonally in a way not unlike the salmon runs of the Pacific Northwest. That reliability has sustained a fishery that extends for centuries back through La Florida and beyond. Starting most recently and working backwards through time, commercial fishing outfits netted massive numbers of the schooling fish throughout the nineteenth and twentieth centuries, dried and cured them, and sent them to market in the United States as well as in Cuba. Before that, Cuban and Native fishermen set up "ranchos" along the coast to do the same thing on much smaller scales during the Spanish and British colonial periods, dating back into the seventeenth century. Cuban fishermen and Natives alike traded salted and smoked fish to Havana merchants, creating a unique regional and informal marketplace that endured for centuries. That makes the Floridian mullet market one of the longest-running industries in the Southeast.[2]

Smoking fish for consumption, and not for sale, has even deeper pre-Columbian roots. While Natives in the interior of the American continent built civilizations off corn production, those along the coast of peninsular Florida and throughout the Caribbean built theirs off seafood, including smoked fish. Those were the societies encountered by the first Spaniards, and indeed, one of the first things European visitors usually saw in the New World, regardless of where they went, was fish smoking on a beach. The men on Columbus's second voyage, for instance, saw smoked fish on Hispaniola in 1493. The sailors, worn out on their shipboard rations, scarfed the fish up, making them not only the first Europeans to reference the word *barbacoa*, from which the modern term barbecue originates, but the first to partake in a New World barbecue. Luis Cáncer de Barbastro's men witnessed fish smoking on the beach among the Tocobaga in the area of Tampa Bay in 1549. The sight and smell was so appetizing that a sailor went ashore to snatch some up. Instead, he was snatched up, drug away by lurking Natives to his certain doom.[3] Then there was Pedro Menéndez de Avilés. After he commemorated the settlement of St. Augustine with a feast, he traveled south in 1566 to enjoy another feast with Calusa chieftain Carlos. While the first feast was Spanish, the second was decidedly Native. According to one account, only fish and oysters were served—the original American seafood buffet. Not far away were the Keys, where the Tequesta did not "plant anything, but live from fish and roots of some fruits of the earth," according to another Spaniard.[4] Everywhere a European looked, it seemed, there was fish. The case for smoked mullet grows stronger yet.

Last but not least there are Europeans' illustrations of Native cooking techniques—the same ones touted by all historians of American barbecue. Two are based off Jacques Le Moyne's time at Fort Carolina in 1564. Another is taken from James White's 1585 watercolor collection, made much farther up the coast in the Outer Banks. All three are strikingly similar: they all feature fish propped up over an open fire. The first images of American barbecue, whether English or Spanish, were all of fish. Perhaps these were mullet as well. All things being equal, it is a strong case indeed for the lowly mullet. Perhaps the official barbecue of the state of Florida should be fish, and perhaps mullet might someday claim a rightful place in the pantheon of American barbecue.

The case for mullet barbecue might be a stretch, but to say that barbecue originated in La Florida is not. Of course, La Florida references not just the modern state of Florida but much of the American Southeast, so that is not too insulting a suggestion to make in the competitive world of American barbecue. Not only did barbecue originate in La Florida, after all, but so did the pigs that typify the Southeastern style of barbecue. Livestock was the product of the Columbian Exchange just as much as were plants and diseases. While certainly not as transformative as smallpox or malaria, the American Southeast would have looked very different without Spanish imports like pigs and cattle. Texas longhorns and Florida "scrub cattle" were Spanish introductions, as were the hogs that terrorize American yards throughout the modern south. American free-range cattle traditions are Spanish traditions, and the first cowboys to work cattle were Natives and enslaved Africans operating out of St. Augustine.

While the cattle tradition in the Southeast pales in comparison to Texas and the plains states, the cattle ranching tradition in the modern-day state of Florida is the oldest in the United States. Another import with clear Spanish roots during the period, citrus, has grown even more uniquely synonymous with Florida, a connection that today Floridians embrace and cherish as if it had always been a part of the state's history. Spanish La Florida, as small and isolated a place in modern American imagination as it was in seventeenth-century reality, is the reason for some of Southeast's most American traditions.

Notes

1. Taylor, *Making Salmon*, 13-38; Mink, *Salmon*, 31-39.
2. *Bulletin of the United States Fish Commission*, 135-137; Stevens, *Pine Island*, 95; Covington, "Trade Relations," 114-128; Hoffman, *Florida Frontiers*, 207; McGoun, *Prehistoric Peoples of South Florida*, 109.
3. Warnes, *Savage Barbecue*, 15-16; Weddle, *Spanish Sea*, 239-241.
4. Hann, *Missions to the Calusa*, 8; Widmer, *The Evolution of Calusa*, 224-225; Arbesú-Fernardez, ed., *Pedro Menéndez De Avilés*, 94; Merás, *Pedro Menéndez de Avilés*, 148.

BBQ, La Florida Style

Barbecue is widely regarded as America's first food, and the case for that is strong indeed. It "entered European consciousness," as one scholar put it, about the same time America itself did.[1] The intertwined history of colonization, enslavement, and immigration all combined to create a uniquely American process of slow roasting meats to glorious culinary perfection. Despite those origins, however, little else is clear. Regional variations have emerged over the centuries that render barbecue perilously difficult to define. What meats and what processes, exactly, constitute America's true barbecue? For starters, is it beef or pork, or perhaps even chicken? What regional hardwoods create a superior smoke? To sauce, or dry rub? These are no trifling questions.

Even leaving out Texas-style beef barbecue and focusing entirely on pork, simply for the sake of simplicity, does little to simplify things. Georgia and South Carolina styles are not to be confused with Memphis, St. Louis, or Kansas City styles, each of which prize different cuts of pig and prepare them differently. And then there are the Virginians, who claim barbecue simply because they claim the first English American colony.[2] To confuse these things would be to slander entire cities, states, and regions, while to suggest that the styles have more in common with each other than not would be to insult the pride of countless American barbecue pit masters and possibly even incite violence. One solution is to acknowledge that the common heritage of pork barbecue lies in La Florida, with the Spaniards who came there and with the Natives who already lived there. That means that all pork barbecue is, more or less, barbecue La Florida style.

First there are the pigs themselves. Along with wheat, wine, and olives of course, there were Black Iberian pigs, *Cerdos Ibericos*. These formed the foundation of the southern Spanish culinary world, the staff of conquistador life. Domesticated for thousands of years by the end of the *Reconquista*, maintaining herds of black-footed hogs was no dishonor among proud Spanish hidalgos. Spaniards were no beginners when it came to a good pig roast, either. In fact, unlike sheep or cows, pigs were ranched for no other reason than for eating. The slaughter and cooking of a pig was a classic community tradition that the men on Columbus's ship would have looked upon fondly as they floated into seeming oblivion on their 1492 voyage. The pig was not necessarily smoked but roasted and eaten in one feast-like sitting. Separate slaughters, known fittingly as *matanzas*, were spread among a community to make sure that food was always around, but never around long enough to spoil. Pork fat could also be rendered to lard for frying, and the fattiness of pork lends well to curing. Cured hams, most notably the legendary *jamón Iberico*, are immensely popular in Spanish culture.[3]

Hogs and pork consumption was so central to Spanish cultural and religious identity that in time it became proof of that identity. While Muslims and Jews were prohibited from consuming pork by their own religious doctrines, Catholic Spaniards absolutely were not. This was such a clear distinction that in the wake of the *Reconquista* the eating of pork became like a litmus test for recently converted Christians. Could you even be Catholic without a love for pork? Apparently not. Publicly claiming conversion, but avoiding pork, could earn you a one-way ticket to an Inquisition tribunal.[4]

The humble porker was also "one of the glories of animal domestication," in the words of one scholar. Pigs were relatively small and easy to transport, and once established they required almost no supervision and reproduced at plague-like rates, providing a stable and reliable food source in even the most uncertain places. A sow might give birth to anywhere from ten piglets to upward of three times that number after just four months of gestation. Within six months the piglets will have grown in size and weight by a staggering 5,000 percent. Pigs store more of their consumed energy as protein and fat than do either cattle or sheep. They render more of their body weight in dressed meat and also provide more calories per ounce of meat than do either of the other two. Few domesticable animals can match the rate of reproduction, growth, or food value of pigs, particularly considering pigs can do it by eating practically anything, and regardless of whether they were tended to or left to range free.[5]

It makes perfect sense, then, for one to see pigs everywhere one saw Spaniards in the New World. That tradition began with Columbus, who brought eight with him on his second voyage to Hispaniola. From that stock, herds of both domesticated and feral pigs quickly spread over the island, and from there across the Caribbean and to Tierra Firme. Diego Velásquez de Cuéllar wrote from nearby Cuba in 1514 that from the pigs he brought to the island only a few years earlier, now there were thirty thousand. Francisco Pizarro brought a stock with him from Panama to Peru. While none of these places produced a Spanish free-range pig's typical diet of tree nuts, the abundance of wild fruits, palms, and other ground foliage was more than enough to make the pigs fat and happy, turning *Cerdos Ibericos* into the "fast, tough, lean, self-sufficient greyhound of a hog," in the words of Alfred Crosby, that are still visible across North and South America. The iconic Arkansas Razorback, it turns out, is not from Arkansas.[6]

The proof is in the numbers. According to one chronicler, de Soto arrived in La Florida carrying just over a dozen Cuban pigs with him. By the time his army was marching north across the modern South Carolina state line the men were "driving three hundred pigs," which multiplied so rapidly that an entire company of cavalry was assigned "especially to herd and guard them." The hogs not only survived the disaster at Mavila years later but their number appeared to have doubled again over the course of the next year. By the time de Soto died on the Mississippi somewhere in southern Arkansas, his estate now contained seven hundred hogs. It is ironic that so many pigs were taken account of so near the future sites of Memphis, St. Louis, and Kansas City—a nod to the barbecue spare rib gods.[7]

With so many pigs on hand, de Soto made it a point to leave a few here and there among several Native communities between Apalachee and Cofitachequi. At two separate chiefdoms he presented a breeding pair as gifts in a show of thanks. Perhaps they died there not long after, but knowing their hardiness, perhaps not. Despite the best efforts to corral their rapidly expanding herd, de Soto's men also lost several pigs that were swept away in river crossings, although it was not described that they drowned. Pigs are actually pretty decent swimmers. More were also "lost along the roads," according to Gracilaso de la Vega. Of course, locals could have dispatched any wayward hogs they ran across, yet it was clear by the movement of the army into Chicaza territory that nearby Natives valued pork almost as much as the Spanish. De Soto had two Natives "shot with arrows" and "the hands of the other cut off" for stealing hogs. All signs pointed to a bright future for the porkers. As de la Vega concluded, "it is probable that, in consideration of the advantages that great kingdom has for breeding them, there are many of them there today," writing as he was years after the de Soto expedition concluded. Historians and anthropologists are generally pretty conservative when it comes to the natural increase among the animals brought by Spaniards, mainly because no one was around to take note of their growth.[8] De la Vega would beg to differ.

Other Spaniards would have brought pigs with them into La Florida, like Tristán de Luna almost certainly did, but the extent to which they would have contributed to a natural population is even more uncertain. Then there was Menéndez, who was the first to consistently import the animals to La Florida. He regularly traveled to from St. Augustine and Santa Elena to Havana, rounding up supplies and having them shipped back to his chronically under-provisioned La Florida outposts. As early as 1567 this included shipments of pigs, chickens, and horses, all of which were done specifically to establish an agricultural base in the colony.[9] Pigs were no doubt part of Santa Elena's food scene, and Franciscans used them at various missions to project a correct Christian lifestyle. That led scholar Amy Turner Bushnell to mention in passing that, based on Spanish sources, at the end of the sixteenth century Guale Natives were living mainly on the mainland. They left the Sea Islands to packs of feral hogs. These appear to be the progenitors of the famed Ossabaw Island hogs, which still live off the coast of Georgia, proving that a direct lineage from the sixteenth century to the twenty-first is not such a longshot at all.[10]

But Spanish pigs alone do not create American barbecue. The second half of this origin story has to do with the word itself. The general consensus is that the word barbecue represents the English adaptation of the Native and Spanish term *barbacoa*. It is a reference to the Native habit of cooking meats over an open fire, which Columbus's men probably witnessed as early as 1493. They could have been cooking the meat in a classic grilled fashion, using high heat, but a wooden grate would not work very long for that. Most of them were probably smoking the meats higher off the coals, at a lower heat, in order to preserve them. Smoking, like salting, removes water from cells, removing the conditions for the spread of bacteria that lead to decomposition.[11]

Yet the barbacoa was not just an American invention. Famous Spanish historian Gonzalo Fernández de Oviedo y Valdés described the practice in Tierra Firme in 1526, in present-day Panama. More specifically, the term did not necessarily refer to the cooking technique as a whole, but rather the apparatus upon which the food was cooked. It was a kind of a wooden rack or scaffolding that was suspended over a pit—an early all-wood barbecue smoker. Whatever meat was available, from fish and iguanas to chunked-up venison, was placed on the scaffolding. "They call these barbacoas, and place fire beneath," and in that manner roasted the meat to their liking. Similar accounts came from Caribs, Arawaks, and Tainos, from Hispaniola and other islands, and from the coastlines of present-day Brazil, Nicaragua, and Colombia. The ubiquity of the barbacoa rack helps confirm for historians and anthropologists just how interconnected the pre-Columbian Caribbean basin truly was. Just about anywhere Europeans encountered Natives, they encountered the barbacoa. As soon as the English began stretching out into Virginia, the Carolinas, and even Florida, they found it there, too.[12]

Although Spaniards saw Natives smoking food on barbacoas practically wherever they went, the first definitive mention of the American barbacoa cooking tradition comes from de Soto. Somewhere in modern-day Georgia the men stumbled upon venison and probably turkey, roasting away on "a *barbacoa*, which is like on a grill."[13] As was the case whenever something like that happened, naturally the men ate it all up and moved on. Charles Hudson and scholars ever since have suggested that the chronicler, in this case Rangel, recorded what very well was the first barbecue ever witnessed by a European in North America, definitely a nod to the Georgia-Carolinas BBQ gods.[14]

This might be true, but it is also evident from the de Soto chronicles that barbacoas were common in the Southeast, and not just for cooking. Not long after their venison feast de Soto's army walked into Cofitachequi, where they set at gorging themselves on the Chieftainess' corn stores. In Rangel's estimation they consumed seven "barbacoas" worth. Another Spanish chronicler described an earlier battle in peninsular Florida, when a Native warrior with a spear "climbed up on a cane floor which they made to hold their maize (which they call a barbacoa)," and attempted to ambush passing Spaniards. The soldiers were not fooled, and promptly killed the Native man with a throwing spear of their own. These structures, clearly not meant for cooking, also correspond with several Spanish usages of the word elsewhere. Oviedo y Valdés described the Tierra Firme Natives using the scaffolding in such a way—as a storage platform. By raising the corn off the ground Natives kept it away from bugs and animals, and the scaffolding might have kept it dryer as well.[15] In Cofitachequi Spaniards witnessed yet a third usage of the platform. In the village's central temple, the bodies of past headmen were "tied on a barbacoa, the breasts and openings and necks and arms and legs covered in pearls." English settlers from the earliest days of Virginia saw barbacoas as well, although they referred to them many times as "hurdles."[16]

Last but not least there was the European fascination with cannibalism, and Bartoleme de las Casas's fascination with the torture of Native Americans by Spaniards. In the first, Theodor de Bry illustrated several cannibalistic scenes taken from Brazil, in which Natives are roasting human body parts on the barbacoa. For his part de las Casas featured the barbacoa in two separate illustrations of death and destruction in his *Short Account*. In the first, a grown man is stretched over a large barbacoa, presumably to be slowly roasted alive by Spaniards, several of which are actively fanning the flames below it. In the second scene, Natives are partaking in more cannibalism while in the background Spaniards are committing all kinds of barbarities. Featured in this second barbacoa is a child, presumably already dead, being roasted in preparation of being eaten by the men who are busy enjoying other body parts.[17] It turns out that the term barbacoa, from which barbecue originates, referenced a simple raised platform that was used in all sorts of ways, including for storing, cooking, and evidently torturing and cannibalizing.

Only one of those uses, obviously, is the reason for American barbecue, yet only when plugged into Native cooking traditions did Spanish pigs birth an American tradition. As one historian suggested, the interplay between the technique and the animals was close indeed. On Hispaniola in the mid sixteenth century pigs abounded, with meat "very sweet and savoury; and so wholesome that they give it to the sick folks to eat," yet that was only possible after the Natives taught the Spaniards the barbacoa tradition.[18]

Natives smoked their meats for the same reasons humans have been doing so since the beginning of time. Rather than use salt to cure, they use smoke. By positioning the barbacoa above the smoldering wood the meat cooked slowly and absorbed smoke in the process. That not only imparted great flavor into the meat but cured it as well, making it "quite dry," and preserving it "from corruption," in the words of interested onlookers. Curing the meat in such a way enabled Natives to store fish for longer periods of time. All Native meats, from venison to fish, could be cooked and preserved in this way, left to stand over a fire for long periods of time to be consumed at the ready, something that Europeans witnessed among Native communities along the coast wherever they went in the sixteenth century.[19]

Historically accurate or not, mullet barbecue is simply too tough a sell for anyone but the proudest Florida native. If the tale of the American barbecue does indeed begin with the combination of European foods and Native techniques, then it was surely Spaniards who arrived in the Caribbean, and then de Soto in the Southeast, who began the American barbecue tradition with the hogs he brought with him. And if he personally treated any of his Native guests to the treat of a pig roast, which is purely conjectural but certainly possible, it probably would have been strapped to a barbacoa. Seldom did Spaniards cook their own food in La Florida, after all. If the acorn and mulberry-fattened hogs were slow roasted over regional hardwoods, like oak and hickory, then everyone was in for a treat. A nod indeed to the Georgia and the Carolina whole-hog BBQ gods.

And then, last but not least, there is Virginia barbecue. For all the cannibalism and torture charges evoked by the imagery of the barbacoa, one of the first American admissions of using it in such a way comes from Jamestown, of all places. In 1609, in a period of disease and famine referred to as the starving time, in the depths of despair one man evidently "did kill his wife, powdered her, and had eaten part of her" before others in the settlement figured it out. The others in turn killed him for the act, obviously, but that did not keep John Smith from pondering the incident with a bit of tongue in cheek. Now "whether she was better roasted, boyled or carbonado'd, I know not, but of such a dish as powdered wife I never heard of," Smith mused.[20] If either "roasted" or "carbonado'd" were synonymous to grilling, then while the first barbecues in La Florida were offerings of smoked fish, venison, or pork, then the first barbecue in Virginia was apparently a human being. Now that is a first.

Notes

1. Warnes, *Savage Barbecue*, 48; Moss, *Barbecue*, 1.
2. Auchmutey, *Smoke Lore*, 21-22; Haynes, *Virginia Barbecue*, 43-44.
3. Warnes, *Savage Barbecue*, 13; Gade, "Hogs (Pigs)," 1: 539; Roberts, *Salted & Cured*, 24-25.
4. Gade, "Hogs (Pigs)," 1: 539-540; Laudan, *Cuisine and Empire*, 167-169, 178-179; Hudson, *Knights of Spain*, 76-78.
5. Hudson, *Knights of Spain*, 76-78; Roberts, *Salted & Cured*, 10-12; Gade, "Hogs (Pigs)," 1: 537; Crosby, *The Columbian Exchange*, 77-78.
6. Gade, "Hogs (Pigs)," 1: 538; Crosby, *The Columbian Exchange*, 75-77; Roberts, *Salted & Cured*, 24-26.
7. "The Account by a Gentleman from Elvas," in Clayton, Knight, and Moore, eds., *The De Soto Chronicles*, 81; Gade, "Hogs (Pigs)," 1: 538; Roberts, *Salted & Cured*, 25-26; Crosby, *The Columbian Exchange*, 77-79.
8. "The Account by a Gentleman from Elvas," in Clayton, Knight, and Moore, eds., *The De Soto Chronicles*, 106; "Account of the Northern Conquest," in Clayton, Knight, and Moore, eds., *The De Soto Chronicles*, 274; "La Florida," in Clayton, Knight, and Moore, eds., *The De Soto Chronicles*, 2: 263; Galloway, *Choctaw Genesis*, 133; Gibson, *Feral Animals*, 29-30.
9. Lyon, *The Enterprise of Florida*, 175.
10. Bushnell, *Situado and Sabana*, 64; Roberts, *Salted & Cured*, 25.
11. Warnes, *Savage Barbecue*, 16-18; Haynes, *Virginia Barbecue*, 41-43, 47-54; Opie, *Hogs and Hominy*, 3; Auchmutey, *Smoke Lore*, 8; Mink, *Salmon*, 34-35.
12. Moss, *Barbecue*, 6; Haynes, *Virginia Barbecue*, 42-43, 72-73, 76-78; Warnes, *Savage Barbecue*, 22-25, 30-31, 48.
13. "Account of the Northern Conquest," in Clayton, Knight, and Moore, eds., *The De Soto Chronicles*, 270.
14. Hudson, *Knights of Spain*, 158; Auchmutey, *Smoke Lore*, 9-10.

15. "Account of the Northern Conquest," in Clayton, Knight, and Moore, eds., *The De Soto Chronicles*, 279; "The Account by a Gentleman from Elvas," in Clayton, Knight, and Moore, eds., *The De Soto Chronicles*, 69; Warnes, *Savage Barbecue*, 22, 25-27; Haynes, *Virginia Barbecue*, 47-49.

16. "Account of the Northern Conquest," in Clayton, Knight, and Moore, eds., *The De Soto Chronicles*, 279; Haynes, *Virginia Barbecue*, 44-49.

17. De Bry, *America, part 3*: 48, 155; Griffin and Pagden, eds., *A Short Account*, 15, 62-63.

18. Opie, *Hogs and Hominy*, 3.

19. Haynes, *Virginia Barbecue*, 68-70, 78-80.

20. Smith, *The Generall Historie of Virginia*, 1: 204-205; Haynes, *Virginia Barbecue*, 55-57.

The Cowboys of the Big Sink

The Spaniards that made up the bulk of the New World's conquistadores were not only swine herders but vaqueros, or cattlemen. In particular, the southern parts of Spain were among the only parts of Western Europe where free range cattle abounded, and the Andalusia and Extremadura regions of modern Spain contain some of the richest and oldest open-range ranching traditions in all of Europe. Vaqueros working on horses shifted herds between marshes and woodlands depending on the season, with a full rotation placing cattle in summer pasturage, where they were left alone for large stretches of time to graze in a semi-feral state. The vaqueros would return in the autumn to drive the herds to different seasonal grazing areas like drier woodlands. This autumn roundup also included a cull, during which some cattle was taken to market. In the spring another roundup would take place, this time to castrate and brand calves, and the herd would be driven back to summer pasturages. So, the seasonal free range went in southern Spain, a tradition "as old as history," as one historian described it. This is the source of the great American cattle tradition. All of the tools and techniques of the trade, in fact, from the skilled usage of horses to the roundup, corral, brand, and drive, were not invented by American cowboys, but imported by Spanish vaqueros into the New World.[1]

And import they did. When pigs arrived at Hispaniola with Columbus in 1493, so did cattle. The same was true with Cuéllar in Cuba. Conquistadores brought cattle to all of the major Caribbean islands by the early sixteenth century, which multiplied rapidly in the "bovine Elysian Fields," according to one historian. With rich grasslands, little competition, and less predation, there was nothing to stop them. In fact, as riverine gold deposits ran dry and mineral-hungry conquistadores moved from the islands to the mainlands, cattle ranching was one of the only industries to remain profitable on Hispaniola and Puerto Rico, and whatever Natives were still alive on those islands probably worked on ranches producing beef products.[2]

Those ranches were granted to Spanish *encomenderos* for commercial use as *haciendas*, *estancias*, or *hatos*.[3] On an island like Hispaniola or Puerto Rico a *hacienda* might produce sugarcane or tobacco, while one in Central Mexico might focus on wheat production. Many of them, however, also produced livestock, while according to some definitions, the terms *estancia* and *hato* were used specifically to refer to livestock operations.[4] Cattle produce a high percentage of meat in proportion to their weight, but their carcasses also produce hides and tallow, both of which were also highly marketable. Hides were widely sought in Europe for all sorts of clothing and utilitarian needs, while tallow made for fine candles. If processed property, in other words, cattle were well worth the investment.[5]

Hopscotching from one island to the next, cattle went everywhere Spaniards went. They were in Panama by the first decade of the sixteenth century. Cortés imported Caribbean cattle into New Spain regularly beginning in 1521, and they were in the modern countries of Colombia and Venezuela within the next few years. The invasion of the Andes then took herds south all the way to Chile and legendary Argentinian Pampa. These imports set into motion the spread of cattle to the farthest reaches of the New World, from Alta California and La Florida to Patagonia. Although they took longer to establish, their numbers soon outgrew both sheep and pigs. While that was the case even on the hot Gulf Coast plains, the cattle really shined the farther they headed into the grasslands of northern Mexico. As onlookers there witnessed around the turn of the seventeenth century, cattle grazed everywhere, and in numbers that seemed to double each year. Individual herds alone numbered in the tens of thousands. By the time Spaniards began moving into the present-day limits of the United States, they found cattle already well-established there.[6]

Every one of those herds originated as Iberian breeds, like the still recognizable *retinto* and *barrenda* subspecies. Lean, hardy, and adaptable, and of course sporting those massive iconic horns, the cattle were more than capable of holding their own wherever Spaniards took them. From the time Spanish established herds in the Caribbean and then transported them to New Spain and La Florida they were something slightly different—*criollo* cattle, yet they can draw their lineage through the Caribbean directly to Canary and Andalusian stocks. Texas Longhorns are the direct descendants of these herds, but would not truly come into their own until the open ranges and legendary cattle drives of the post–Civil War American southwest.[7]

Cattle were in peninsular La Florida much sooner, and possibly as early as Juan Ponce de León, at least as the legend goes. While de León would have carried cattle with him on his 1521 colonization expedition, it is unclear whether they even landed. If they were landed, it is unclear whether they were killed in the Calusa assault that crippled the expedition and ultimately killed de León. It is doubtful they lived much longer even if they did survive. If the Calusa did not kill them immediately, the cattle probably did not live long enough to produce a feral herd. The exact same could be said for Ayllón's Chicora settlement, and it is unlikely Narváez or de Soto brought cattle with them.[8] These early years were important for several developments, but probably not cattle.

Cattle did not even do particularly well in the early years of St. Augustine. They were imported regularly beginning in the 1560s, and Menéndez and others placed Cuban cattle on the various Sea Islands off the Florida and Georgia coast in the hopes of creating a viable stock. By all accounts, however, they did not last long there. Apparently even Andalusian cattle had their limits, and the sandy, poorly watered Sea Islands were beyond it. With no stable stock herd around, St. Augustine's population had to rely for decades on dried beef shipped in from Havana, or from beef locally slaughtered from within the town itself, and even that became a problem as the amount of land available for farming or ranching in the city's commons slowly shrank.[9]

The problem was not the quality of the land outside the city walls. The savannahs, hammocks, and wetlands that stretch across the northern portion of Florida from Ocala into Georgia provided excellent pasturage for cattle, and the Native tradition of burning the land to stimulate new growth made the rich grasslands even richer. Naturalist William Bartram passed through one such savanna in 1774. Although he did so a century after the height of the Spanish *estancias* there, from what he described it certainly was a beautiful and rich place that was being managed as it had for generations. Moving through an orange grove and stands of oaks and magnolias late in the evening on the banks of the St. Johns River, he wrote, "I penetrated the grove, and afterwards entered some almost unlimited savannas and plains, which were absolutely enchanting; they had been lately burnt by the Indian hunters and had just now recovered their vernal verdure and gaiety." The region was basically perfect for cattle ranching, which Spanish and English visitors alike quickly realized.[10]

The problem with the land was that people already lived there—Potano, Timucua, and Apalachee people, to be exact. In the decades before the successful Franciscan missions, very little of the La Florida interior was considered safe enough to pass through, let alone release cattle into, by entrepreneuring Spaniards. Quite to the contrary, Natives were in the habit of killing anything that wandered too far from St. Augustine's defenses, either human or animal.[11] Was epidemic disease not a thing in the New World, none of that would have changed. Unfortunately, it was, and the rising population of grazing animals like cattle, horses, and pigs was only possible as the Native populations of the same areas plummeted. This began on the Caribbean islands, and if aliens were looking down on an island like Hispaniola, wrote Alfred Crosby, the rise of animal numbers and the decline of human numbers corresponded so closely they would have concluded that Spaniards were doing it on purpose. They weren't doing it on purpose, of course, but the reality is they probably couldn't have killed off the Native populations much faster, or introduced domesticated animals much faster, had they been trying.

At least for Spanish colonial authorities there was a silver lining to all the death and destruction devastating La Florida's Native people. The more the population fell, the more grazing land was available for free-range ranching. That was the case everywhere Spaniards went, from the Caribbean to New Spain and Peru. Through disease, enslavement, and massacre, writes one historian, Spaniards "cleared vast tracks of the Yucatan Peninsula of people. The inheritors were cows." Unfortunately, much the same was true in La Florida.[12]

The Potano savannahs so coveted by St. Augustine Spaniards, for instance, were opening up to ranchers early in the seventeenth century after missionaries made inroads, certainly, but also because epidemics that began in 1614 wiped out half the population. After another wave of disease in the 1670s, weeds were growing up through Potano corn fields. If the land was going to be repopulated at all, according to one historian, "it would have to be by ranchers." The Spanish residents of La Florida, desperate to create a stable food supply, quickly moved in. After Dutch pirates captured the entire 1628 treasure fleet, the Crown cut the financial support that sustained outposts like St. Augustine. Without that support, the province was on its own, and royal officials responded by issuing *estancias*. Native corn fields were turning into Spanish cattle ranches.[13]

Ranches were operating in Potano and Timucua prairies started as early as the 1630s, but the conditions were still far from favorable. Just when ranches started to expand the colony was racked again in mid-century by waves of epidemic disease, Native uprisings, and resulting famine. The 1656 Timucua uprising was at least partially initiated by the raiding of La Chua and the killing of three workers there by a disgruntled Timucua headman, proof that cattle ranching on Native American lands was still an exploitative and dangerous Spanish dream. The uprising, quelled eventually by Governor Don Diego de Rebodello, was one of many catastrophes that kept a cattle ranching industry from taking hold in the region through midcentury. As was the case with the town and economy of St. Augustine, just when it seemed that cattle ranches were making inroads, some sort of calamity swept through the colony. In the wake of the epidemics and the Apalachee and Timucua rebellions, it would take years for the missions to be rebuilt and Native towns consolidated into smaller *reduccion* mission towns, the roads and farms rebuilt, and breeding stocks established. In time, however, it did happen. Hundreds of yearlings were being branded just west of St. Augustine, creating a breeding base for the interior of the colony, and when the Viceroy of New Spain sent a company of Mexican *mestizo* soldiers renowned as horsemen to the St. Augustine garrison, many of them took to ranching instead. As St. Augustine slowly pulled out of a midcentury period of despair, small ranches again began to stretch west.[14]

The biggest influx of cattle and cattlemen, and the resulting ranching boom, coincided with the royal investment in St. Augustine that came late in the seventeenth century. Along with the enlargement of the St. Augustine garrison and the construction of the Castillo de San Marcos came laborers and soldiers by the hundreds, and ranchers expanded their operations to meet the demand. The corresponding influx of laborers and money brought a higher demand for fresh beef. That increase also allowed for the production of more dried beef, hides, and tallow, all of which were soon being shipped from the ranches to St. Augustine. Pork production increased as well. St. Augustine finally had an agricultural base it could rely on for tax revenue, with treasury officials charging ranchers at different times of beef production according to the head of cattle, acreage of plowed land, fees for *estancias*, fees for inheritable titles to more land, etc. Ranchers gained enduring titles to land and St. Augustine finally made a little bit of money. The boom days of St. Augustine were also the boom days of early Florida cattle ranching.[15]

At its height around the turn of the eighteenth century, according to one historian, over thirty separate ranches were on St. Augustine's tax records, herding upward of twenty thousand head of cattle. Some operated along the coast north of St. Augustine, and more were to the west, along the banks of the St. Johns River. The largest clusters were in central Florida, in Timucua province, and still more were farther to the west, into the Florida panhandle, where missions tended their own herds, some of them sizeable.[16]

Among the smaller *estancias* and *haciendas* stood La Chua, by far the largest of La Florida's cattle ranches. Owned by relatives of Menéndez and operating late in the 1640s, the ranch was named after a swampy section of north central Florida, known as Payne's Prairie near present-day Gainesville. The name Alachua is taken directly from it, and as one historian once suggested it is perfectly plausible that the University of Florida, "with its excellent Department of Animal Husbandry," sits directly on the spot "of a large Spanish cattle ranch," perhaps La Chua itself. From that ranch and others, herds were transported east over the St. Johns River in flatboats to St. Augustine, where they were taken into the city and slaughtered. After the meat was sold or preserved the hide and tallow work began. The latter two were done primarily for export, with ships leaving for Cuba and even Spain on occasion. Occasionally the ranch sold meat to Apalachee, and the owners also opened a small port on the Suwanee River, named San Martín, to ship their product from La Chua to Havana directly, away from the prying eyes of tax officials in St. Augustine.[17] The ranch was at least profitable enough to have its own black market.

In the years before British and Native raiding devastated La Florida, La Chua and the many smaller *haciendas* around it squeezed out a modest profitability, just as St. Augustine did. Several lists of cattle herds were made in complaints of Natives who were angered by cattle destroying their crops in Apalachee province and around San Luis de Talimali, proving the ranches were spreading west fast enough to irritate the remaining Apalachees and eventually overtake most of their traditional farming lands. Thousands of head of cattle roamed the prairies and were so numerous and valuable that ranch hands and overseers were paid royally for keeping the ranches secure. Many of the small *haciendas* were fortified, and La Chua eventually included a blockhouse.[18]

This boom period did not come without a price. Whatever Native resistance to the ranches had existed at midcentury slowly melted away. The expansion of the *estancias* from the St. Johns River to Apalachee Province that took place later in the century would never have been possible, either legally or practically, had the Native population not plummeted to such lengths that they were basically gone. Nevertheless, some Natives did remain, and as was the case elsewhere in the Spanish ranching world, many of them turned into cattlemen. America's first cattlemen were not only Spaniards, in other words, but the Natives that were forced to work for them. While the *encomiendas* that would have truly forced Natives to work on the ranches did not really exist in La Florida, *repartimiento* labor drafts and Franciscan demands certainly did. These labors were so despised that both civil and religious authorities soon complained of Apalachee and Timucua Natives running away to the ranches to work there, either free or on a contract basis, rather than submit to *repartimiento* work in the mission fields or in St. Augustine. At the turn of the eighteenth century there were so many Natives among the *haciendas* that church authorities feared religious observations were being overlooked.[19]

These first American cowboys were a remarkably multicultural lot, as were the American cowboys of the post-Civil War west. La Florida *haciendas* and *estancias* operated with a mix of laborers that ranged from free Floridanos and creoles, to quasi-enslaved Native laborers, to completely enslaved Africans. All three would have been visible at a place like La Chua, making America's first cowboys not only Spanish and Native, but African American as well. When Timucua rebels attacked La Chua in the 1655 revolt, for instance, they left four Spaniards, one Mexican from Tabasco region, and two African slaves dead. The dead were all ranch hands, providing an enticing glimpse into the multiethnic nature of America's first cow culture.[20]

Just as cattle ranching moved into La Florida from the Caribbean, so did enslaved African vaqueros. Enslaved African cowmen came to the Caribbean islands shortly after cattle did and were commonplace by the mid-1500s. There were well over a thousand on Hispaniola alone, and hundreds on each of the other significant Caribbean islands, like Puerto Rico and Cuba. By the late sixteenth century vaqueros of mixed African race dominated coastal New Spain ranches, some transitioning in time from slaves to highly specialized and independent wage laborers. "Disparaged by the privileged class as vagrants and 'low fellows' given to orgies of drink and sex," wrote one ranching historian, these early southwestern cowmen "had already become the stuff of which western dime novels could be made."[21]

As historian Amy Turner Bushnell took from ranching records, one of these African or mixed-race slaves was considered an important addition to a La Florida *hacienda*, and at least one was part of the sizeable startup cost. According to one slave sale at midcentury, a thirty-year-old ranch hand from West Africa sold for the considerable sum of five hundred pesos, and a *mulatto* overseer for one hundred pesos more. That clearly seemed to be the case with La Chua, and it seems reasonable that of the enslaved Africans that existed on the fringe of society in St. Augustine, as royal slaves, private chattel, or hired laborers, their numbers were among La Florida's original cowmen.[22]

Like most of La Florida, cattle ranching was almost entirely annihilated in the British raids that took place not long after the boom days of the La Chua *hacienda*. Some cattle were driven into the newly built castillo for protection and some were driven west towards Pensacola. While that protected St. Augustine's residents, the *haciendas* did not fare nearly as well. Most, like La Chua, were either burned or abandoned, and would never rebuild. Like the rest of St. Augustine, residents held on to cattle ranching right up until the end of La Florida, yet with the loss of the missions the ranches never functioned well very far from the city. In the meantime cattle also roamed the empty Potano and Timucua fields, slowly making their way south across the peninsula. In 1774 William Bartram found them "large, sleek, sprightly, and as fat as can be in general." These would become the Florida "scrub" of late centuries and of Florida cowboy lore.[23]

Notes

1. Rimas and Fraser, *Beef*, 126-128; Crosby, *The Columbian Exchange*, 86-87; Jordan, *North American Cattle-Ranching Frontiers*, 14-30, 92-95; Rouse, *The Criollo*, 9-21.
2. Crosby, *The Columbian Exchange*, 76, 85-92; Gade, "Cattle," 1: 493-494; Jordan, *North American Cattle-Ranching Frontiers*, 65-72; Rouse, *The Criollo*, 21-24, 30-42.
3. Bushnell, "The Menendez Marquez Cattle Barony," 410.
4. Jordan, *North American Cattle-Ranching Frontiers*, 30-33, 75-76.
5. Jordan, *North American Cattle-Ranching Frontiers*, 73-74; Crosby, *The Columbian Exchange*, 86.
6. Jordan, *North American Cattle-Ranching Frontiers*, 86-104; Rouse, *The Criollo*, 43-73; Rimas and Fraser, *Beef*, 122-126, 129-130; Crosby, *The Columbian Exchange*, 87-88.
7. Jordan, *North American Cattle-Ranching Frontiers*, 67; Rimas and Fraser, *Beef*, 128-129; Rouse, *The Criollo*, 3-5,18-19.
8. Jordan, *North American Cattle-Ranching Frontiers*, 105-106; Arnade, "Cattle Raising," 117-118; Rouse, *The Criollo*, 73-74.
9. Bushnell, "The Menendez Marquez Cattle Barony," 408-410; Jordan, *North American Cattle-Ranching Frontiers*, 106.
10. Hallock and Franz, eds., *Travels on the St. Johns River*, 76; Bushnell, "The Menendez Marquez Cattle Barony," 410; Arnade, "Cattle Raising," 118; Jordan, *North American Cattle-Ranching Frontiers*, 105-106.
11. Bushnell, "The Menendez Marquez Cattle Barony," 410; Jordan, *North American Cattle-Ranching Frontiers*, 66, 70, 88.
12. Crosby, *The Columbian Exchange*, 75; Rimas and Fraser, *Beef*, 122.
13. Bushnell, "The Menendez Marquez Cattle Barony," 416-420.
14. Hoffman, *Florida Frontiers*, 117; Blanton, "The Role of Cattle Ranching," 667-685; Bushnell, "The Menendez Marquez Cattle Barony," 417-422.
15. Bushnell, *Situado and Sabana*, 139; Bushnell, "The Menendez Marquez Cattle Barony," 422-423, 426-428; Arnade, "Cattle Raising," 122-123; Parker, "St. Augustine in the Seventeenth Century," 574-575; Hann, *Apalachee*, 240; Bushnell, *The King's Coffer*, 80-81.
16. Arnade, "Cattle Raising," 118; Jordan, *North American Cattle-Ranching Frontiers*, 106-107; Hann, *Apalachee*, 239-240.

17. Bushnell, "The Menendez Marquez Cattle Barony," 423-424; Hoffman, *Florida Frontiers*, 119.

18. Bushnell, *Situado and Sabana*, 141-142; Hann, *Apalachee*, 53, 59, 232; Bushnell, "The Menendez Marquez Cattle Barony," 429-430; Jordan, *North American Cattle-Ranching Frontiers*, 106.

19. Hoffman, *Florida Frontiers*, 136; Bushnell, *Situado and Sabana*, 139; Bushnell, "The Menendez Marquez Cattle Barony," 430; Hann, *Apalachee*, 232-233.

20. Hoffman, *Florida Frontiers*, 130; Landers, *Black Society*, 20; Landers, "Africans and Native Americans," 57; Bushnell, "The Menendez Marquez Cattle Barony," 418; Bushnell, *The King's Coffer*, 23.

21. Jordan, *North American Cattle-Ranching Frontiers*, 66-67, 92.

22. Bushnell, "The Menendez Marquez Cattle Barony," 418; Bushnell, *The King's Coffer*, 23; Hoffman, *Florida Frontiers*, 130; Landers, *Black Society*, 20; Landers, "Africans and Native Americans," 57.

23. Hoffman, *Florida Frontiers*, 136; Rouse, *The Criollo*, 76-77, 186-187; Bushnell, "The Menendez Marquez Cattle Barony," 429-431; Jordan, *North American Cattle-Ranching Frontiers*, 107-108; Van Doren, ed., *The Travels of William Bartram*, 179.

Citrus aurantium, La Florida's Fruit

"ORANGES MAY NOT BE THE ONLY FRUIT," WROTE ONE RECENT HISTORIAN OF Florida's most famous plant, "but they are one of the most romantic." William Bartram clearly thought so as he painted a positively divine scene just south of St. Augustine in 1774. He was somewhere on the shores of Lake George, the swampy headwaters of the St. Johns River. "This delightful spot, planted by nature," he described, was full of palms, magnolias, oaks, and of course orange trees. The sights and the aromas had him enchanted. What a "fascinating atmosphere surrounds this blissful garden," he penned. "What a beautiful retreat is here! Blessed unviolated spot of earth!" The feeling hasn't changed much for modern-day Floridians, who despite the retreat of orange groves south down the peninsula, remain as enchanted as ever. So intertwined is the orange in the state's cultural fabric, that many Americans consider them native.[1]

While another more recent scholar acknowledged Florida as the undisputed birthplace of the orange industry in a clear check on the more recent California competition, she still had to concede that Florida citrus too had its beginnings elsewhere. "The industry that grew there was centuries in the making," yet even then "first the orange had to find its way to North America."[2] Like many of the other vegetables grown either commercially or for fun anywhere in the United States, oranges are not actually from Florida. They are the product of the same Columbian Exchange that brought cattle and pigs to America as well as the diseases that wiped out much of the Native population. And similarly, much of this was done by Spaniards. Why else would famous orange varietals be named the Seville, or the Valencia?

The history of citrus is long and the fruit well-traveled. Just as oranges did not begin in La Florida, in fact, neither did they begin in Spain. Their origin is somewhere much farther east, among the modern-day countries of India, Burma/Myanmar, and southern China. Chinese sources dating into the BCE mention the peeling and eating of oranges, with one already describing over two dozen varietals. Most of these were produced for their aesthetic value and fragrant nature. They were excellent preserved with sugar or used to flavor teas, wines, and other drinks. The terms *naranga*, or *narangi*, from which the Spanish *naranja* presumably originates, were seen in Sanskrit in India and referred to the fruits' fragrant qualities.[3]

Various citrus varietals made their way west into Europe by way of trade routes and with invading armies, making them part of Europe's wars of religion and particularly the *Reconquista*. While citrus was traded along the Silk Road, the plants themselves were probably first admired by Europeans during the Crusades. The orange tree was incredibly popular among Muslims, "being loved for its graceful form, the intensity of its evergreen leaves and its hedonistic blossoms." All parts of the plant, from the fruit to the blossoms to the branches, were used medicinally as well as cosmetically and even in the construction of furniture. Crusade-era Christian warriors clearly took a liking to the trees, bringing oranges back with them in the twelfth and thirteenth centuries, and spreading seeds through the modern-day country of Israel into the Mediterranean and eventually through Italy. Oranges arrived into Barcelona, Seville, Lisbon, and other Iberian ports not long after.[4]

In a surprising early chapter of the *Reconquista*, however, the Muslim invaders of the Iberian Peninsula were the ones to introduce oranges to what would become modern Spain, bringing orange trees with them in their conquest of southern Iberia. The imposing Islamic structures in the south of Spain, including in Córdoba, the Alcazar in Seville, the Alhambra in Granada, and the Alcazaba of Málaga, all feature magnificent gardens and planted walkways, "a form of paradise on earth" in the words of one historian, designed for spiritual repose. Many of them were often adorned with stands of citrus trees.[5]

How the trees got from the Old World to the New World is also pretty clear. One reason seafaring Europeans might have carried citrus on their ships would have been to combat the vitamin C deficiency that would, sooner or later, have caused their teeth to fall out of their heads and their bones to turn to jelly. Eventually the result was scurvy, which if left untreated led to a painful and downright disgusting death. It took months for the effects of the deficiency to become notable, but sailors on transatlantic voyages frequently had that sort of time on their hands. They also tended to not eat that well. Vitamin C was not in salted pork or cod, was not in simple flour biscuit, and was not in booze, and those three constituted the majority of a sailor's diet for possibly months at a time. When that led to scurvy, many of the illness's symptoms included lethargy, joint pain, aching and weak muscles, bleeding gums and loose teeth, and bloody sores on the body. Yet these symptoms presented for countless other common diseases, like syphilis, leaving surgeons confused and frustrated. The disease took far too long for navies to tackle because it was so little understood, even when the cure was so simple. As surgeons came to realize, the answer was as easy as eating an orange.[6]

On Vasco de Gama's legendary 1498 journey around the Cape of Good Hope and into the Indian Ocean, for instance, he lost half his men to scurvy. Contemporary sixteenth- and seventeenth-century accounts demonstrated how little had changed over the course of the next century. One sailor recalled how those afflicted suffered: "their gums wax great, and swell," legs swelled, "and all the body becometh sore, and so benumbed, that they can not stir hand nor foot, and they die for weakness, or fall into fluxes and agues, and die thereby." Another referenced widespread body pain, heavy bruising, and then obviously the teeth. The gums "in the inside of the mouth and outside the teeth, become so swollen to such a size that neither teeth not the molars can be brought together. The teeth become so loose and without support that they move while moving the head." The men on Magellan's circumnavigation even lanced their gums when they began swelling and rinsed them with urine in an attempt to remedy the situation.[7] Scurvy was no fun.

Most of these early examples all came from Portuguese and Spanish sources. Scurvy was the curse of discovery, and the Portuguese and Spanish were the discoverers. They were the pioneers of long-distance sea travel and trade, although in time there would be others. Jacques Cartier's men suffered terribly from scurvy on his North American voyages, and the English would come to dread scurvy soon enough. By that time, however, the Spanish seemed already to have a handle on the malady. De Gama's surviving men were saved when Moorish traders provided them with oranges on the east coast of Africa, and as soon as the symptoms reappeared on the way home back, one of the officers "sent a man on shore to bring off a supply of oranges which were much desired by our sick." It was clear to those men that citrus held the key to their salvation, and they were right. The remedy, almost too simple to rely on, was a good shot of citrus juice, which perhaps explains why it took generations longer for British sailors to consistently stock their ships with citrus.[8]

While Spanish and Portuguese mariners set records for time at sea on their way to the edges of the earth, sailors seldom suffered from scurvy on the Atlantic crossing. That particular route, although miserable and deadly for all sorts of reasons, was not usually long enough to generate a vitamin C deficiency debilitating enough to produce scorbutic symptoms. Although a return trip to Spain could take months, ships were seldom too far from the coast to seek help, a coast that by the mid-sixteenth century was apparently lined with citrus trees. That transfer began with Columbus, who supposedly brought citrus seeds with him to Hispaniola on his second voyage. According to some sources, Spaniards were legally required to bring citrus in some form with them on all long-haul voyages specifically to propagate the trees, so important was the prevention of scurvy and so obvious was the connection between that and citrus. Even if the legal requirement to do so was not real, Columbus's voyage was still one of colonization, and in addition to livestock Columbus brought all sorts of European seeds, clippings, and other food stores with him. Citrus, if only because Spaniards liked it, would have been an obvious choice. And like everything else, citrus did great in the Caribbean, of which Brazil's current orange industry is a clear testament.[9]

Both the modern-day states of Florida and California have long histories with the fruit because they have long histories with the Spanish. Some have suggested that, like cattle, the story of Florida oranges began with Juan Ponce de León. Like cattle, that probably didn't happen. The same could be said about de Soto. It is uncertain but highly unlikely that any of the citrus seeds or plants brought by de León, de Soto, or de Luna took root in La Florida. Citrus seeds are not particularly hardy. They do not store well and they spoil easily. If any were discarded by passing Spaniards, who might consider eating a fruit and spitting out the seeds, nothing would have materialized.[10]

The exact date of citrus introduction in America, like cattle, will forever remain elusive. Yet it seems most reasonable that it was the permanent settlement at St. Augustine that opened the door for the first orange groves. It was not in the southern portion of the present state of Florida, but in the northeast, where orange groves first flourished. They not only grew well there, but apparently all the way up the coast into South Carolina. According to historical evidence, both St. Augustine and Santa Elena included groves in the 1580s, although their remains have been difficult to locate since. There were certainly groves in St. Augustine in 1586, because Sir Francis Drake's men made it a point to chop all of them down during his attack, "even the trees and plantings," one survivor described. The hardy and resourceful trees would have just re-sprouted right out of the old stumps, an excellent metaphor for the scrappy St. Augustine settlement itself.[11]

Oranges of course are not the only kinds of citrus grown, but they are by far the most popular. Among the most important and influential varietals are the sweet (*Citrus sinensis*) and the bitter orange (*Citrus aurantium*). The former is known as the Valencia, and the latter the Seville. The Valencia is the most common commercial orange grown in the world, including for the modern Florida juice industry. It does not actually originate from Valencia but was named so after a Spaniard who evidently found it similar to trees back home. Although cultivars introduced the Valencia from the Azores and Portugal, they did so commercially in the nineteenth century—far too late to be an early American story.[12]

The real La Florida gem was the bitter orange, the Seville, which is still widely produced in Spain and exported because of its aromatic qualities and high pectin content. It makes an excellent marmalade. It is also commonly referred to as "sour," or "bittersweet," and while not so great for casual eating, the acidic and aromatic bitter orange was, and still is, fantastic for cooking. Naturalist William Bartram learned so in 1774 while on one of his legendary Florida treks. As he sat on the shore of the St. Johns River, he considered eating the fish he cooked the last night, "though the sultry heats of the day had injured them." Fish does not last long in the Florida sun, Bartram was coming to realize. Yet, "by stewing them up afresh with the lively juice of Oranges, they served well enough for my supper." By pairing strong meats with bold citrus flavors, Bartram had wandered into the Caribbean-Creole world of mojo cuisine. Had he tried it during a pork roast, he would have been really impressed.[13]

This was the tree that remade the New World and is the one that apparently grew like a weed in La Florida—all parts of La Florida. In fact, while much of the orange's commercial story takes place long after the end of La Florida, there was a time when orange groves extended across much of peninsular Florida and up the coastal Atlantic. Frosts can damage or even destroy orange groves if they strike at the wrong time, making it seem strange to see so many references to orange stands so far to the north. Yet they were there, all the way into South Carolina. The English in Charleston might have hated the Spanish in St. Augustine, but apparently not enough to turn away shipments of La Florida oranges, which delighted South Carolinians until the outbreak of the War of Jenkin's Ear in 1739. For a while Charleston even had its own orange export, and Georgia and South Carolinian groves existed for generations, no doubt a legacy of the original Spanish La Florida settlements. Like every other part of Spanish colonialism in North America, however, oranges eventually shrunk back into the present-day limits of the state of Florida.[14]

Aside from those planted in backyards, modern orange groves are basically unheard of north of present-day Orlando. Climate stability and land development might have forced commercial growers out of north Florida, but that is a relatively new development in the long history of citrus in the peninsula. Take, for instance, William Bartram and his time on the St. Johns watershed. His father, famed British naturalist John Bartram, first toured it with William in 1766. William made his own separate journey over much of the same river again in 1774. On both trips it was rare for the men to go more than a few days before making some mention of citrus. Within days of setting out from St. Augustine on the first expedition, for instance, the Bartram party camped on a bluff "amongst plenty of bitter-sweet oranges, next in goodness to China, and here the woods are full of them." When William set out on his own adventure he barely got out of St. Augustine before mentioning that the surrounding orange trees "were in full bloom and filled the air with fragrance."[15]

Some of the groves were unexceptional and mentioned in passing, a testament to their seeming omnipresence along the St. Johns River. Such was the case near an isolated Seminole trading post owned by James Spalding and referred to as Spalding's Upper Store. There the Bartrams ran across "an orange grove on a bluff, where we gathered good bitter-sweets," with the fruit scattered along the ground. That pitiful grove differed greatly from the sight the men beheld just a bit farther down the river, where they encamped "at a great orange-grove, where thousands of orange trees grow as thick as possible, and full of sour and bitter-sweet fruits."[16] This abandoned grove was massive. Apparently, oranges were everywhere.

A decade later, little had changed. Consider one sprawling grove William enjoyed in 1774. William and his party decided to make a visit to the plantation of a British rice and indigo planter after running across a Seminole who was out hunting food for it. In the afternoon, Bartram wrote, he and his fellow travelers "retired to the fragrant shades of an Orange grove," which was apparently quite impressive. It was right next to the plantation house and consisted of "many hundred trees, natives of the place," which were large, "flourishing and in perfect bloom, and loaded with their ripe golden fruit." All of this suggests that the grove was already standing when the planter took possession of the land and built the plantation and gardens around it.[17]

How did those trees get there? Who was taking care of them? There are several possible answers. Perhaps what the enterprising planter beheld on his newly acquired property resembled what John Bartram had noticed in 1766, "a point of high ground, which has been an ancient plantation of Indians or Spaniards." Growing there were several sizeable oaks "and plenty of oranges."[18] Perhaps these were the remnants of a Native grove or even a Native community, or perhaps the ruins of an abandoned Spanish *hacienda*. Considering how close the land was to St. Augustine, either tenant would have made sense. Before

Seminoles entered the region this was not only prized grazing land but Timucua and Potano territory. Coming upon an active Seminole community, the younger Bartram described a "large orange grove at the upper end of their village; the trees were large, carefully pruned, and the ground under them clean, open, and airy." Another, still abandoned, was "betwixt the riverbanks and ancient Indian fields, where there are evident traces of the inhabitants of the ancients." Bartram stumbled across a Native burial ground while wandering through another grove in the dark.[19]

Then again, St. Johns River was also lined with small Spanish *haciendas* by the turn of the eighteenth century, and Spaniards may indeed have been the ones to plant the trees. However they got there, sometimes plantation owners removed the groves "to make room for planting ground," as William noticed farther down the river. That was the case with one plantation he passed near a place called Mount Hope, "so named by my father John Bartram" when he made his trip a decade earlier. "It was at that time a fine Orange grove, but now cleared and converted into a large Indigo plantation, the property of an English gentleman, under the care of an agent." However, as was also clear from the fine plantation they rested on, which was basically built around the grove, oftentimes the new British tenants kept them, both for their production and no doubt for their aesthetics.[20] It was an aesthetic that William Bartram appreciated in 1774.

As the travels of both the Bartrams revealed, the St. Johns River was the place for ambitious and ruthless entrepreneurs. After the turnover of La Florida to the British, Northeast Florida became British East Florida, and prospective planters entered with dreams of rice and indigo riches. Apparently, some of them also looked to oranges. Among them was trader and grower Jesse Fish, who shipped 65,000 oranges to England in 1776. Settlers planted more commercial groves during Florida's territorial period, beginning in 1821, yet only much later in the nineteenth century did a thriving citrus industry really take off.[21]

The Valencia brand that swept through Florida arrived later in the nineteenth century, but not necessarily in seed form. The Valencia, not a La Florida varietal, might not have taken off at all had grove planters not grafted the European varietal to local rootstock. Grafting was a far superior way to quickly grow orange trees from preexisting seedlings by taking the roots of already established and thriving orange trees derived from the much older Spanish imports, called rootstock, and grafting Valencia shoots onto them. Not only does the resulting tree fruit much faster than a tree sown from seed, but incorporates the hardiness and resistance of the established stock.[22] In the case of Florida oranges, that was La Florida rootstock.

There was no denying that citrus did exceptionally well in the wet Florida heat, and particularly so once Valencias were grafted to Florida rootstock. With the expansion of railroads down both the east and west coasts of Florida in the Gilded Age, the conditions were finally right for a booming Citrus economy. Fruit stands popped up along the coast, and brands like Indian River are still recognizable across the country.[23] Just about four hundred years after the first oranges hit the shores of La Florida, Tropicana began the bulk processing of oranges specifically for juice, revolutionizing the market with frozen concentrated orange juice. Despite increased foreign competition and booming housing markets, Tropicana trains still ship Florida orange juice all over the country, and citrus is still tied inextricably to state identity. If it does anywhere, La Florida lives on in Florida orange juice.[24]

Notes

1. Hyman, *Oranges*, 7; Thursby, *Florida Oranges*, 9; Hallock and Franz, eds., *Travels on the St. Johns River*, 106.
2. Hamilton, *Squeezed*, 4.
3. Hyman, *Oranges*, 7-10.
4. Hamilton, *Squeezed*, 4-5; Hyman, *Oranges*, 11-19; Laszlo, *Citrus*, 15-19.
5. Hamilton, *Squeezed*, 4-5; Hyman, *Oranges*, 23-25; Laudan, *Cuisine and Empire*, 143; Ruhl, "Oranges and Wheat," 40.
6. Gratzer, *Terrors of the Table*, 16-18; Bown, *Scurvy*, 34-38; Davies et al., *Vitamin C*, 7-14; Carpenter, *The History of Scurvy*, 1-28; Bushnell, *Situado and Sabana*, 56.
7. Davies et al., *Vitamin C*, 7-8; Carpenter, *The History of Scurvy*, 3-5; Laudan, *Cuisine and Empire*, 190.
8. Davies et al., *Vitamin C*, 7-14; Carpenter, *The History of Scurvy*, 1-28.
9. Hyman, *Oranges*, 19; Ruhl, "Oranges and Wheat," 40; Thursby, *Florida Oranges*, 15.
10. Hamilton, *Squeezed*, 5; Ruhl, "Oranges and Wheat," 40-41; Hyman, *Oranges*, 19; Thursby, *Florida Oranges*, 14.
11. Ruhl, "Oranges and Wheat," 40-41; Covington, "Drake Destroys St. Augustine," 92; Document 43, in Wright, *Further Voyages*, 183.
12. Hamilton, *Squeezed*, 5; Hyman, *Oranges*, 34-38; Laszlo, *Citrus*, 34.
13. Hamilton, *Squeezed*, 5; Hyman, *Oranges*, 34-38; Thursby, *Florida Oranges*, 15.
14. Thursby, *Florida Oranges*, 14-15; Ruhl, "Oranges and Wheat," 41-42.
15. Hallock and Franz, eds., *Travels on the St. Johns River*, 20, 54; Thursby, *Florida Oranges*, 15.
16. Hallock and Franz, eds., *Travels on the St. Johns River*, 33, 37.
17. Hallock and Franz, eds., *Travels on the St. Johns River*, 56.
18. Hallock and Franz, eds., *Travels on the St. Johns River*, 16.
19. Hallock and Franz, eds., *Travels on the St. Johns River*, 65, 95, 103, 105; Thursby, *Florida Oranges*, 9.
20. Hallock and Franz, eds., *Travels on the St. Johns River*, 70.
21. Thursby, *Florida Oranges*, 15-16; Hamilton, *Squeezed*, 5; Hyman, *Oranges*, 19; Hoffman, *Florida's Frontiers*, 229-230.

22. Thursby, *Florida Oranges*, 9-12.
23. Hyman, *Oranges*, 48-53.
24. Hyman, *Oranges*, 62-71.

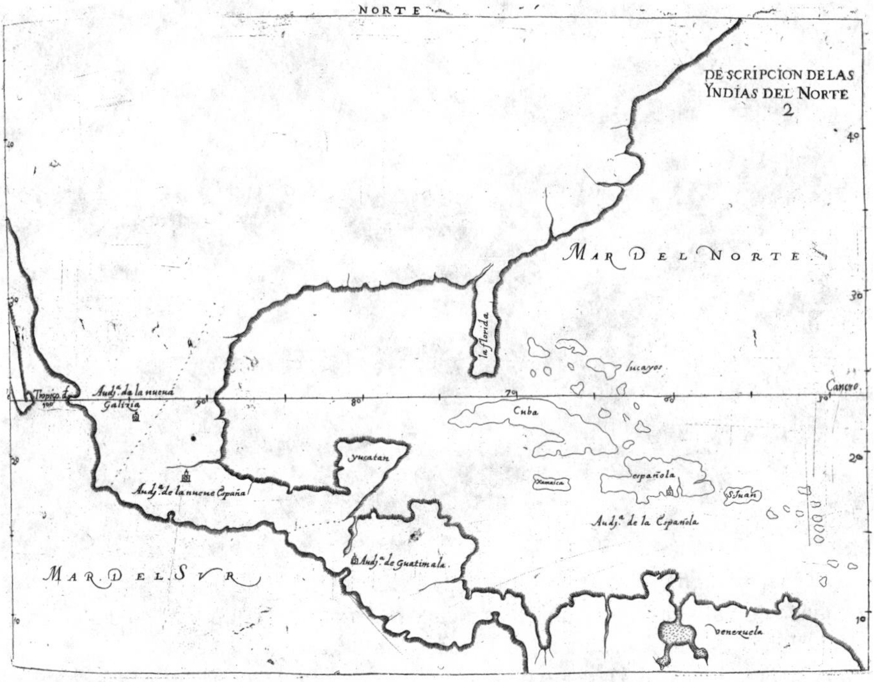

MAP 4.1. An Unknown La Florida

As can be seen in this turn of the century map, very little was understood about the interior of La Florida, even though by that point several entradas had penetrated the continent, St. Augustine existed, and Franciscan missions were beginning to stretch up the Georgia and Carolinian coastlines.

"DESCRIPCION DE LAS YNDIAS DEL NORTE." MADRID, 1601. ACCESSION NUMBER 01808-007. JOHN CARTER BROWN LIBRARY—BROWN UNIVERSITY.

PHOTO 4.1. Hernando de Soto and the Black Legend
Hernando de Soto torturing Native Americans in various ways. Certainly a depiction of the "Black Legend," according to Theodore de Bry.

"FERDINANDUS SOTTO CRUDELITER IN FLORIDA..." *[AMERICA. PT 5. LATIN] AMERICAE PARS QUINTA NOBILIS & ADMIRATIONE PLENA HIERONYMI BEZONI MEDIOLANENSIS SECUNDAE SETIONIS HISPANORUM* ... RECORD NUMBER 34724-18. JOHN CARTER BROWN LIBRARY—BROWN UNIVERSITY.

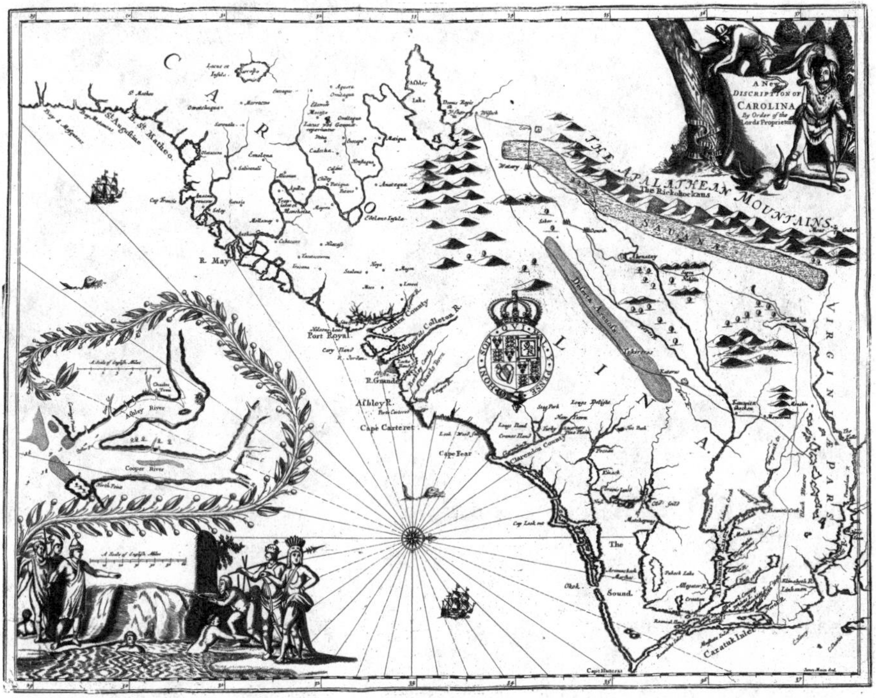

PHOTO 4.2. Carolina

This early map demonstrates contentious and overlapping claims to the Southeast. According to it, the Carolina grant extended down the East Coast well into La Florida, past St. Augustine.

"A NEW DISCRIPTION OF CAROLINA BY ORDER OF THE LORDS PROPRIETORS." LONDON, 1672. ACCESSION NUMBER 4820. JOHN CARTER BROWN LIBRARY—BROWN UNIVERSITY.

PHOTO: 4.3. Timucuan BBQ

An early La Florida depiction of Natives cooking and drying fish and various game with smoke on a barbacoa.

"WIE SIE IRE FISCH WILDPRET ..." *[AMERICA. PT 2. GERMAN] DER ANDER THEIL DER NEWLICH ERFUNDENEN LANDTSCHAFFT AMERICAE, VON DREYEN SCHIFFAHRTEN, SO DIE FRANTZOSEN IN FLORIDAM ... GETHAN* ... RECORD NUMBER 08915-29. JOHN CARTER BROWN LIBRARY—BROWN UNIVERSITY.

PHOTO 4.4. Oranges on the St. Johns River
A late nineteenth-century Florida print shows a thriving orange grove on the St. Johns River.
SKETCHES IN AN ORANGE GROVE BY E. A. ABBEY—CITRUS COUNTY, FLORIDA. 1875 (CIRCA). IMAGE NUMBER RC10895. STATE ARCHIVES OF FLORIDA, FLORIDA MEMORY.

Conclusion

"20. AND ODD NEGROES"

The 1619 sale of enslaved Africans to the English in Virginia is widely considered the beginning of American slavery and the beginning of African American history. According to famous Virginian John Rolfe, that moment took place when Captain John Colyn Jope and the *White Lion* arrived at Point Comfort in August of 1619. Captain Daniel Elfrith and the *Treasurer* made port a few days later. As Rolfe recalled, Jope and the *White Lion* were desperate to trade for provisions but had on board nothing with which to trade for them except "20. and odd Negroes." Planters obliged the captain and traded for the slaves "at the best and easiest rates they could," as Rolfe explained it, and the *White Lion* was soon on its way. The *Treasurer* arrived in the same condition and pulled away around the same time, having left "two or three of negroes" in Virginia, presumably also in exchange for supplies. The *White Lion* and the *Treasurer* pushed off from Point Comfort and out of the history books, leaving Virginians with English America's first African slaves.[1]

This episode provides an excellent opportunity to close *La Florida* with another intriguing American counter-narrative—a counterpoint to the Thanksgiving Day massacre. Evidence of the 1619 sale is based on sources not much longer or more detailed than those of the First Thanksgiving. Only a few short passages describe the transactions, leaving historians with questions about the first days of English slavery that might never be answered. Yet knowing what we know now about the way things worked in the region, it is easy to add context to this momentous American first by looking not to Jamestown, but to the nearby Spanish. At 160 tons the *White Lion* was nowhere near the largest ship cruising the Atlantic, but then again pirate ships usually weren't. Indeed, while Rolfe described the *White Lion* as a Dutch "man of Warr," it was most certainly a privateer. The ship's pilot "for the West Indies" was an Englishman by the name of Mr. Marmaduke. He was definitely a pirate. How else would an Englishman have a reputation for his Caribbean sailing chops? Neither England nor the Netherlands had any colonies in the Caribbean early in the seventeenth century, save Bermuda, and in 1619 Bermuda was not much to look at. There were no other reasons for an Englishman to be in the region other than to engage in illicit trade and of course to pillage Spanish shipping. That is in fact exactly just what happened. African slaves ended up in Virginia because Jope and Elfrith had just robbed a Portuguese slave ship.

James I and Philip II wrapped up the Anglo-Spanish "sea war" fifteen years previous, so what were English privateers doing robbing Portuguese and Spanish shipping interests in Caribbean waters in 1619? As Philip D. Morgan suggested in his own work on the subject, the *Treasurer* probably lacked a legitimate letter of marque when it arrived at Point Comfort. That would have raised eyebrows even in Virginia. Without such paperwork, Captain Elfrith's seizure of the Spanish slaves constituted an act of absolute piracy, even according to British standards. If anyone who cared caught wind of the attack, Elfrith and most of his pirate crew would probably end up hanging somewhere. Perhaps that was why Elfrith and the *Treasurer* slinked out of Chesapeake Bay and towards Bermuda without staying long at all in Virginia.

Then there was Captain Jope and the *White Lion*. His ship was English too, but he sailed under a letter of marque issued by the Dutch government. While England and Spain were technically at peace since 1604, the Spanish and Dutch were still tied up in an intense struggle for Dutch independence. A 1609 ceasefire ended fighting that began in the 1580s only to have it pick back up again just a few years later. With the Dutch basically almost never at peace with the Spanish, Dutch authorities were giving away letters of marque to anyone who asked, the same tactic Elizabeth used in the 1580s. The Portuguese, aligned closely with Spain and the ones currently contracted to run the slave trade into the Spanish colonies, were fair game as well. That made the *White Lion* an English ship with an English crew, engaging in piracy against combined Spanish-Portuguese shipping, in the Caribbean, on behalf of the Dutch. It all was so fantastically elaborate, corrupt, and opportunistic, yet so perfectly ordinary for the period.

As the story went, the *White Lion* and the *Treasurer* met up in the Caribbean and went about privateering together, making their way into the Gulf of Mexico in search of enemy shipping. There the two ran across the *São João Bautista*, known in Spanish as the *San Juan Bautista*. That ship, skippered by Manuel Mendes da Cunha (also de Acunha, in Spanish), was underway to Vera Cruz from São Paulo de Luanda, a major slaving port in Portuguese Angola. At

Luanda, da Cunha loaded 350 enslaved Africans onboard the *Bautista* and cast off, beginning a perfectly legal slave trading expedition that would lead him to Vera Cruz, one of the only ports in New Spain where merchants could legally dispose of enslaved Africans.

Enter the *White Lion* and the *Treasurer*, which overtook da Cunha and the *Bautista* off Campeche. This was cut and dry English privateering, something that had made English merchants money for decades at the expense of Spanish colonial interests. For the Spanish in the early seventeenth century, this was still very much the treacherous Gulf. The "English corsairs" relieved Captain da Cunha of much of his human cargo, according to a Spanish report, and moved on. While a ship full of silver bars would have been preferable, human cargos could be seized and resold for handsome profits if the pirates were so inclined, which both Jope and Elfrith clearly were. From the 350 enslaved Angolans Acunha had originally packed on the ship, "large and small," the pirates left him with less than 150. Perhaps the captains had already hopscotched backwater slave ports on their way to Point Comfort, dispensing of their human cargo to labor-hungry Spaniards. Otherwise, the *White Lion* should have had many more than "20. and odd Negroes" locked away in its hold.

None of this was unordinary, either for the time or for the place. English privateers sacking Spanish and Portuguese shipping in the Caribbean was nothing new. Neither was the route the two took to escape with their booty. The two ships passed through the Gulf, the Florida Straits, and the Bahamian channel unchecked, just as countless English pirates had done before them. They sailed right past St. Augustine and probably in sight of the beach on Anastasia Island. Regional officials, recovering from several waves of epidemics that ravaged La Florida in the sixteen-teens, probably had bigger problems to worry about than keeping an eye on small ships passing up the coast. The outpost of St. Augustine, built and maintained explicitly to stop every part of this story so far, had proven itself useless once again.

Up the coast was Jamestown. Settled a little more than a decade previous, Jamestown was still very much a disappointment of a colony in 1619, with its planters having just recently discovered tobacco as a possible cash crop. Tobacco would make Virginians among the richest English colonials in the seventeenth and eighteenth centuries, but that was a long way away from the Virginia Jope and Elfrith laid eyes on in 1619. For these two captains, however, Jamestown was functioning just as Virginia's very first colonial boosters had intended. It was a sanctuary and re-provisioning outpost for privateers preying on Spanish shipping in the Caribbean and the Florida Straits. Both ships did, in the end, get what they came to Virginia to get. They loaded up with food and water and went on their way. The *Treasurer* made for Bermuda and the *White Lion* went back on the prowl. Both ships sold slaves to pay for their provisioning, but that was only because slaves were all they had to sell. Had the *Bautista* carried silver, tobacco, log wood, or animal hides in their holds, then Jope and Elfrith would have paid for their food with those stolen valuables. This is what historians like Philip D. Morgan mean when they say that the 1619 introduction of slavery came about only by happenstance. Had Jope and Elfrith not raided a Spanish slave ship, the trajectory of slavery in English America might have been entirely different. Slavery in English America was, in this light, not only a coincidence. It was a product of English privateering in the Gulf of Mexico—a product, in one way or another, of La Florida.[2]

Even this story of the American origins of slavery, in short, is woven with Spanish thread. By the seventeenth century the *asiento* was in full operation, and thousands of slaves a year were being freighted across the Atlantic on Portuguese and Spanish ships—ships that were often the target of English pirates. The colonies, the ships, the slaves, the letters of marque, even the Florida Straits, are familiar chapters in the history of Spanish colonialism in America. While the particular story of the *White Lion* and the *Treasurer* does not directly involve La Florida, it explains precisely why Spanish authorities clung so tenaciously to St. Augustine and a colony that never made anyone in Spain happy. If colonial authorities had pumped enough money into the colony to make it self-sustaining and strategically effective, neither the *White Lion* nor the *Treasurer* might have slipped past it and again, the trajectory of the American South might look entirely different.

That did not happen, of course, and the contingency sale of slaves to Virginians in 1619 is perhaps the single most important moment in the development of the massive and massively influential slave society that the Chesapeake Tidewater became. Not much else is clear about the sale, leading historians in the present to ponder the immediate and long-term implications of that moment in 1619. Did the enslaved Africans sold in Virginia stay enslaved, or were they freed? If they were freed, what kinds of freedom did they enjoy? These are the questions that modern historians of race and slavery in America still grapple with. On the one hand, it would have been difficult to keep them enslaved since Englishmen had never used African slaves before and Virginia did not have a slave code that would have cemented the legal permanency of the enslaved. As

Morgan suggested, however, records indicated that the planters of the period continually listed the Africans they received as servants and as property. Many were sold or otherwise legally transferred to other planters and their families as late as midcentury. From those records it seems pretty clear that neither the Africans nor their children were considered entirely free people.[3]

No doubt this is an argument of historical concern in Virginia, but from the perspective of St. Augustine and the larger Southeast, none of it would have changed much. Again, think the First Thanksgiving. Both the *White Lion* and the *Treasurer* passed right by St. Augustine on their way to Virginia, after all. If any of the enslaved men and women trapped on those two ships caught a glimpse of the coastline, they would have beheld a place where many of their countrymen had already been forcibly taken and now lived in bondage. Or rather, perhaps from St. Augustine, María Angola or Juan Angola might have caught a glimpse of the boats passing in the distance as they made their way up the coast. Both María and Juan were enslaved Africans who lived in St. Augustine, whose names appear in the town's baptismal records, and who might have been alive in 1619. In 1606 "María Angola slave of Vicente Morera" served as the sponsor of newborn Sussana. The next year an enslaved "María Angola" gave birth to a daughter, Andrea. If this was the same María, she was now owned by Luis Diaz, and she was now a mother. Ten years later Juan Angola, "slave of the king" served as sponsor to another newborn, Sebastian.[4] These slaves' lives are illuminated for only the briefest moment in time, for only a sentence or two in baptismal records. Yet there they were, African slaves alive and living in St. Augustine.

First, the names "Angola." María and Juan were not related, at least as far as we can tell. The place references in slaves' names commonly referred to their countries of origin. In this case, it was the same Angola from which Virginia's 1619 slaves originated. María and Juan were not Islamic "Moorish" slaves taken from North African or Southern Spanish ports, and therefore undeserving of a place in the very first chapter of America's history of slavery. They were most likely *bozales*, first generation slaves taken directly from West Africa on a slave ship very similar to the *Bautista*. They might even have been shipped out of the very same port, São Paulo de Luanda, from which Virginia's slaves originated. The Africans who were forced on shore at Point Comfort in 1619, in all likelihood, came from the very same region as the Africans that were forced on shore in St. Augustine decades previous.

Second, the first slaves in Virginia might have stayed slaves. The planters might have treated them like indentured laborers, or they might have freed them altogether. Because Virginians had no experience with slavery, or had a legal framework to deal with it, we are not exactly sure just how Virginia's planters approached their newly acquired property. Neither ambiguity nor inexperience was the case when it came to María and Juan. María was a privately owned slave and Juan publicly owned. They were slaves living in a slave society that was operating for generations already, and which had strong legal precedence. This was chattel slavery, no different from the slave system that would eventually dominate English colonies in the Caribbean and the American South. Whether María, a woman, was a domestic slave or a field slave mattered little, just as whether Juan toiled for the Crown inside the walls of St. Augustine or outside them. And while María, Sussana, Andrea, Sebastian, and Juan all appeared in church records, that made them no less enslaved. They were just Catholic slaves. These documents leave little room for equivocation: St. Augustine, their existence confirms, was the birthplace of American slavery.

Lastly, these records portray an enslaved population of St. Augustine that for decades already was becoming the African American population of St. Augustine. The births of babies Andrea, Sussana, or Sebastian, the ones mentioned in those same records, were no outliers. Before them all was Augustin, who was born on Sunday, August 20, 1606, "legitimate son of Augustine slave and Francisca slave," and was baptized in St. Augustine's main church. Perhaps Esteban, who was born more than a decade earlier in 1595, was enslaved, but the portion of the page that would have said so is missing. The difference of a decade, while significant, changes the narrative little. Not only were Africans not landed in Virginia until thirteen years after Augustin's birth, but Jamestown itself would not exist for another year after his birth. Think of the implications there: St. Augustine was not just the birthplace of American slavery, and African American heritage in what would become the United States was not just older than 1619. If Augustin's birth occurred a year before Jamestown even existed, then the United States' African American history is actually older than its English American history.

The transaction that brought the first African slaves into Virginia society is much better understood once the Spanish are included in the story. American slavery, just like many of the foodways, Native identities, religious traditions, etc., that originated in the south, had Spanish influences. Without understanding those influences, how can one understand something as complex and important to the country as slavery? Spanish-American history is not just the country's first Euro-American history, it is highly relevant history. It is history with a clear modern-day legacy. Just like the Thanksgiving story, Augustin's birth might not change the way American history is taught and understood. Perhaps it should.

Tales of Thanksgivings and of slavery bookend *La Florida: Catholics, Conquistadores, and other American Origin Stories.* Its narrative path not only follows "connections," but "origins," "transitions," and "legacies," all in the hopes of revealing and re-centering for modern Americans a complicated Spanish-American history that was in many ways this country's first colonizing history, yet is now just a lost history. The narrative path winds its way through several centuries, beginning when La Florida was much of the American Southeast, and a product of Spanish desires elsewhere in the Caribbean and in Latin America. The path leads eventually to 1763, when for reasons of international diplomacy, Spain finally gave up on La Florida. By that time there was not much left to give up on, really, only the isolated outposts of St. Augustine and Pensacola. Even long after La Florida had shrunk territorially to a mere sliver of its former size, however, the Spanish presence in North America was a shaping force elsewhere in the continent, like in say South Carolina.

These connecting threads, which have ranged from discussions of slavery in the Spanish Caribbean to barbecue in the Carolinas, are all designed to bring a renewed focus on America's Spanish, Catholic heritage. Some, evoking the violence of conquest or the dawn of American slavery, are historical arguments of incredible weight that Americans should be grappling with in the most honest discussions they have about their past. Others, like the Seminole Tribe of Florida, evoke more positive stories of creation and resilience. And some, like orange juice and the venerable Florida scrub cattle, are just downright fun. Even though most of that heritage might have faded from the national view, it is not gone, and it is not hard at all to evoke the oldest of America's Spanish traditions. A good pulled pork sandwich or even a glass of orange juice will do.

Notes

1. Billings, ed., *The Old Dominion*, 180.
2. Billings, ed., *The Old Dominion*, 180; Morgan, "Virginia Slavery in Atlantic Context, 1550-1650," 85; Sluiter, "New Light on the '20. and Odd Negroes' Arriving in Virginia," 395-398.
3. Morgan, "Virginia Slavery in Atlantic Context, 1550-1650," 86.
4. *Baptisms, 1594-1763*, 1: 24, 29.

Bibliography

Adorno, Rolena. "The Polemics of Possession: Spain on America, Circa 1550," in Gregerson and Juster, eds., *Empires of God*. Philadelphia: University of Pennsylvania Press, 2010.

Adorno, Rolena, and Patrick Charles Pautz, eds., *The Narrative of Cabeza de Vaca*. Lincoln: University of Nebraska Press, 2003.

Altman, Ida. "Towns and the Forging of the Spanish Caribbean," in Lynn and Rowe, eds., *The Early Modern Hispanic World*. New York: Cambridge University Press, 2017.

Anderson, David G. "Stability and Change in Chiefdom-Level Societies: An Examination of Mississippian Political Evolution on the South Atlantic Slope," in Williams and Shapiro, eds., *Lamar Archaeology*. Tuscaloosa: University of Alabama Press, 2010.

Andrews, Kenneth R. *Elizabethan Privateering: English Privateering during the Spanish War, 1585-1603*. Cambridge, UK: Cambridge University Press, 1964.

Arana, Luis Rafael. "The Exploration of Florida and Sources on the Founding of St. Augustine." *The Florida Historical Quarterly* 44, no. 1/2 (1965): 1-16.

Arbesú-Fernardez, ed., *Pedro Menéndez De Avilés and the Conquest of Florida: A New Manuscript*. Gainesville: University Press of Florida, 2017.

Armelagos, George, and Cassandra Hill. "An Evaluation of the Biocultural Consequences of the Mississippian Transformation," in Dye and Cox, eds., *Towns and Temples along the Mississippi*. Tuscaloosa: University of Alabama Press, 2009.

Arnade, Charles. "Cattle Raising in Spanish Florida, 1513-1763." *Agricultural History* 35, no. 3 (1961): 116-124.

Auchmutey, Jim. *Smoke Lore: A Short History of Barbecue in America*. Athens: University of Georgia Press, 2019.

Baker-Benfield, G. J., and Catherine Clinton, eds. *Portraits of American Women: From Settlement to Present*. New York: Oxford University Press, 1998.

Balsera, Viviana Díaz, and Rachel May, eds. *La Florida: Five Hundred Years of Hispanic Presence*. Gainesville: University Press of Florida, 2014.

Baptisms, 1594-1763. Cathedral Parish Records Abstracts: Baptisms. St. Augustine Restoration, Inc. http://ufdc.ufl.edu/USACH00588/00001.

Beck, Robin A. Jr. "Catawba Coalescence and the Shattering of the Carolina Piedmont," in Ethridge and Shuck-Hall, eds., *Mapping the Mississippian Shatter Zone*. Lincoln: University of Nebraska Press, 2009.

Beck, Robin A. Jr. *Chiefdoms, Collapse, and Coalescence in the Early American South*. Cambridge, UK: Cambridge University Press, 2013.

Bennett, Charles E., ed. *Settlement of Florida*. Gainesville: University of Florida Press, 1968.

Bense, Judith A. "Presidio Santa María de Galve (1698-1719): A Frontier Garrison in Spanish West Florida." *Historical Archaeology* 38, no. 3 (2004): 47-64.

Bense, Judith A. *Presidios of Spanish West Florida*. Gainesville: University Press of Florida, 2022.

Berlin, Ira. *Many Thousands Gone: The First Two Centuries of Slavery in North America*. New York: Belknap, 1998.

Billings, Warren M., ed. *The Old Dominion in the Seventeenth Century*. Chapel Hill: University of North Carolina Press, 1975.

Blanton, Justin. "The Role of Cattle Ranching in the 1656 Timucuan Rebellion: A Struggle for Land, Labor, and Chiefly Power." *The Florida Historical Quarterly* 92, no. 4 (2014): 667-684.

Borchard, Kimberly C. *Appalachia as Contested Borderland of the Early Modern Atlantic, 1528-1715*. Tempe, AZ: Arizona Center for Medieval and Renaissance Studies, 2001.

Borucki, Alex. *From Shipmates to Soldiers: Emerging Black Identities in the Rio de la Plata*. Albuquerque: University of New Mexico Press, 2015.

Bossy, Denise. "Yamasee Mobility: Mississippian Roots, Seventeenth-Century Strategies," in Edmond, Boudreaux, Meyers, and Johnson, eds., *Contact, Colonialism, and Native Communities*. Gainesville: University of Florida Press, 2020.

Bossy, Denise, ed. *The Yamasee Indians: From Florida to South Carolina*. Lincoln: University of Nebraska Press, 2018.

Boudreaux, Edmund, Maureen S. Meyers, and Jay K. Johnson, eds. *Contact, Colonialism, and Native Communities in the Southeastern United States*. Gainesville: University of Florida Press, 2020.

Bown, Stephen R. *Scurvy: How a Surgeon, a Mariner and a Gentleman Solved the Great Medical Mystery of the Age of Sail*. New York: Penguin, 2004.

Bowne, Eric E. *The Westo Indians: Slave Traders of the Early Colonial South*. Tuscaloosa: The University of Alabama Press, 2005.

Boyd, Mark. "Diego Pena's Expedition to Apalachee and Apalachicola in 1716: A Journal Translated and with an Introduction." *The Florida Historical Quarterly* 28, no. 1 (July 1949): 1-27.

Boyd, Mark, ed. *Here They Once Stood: The Tragic End of the Apalachee Missions*. Gainesville: University of Florida Press, 1951.

Bradford, William. *Bradford's History "Of Plimoth Plantation."* Boston: Wright & Potter Publishing Co., State Printers, 1898.

Bradley, Peter T. *British Maritime Enterprise in the New World: From the Late Fifteenth to the Mid-Eighteenth Century*. Lewiston, NY: Edwin Mellen Press, 1999.

Braund, Kathryn E. Holland. *Deerskins & Duffels: The Creek Indian Trade with Anglo-America, 1658-1815*. Lincoln: University of Nebraska Press, 1993.

Briggs, Rachel V. "The Civil Cooking Pot: Hominy and the Mississippian Standard Jar in the Black Warrior Valley, Alabama." *American Antiquity* 81, no. 2 (April 2016): 316–332

Bulletin of the United States Fish Commission, Volume 4, for 1884. Washington: GPO, 1884.

Burrage, Henry S., ed. *Early English and French Voyages: Chiefly from Hakluyt, 1534-1608*. New York: Charles Scribner's Sons, 1906.

Bushnell, Amy Turner. *The King's Coffer: Proprietors of the Spanish Florida Treasury, 1565-1702*. Gainesville: University Press of Florida, 1981.

Bushnell, Amy Turner. "Living at Liberty: The Ungovernable Yamasees of Spanish Florida," in Bossy, ed., *The Yamasee Indians*. Lincoln: University of Nebraska Press, 2018.

Bushnell, Amy Turner. "The Menéndez Marquez Cattle Barony at La Chua and the Determinants of Economic Expansion in Seventeenth-Century Florida." *The Florida Historical Quarterly* 56, no. 4 (1978): 407-431.

Bushnell, Amy Turner. "Ruling 'the Republic of Indians,'" in Wood, Waselkov, and Hatley, eds., *Powhatan's Mantle*. Lincoln: University of Nebraska Press, 1989.

Bushnell, Amy Turner. *Situado and Sabana: Spain's Support System for the Presidio and Mission Provinces of Florida*. New York: American Museum of Natural History, 1994.

Cadava, Geraldo. "Entrepreneurs from the Beginning: Latino Business and Commerce since the Sixteenth Century," in Orozco, Morales, Pisani, and Porras, eds., *Advancing U.S. Latino Entrepreneurship*. West Lafayette, IN: Purdue University Press, 2020.

Calloway, Colin G. *The American Revolution in Indian Country: Crisis and Diversity in Native American Communities*. Cambridge, UK: Cambridge University Press, 1995.

Calloway, Colin G. *New Worlds for All: Indians, Europeans, and the Remaking of Early America*. Baltimore: Johns Hopkins University Press, 1997.

Cameron, Catherine, Paul Kelton, and Alan Swedlund, eds. *Beyond Germs: Native Depopulation in North America*. Tucson: University of Arizona Press, 2016.

Canny, Nicholas P., ed. *The Oxford History of the British Empire: Volume 1, The Origins of Empire*. Oxford, UK: Oxford University Press, 2001.

Carpenter, Kenneth J. *The History of Scurvy and Vitamin C*. Cambridge, UK: Cambridge University Press, 2003.

Chacon, Richard J., and Rubén G. Mendoza. *North American Indigenous Warfare and Ritual Violence*. Tucson: University of Arizona Press, 2007.

Chatelain, Verne E. *The Defenses of Spanish Florida, 1565 to 1763*. Washington, DC: Carnegie Institution of Washington, 1941.

Childers, Ronald Wayne. "The Presidio System in Spanish Florida, 1565-1763." *Historical Archaeology* 38, no. 3 (2014): 24-32.

Claassen, Cheryl. "Changing Venue: Women's Lives in Prehistoric North America," in Claassen and Joyce, eds., *Women in Prehistory*. Philadelphia: University of Pennsylvania Press, 1997.

Claassen, Cheryl, and Rosemary A. Joyce. *Women in Prehistory: North America and Mesoamerica*. Philadelphia: University of Pennsylvania Press, 1997.

Clavin, Matthew J. *Aiming for Pensacola: Fugitive Slaves on the Atlantic and Southern Frontiers*. Cambridge, MA: Harvard University Press, 2015.

Clayton, Lawrence A., Vernon Knight, and Edward C. Moore, eds. *The De Soto Chronicles: The Expedition of Hernando de Soto to North America in 1539-1543*. Tuscaloosa: University of Alabama Press, 1993.

Clayton, Lawrence A., and David Lantigua, eds., *Bartolemé de las Casas and the Defense of Amerindian Rights: A Brief History with Documents*. Tuscaloosa: University of Alabama Press, 2020.

Cofer, Judith Ortiz. "A Brief Account of the Adventures of My Appropriated Kinsman, Juan Ortiz, Indian Captive, Soldier, and Guide to General Hernando de Soto," *Georgia Review* 66, no. 3 (Fall 2012): 655-666.

Colburn, David, and Jane Landers, eds. *The African American Heritage of Florida*. Gainesville: University Press of Florida, 1995.

Comer, James. "North America from 1492 to the Present," in Kiple and Ornelas, eds., *The Cambridge World History of Food*. Cambridge, UK: Cambridge University Press, 2000.

Cook, David Noble, and George Lovell, eds. *"Secret Judgments of God": Old World Disease in Colonial Spanish America*. Norman: University of Oklahoma Press, 1991.

Corkran, David H. *The Creek Frontier, 1540-1783*. Norman: University of Oklahoma Press, 1967.

Covington, James. "Drake Destroys St. Augustine: 1586." *The Florida Historical Quarterly* 44, no. 1/2 (1965): 81-93.

Covington, James. "Migration of the Seminoles into Florida, 1700-1820." *The Florida Historical Quarterly* 46, no. 4 (1968): 340-357.

Covington, James. *The Seminoles of Florida*. Gainesville: University Press of Florida, 1993.

Covington, James. "Trade Relations between Southwestern Florida and Cuba: 1600-1840." *The Florida Historical Quarterly* 38, no. 2 (1959): 114-128.

Crane, Verner W. *The Southern Frontier, 1670-1732*. Tuscaloosa: University of Alabama Press, 2004 [1929].

Crosby, Alfred. *The Columbian Exchange: Biological and Cultural Consequences of 1492*. Westport, CT: Praeger, 2003 [1973].

Crosby, Alfred. *Ecological Imperialism: The Biological Expansion of Europe, 900-1900*. Cambridge, UK: Cambridge University Press, 1993.

Crosby, Alfred. "Virgin Soil Epidemics as a Factor in the Aboriginal Depopulation in America." *William and Mary Quarterly*, 3d Ser., 33, no. 2 (April 1976): 289-299.

Cusick, James, and Sherry Johnson, eds. *The Voyages of Ponce de León: Scholarly Perspectives*. Cocoa Beach: Florida Historical Society Press, 2012.

Davenport, Frances Gardiner. *European Treaties Bearing on the United States and Its Dependencies to 1648*. Gloucester, MA: Peter Smith, 1967.

Davies, Michael B., John Austin, and David A. Partridge. *Vitamin C: Its Chemistry and Biochemistry*. Cambridge, UK: Royal Society of Chemistry, 1991.

Davis, R. P. Stephen Jr. "The Cultural Landscape of the North Carolina Piedmont at Contact," in Ethridge and Hudson, eds., *The Transformation of the Southeastern Indians*. Oxford: University Press of Mississippi, 2002.

Davis, T. Frederick. "Ponce de León's First Voyage and Discovery of Florida." *The Florida Historical Society Quarterly* 14, no. 1 (1935): 7-49.

Davis, T. Frederick. "Ponce de León's Second Voyage and Attempt to Colonize Florida." *The Florida Historical Society Quarterly* 14, no. 1 (1935): 51-66.

Davis, T. Frederick. "The Record of Ponce de León's Discovery of Florida, 1513." *The Florida Historical Society Quarterly* 11, no. 1 (1932): 5-15.

De Bry, Theodore. *America, part 3*. Frankfurt, Germany: 1593.

Deagan, Kathleen. *America's Ancient City: Spanish St. Augustine, 1565-1763*. New York: Garland, 1991.

Deagan, Kathleen. "The Historical Archaeology of Sixteenth-Century La Florida." *The Florida Historical Quarterly* 91, no. 3 (2013): 349-374.

Deagan, Kathleen. "Mestizaje in Colonial St. Augustine." *Ethnohistory* 20, no. 1 (1973): 55-65.

Deagan, Kathleen. "St. Augustine and the Mission Frontier," in McEwan, ed., *The Spanish Missions of La Florida*. Gainesville: University Press of Florida, 1993.

Deagan, Kathleen, Joan K. Koch, et al. *Spanish St. Augustine: The Archaeology of a Colonial Creole Community*. New York: Academic Press, 1983.

DePratter, Chester. "The Chiefdom of Cofitachequi," in Hudson and Tesser, eds., *The Forgotten Centuries*. Athens: University of Georgia Press, 1994.

Dexter, Henry Martyn. *Mourt's Relation, or Journal of the Plantation at Plymouth*. Boston: John Kimball Wiggin, 1865.

Diamond, Jared M. *Guns, Germs, and Steel: The Fates of Human Societies*. New York: W.W. Norton, 2017 [1997].

Dobyns, Henry. "The Invasion of Florida," in Henderson and Mormino, eds., *Spanish Pathways in Florida*. Sarasota: Pineapple Press, 1991.

Dobyns, Henry. *Their Number Become Thinned: Native American Population Dynamics in Eastern North America*. Knoxville: University of Tennessee Press, 1983.

Douglas-Lithgow, R. A. *Native American Place Names of Massachusetts*. Bedford, MA: Applewood Books, 2001.

Dubcovsky, Alejandra. "The Testimony of Thomas de la Torre, a Spanish Slave." *William and Mary Quarterly* 70, no. 3 (2013): 559-580.

Duncan, David Ewing. *Hernándo de Soto: A Savage Quest in the Americas*. Norman: University of Oklahoma Press, 1997.

Dye, David H., and Adam King. "Desecrating the Sacred Ancestor Temples: Chiefly Conflict and Violence in the American Southeast," in Chacon and Mendoza, eds., *North American Indigenous Warfare and Ritual Violence*. Tucson: University of Arizona Press, 2007.

Dye, David H., and Cheryl Anne Cox, eds. *Towns and Temples along the Mississippi*. Tuscaloosa: University of Alabama Press, 2009.

Elliott, J. H. *Empires of the Atlantic World: Britain and Spain in America, 1492-1830*. New Haven, CT: Yale University Press, 2007.

Ethridge, Robbie. "A Brief Sketch of Creek Country," in Paredes, ed., *Red Eagle's Children*. Tuscaloosa: University of Alabama Press, 2012.

Ethridge, Robbie. "Differential Responses Across the Southeast to European Incursions," in Boudreaux, Meyers, and Johnson, eds., *Contact, Colonialism, and Native Communities*. Gainesville: University of Florida Press, 2020.

Ethridge, Robbie. *From Chicaza to Chickasaw: The European Invasion and the Transformation of the Mississippian World, 1540-1715*. Chapel Hill: University of North Carolina Press, 2010.

Ethridge, Robbie. "Introduction: Mapping the Mississippi Shatter Zone," in Ethridge and Shuck-Hall, eds., *Mapping the Mississippian Shatter Zone*. Lincoln: University of Nebraska Press, 2009.

Ethridge, Robbie. "Navigating the Mississippian World: Infrastructure in the Sixteenth-Century Native South," in Waselkov and Smith, eds., *Forging Southeastern Identities*. University of Alabama Press, 2017.

Ethridge, Robbie, and Charles Hudson, eds. *The Transformation of the Southeastern Indians, 1540-1760*. Oxford: University Press of Mississippi, 2002.

Ethridge, Robbie, and Sheri Marie Shuck-Hall, eds. *Mapping the Mississippian Shatter Zone: The Colonial Indian Slave Trade and Regional Instability in the American South*. Lincoln: University of Nebraska Press, 2009.

Ewen, Charles. "Continuity and Change: De Soto and the Apalachee." *Historical Archaeology* 30, no. 2 (1996): 41-53.

Ferdinando, Peter. "A Translation History of Fontaneda." *Florida Historical Quarterly* 89, no. 2 (Fall 2010): 210-251.

Figueredo, D. H. *Revolvers and Pistolas, Vaqueros and Caballeros: Debunking the Old West.* Santa Barbara, CA: Praeger, 2015.

Foner, Eric, ed. *The New American History*, rev. ed. Philadelphia, PA: Temple University Press, 1997.

Forbes, Jack D. *Africans and Native Americans: Color, Race, and Caste in the Evolution of Red-Black Peoples.* Urbana: University of Illinois Press, 1993.

Francis, J. Michael. "Juan Ponce de León and the Fountain of Youth," in Cusick and Johnson, eds., *The Voyages of Ponce de León.* Cocoa Beach: Florida Historical Society Press, 2012.

French, B. F., ed. *Historical Collections of Louisiana and Florida.* New York: Albert Mason, 1875.

Friede, Juan, and Benjamin Keen, eds., *Bartolomé de las Casas in History: Toward an Understanding of the Man and His Work.* Dekalb, IL: Northern Illinois University Press, 2008 [1971].

Fritz, Gayle J. *Feeding Cahokia: Early Agriculture in the North American Heartland.* Tuscaloosa: University of Alabama Press, 2019.

Gade, Daniel W. "Cattle," in Kiple and Ornelas, eds., *The Cambridge World History of Food.* Cambridge, UK: Cambridge University Press, 2000.

Gade, Daniel W. "Hogs (Pigs)," in Kiple and Ornelas, eds., *The Cambridge World History of Food.* Cambridge, UK: Cambridge University Press, 2000.

Galgano, Robert. *Feast of Souls: Indians and Spaniards in the Seventeenth-Century Missions of Florida and Mexico.* Albuquerque: University of New Mexico Press, 2005.

Gallay, Alan. *Indian Slave Trade: The Rise of the English Empire in the American South, 1670-1717.* New Haven, CT: Yale University Press, 2003.

Galloway, Patricia Key. *Choctaw Genesis, 1500-1700.* Lincoln: University of Nebraska Press, 1995.

Galloway, Patricia Key. "Colonial Period Transformations in the Mississippi Valley: Disintegration, Alliance, Confederation, Playoff," in Ethridge and Hudson, eds., *The Transformation of the Southeastern Indians.* Oxford: University Press of Mississippi, 2002.

Gannon, Michael. "Altar and Hearth: The Coming of Christianity, 1521-1565." *Florida Historical Quarterly* 44, no. 1/2 (1965): 17-44.

Gannon, Michael. *The Cross in the Sand: The Early Catholic Church in Florida, 1513-1870.* Gainesville: University of Florida Press, 1967.

Gannon, Michael. "First European Contacts," in Gannon, ed., *A New History of Florida.* Gainesville: University of Florida Press, 1967.

Gannon, Michael. *A New History of Florida.* Gainesville: University Press of Florida, 1996.

Gerhard, Peter. "A Black Conquistador in Mexico." *The Hispanic American Historical Review* 58, no. 3 (1978): 451-459.

Gibson, Abraham. *Feral Animals in the American South: An Evolutionary History.* Cambridge, UK: Cambridge University Press, 2018.

Gillaspie, William. "Survival of a Frontier Presidio: St. Augustine and the Subsidy and Private Contract Systems, 1680-1702." *Florida Historical Quarterly* 62, no. 3 (1984): 273-295.

Giménez Fernández, Manuel. "Fray Bartolomé de Las Casas: A Biographical Sketch," in Friede and Keen, eds., *Bartolomé de las Casas in History: Toward an Understanding of the Man and his Work.* Dekalb, IL: Northern Illinois University Press, 2008 [1971].

Gradie, Charlotte M. "Spanish Jesuits in Virginia: The Mission That Failed." *Virginia Magazine of History and Biography* 96, no. 2 (April 1988): 131-156.

Gratzer, Walter. *Terrors of the Table: The Curious History of Nutrition.* Oxford, UK: Oxford University Press, 2009.

Green, Michael D. *The Politics of Indian Removal: Creek Government and Society in Crisis.* Lincoln: University of Nebraska Press, 1985.

Gregerson, Linda, and Susan Juster. *Empires of God: Religious Encounters in the Early Modern Atlantic.* Philadelphia: University of Pennsylvania Press, 2010.

Griffin, Nigel, and Anthony Pagden, eds. *A Short Account of the Destruction of the Indies.* London, UK: Penguin Books, 2004.

Hahn, Steven C. *The Invention of the Creek Nation, 1670-1763.* Lincoln: University of Nebraska Press, 2004.

Hakluyt, Richard. *A Discourse Concerning Western Planting.* Cambridge, UK: Press of John Wilson and Son, 1877.

Halbirt, Carl. "La Ciudad de San Augustin: A European Fighting Presidio in Eighteenth-Century 'La Florida.'" *Historical Archaeology* 38, no. 3 (2004): 33-46.

Halley, David. "The Chiefdom of Coosa," in Hudson and Chaves Tesser, eds., *The Forgotten Centuries.* Athens: University of Georgia Press, 1994.

Hallock, Thomas, and Richard Franz, eds. *Travels on the St. Johns River.* Gainesville: University Press of Florida, 2017.

Hamilton, Alissa. *Squeezed: What You Don't Know About Orange Juice.* New Haven, CT: Yale University Press, 2009.

Hann, John. "Apalachee Counterfeiters in St. Augustine." *Florida Historical Quarterly* 67, no. 1 (July 1988): 52-68.

Hann, John. *Apalachee: The Land Between the Waters.* Gainesville: University Press of Florida, 1988.

Hann, John. "Demographic Patterns and Changes in Mid-Seventeenth Century Timucua and Apalachee." *Florida Historical Quarterly* 64, no. 4 (April 1986): 371-392.

Hann, John. "The Mayaca and Jororo and Missions to Them," in McEwan, ed., *The Spanish Missions of La Florida.* Gainesville: University Press of Florida, 1993.

Hann, John. *Missions to the Calusa.* Gainesville: University of Florida Press, 1991.

Hann, John, and Bonnie McEwan. *The Apalachee Indians and Mission San Luis.* Gainesville: University Press of Florida, 1998.

Hart, J. *Comparing Empires: European Colonialism from Portuguese Expansion to the Spanish-American War.* New York: Palgrave Macmillan, 2003.

Hastings, Adrian. *A World History of Christianity.* Grand Rapids, MI: W.B. Eerdmans, 2000.

Hatley, Tom. *The Dividing Paths: Cherokees and South Carolinians through the Era of Revolution.* Oxford, UK: Oxford University Press, 1993.

Haynes, Joseph. *Virginia Barbecue.* Charleston, SC: Arcadia Publishing, 2016.

Hazlewood, Nick. *The Queen's Slave Trader: John Hawkyns, Elizabeth I, and the Trafficking in Human Souls.* New York: Harper Perennial, 2004.

Heldman, Donald P. "Fort Toulouse of the Alabamas and the Eighteenth-Century Indian Trade." *World Archaeology* 5, no. 2 (October 1973): 163-169.

Helg, Aline, and Lara Vernaug. *Slave No More: Self-Liberation Before Abolitionism in the Americas.* Chapel Hill: University of North Carolina Press, 2019.

Henderson, Ann, and Gary Mormino, eds. *Spanish Pathways in Florida, 1492-1992.* Sarasota: Pineapple Press, 1991.

Herrick, Dennis. *Esteban: The African Slave Who Explored America.* Albuquerque: University of New Mexico Press, 2018.

Hill, Jonathan David, ed. *History, Power, and Identity: Ethnogenesis in the Americas, 1492-1992.* Iowa City: University of Iowa Press, 1996.

Hoffman, Michael P. "The Terminal Mississippian Period in the Arkansas River Valley and Quapaw Ethnogenesis," in Dye, et al., eds., *Towns and Temples along the Mississippi.* Tuscaloosa: University of Alabama Press, 2009.

Hoffman, Paul. "The Chicora Legend and Franco-Spanish Rivalry in La Florida." *Florida Historical Quarterly* 62, no. 4 (April 1984): 419-438.

Hoffman, Paul. *Florida's Frontiers*: Bloomington: Indiana University Press, 2002.

Hoffman, Paul. "Legend, Religious Idealism, and Colonies: The Point of Santa Elena in History, 1552-1566." *South Carolina Historical Magazine* 84, no. 2 (1983): 59-71.

Hoffman, Paul. "Lucas Vázquez de Ayllón's Discovery and Colony," in Hudson and Chaves Tesser, eds., *The Forgotten Centuries.* Athens: University of Georgia Press, 1994.

Hoffman, Paul. "Narváez and Cabeza de Vaca in Florida," in Hudson and Chaves Tesser, eds., *The Forgotten Centuries.* Athens: University of Georgia Press, 1994.

Hoffman, Paul. *A New Andalucia and a Way to the Orient: The American Southeast during the Sixteenth Century.* Baton Rouge: Louisiana State University Press, 2004.

Hoffman, Paul. "'Until the Land Was Understood': Spaniards Confront La Florida, 1500-1600," in Balsara and May, eds., *La Florida.* Gainesville: University Press of Florida, 2014.

Horn, James. *A Kingdom Strange: The Brief and Tragic History of the Lost Colony of Roanoke.* New York: Basic Books, 2011.

Hoshower, Lisa, and Jerald Milanich. "Excavations in the Fig Springs Mission Burial Area," in McEwan, ed., *The Spanish Missions of La Florida.* Gainesville: University Press of Florida, 1993.

Hudson, Charles. "Coosa: A Chiefdom in the Sixteenth-Century Southeastern United States." *American Antiquity* 50, no. 4 (1985): 723-737.

Hudson, Charles. *The Juan Pardo Expeditions*: *Exploration of the Carolinas and Tennessee, 1566-1568.* Tuscaloosa: University of Alabama Press, 2009.

Hudson, Charles. *Knights of Spain, Warriors of the Sun: Hernándo De Soto and the South's Ancient Chiefdoms.* Athens: University of Georgia Press, 2018.

Hudson, Charles. *The Southeastern Indians.* Knoxville: University of Tennessee Press, 2007 [1976].

Hudson, Charles, Marvin Smith, and Chester DePratter. "The Hernándo de Soto Expedition: From Apalachee to Chiaha." *Southeastern Archaeology* 3, no. 1 (1984): 65-77.

Hudson, Charles, and Carmen Chaves Tesser, eds. *The Forgotten Centuries: Indians and Europeans in the American South: 1521-1704.* Athens: University of Georgia Press, 1994.

Hyman, Clarissa. *Oranges: A Global History.* London: Reaktion Books, 2013.

Jenkins, Ned J. "Tracing the Origins of the Early Creeks, 1050-1700 CE," in Ethridge and Shuck-Hall, eds., *Mapping the Mississippian Shatter Zone.* Lincoln: University of Nebraska Press, 2009.

Jennings, Matthew. "Cutting One Another's Throats," in LeMaster and Wood, eds., *Creating and Contesting Carolina.* Columbia: University of South Carolina Press, 2013.

Jennings, Matthew. *New Worlds of Violence: Cultures and Conquests in the Early American Southeast*. Knoxville: University of Tennessee Press, 2011.

Johnson, Kenneth. "Mission Santa Fé de Toloca," in McEwan, ed., *The Spanish Missions of La Florida*. Gainesville: University Press of Florida, 1993.

Jones, David S. "Virgin Soils Revisited." *William and Mary Quarterly* 60, no. 4 (October 2003): 703-742.

Jordan, Terry. *North American Cattle-Ranching Frontiers: Origins, Diffusion, and Differentiation*. Albuquerque: University of New Mexico Press, 2000.

Kamen, Henry. *Empire: How Spain Became a World Power, 1492-1763*. New York: Perennial, 2004.

Kamen, Henry. *Golden Age Spain*. Basingstoke: Palgrave Macmillan, 2005.

Kamen, Henry: *Imagining Spain: Historical Myth & National Identity*. New Haven, CT: Yale University Press, 2008.

Kelton, Paul. "Avoiding the Smallpox Spirits: Colonial Epidemics and Southeastern Indian Survival." *Ethnohistory* 51, no. 1 (Winter 2004): 45-71.

Kelton, Paul. *Epidemics and Enslavement: Biological Catastrophe in the Native Southeast, 1492-1715*. Lincoln: University of Nebraska Press, 2007.

King, Adam. "Historic Period Transformation," in Pluckhahn and Ethridge, eds., *Light on the Path*. Tuscaloosa: University of Alabama Press, 2006.

Kiple, Kenneth F., and Kriemhild Coneè Ornelas, eds. *The Cambridge World History of Food*. Cambridge, UK: Cambridge University Press, 2000.

Klasko, George. *The Oxford Handbook of the History of Political Philosophy*. Oxford, UK: Oxford University, 2011.

Knight, Franklin W., and Andrew Hurley, eds. *An Account, Much Abbreviated, of the Destruction of the Indies, with Related Texts*. Indianapolis, IN: Hackett, 2003.

Kornworlf, James D. and Georgiana Wallis. *Architecture and Town Planning in Colonial North America*. 3 volumes. Johns Hopkins University Press, 2002.

Kowalewski, Stephen. "Coalescent Societies," in Pluckhahn and Ethridge, eds., *Light on the Path*. Tuscaloosa: University of Alabama Press, 2006.

Krech, Shepard III. *The Ecological Indian: Myth and History*. London, UK: Norton, 2001.

Kupperman, Karen Ordahl. *Roanoke: The Abandoned Colony*. New York: Rowman & Littlefield Publishers, 2007.

Landers, Jane. "Africans and Native Americans," in Restall, ed., *Beyond Black and Red*. Albuquerque: University of New Mexico Press, 2005.

Landers, Jane. "Africans in the Spanish Colonies." *Historical Archaeology* 31, no. 1 (1997): 84-103.

Landers, Jane. *Black Society in Spanish Florida*: Urbana: University of Illinois Press, 1999.

Landers, Jane. "The Geopolitics of Seventeenth-Century Florida." *Florida Historical Quarterly* 92, no. 3 (2014): 480-490.

Landers, Jane. "Gracia Real de Santa Teresa de Mose: A Free Black Town in Spanish Colonial Florida." *American Historical Review* 95, no. 1 (1990): 9-30.

Landers, Jane. "Traditions of African American Freedom and Community in Spanish Colonial Florida," in Colburn and Landers, eds., *The African American Heritage of Florida*. Gainesville: University Press of Florida, 1995.

Lane, Kris. *Pillaging the Empire: Global Piracy on the High Seas, 1500-1750*. New York: Routledge, 2016.

Lantigua, David. *Infidels and Empires in a New World Order: Early Modern Spanish Contributions to International Legal Thought*. Cambridge, UK: Cambridge University Press, 2020.

Larson, Clark Spencer. "On the Frontier of Contact: Mission Bioarcheology in La Florida," in McEwan, ed., *The Spanish Missions of La Florida*. Gainesville: University Press of Florida, 1993.

Laszlo, Pierre. *Citrus: A History*. Chicago: University of Chicago Press, 2008.

Laudan, Rachel. *Cuisine and Empire: Cooking in World History*. Berkeley: University of California Press, 2015.

LeMaster, Michelle, and Bradford Wood, eds. *Creating and Contesting Carolina*. Columbia: University of South Carolina Press, 2013.

Lewis, Clifford Merle, and Albert Joseph Loomie. *The Spanish Jesuit Mission in Virginia, 1570-1572*. Chapel Hill: University of North Carolina Press, 1953.

Loucks, L. Jill. "Spanish-Indian Interaction on the Florida Missions: The Archaeology of Baptizing Spring," in McEwan, ed., *The Spanish Missions of La Florida*. Gainesville: University Press of Florida, 1993.

Lowery, Woodbury. *The Spanish Settlements Within the Present Limits of the United States, 1513-1561*. New York: G.P. Putnam's Sons, 1901.

Lynch, John. *New Worlds: A Religious History of Latin America*. New Haven, CT: Yale University Press, 2012.

Lynn, Kimberly, and Erin Kathleen Rowe, eds. *The Early Modern Hispanic World: Transnational and Interdisciplinary Approaches*. New York: Cambridge University Press, 2017.

Lyon, Eugene. *The Enterprise of Florida: Pedro Menéndez de Avilés and the Spanish Conquest of 1565-1568*. Gainesville: University Press of Florida, 1999.

Mahon, John. *History of the Second Seminole War, 1835-1842*. Gainesville: University Press of Florida, 1990.

Malouchos, Elizabeth Watts, and Alleen Betzenhauser, eds. *Reconsidering Mississippian Communities and Households*. Tuscaloosa: University of Alabama Press, 2021.

Marley, David. *Wars of the Americas: A Chronology of Armed Conflict in the Western Hemisphere*. Santa Barbara, CA: ABC-CLIO, 2008.

Martin, Joel W., and Mark A. Nicholas, eds. *Native Americans, Christianity, and the Reshaping of the American Religious Landscape*. Chapel Hill: University of North Carolina Press, 2010.

Martyr D'Anghera, Peter. *De Orbe Novo*. 2 Volumes. New York: G.P. Putnam's Sons, 1912.

Marx, Robert. *Shipwrecks in the Americas*. New York: Dover, 2016 [1983].

McCord, David. *The Statutes at Large of South Carolina*, *Volume 7*. Charleston, SC: A.S. Johnston, 1840.

McEwan, Bonnie. "Hispanic Life on the Seventeenth-Century Florida Frontier," in McEwan, ed., *The Spanish Missions of La Florida*. Gainesville: University Press of Florida, 1993.

McEwan, Bonnie. "The Historical Archaeology of Seventeenth-Century La Florida." *Florida Historical Quarterly* 92, no. 3 (Winter 2014): 491-523.

McEwan, Bonnie, ed. *Indians of the Greater Southeast*. Gainesville: University Press of Florida, 2000.

McEwan, Bonnie, ed. *The Spanish Missions of La Florida*. Gainesville: University Press of Florida, 1993.

McGoun, William. *Prehistoric Peoples of South Florida*. Tuscaloosa: University of Alabama Press, 2010 [1993].

McLoughlin, William G. *Cherokee Renascence in the New Republic*. Princeton, NJ: Princeton University Press, 2018.

McReynolds, Edwin C. *The Seminoles*. Norman: The University of Oklahoma Press, 1957.

Mentzer, Raymond A. "The French Wars of Religion," in Pettegree, ed., *The Reformation World*. London, UK: Routledge, 2006.

Merás, Gonzalo Solís de. *Pedro Menéndez de Avilés: Adelantado Governor and Captain-General of Florida*. Deland, FL: Florida State Historical Society, 1923.

Merrell, James. *The Indians' New World: Catawbas and Their Neighbors from European Contact through the Era of Removal*. Chapel Hill: University of North Carolina Press, 2012 [1989].

Meyers, Maureen. "The Seventeenth-Century Native-Colonial Borderlands of the Savannah River Valley," in Boudreaux, Meyers, and Johnson, eds., *Contact, Colonialism, and Native Communities*. Gainesville: University of Florida Press, 2020.

Milanich, Jerald T. "Franciscan Missions and Native Peoples in Spanish Florida," in Hudson and Chaves Tesser, eds., *The Forgotten Centuries*. Athens: University of Georgia Press, 1994.

Milanich, Jerald T. *Laboring in the Fields of the Lord: Spanish Missions and Southeastern Indians*. Gainesville: University Press of Florida, 2006.

Milanich, Jerald T. "The Timucua Indians," in McEwan, ed., *Indians of the Greater Southeast: Historical Archaeology and Ethnohistory*. Gainesville: University Press of Florida, 2001.

Milanich, Jerald T., and Susan Milbrath. *First Encounters: Spanish Explorations in the Caribbean and the United States, 1492-1570*. Gainesville: University of Florida Press, 1989.

Milanich, Jerald, and William Sturtevant, eds. *Francisco Pareja's 1613 Confessionario: A Documentary Source for Timucuan Ethnography*. Tallahassee, FL: Florida Division of Archives, History, and Records Management, 1972.

Milton, Giles. *Big Chief Elizabeth: The Adventures and Fate of the First English Colonists in America*. New York: Farrar, Straus and Giroux, 2000.

Mink, Nicholas. *Salmon: A Global History*. London, UK: Reaktion Books, 2013.

Moorhead, Max, and David Weber. *The Presidio: Bastion of the Spanish Borderlands*. Norman: University of Oklahoma Press, 1975.

Morgan, Philip D. "Virginia Slavery in Atlantic Context, 1550-1650," in Musselwhite, Mancall, and Horn, eds., *Virginia 1619*. Chapel Hill: Omohundro Institute of Early American History and Culture and University of North Carolina Press, 2019.

Morris, Brent. *Yes, Lord, I Know the Road: A Documentary History of African Americans in South Carolina, 1526-2008*. Columbia: University of South Carolina Press, 2017.

Moss, Robert. *Barbecue: The History of an American Institution*. Tuscaloosa: University of Alabama Press, 2020.

Mt. Pleasant, Jane. "A New Paradigm for Pre-Columbian Agriculture in North America." *Early American Places* 13, no. 2 (Spring, 2015): 374-412.

Mulroy, Kevin. *Freedom on the Border: The Seminole Maroons in Florida, the Indian Territory, Coahuila, and Texas*. Lubbock: Texas Tech University Press, 1993.

Murrin, John M. "Beneficiaries of Catastrophe: The English Colonies in America," in Foner, ed., *The New American History*, rev. ed. Philadelphia, 1997.

Musselwhite, Paul, Peter C. Mancall, and James Horn, eds. *Virginia, 1619: Slavery and Freedom in the Making of Early America*. Chapel Hill: Omohundro Institute of Early American History and Culture and University of North Carolina Press, 2019.

Muthu, Sankar, ed. *Empire and Modern Political Thought*. New York: Cambridge University Press, 2014.

Navin, John. *The Grim Years: Settling South Carolina, 1670-1720*: Columbia: University of South Carolina Press, 2020.

Noll, Steven, and David Tegeder. *Ditch of Dreams: The Cross Florida Barge Canal and the Struggle for Florida's Future.* Gainesville: University Press of Florida, 2015.

Oatis, Steven J. *A Colonial Complex: South Carolina's Frontiers in the Era of the Yamasee War, 1680-1730*. Lincoln: University of Nebraska Press, 2004.

O'Brien, Greg. *Pre-Removal Choctaw History: Exploring New Paths*. Norman: University of Oklahoma Press, 2008.

O'Daniel, V. F. *Dominicans in Early Florida*. New York: United States Catholic Historical Society, 1930.

Opie, Frederick Douglass. *Hogs and Hominy: Soul Food from Africa to America*. New York: Columbia University Press, 2010.

Orozco, Marlene, Alfonso Morales, Michael J. Pisani, and Jerry I. Porras, eds. *Advancing U.S. Latino Entrepreneurship: A New National Economic Imperative*. West Lafayette, IN: Purdue University Press, 2020.

Oviedo y Valdés, Gonzalo Fernández. *Historia General y Natural de las Indias. Tercero de la Obra*, Volume 3. Madrid: Imprenta de la Real Academia de la Historia, 1853.

Pagden, Anthony. *The Burdens of Empire, 1539 to the Present*. Cambridge, UK: Cambridge University Press, 2015.

Pagden, Anthony. "Conquest and the Just War: The 'School of Salamanca' and the 'Affair of the Indies,'" in Muthu, ed., *Empire and Modern Political Thought*. New York: Cambridge University Press, 2014.

Pagden, Anthony. "The School of Salamanca," in Klosko, ed., *The Oxford Handbook of the History of Political Philosophy*. Oxford, UK: Oxford University Press, 2011.

Pagden, Anthony. "The Struggle for Legitimacy," in Canney, ed., *The Oxford History of the British Empire: Volume 1*. Oxford, UK: Oxford University Press, 2001.

Paredes, Anthony, and Judith Knight, eds. *Red Eagle's Children: Weatherford vs. Weatherford, et al.* Tuscaloosa: University of Alabama Press, 2012.

Parker, Susan Richbourg. "St. Augustine in the Seventeenth-Century: Capital of La Florida." *Florida Historical Quarterly* 92, no. 3 (Winter 2014): 554-576.

Peck, Douglas. "Lucas Vasquez de Ayllón's Doomed Colony of San Miguel de Gualdape." *Georgia Historical Quarterly* 85, no. 2 (Summer 2001): 183-198.

Perttula, Timothy K. "Social Changes among the Caddo Indians in the Sixteenth and Seventeenth Centuries," in Ethridge and Hudson, eds., *The Transformation of the Southeastern Indians*. Oxford: University Press of Mississippi, 2002.

Pettegree, Andrew. *Europe in the Sixteenth Century*. Oxford, UK: Blackwell, 2002.

Pettegree, Andrew, ed. *The Reformation World*. London, UK: Routledge, 2006.

Piker, Joshua. *Okfuskee: A Creek Indian Town in Colonial America*. Cambridge, MA: Harvard University Press, 2006.

Pluckhahn, Thomas J., and Robbie Ethridge, eds. *Light on the Path: The Anthropology and History of the Southeastern Natives*. Tuscaloosa: University of Alabama Press, 2006.

Porter, Kenneth. "The Cowkeeper Dynasty of the Seminole Nation." *Florida Historical Quarterly* 30, no. 4 (April 1952): 341-349.

Porter, Kenneth. "The Founder of the 'Seminole Nation' Secoffee or Cowkeeper." *Florida Historical Quarterly* 27, no. 4 (April 1949): 362-384.

Priestly, Herbert Ingram, ed. *The Luna Papers, 1559-1561.* Tuscaloosa: University of Alabama Press, 2010.

Pringle, Patrick. *Jolly Roger: The Story of the Great Age of Piracy.* New York: Norton, 1953.

Quinn, David Beers. *Set Fair for Roanoke: Voyages and Colonies, 1584-1606.* Chapel Hill: University of North Carolina Press, 1986.

Quinn, David Beers, ed. *The Roanoke Voyages, 1584-1590.* London, UK: Hakluyt Society, 1995.

Ramsey, William L. *The Yamasee War: A Study of Culture, Economy, and Conflict in the Colonial South.* Lincoln: University of Nebraska Press, 2008.

Rankin, Hugh. *The Golden Age of Piracy.* New York: Holt, Rinehart and Winston, Published for the Colonial Williamsburg Society, 1969.

Records in the British Public Record Office Relating to South Carolina, 1663-1690. Atlanta, GA: Printed for the Historical Commission of South Carolina by Foote & Davies Company, 1928-1929.

Reeves, Carolyn: *The Choctaw Before Removal.* Jackson: University Press of Mississippi, 1985.

Reid, Jonathan. "France," in Pettegree, ed., *The Reformation World.* London, UK: Routledge, 2006.

Reitz, Elizabeth. "Evidence for Animal Use at the Missions of Spanish Florida," in McEwan, ed., *The Spanish Missions of La Florida.* Gainesville: University Press of Florida, 1993.

Reitz, Elizabeth. "Vertebrate Fauna from Seventeenth-Century St. Augustine." *Southeastern Archaeology* 11, no. 2 (Winter 1992): 79-94.

Reséndez, Andrés. *The Other Slavery: The Uncovered Story of Indian Enslavement in America.* New York: Houghton Mifflin Harcourt, 2016.

Restall, Matthew, ed. *Beyond Black and Red: African-Native Relations in Colonial Latin America.* Albuquerque: University of New Mexico Press, 2005.

Restall, Matthew. "Black Conquistadors: Armed Africans in Early Spanish America." *The Americas* 57, no. 2 (October 2000): 171-205.

Restall, Matthew. *Seven Myths of the Spanish Conquest.* Oxford, UK: Oxford University Press, 2003.

Richter, Daniel K. *Facing East from Indian Country: A Native History of Early America.* Cambridge, MA: Harvard University Press, 2001.

Riegelsperger, Diana. "Pirate, Priest, and Slave: Spanish Florida in the 1668 Searles Raid." *Florida Historical Quarterly* 92, no. 3 (Winter 2014): 577-590.

Rimas, Andrew, and Evan D. G. Fraser. *Beef: The Untold Story of How Milk, Meat, and Muscle Shaped the World.* New York: HarperCollins, 2009.

Rivers, Larry. *Slavery in Florida: Territorial Days to Emancipation.* Gainesville: University Press of Florida, 2009.

Roberts, Jeffrey. *Salted & Cured: Savoring the Culture, Heritage, and Flavor of America's Preserved Meats.* White River Junction, VT: Chelsea Green Publishing, 2017.

Roberts, Justin, and Ian Beamish. "Venturing Out," in LeMaster and Wood, eds., *Creating and Contesting Carolina.* Columbia: University of South Carolina Press, 2013.

Rodning, Christopher B. "Restructuring the Coalescence of Cherokee Communities in Southern Appalachia," in Ethridge and Hudson, eds., *The Transformation of the Southeastern Indians, 1540–1760.* Oxford: University of Mississippi Press, 2002.

Rouse, John. *The Criollo: Spanish Cattle in America*. Norman: University of Oklahoma Press, 1977.

Rowe, Erin Kathleen. *Saint and Nation: Santiago, Teresa of Avila, and Plural Identities in Early Modern Spain*. University Park: Pennsylvania State University Press, 2011.

Rugemer, Edward Bartlett. *Slave Law and the Politics of Resistance in the Early Atlantic World*. Cambridge, MA: Harvard University Press, 2018.

Ruhl, Donna. "Oranges and Wheat: Spanish Attempts at Agriculture in La Florida." *Historical Archaeology* 31, no. 1 (1997): 36-45.

Sale, Kirkpatrick. *The Conquest of Paradise: Christopher Columbus and the Columbian Legacy*. New York: Plume, 1990.

Salley, Alexander, and W. Noel Sainsbury, eds. *Records in the British Public Record Office Relating to South Carolina, 1663-1690*. Atlanta, GA: Printed for the Historical Commission of South Carolina by Foote & Davies Co., 1928-1929.

Sanchez, Joseph. *The Spanish Black Legend: Origins of Anti-Hispanic Stereotypes*. Albuquerque, NM: National Park Service, 1987 [1979].

Sattler, Richard A. "Cowboys and Indians: Creek and Seminole Stock Raising, 1700-1900." *American Indian Culture and Research Journal* 22, no. 3 (1998): 79-99.

Sattler, Richard A. "Remnants, Renegades, and Runaways: Seminole Ethnogenesis Reconsidered," in Hill, ed., *History, Power, and Identity*. Iowa City: University of Iowa Press, 1996.

Saunders, Rebecca. "Architecture of the Missions Santa María and Santa Cataline de Amelia," in McEwan, ed., *The Spanish Missions of La Florida*. Gainesville: University Press of Florida, 1993.

Saunders, Rebecca. "The Guale Indians," in McEwan, ed., *Indians of the Great Southeast*. Gainesville: University Press of Florida, 2000.

Saunt, Claudio. *A New Order of Things: Property, Power, and the Transformation of the Creek Indians, 1733-1816*. Cambridge, UK: Cambridge University Press, 1999.

Scarry, C. Margaret. "Plant Production and Procurement in Apalachee Province," in McEwan, ed., *The Spanish Missions of La Florida*. Gainesville: University Press of Florida, 1993.

Scarry, John. "Late Prehistoric Southeast," Hudson and Tesser, eds., *The Forgotten Centuries*. Athens: University of Georgia Press, 1994.

Scarry, John. "The Rise, Transformation, and Fall of Apalachee: A Case Study of Political Change in a Chiefly Society," in Williams and Shapiro, eds., *Lamar Archaeology*. Tuscaloosa: University of Alabama Press, 2010.

Schwaller, John Frederick. *The History of the Catholic Church in Latin America: From Conquest to Revolution and Beyond*. New York: New York University Press, 2011.

Schwartz, Stuart B. *Sea of Storms: A History of Hurricanes in the Greater Caribbean from Columbus to Katrina*. Princeton, NJ: Princeton University Press, 2015.

Seed, Patricia. *Ceremonies of Possession in Europe's Conquest of the New World, 1492-1640*. Cambridge, UK: Cambridge University Press, 1995.

Shephard, Stephen. "The Spanish Criollo Majority," in Deagan, ed., *America's Ancient City: Spanish St. Augustine*. New York: Garland, 1991.

Shuck-Hall, Sheri M. "Alabama and Coushatta Diaspora and Coalescence in the Mississippian Shatter Zone," in Ethridge and Shuck-Hall, eds., *Mapping the Mississippian Shatter Zone*. Lincoln: University of Nebraska Press, 2009.

Siebert, Wilbur. "Slavery and White Servitude in East Florida, 1726 to 1776." *Florida Historical Quarterly* 10, no. 1 (July 1931): 2-23.

Sledge, John. *The Gulf of Mexico: A Maritime History*. Columbia, SC: University of South Carolina Press, 2019.

Slotte, Pamela, and John Haskell. *Christianity and International Law: An Introduction*. Cambridge, UK: Cambridge University Press, 2021.

Sluiter, Engel. "New Light on the '20. and Odd Negroes' Arriving in Virginia, August 1619." *William and Mary Quarterly* 54, no. 2 (1997): 395-398.

Smith, Bruce D., ed. *Rivers of Change: Essays on Early Agriculture in Eastern North America*. Tuscaloosa: University of Alabama Press, 2007.

Smith, Cassander. "Beyond the Mediation: Esteban, Cabeza de Vaca's 'Relación,' and a Narrative Negotiation." *Early American Literature* 47, no. 2 (2012): 267-291.

Smith, Jonathan. *The Generall Historie of Virginia, New England & the Summer Isles, Together with The True Travels, Adventures and Observations, and A Sea Grammar*. New York: Macmillan, 1907.

Smith, Mark, ed. *Stono: Documenting and Interpreting a Southern Slave Revolt*. Columbia: University of South Carolina Press, 2005.

Smith, Marvin. "Aboriginal Depopulation in the Postcontact Southeast," in Hudson and Tesser, eds., *The Forgotten Centuries*. Athens: University of Georgia Press, 1994.

Smith, Marvin. "Aboriginal Population Movements in the Early Historic Period," in Wood, Waselkov, and Hatley, eds., *Powhatan's Mantle*. Lincoln: University of Nebraska Press, 1989.

Smith, Marvin. "Aboriginal Population Movements in the Postcontact Southeast," in Ethridge and Hudson, eds., *The Transformation of the Southeastern Indians*. Oxford: University Press of Mississippi, 2002.

Spate, Oskar Hermann Khristian. *The Spanish Lake*. Canberra: Australian National University, 2004.

Starna, William A. "The Biological Encounter: Disease and the Ideological Domain." *American Indian Quarterly*, 16 (1992): 513.

Stevens, Mary Kaye. *Pine Island*. Charleston, SC: Arcadia Publishing, 2008.

Sugden, John. *Sir Francis Drake*. London, UK: Pimlico, 1996.

Swanton, John Reed. *The Indian Tribes of North America*. Baltimore, MD: Genealogical Publications Company, 2003 [1979].

Swanton, John Reed. *The Indians of the Southeastern United States*. Washington, DC: Government Printing Office, 1946.

Sweet, Julie Anne. *Negotiating for Georgia: British-Creek Relations in the Trustee Era, 1733-1752*. Athens: University of Georgia Press, 2005.

Taylor, Joseph E. III. *Making Salmon: An Environmental History of the Northwest Fisheries Crisis*. Seattle: University of Washington Press, 2015 [1999].

Thomas, David Hurst. "The Archaeology of Mission Santa Catalina de Guale: Our First 15 Years," in McEwan, ed., *The Spanish Missions of La Florida*. Gainesville: University Press of Florida, 1993.

Thursby, Erin. *Florida Oranges: A Colorful History*. Charleston, SC: Arcadia Publishing, 2019.

Truman, Carl. "Luther and the Reformation in Germany," in Pettegree, ed., *The Reformation World*. London, UK: Routledge, 2006.

Turner, Samuel. "Juan Ponce de León and the Discovery of Florida Reconsidered." *Florida Historical Quarterly* 92, no. 1 (Summer 2013): 1-31.

Twinam, Ann. *Purchasing Whiteness: Pardos, Mulattos, and the Quest for Social Mobility in the Spanish Indies*. Stanford, CA: Stanford University Press, 2015.

Vanderwarker, Amber M., Dana N. Bardolph, and C. Margaret Scarry. "Maize and Mississippian Beginnings," in Wilson, ed., *Mississippian Beginnings*. Gainesville: University of Florida Press, 2017.

Van Doren, Mark. *The Travels of William Bartram*. New York: Dover Publications, 1928.

Vinson, Ben III, and Matthew Restall. "Black Soldiers, Native Soldiers," in Restall, ed., *Beyond Black and Red*. Albuquerque: University of New Mexico Press, 2005.

Voigt, Lisa. *Writing Captivity in the Early Modern Atlantic: Circulations of Knowledge and Authority in the Iberian and English Imperial Worlds*. Chapel Hill: University of North Carolina Press, 2009.

Walton, Timothy. *The Spanish Treasure Fleets*. Sarasota, FL: Pineapple Press, 1994.

Warnes, Andrew. *Savage Barbecue: Race, Culture, and the Invention of America's First Food*. Athens: University of Georgia Press, 2010.

Waselkov, Gregory. "Seventeenth-Century Trade in the Colonial Southeast." *Southeastern Archaeology* 8, no. 2 (1989): 117-133.

Waselkov, Gregory, et al., eds. *Forging Southeastern Identities: Social Archaeology, Ethnohistory, and Folklore of the Mississippian to Early Historic South*. Tuscaloosa: University of Alabama Press, 2017.

Weber, David J. *The Spanish Frontier in North America*. New Haven, CT: Yale University Press, 1992.

Weddle, Robert Samuel. *Spanish Sea: The Gulf of Mexico in North American Discovery, 1500-1685*. College Station: Texas A&M University Press, 1995.

Weisman, Breant. "Nativism, Resistance, and Ethnogenesis of the Florida Seminole Indian Identity." *Historical Archaeology* 41, no. 4 (2007): 198-212.

West, Patsy. *The Enduring Seminoles: From Alligator Wrestling to Ecotourism*. Gainesville: University Press of Florida, 1998.

White, Richard. *Roots of Dependency: Subsistence, Environment, and Social Change among the Choctaws, Pawnees, and Navajos*. Lincoln: University of Nebraska Press, 1988.

Whitehead, Alfred. *Gaspard de Coligny, Admiral of France*. London, UK: Methuen, 1904.

Widmer, Randolph. *The Evolution of Calusa: A Nonagricultural Chiefdom on the Southwest Florida Coast*. Tuscaloosa: University of Alabama Press, 1988.

Widmer, Randolph. "The Structure of Southeastern Chiefdoms," in Hudson and Tesser, eds., *The Forgotten Centuries*. Athens: University of Georgia Press, 1994.

Williams, Mark. "Growth and Decline of the Oconee Province," in Hudson and Tesser, eds., *The Forgotten Centuries*. Athens: University of Georgia Press, 1994.

Williams, Mark, and Gary Shapiro, eds. *Lamar Archaeology: Mississippian Chiefdoms in the Deep South*. Tuscaloosa: University of Alabama Press, 2010.

Williamson, Margaret Holmes. *Powhatan Lords of Life and Death: Command and Consent in Seventeenth-Century Virginia*. Lincoln: University of Nebraska Press, 2003.

Wilson, Gregory D., ed. *Mississippian Beginnings*. Gainesville: University of Florida Press, 2017.

Wood, Peter. *Black Majority: Negroes in Colonial South Carolina from 1670 through the Stono Rebellion*. New York: W.W. Norton, 1996.

Wood, Peter. "Changing Population," in Wood, Waselkov, and Hatley, eds., *Powhatan's Mantle*. Lincoln: University of Nebraska Press, 1989.

Wood, Peter, Gregory Waselkov, and Thomas Hatley, eds. *Powhatan's Mantle: Indians in the Colonial Southeast*. Lincoln: University of Nebraska Press, 1989.

Woodard, Colin. *The Republic of Pirates: Being the True and Surprising Story of the Caribbean Pirates and the Man Who Brought Them Down*. London, UK: Pan Books, 2007.

Worth, John. "Bridging Prehistory and History," in Pluckhahn and Ethridge, eds., *Light on the Path*. Tuscaloosa: University of Alabama Press, 2006.

Worth, John. *Discovering Florida: First-Contact Narratives from Spanish Expeditions along the Lower Gulf Coast*. Gainesville: University Press of Florida, 2014.

Worth, John. "Late Spanish Military Expeditions in the Interior Southeast, 1597-1628," in Hudson and Tesser, eds., *The Forgotten Centuries*. Athens: University of Georgia Press, 1994.

Worth, John. "Spanish Florida and the Southeastern Indians, 1513-1650," in Boudreaux, Meyers, and Johnson, eds., *Contact, Colonialism, and Native Communities*. Gainesville: University of Florida Press, 2020.

Worth, John. "Spanish Missions and the Persistence of Chiefly Power," in Ethridge and Hudson, eds., *The Transformation of the Southeastern Indians*. Oxford: University Press of Mississippi, 2002.

Worth, John. *The Struggle for the Georgia Coast*. Tuscaloosa: University of Alabama Press, 2009.

Wright, Irene Aloha. *Further English Voyages to America, 1583-1594*. London, UK: Hakluyt Society, 2010 [1967].

Wright, James Leitch Jr. *Creeks & Seminoles: The Destruction and Regeneration of the Muscogulge People*. Lincoln: University of Nebraska Press, 1990.

Young, Philip. "Pocahontas," in Barker-Benfield and Clinton, eds., *Portraits of American Women*. New York: Oxford University Press, 1998.

Index

Adelantado, 10–11, 13, 15–16, 19–20, 37, 51, 54, 70, 201–02
Ajacán, mission of, 56, 58, 187–89, 283
Alachua Savanna, 231–34, 257–59, 368
Alaminos, Antón de, 27, 35, 41, 279, 285
Altamaha, chiefdom of, 22, 140, 162
Apalachee, chiefdom of, 3, 17–18, 22–24, 85, 103, 114–15, 137, 147–49, 153, 155, 161, 164–165, 173, 175, 189–92, 194–95, 237, 243–44, 253–54, 283, 355, 363, 366;
  disease among, 210, 239
  missionizing in, 189–92
  rebellion in, 194, 238, 365
  slave raiding in, 344–45
Apalache, Fort San Marcos de, 212–13, 342–43, 345–46
Atahualpa, 77–78
Aute, chiefdom of, 17–18, 103–04, 145–48
Ayllón, Lucas Vázquez de, 12–13, 15, 21, 23, 49, 53, 113–14, 118, 281, 363;
  and the Order of St. James, 72
  requerimiento, 82

Barbacoa, 350, 356–58
Barbecue, 349–50, 358–59
Bahamas. *See* Lucayos
Bahamian Channel. *See* Gulf Stream
Barbastro, Fray Luis Cáncer de, 187, 350
Bartram, William, 231, 363, 368, 371
Bimini, island of, 9–10, 111–12, 284, 292
Black Legend, the, 293–98
Bowlegs, 263
Bowlegs, Billy, 263–64
Burgos, 1512 Law of, 109–10, 293
Cabeza de Vaca, Álvar Núñez, 17–20, 29–31, 51, 126, 280
Cabrera, Governor Juan Marquez, 212
Calusa, chiefdom of, 10, 12, 56, 112–13, 362
Camino Real, 55–57, 190
Canço, Governor Mendez de, 191
capitulacion, 10–11, 54, 74, 81, 108, 118, 201
Carey, Sir George, 315
Caroline, Fort, 54
Carrera de Indias, 33
Casas, Bartolemé de las, 110, 293–98
Casqui, chiefdom of, 89, 167–69, 250. *See also* Pacaha, chiefdom of
Castillo de San Marcos, 211–13, 321, 330
Catawba Indians, 250
Catholic Church, 68–69, 187–98;
  conflict with Protestants, 93–96, 101
  and conquest, 74–78, 85–86
  exploitation by, 192–94
  missions of, 187–95
  sacraments of, 87–89
  and Spanish identity, 91–92
  and slavery, 107
cattle, 361–68;
  ranches, 365–66
  Spanish ranching tradition, 361–62. *See also criollo*
Charles V, 81
Charlesfort, 54
Charleston, 322. *See also* South Carolina, colony of
Cherokee Indians, 250, 343
Chesapeake Bay. *See* Santa María, Bahia de
Chiaha, chiefdom of, 152, 157, 161
Chicaza, chiefdom of, 23–25, 153, 235

Chickasaw Indians, 250
Chicora, 12, 112
Chisca, chiefdom of, 161
Choctaw Indians, 235, 250
coalescence, 249, 251–52, 339
Cofaqui, chiefdom of, 137–138, 166
Cofitachequi, chiefdom of, 3–4, 22–23, 117–18, 144–45, 163, 166–67, 357;
 and disease, 144–145
 lady of, 22, 163
 and pearls, 115
Coligny, Gaspard de, 95–96
Columbian Exchange, 141
Columbus, Christopher, 5, 7, 107, 141, 356
Contratacion, Casa de, 33
convento, *See* Catholic Church
Coosa, chiefdom of, 23–24, 115, 153, 158, 163, 166, 235–36
Córdoba, Francisco Hernández, 10
corn, agriculture of, 148–52
Cortés, Hernán, 10–11, 13, 15–16, 41
Coweta Resolution, 342
Cowkeeper, the, 231–32, 257–59, 261–62, 264
Creek Indians, 148, 235, 244, 250, 252, 263, 337–47
criollo, 218, 361.
 See also cattle
 See also floridano
Crosby, Alfred, 141–44
Cuéllar, Diego Velázquez de, 9, 15, 109, 111, 113, 294
current system, Caribbean, 7, 33–35, 50–51
Cuscowilla, 231–33

De León. *See* León, Juan Ponce
De Soto. *See* Soto, Hernando de
disease, 141–45, 238–40;
 and cattle ranching, 364, 366
 and missions, 238–40
Dobyns, Henry, 143–44, 148–49, 249
doctrina. *See* Catholic Church
Donation, Bulls of, 71–72, 76, 78
Drake, Sir Francis, 206–07, 307, 309–10, 312, 314, 316, 374

Edisto Island, 212, 282, 321, 326
Elfrith, Captain Daniel, 385–87
Elizabeth, Queen, 289, 308–10
encomienda, 9, 54, 106–12, 114, 117, 121, 153, 193–94, 204, 206–07, 217, 293–94, 366
estancia, 207, 362–367
Esteban the Moor, 103–05, 125–26, 128

Feliú, Governor Melchor, 331
Fish, Jesse, 377
Floréncia, Claudio Luís de, 190
floridano, 206–207, 210–217, 218, 367
Flota de Indias, 41–42
Fountain of Youth, legend of, 291–93
Franciscans, order of, 82, 188–90, 237–39, 244, 285, 356, 363, 366
French, 43, 49–54, 67–68, 93, 95–97;
 pirates, 45, 54, 93
 Charlesfort, 49.
 See also Caroline, Fort
 See also Huguenots
Fontaneda, Hernándo d'Escalante, 40, 55, 292

Galve, Presidio Santa María de, *See* Pensacola
Garrido, Juan, 124–25
Georgia, colony of, 330, 345–46
Gilbert, Sir Humphrey, 310
Gordillo, Francisco, 12, 113
Grajales, Francisco López de Mendoza, 97, 99, 187
Grenville, Richard, 307, 312–14
Grijalva, Juan de, 10
Guadalpe, San Miguel de, 13, 72, 117, 126–28, 227
Guale, chiefdom of, 187–89, 238–40, 253–54
Gulf of Mexico, 34–36, 38;
 danger of, 36–39
Gulf Stream, 35, 37, 50, 55

hacienda, 42, 108, 117, 122, 207, 217, 231, 257–59, 303, 362, 365–67, 376
Hakluyt, Richard, 298, 311–12
Hawkins, John, 35, 316
Heyn, Piet, 209
Hispaniola, 7, 8, 9, 34, 42, 54, 68, 107, 109, 202, 295
Horruytiner, Governor Luis de, 209
horses, 172, 178–79
Huguenots, xii-xiii, 67, 70, 94–97, 100
hurricanes, 39–40;
  and Pensacola, 52–53

Inquisition, Spanish, 69, 94, 354

Jacksonville. *See* Fort Caroline
Jesuits, order of, 187–89, 193, 195, 198
Jope, Captain John Colyn, 385–87

Kelton, Paul, 144–45

La Chua, 231, 257–59, 261, 264, 364–68. *See also* Alachua
Lane, Richard, 307
Laudonnière, René Goulaine, 53, 95–96
León, Juan Ponce de, 5, 7, 9–12, 15, 18, 23, 35, 38, 81–82, 109, 111–14, 125, 143–44, 187, 279, 282–85, 291–93, 295–96, 362, 374;
  and *encomienda*, 112–13
  and the Fountain of Youth, 292–93
Limpieza de Sangre, 94, 219, 221, 224
Lords Proprietors, 319–20
Lucayos, 109–11
Luna y Arellano, Tristán de, 49–53, 56, 105, 129, 144, 187, 213, 235–36, 285, 355, 374
Lutherans. *See* Huguenots

Marqués, Governor Pedro Menéndez, 315
Matamoros, Santiago. *See* St. James, Order of
matanza, la, 96–101, 283
Mavila, 115, 153, 173–79;
  battle of, 24–25, 87–88, 173–179
Menéndez de Avilés, Pedro, x-xiii, 37, 40, 54–56, 58, 67, 69, 72, 93–94, 96–100, 129, 185, 187–88, 201–02, 236, 282, 350, 356, 365;
  founding St. Augustine, 54–55
  and la matanza, 97–101
  and St. James, Order of, 98
  and slavery, 220
mestizo, 218–20, 224–25, 365
Micanopy, 263
Miccosukee (Mikasuki), 260, 263
Miruelo, Diego, 110
Mississippian chiefdoms, 150–54, 162–69, 189,
  collapse of, 235–37
  conflict in, 165–69
  corn reliance in, 148–52
  chieftains of, 161–65
  men as farmers, 154
  role of women, 155–59
  Spanish support of, 253–54
  weapons of, 171–72.
  See also individual chiefdoms
Montesinos, Antonio, 110, 293–94
Montiano, Governor Manuel, 327, 329–30, 346
Moore, James, 213, 219–20, 243–45
moreno, 224–25
Mosé, Gracia Real de Santa Teresa de, 227–28, 326–28, 330–31
Moyne, Jacques le, 98, 100, 350
mulatto, 224–25
mullet, 349–50
Mt. Pleasant, Jane, 148

Narváez, Panfilo de, 5, 13, 15–20, 51, 82–83, 103, 114, 147–48, 155, 280;
Nairne, Thomas, 245–46
Napetuca, 114–15, 117, 141, 171–75, 179, 283, 297;
  destruction of, 173–75
New Laws of 1542, 108
Newport, Christopher, 310–11, 316
Northwest Passage, 56

Ocale, chiefdom of, 149, 154, 164–65, 259, 282
Ochese, chiefdom of, 86, 137–38
Ochuse, Santa María de. *See* Pensacola
Ocute, chiefdom of, 22–23, 86, 138, 163, 166, 250
Oglethorpe, James, 330, 346
oranges, 371–78;
  and the *Reconquista*, 372–73
  for scurvy, 372–74
  on the St. John's River, 375–77
Ortiz, Juan, 275–77.
  See also Pocahontas, legend of
Ossabaw Island, 356
Ovando, Nicolás de, 107–10, 123–24, 202, 294

Pacaha, chiefdom of, 167–69, 250
Paracoxi, chiefdom of, 117, 174
Pareja, Father Francisco, 195–199
pardo, 183, 225–26
Pardo, Juan, 56–58, 236, 239,
Patofa, chiefdom of, 138, 153
Payne, King, 262
peninsular, 217–18
Pensacola, 52–53, 212–13
Phillip II, King, 54, 95–97
pigs, 138, 192, 204, 238, 350, 353–56
Pineda, Alonso Álvarez de, 11, 51
piracy, 45–46, 49, 58;
  French, 45, 54, 94.
  See also privateering
Pizarro, Francisco, 21, 71–72, 77–78, 81, 104, 107–08, 162, 253, 354
place names, 282–88;
  Catholic origins of, 284–87
  and Florida, 284
play-off diplomacy, 304, 338
Pocahontas, legend of, 275–77, 291
Port Royal, 54.
  See also Santa Elena
Potano, chiefdom of, 189, 205, 219, 227, 239, 259, 363–64, 368, 377
Prieto, Father Martin, 188
privateering, 308–17, 387–88

Puerto Rico, 7, 9, 10, 34, 42, 45, 46, 67, 107, 123

Quapaw Indians, 252
Quejo (Quexo), Pedro de, 12–13, 113
Quiroga y Losada, Governor Diego de, 212, 321

Raleigh, Sir Walter, 310, 316
reconquista, 8, 69, 71–72, 123, 372–73
Reformation, xiii, 95–96
repartimiento, 54, 154, 193–94, 237–39, 367
requerimiento, 76–77, 81–83, 109
Rios, Isavel de los, 183–84
Ribault, Jean, 53–54, 68, 100–01
Ribero, Diego map, 286
Roanoke, 56, 297, 307–17;
  and piracy, 311

St. James, Order of, 71–72, 87, 185
St. Augustine, 97, 183–85, 203–13, 221–26, 310, 315, 320–21, 324–25, 344, 363–64, 374, 389–90;
  attacked, 206, 210, 213, 219
  disease in, 210
  founding, 97, 201–02
  government of, 203–04
  growth of, 211–13
  runaway slaves to, 321–24, 328–30
  slavery in, 221–23, 388–90
  structure of, 207–09
sabana, 205, 210
Santa Elena, 49–57, 206, 212, 281
Santa María, Bahia de, 53
scurvy, 372–73
Sea War, Anglo-Spanish, 309–11
Searles, Robert, 210
Seminole Indians, 231–32, 257–64;
  creation of, 260–262
  and ranching, 257–260
Shawnee Indians, 249
shipwrecks, 37–40, 43–44;
  cost of, 41, 43–44
silk road, 7

situado, 204–05, 209
slave laws, 322–24, 329–30
slave trade, 119–20
slave trade, Indian, 240–46
slavery:
  and Native barbarism, 110
  and Columbus, 107
  in the Caribbean, 109
  and Florida, 111–112, 388–90
  and mortality, 226–27
  resistance to Spanish, 227
  runaways from Spanish, 125–27, 227
  in St. Augustine, 223–25
  in Spanish culture, 121–22, 221–23
  in Virginia, 385–89
  and women, 155–59.
  See also asiento
  See also encomienda
  See also slave trade, Indian
Smith, John, *see* Pocahontas, legend of
Soto, Hernando de, 3–5, 20–25, 83–89, 137, 152–58, 161, 165–69, 173, 280–81, 296–97, 355;
  and the Black Legend, 296–97
  and *encomienda*, 114
  and Order of St. James, 72
  past, 20–21, 163–64
  requerimiento, 83–84
  treatment of chieftains, 163–65
  treatment of native laborers, 153–54
  treatment of slaves, 112–14
South Carolina, colony of, 240–41, 254, 319–30;
  Barbados connection, 319–20
  runaway slaves from, 321–22, 325, 327–28, 330
  and slavery, 320–24, 328
Spanish:
  cattle tradition, 361–62
  countering British traders, 339–40
  government style of, 202–03
  missionizing by, 187–95
  racial caste system of, 217
  and slavery, 222–23
  weaponry of, 172.
  See also Catholic Church
Stono Rebellion, 301–03, 329–30
straights, Florida, 35, 37–38, 55
Succor, town of, 138–39, 166

Talimali, Mission San Luis de, 191–92, 195, 211, 219, 243–45, 366.
  See also Catholic Church
Talisi, chiefdom of, 158, 163, 166, 176
Tapia, Crispin de, 183–85, 225–26
Tascalusa, chiefdom of, 163, 166, 235.
  See also Mavila
Thanksgiving Day:
  first, ix–xiv, 390–91
  massacre, xi–xii, 100
trade, deerskin, 335–38
Timucua, chiefdom of, 189, 238–39, 244–45, 253–54, 364
Tropicana, 378

Vega, Gracilaso de la, 277, 292
Velasco, Diego de, 49–50, 53
Verrazano, Giovanni de, 49
Villafañe, Ángel de, 52–53
visita. *See* Catholic Church

Watts, John, 310, 316
Westo Indians, 242–43, 249, 25
White, John, 307, 316
Winyah Bay, 111

Yamasee Indians, 242–246, 249, 258, 339, 343–44
Yamasee War, 259–60, 304, 324, 335, 338, 340–42